Madame Jazz

Madame

New York   Oxford
OXFORD UNIVERSITY PRESS
1995

Jazz

Contemporary Women Instrumentalists

Leslie Gourse

Oxford University Press

Oxford   New York   Toronto
Delhi   Bombay   Calcutta   Madras   Karachi
Kuala Lumpur   Singapore   Hong Kong   Tokyo
Nairobi   Dar es Salaam   Cape Town
Melbourne   Auckland

and associated companies in
Berlin   Ibadan

Published by Oxford University Press, Inc.
200 Madison Avenue, New York, New York 10016

Oxford is a registered trademark of Oxford University Press

Library of Congress Cataloging-in-Publication Data
Gourse, Leslie.
Madame Jazz : contemporary women instrumentalists / Leslie Gourse.
p.   cm.
Includes bibliographical references and index.
ISBN 0-19-508696-1
1. Women jazz musicians—United States.
2. Jazz—United States—History and criticism.
I. Title.
ML82.G69   1995   781.65'082—dc20   93-40360

Fulman's review (Chapter Three) © New York Daily News. Used with permission.

Jeske's review (Chapter Twenty) from the New York Post. Used with permission.

Palmer's review (Chapter Three) Copyright © by The New York Times Company, reprinted by
permission, for "Women Who Make Jazz," by Robert Palmer, Jan. 21, 1977, and "Women Prove
They Are Equal To Men In Jazz," by Robert Palmer.

Drawings on pages ii and iii by Samuel Gourse.

9 8 7 6 5 4 3 2 1

Printed in the United States of America
on acid-free paper

For all the people who contributed to this book
and for Dr. Edward Holtzman,
trumpeter Johnny Parker,
and photographer Ray Ross

/ / / Preface

Drummer Terri Lyne Carrington, one of the most successful young instrumentalists in jazz and pop, noticed a striking change in the status of
women instrumentalists between the end of the 1980s and the early
1990s. By 1994, she had lost count of the new players. "There are a lot
more women playing and coming into their own. It's no longer a matter of
women being fashionable or a fad. It's really serious. When a woman says
she plays, you have to listen and find out now," Terri said.

Drummer Dottie Dodgion, who began her career in the 1950s, was
playing on the West Coast in the late 1980s and early 1990s, hired by male
musicians whom she had known for a long time. Even so, she was certain
that the attitude of male chauvinism against women instrumentalists
"would go on forever."

These views are not necessarily mutually exclusive. Dottie was speaking from long experience. Prejudice against women jazz instrumentalists
had sometimes frozen her out of high-profile jobs. In the 1990s, women
were still experiencing incidences of traditional discrimination, though it
usually manifested itself in far more subtle ways than when Dottie had
begun playing. The burden of guaranteed, relentless, and depressing frus-
tration had lifted from women's shoulders.

Quite a few lucky women could even say they had rarely encountered
overt discrimination. The National Endowment for the Arts gave awards
to women. Many were building careers successfully, using the door-to-
door method for advancement. That is, if they were turned away at one
door, they were welcomed at the next. They looked for jobs in places
where men didn't always go. And there were deepening, widening pock-
ets of real support—male musicians who could be counted on to call
women to play and rarely give gender a second thought. Women found out
there were no longer any immutable rules. All they had to do to succeed
was count indisputably among the best and the brightest players, the most
persistent job seekers, and the most agreeable people. Naturally, they had
to be lucky too, and catch the attention of the right people. And if the

gifted women had good connections, or roots in the jazz world, through family or friends, all the better for their prospects—usually.

This book is about the history that women jazz instrumentalists are making now. And so many women are playing that, although this book is not intended as an encyclopedia, a list of many active players, primarily in New York, with a sampling of the rest of the country, is included.

New York   *L.G.*
April 1994

/// Acknowledgments

Thanks to all the instrumentalists—men and women—for their enthusiastic support and conscientious contributions of their experiences and ideas and their references to colleagues, among them Marian McPartland, pianist, and Kim Clarke, bassist; to Audreen Ballard, former managing editor of *Lear's* magazine for guidance leading to Chapter four; to W. Royal Stokes for his assignments of pieces on women jazz musicians to me for *Jazz Times;* to Frankie Nemko for her painstaking assistance; to Sheldon Meyer for his unique commitment to a book about this facet of jazz history, and to Helen Keane, Karen Wolny, Ellen Fuchs, Joellyn Ausanka, and Rosemary Wellner for their help with the manuscript.

/ / / Contents

Introduction
Diva, 3

Chapter One
A Status Report on the Contemporary Scene: Part One, 7

Chapter Two
A Status Report: Part Two, 13

Chapter Three
Remembrance of Things Passé: Jill McManus Recalls the Frustrations
of the Jazz Sisters in the 1970s, 24

Chapter Four
Several Successful Contemporary Young Women Musicians Talk About
Their Inspiration and Commitment, 33

Chapter Five
Pianists Renee Rosnes and Rachel Z, Rising to the Top in the 1990s,
Ruminate About Their Worlds, 43

Chapter Six
A View from the Business Women, 48

Chapter Seven
The Instrument Is the Image, 66

INTRODUCTION TO THE PROFILES, 73

Chapter Eight
Kit McClure, Big-Band Leader: "You Did the Right Thing", 75

INTRODUCTION TO THE STRING PLAYERS, 83

Chapter Nine
Tracy Wormworth, Bassist: "Doors Just Opened", 87

Chapter Ten
Emily Remler and the Guitarists, 92

INTRODUCTION TO THE HORN PLAYERS, 97

Chapter Eleven
Focusing on Trumpeter Rebecca Coupe Franks, Alto Saxophonists
Virginia Mayhew, Carol Chaikin, and Sue Terry, French Horn Player
Stephanie Fauber, Oboist Kathy Halvorson, and Saxophonists Laura
Dreyer and Paula Atherton, 99

Chapter Twelve
Trumpeters Laurie Frink and Stacy Rowles, 106

Chapter Thirteen
Flautists Elise Wood and Ali Ryerson, 114

Chapter Fourteen
Carol Sudhalter, A Role Model, 117

Chapter Fifteen
Jane Ira Bloom, Soprano Saxophonist and Experimentalist, 124

INTRODUCTION TO THE DRUMMERS, 129

Chapter Sixteen
Terri Lyne Carrington, 131

Chapter Seventeen
Cindy Blackman and Sylvia Cuenca, 136

Chapter Eighteen
Percussionist Carol Steele, 143

Chapter Nineteen
Individualists, 150

VIEWS FROM WOMEN AT THE TOP, 171

Chapter Twenty
Shirley Horn: "I Got Older and Bolder", 173

Chapter Twenty-One
Joanne Brackeen Lives and Plays Without Any Dos and Don'ts, 178

Chapter Twenty-Two
The Wily Miss Dorothy Donegan, Mistress of Fiery Medleys, 183

Chapter Twenty-Three
Marian McPartland: " . . . Something You Really Need in Life,
Someone to Encourage You", 190

Chapter Twenty-Four
A Few Words About Love, Marriage, and Motherhood, 201
A View from the West Coast, by Frankie Nemko, 208

Appendix:
Women Instrumentalists Active in the 1980s and Early 1990s, 211

Bibliography, 265

Index, 267

Madame Jazz

■ ■ ■ ■ ■ ■ ■ ■ ■ ■

Duke Ellington named a character in one of his suites "Madame Zajj," which is jazz spelled fancifully backward. Ellington cast her in the role of the muse of the male musician, "Carribee Joe." By 1994, however, the tables had been turned. Ellington's music was a universal inspiration, and the former muse, Madame Zajj, had become the musician.

Introduction / / / Diva

Suddenly several audiences became alerted to the emergence of women musicians as a first-rate force in jazz, when a big band named Diva made its debut at Loeb Student Center at New York University on March 30, 1993. Diva then played for a fund-raiser at the Village Gate the next night and made such a good impression that it was immediately booked to play at Carnegie Hall the next year.

Moments after Diva's debut at NYU, Stanley Kay, the band's founder, confided to the audience about the instrumentalists who had become his cherished project. "I can't call them girls, and they call each other 'man' or 'guys'." He had been Buddy Rich's drummer and managed Rich's two New York nightclubs and also a Greenwich Village club, Hopper's. His joke poked fun at the lingering controversy about the position of women in the jazz world.

But there was no doubt that flugelhorn and trumpet player Clark Terry, the guest artist for the Gate benefit, enjoyed it very much when Sue Terry, a saxophonist playing alto in Diva and acting as the leader that night, called him "my honorary brother." The remark was amusing because Clark Terry, an African-American, is about thirty-five years older than Sue, who is white. In the audience, trumpeter Jonah Jones, pianist Junior Mance, and bandleader Skitch Henderson had clearly loved the band's brilliance. Junior had a rapt smile on his face; his head bobbed to the time kept by bassist Melissa Slocum.

"I thought the band was very, very good," he said later. "Art D'Lugoff [owner of the Village Gate] called me to come to hear them. I had heard about the band from (saxophonist) Virginia Mayhew; they were rehearsing. Ingrid Jensen is wonderful. She came by and sat in with us for the The Golden Men of Jazz [a group of eminent older players]. Ingrid's a protégé of Clark Terry. The piano player is good. The bass player, Melissa Slocum, sounds . . . strong, she swings. As soloists and a unit, they were quite good . . . I was really surprised . . . I knew a few, but I didn't know most of the people in the band."

The women were pleased too. Lolly Bienenfeld, a trombonist who had once worked with the Thad Jones-Mel Lewis Orchestra and played with the circus in the 1990s—a demanding job—had been chosen to play lead trombone in Diva. She was happy to work with a concert jazz band that was so good.

Kay knew of only a few good all-women's bands in the past—Ina Rae Hutton's and Anna Mae Winburn's International Sweethearts of Rhythm, and, the all-girl orchestra led by Phil Spitalny. Kay wasn't familiar with Kit McClure's contemporary all-women's band or Maiden Voyage, the women's big band on the West Coast. On May 12, 1990, Kay had walked into the Shubert Theatre, where Sherrie Maricle, a drummer, was auditioning for Skitch Henderson's New York Pops Orchestra. She got the job. Kay didn't know Sherrie, nor had he ever heard a woman play drums for any of his productions. He was very impressed with Sherrie's playing, and he thought, "If she's that good, there have to be other women out there who can play all the instruments just as well." He knew only about women piano players, harpists, flutists, and violinists.

He also didn't know that Sherrie, at age nineteen in her hometown, Binghamton, New York in 1984, had been fired from a trio scheduled to play for a performance by a famous comedian; a member of the comedian's staff had told her, "He doesn't work with any women musicians." She persisted in her career and chalked up a long list of impressive credits. She has led groups on recordings, taught at New York University, and plays the drumset in the New York Pops regularly.

Eventually Kay called Sherrie and told her he would like to audition women for a big band, and wanted her to work as the straw boss. John LaBarbera, who had written arrangements for Buddy Rich, would write for the women's band. Women came from all over the country and Europe to audition at the historic Nola Recording Studios on West 57th Street in June 1992. Hearing the women play, LaBarbera told Kay, "We've really got something." Kay made a video of the band, with its fifteen instrumentalists, to try to get people to believe in it and present it. He also called the LRC record label in New York and suggested that the owner, Sonny Lester, an old friend, make a recording of four musicians from the band— Melissa, pianist Jill McCarron, alto saxophonist Carol Chaikin, and Sherrie. The result was a recording of standards—well-rehearsed, polished, exciting music—done in 1992. Called "Dedication," it was aired on the radio, and the quartet, named Unpredictable Nature, performed to large audiences for three sets at the Blue Note on a Monday night in March in New York City.

As he organized Diva, Kay became aware of "how difficult the women's lives had been, how much dues they had paid, and how much they were put down." Buoyed by the auspicious debut, Kay recommitted himself to the band: "I'm going to do everything I can to make this happen." He was exploring the possibility of finding funds and sponsorship from famous fashion designers for the costly enterprise. He booked Diva to play at the Smithsonian Institution, and in August 1993, then again that year at Tavern on the Green, and in spring and summer 1994. The band's first CD, "Something's Coming," was scheduled for release in 1994. "They're my family now . . . If it goes well, and we get lucky, my ambition is to offer them a pension plan and a health plan. It gives them incentive and a stake in the band."

Diva's personnel are listed at the end of this book. There continue to be changes.

Chapter One /// A Status Report on the Contemporary Scene: Part One

This is a report on the position of women in jazz from the late 1970s to the early 1990s, an exciting and crucial time of transition. With few exceptions, before the mid-1980s, women were always second-class citizens in jazz, the most macho of all the arts. That has been well documented in Sally Placksin's book *American Women in Jazz,* and Linda Dahl's *Stormy Weather,* both of which ended in approximately 1980. They chronicled the history and plight of women musicians from early blues singers to contemporary singers and instrumentalists.

Long after women became accepted as writers and, to a lesser extent, as visual artists, women in music—classical, jazz, and pop—faced the nearly insuperable barrier of male chauvinism. In music, nobody except a concert soloist gets a chance to play in public unless he or she is hired by someone for a group, whether a huge orchestra or a duo. Historically, men in jazz rarely hired women musicians. They did so increasingly in the 1990s.

Before the 1970s, women who crossed the gender barrier with seeming ease were usually pianists. They were either married or related to male stars, or were singers who could accompany themselves on piano, or band-singers who often received little or no respect from men in the industry and derived their influence from their popularity with the public. Singers who couldn't read music compounded the prejudice. Few women became managers or operated on the business side of music until the late 1970s, unless they were married to the musicians they managed. Although women in record companies still rarely function as anything but publicists, the women's movement has, in general, changed the status and prospects for women in every part of the music world since the mid-1970s.

At that time, even though it was still a well-kept secret, musically talented women no longer thought they had to be confined to teaching or playing as amateurs in churches and other community organizations if they decided to study music for a profession. So they began attending conservatories and colleges, which had previously discriminated against them; either the schools hadn't accepted them or professors and male students barely talked to the few women who were accepted. Now there were more jazz faculties. Prestigious music schools along with liberal arts colleges and universities had begun to teach jazz performance, theory, composition, and history—innovative courses created in the days when equal opportunity laws were new and the National Endowment for the Arts started to grant awards to jazz musicians in the late 1960s. The schools tentatively encouraged women students while they simultaneously actively sought minority group musicians to become degree candidates. Well-known jazz musicians became visiting clinicians, staff teachers, professors, and administrators. Jazz itself was on its way to becoming Establishment and trendy in the public perception. With the music held in increasingly higher esteem, women felt freer than ever to try to indulge their aspirations to be included in the jazz world.

Emboldened—and even deluded to a degree—by the changing atmosphere in society, they began to play instruments other than the piano—horns, percussion, guitars, and basses—that were formerly regarded as male preserves. Many people still feel it's unacceptable to see a woman with a horn, especially a saxophone or trumpet, in her mouth. Nadine Jansen, a flugelhornist and pianist, remembers a night in the 1940s when a man came out of an audience and hit the end of her horn, saying, "I hate to see a woman do that." He may have chipped a tooth; although he didn't hurt her, he upset her. And her experience wasn't unique.

Of the women who became famous in jazz before the 1960s, most played piano—Lil Hardin Armstrong, Mary Lou Williams, Dorothy Donegan, Marian McPartland, and Hazel Scott. Also respected, Dardanelle Hadley, a vibrist and pianist, led her own popular, Nat King Cole-style trio in the 1940s. In the 1950s, Shirley Scott played the organ in Eddie "Lockjaw" Davis's band. She would become one of the relatively few women to lead her own group in the Village Vanguard. Of the younger women who became prominent in the 1960s and 1970s, Joanne Brackeen, Patti Bown, Toshiko Akiyoshi, and Carla Bley play piano. Shirley Horn, singer and pianist, had her following, but she would not become nationally prominent until the 1980s and especially the 1990s.

The only woman horn player who consistently stood on important bandstands alongside men was trombonist Melba Liston. She had attended music school in Los Angeles in the 1940s, where she had become friends with saxophonist Dexter Gordon, her earliest mentor. Count Basie and Dizzy Gillespie, among others, hired her in the 1950s, not just because she was a formidable player—"one of the best jazz musicians, not just one of the best women jazz musicians," as pianist Junior Mance summed up the jazz world's regard for her—but because Melba was also a superior arranger. A bandleader on the road liked to take along an arranger who knew the musicians' strengths and could eliminate the complications and costs of having arrangements sent from the East and West Coasts.

The combination of musical education and psychological orientation in the 1970s—the feeling that it was acceptable for women to be competitive with men—helped transform women into strong players, leaders, arrangers, and composers. Women felt free to try their best. They began to play more frequently in jazz clubs and concert halls. Trumpeter Clark Terry chose musicians for a band that played in a JVC Jazz Festival in New York in the late 1980s by auditioning their tapes. Without knowing whom he was listening to, he hired the band's personnel including Dianne DeRosa, a baritone saxophonist. Terry had first met her when he taught in a school clinic but he didn't know whose tape he was listening to when he auditioned hers for his festival band. Some women now work steadily in groups led by men, often crossing the lines from classical to jazz to pop, rhythm and blues, funk, and rock and roll, taking advantage of every opportunity to earn a living. Some have become stars in jazz, overriding the lingering, occasionally almost pernicious prejudice.

"Now it's all subtle, because it's not cool to be sexist or racist. It's all under the table," says pianist Rachel Z. "It's more like being left out," as French horn player Stephanie Fauber, among others, describes the way discrimination manifests itself in the music business. Men who still feel bias rarely say anything directly to women. But an excellent jazz guitarist, Peter Leitch, a group leader and recording artist, had to endure a bit of heckling from his male musician friends when he played as a sideman in a New York-based group led by a woman saxophonist with a male bassist and woman drummer. And drummer Charli Persip, who established himself in the 1950s with Dizzy Gillespie and went on to get his teaching degree and form his own big band, admits he has taken "flak" because he hired eight women for his Superband in the 1980s.

Passing through his band have been bassist Melissa Slocum, who took her college tuition money for graduate art school and bought a bass in the early 1980s, and composer, French horn player, and keyboardist Sharon Freeman, saxophonist Sue Terry, and Fostina Dixon who plays baritone, alto, and soprano saxes and sings, composes, and has led her own group, Winds of Change, and has traveled with singer-guitarist James

Blood Ulmer. Persip knows that most established jazz leaders still don't call these women for gigs. "Some musicians think that women are inferior to men musically. But men are superior only in brute strength, and it's not that necessary in today's economy and society. Men feel fear, jealousy, and resentment of that. All I care about is respect, dedication, playing ability and talent. I frequently find that women have more sensitivity and dedication to jazz than men. And jazz is about sensitivity."

Clearly a few men really haven't changed their attitudes at all since the 1950s, when Melba Liston, who was leading her own group, brought a promising young pianist, Kirk Lightsey, to New York for the first time. He knew it wasn't the best way to show up in New York—working for a woman—but he decided to brave the criticism, because Melba was such a good musician and she afforded him the chance to play in the Big Apple. He has since became a star in his own right.

The men who accept invitations to play in women's groups still rarely think about paying the women back by calling them for work. Only if a woman succeeds spectacularly are men delighted to play in her group—Roberta Flack is a good example; so are Shirley Horn, Nina Simone, Ella Fitzgerald, Carmen McRae, and Nancy Wilson—women singers, some of them also instrumentalists, who can pay top salaries and have their pick of the best instrumentalists in the country. Sarah Vaughan, who played piano very well (albeit with the wrong part of her fingers because she liked to keep her nails long), was viewed as a master class by the male musicians who played for her. Natalie Cole acquired the trappings of success that give her the luxury of inviting anyone she chooses to play for her. Cassandra Wilson's musicians are also in the limelight.

Of the older stars still playing throughout the 1980s, pianists Marian McPartland and Dorothy Donegan have the musical mastery, charisma, and prestige to impress any man they call to play for their groups. Marian also hosts a Peabody Award-winning radio show, "Piano Jazz," on National Public Radio, which has added luster and influence to her reputation. Dorothy Donegan has had her share of awards in the past few years. Singer and pianist Shirley Horn records hit albums; anyone would love to play in her groups.

Among the younger women transcending prejudice now, drummer Terri Lyne Carrington has played in late-night talk show host Arsenio Hall's studio band on television. She has been included—along with dozens of other women instrumentalists on all the instruments—in jazz festivals. She's in demand as a sideperson in the most famous jazz and pop groups. Drummer and percussionist Sue Evans and conguero Carol Steele have made their marks playing with stars in the studios. Sue plays with jazz, pop, and classical groups too. Drummer Cindy Blackman has been the regular drummer in jazz trombonist Al Grey's group, and now travels with pop star Lenny Kravitz.

Jazz pianist Patrice Rushen, who earned her commercial viability as a composer and singer in rock and r&b, has played keyboards in Wayne Shorter's groups in concert halls and on recordings. (It's the rare musician who hasn't aspired to work with Shorter.) Filmmaker Robert Townsend hired her, in 1992, to work as his musical director for a television show. As an arranger, she has also built a strong reputation. Pianist Renee Rosnes, who arrived in New York in 1985 and became prominent in the 1990s, hires grateful men for her groups, and some *do* call her for theirs.

Trumpeter Rebecca Coupe Franks has been called for a record date by Bill Cosby, for club dates with such musicians as saxophonist Lou Donaldson, and has a recording contract with the Justice label. Jobs often materialize once men hear her play. Electric bass player Tracy Wormworth, daughter of a professional drummer, has played for Cosby's TV studio band and for Sting's group. She works regularly with very popular groups.

In New York City's prestigious JVC Jazz Festival, in the mid-1980s, Miles Davis set lithe Marilyn Mazur, a black, American-born percussionist, who was raised in Copenhagen and bristles with energy, high on a back podium with her congas, bongos, and timbales. The audience saw her flailing arms clearly. At the end of the set, she seized a drum and danced to centerstage. Miles got out of her way, as she writhed in a tight black leotard and simultaneously played. (Miles's groups were always rife with costumes.) Mazur's welcome didn't come as a total shock to anyone familiar with the evolving popular music scene. Sheila E had paved the way a few years earlier for women to play percussion as featured artists in top-notch groups when she worked with pop star Prince. All the women drummers have thanked her.

A few nights later on the same Lincoln Center stage, Patrice Rushen, who had single records in the Top Ten popular lists and two Grammy nominations by 1990, never let up her barrage on an electric keyboard for the Carlos Santana/Wayne Shorter group. It's difficult to be articulate and communicate jazz intimacy, style, and feeling on an electric instrument. But Rushen did it. The next year, pianist Rachel Z dazzled the critics in a JVC festival concert featuring the jazz group Steps Ahead—Rachel's gig since 1989; she followed the "bad" and the beautiful Eliane Elias as the keyboardist in Steps Ahead. Rachel also plays with funk groups, keeping herself versatile. Her debut album came out after she had been paying dues as a performer for years. By the 1990s, audiences still noted the presence of a woman on the bandstand as fascinating but without any shock value.

These are a small fraction of the success stories—the many women who have found themselves accepted and even taken for granted in the man's world of jazz. Subtly but increasingly, that world was in flux in the 1980s and early 1990s.

For a while, women had their own jazz festivals; especially notable was the relatively long-lived Women's Jazz Festival founded by Cobi Narita in New York City in the late 1970s. Gaining confidence from their exposure and good reviews, women musicians felt assured enough to ask if they could sit in with groups of established leaders in nightclubs. That's how drummer Sylvia Cuenca came to impress Clark Terry in New York's Village Vanguard. Afterward he called her for gigs in the New York area.

It isn't necessarily chauvinism alone that still keeps most men playing with men. Habit usually guides them. They have the tradition of jazz as the creation of black men, with assistance in development from white men, along with the bonding instinct developed by those men for survival of music industry politics and the hard realities of musicians' lives spent primarily on the road. Many men simply haven't realized the extent to which women players have become equals—available, eager, and able to play in the 1980s and 1990s. So men usually play with musicians they have always worked with: other men. Emergent men players on the scene have met the new women players in schools, but the young men face so much competition for gigs that they often never give the women a second thought unless it's to hope that men will get preferential treatment—the chance to work, accumulate publicity and honors, earn a living, and become a star.

For the women players, the breaks have to come from leaders who, for one reason or another, keep their minds and options open. Or the women must get their own gigs as leaders. And they are getting them, especially in smaller clubs.

Chapter Two / / / A Status Report: Part Two

After veteran jazz drummer Charli Persip's seventeen-piece Superband finished swinging with brassiness and sophistication through a summer night in 1988 at Visiones, a Greenwich Village club, his musicians went to the bar to calm down from their high-energy performance. Visiones is on Macdougal Street in a neighborhood long famous for sheltering creative upstarts. One young male hornplayer banged into Melissa Slocum's bass fiddle and amplifiers. He said, "Man, I didn't mean to do that."

Melissa, then in her mid-twenties and one of three women in the group that year, replied, "That's all right, man." She gave him a sloe-eyed warning glance with a little smile and kept going to the bar. She was wearing a little black leather beanie, which gave her an offbeat appearance. Sharon Freeman, who played an electric keyboard with the group that night (though she prefers an acoustic piano and is also well known as a French horn player), and alto saxophonist Sue Terry had already ordered their drinks. The women started talking a bit of shop, occasionally calling each other "man."

Everyone still says "man" in the jazz world. It's the tradition. It may have started as a tribute to someone's great playing abilities, which gave him authority and stature in the eyes of his admirers. And in jazz, especially in bebop-rooted jazz, which is the main style in New York City, and in New Orleans-rooted Swing Era jazz too, tradition means a lot. All youngsters are advised to know the classic jazz repertoire from, for example, "St. James Infirmary" from Louis "Pops" Armstrong's band book in the 1920s to Thelonious Monk's "Round Midnight" written in the bebop era, to John Coltrane's "Giant Steps" and much more. Fledgling professional pianist Beatriz DeMello from Brazil impressed trombonist Al Gray because she knew how to play Dizzy Gillespie's "Ow" at a club in Boston; he later invited her to sit in when he spotted her in his audience at Fat Tuesday's in New York. Youngsters who don't know the jazz repertoire—

the tradition—are disparaged. With a good background in the music, which they must play wonderfully well, they can catch the attention of veteran musicians, who hire them for gigs. Then their colleagues, or hip managers, or critics, or clubowners may be alerted, and executives may arrange recording contracts.

For the women at Visiones, talking shop meant sharing information about what other women jazz musicians were doing. Many women hire each other to play in groups. That method of connecting, or bonding, is especially important for women; they have to overcome their own compliance with the traditional prejudice against their playing at all. They also hire men for sexually integrated groups. That way, too, they avoid the old-fashioned pigeonhole of the all-women's group—the novelty act—virtually the only choice, until the 1980s, for most women who wanted to play professionally.

Some women never agree to play in all-women's groups or all-women's festivals out of an unwillingness to be ghettoized. For that reason, several musicians, primarily those who play in pop groups and studios and occasionally play jazz too, have taken a firm anti-women's group stand. If the forum has sexism and not music as its raison d'être, all women jazz musicians like to avoid it. And they try to brave their lonesome ways through the dissonance of rejections based sometimes solely on sexual discrimination. So complicated and volatile an issue is women's presence in jazz that women, the wives of jazz musicians, have occasionally compounded matters by objecting to their husbands' taking women instrumentalists on the road. Some women instrumentalists know they have been passed over for jobs because of pressure from the leaders' wives. That's part of the dues women musicians pay in a field where everybody pays dues. Many women handle the sexual discrimination aspect of their careers by "wearing blinders," as Sue Evans called the technique of ignoring prejudice and forging ahead with music. Usually women arrive at budding acceptance in jazz circles, from which the invitations for jobs must first come from peers, by gladly playing in any situation—all-women's groups or not. A fine all-woman's group such as the big band Diva is indisputably a wonderful way to make a good impression. So are Kit McClure's band, Maiden Voyage, and Straight Ahead, an all-women's quintet that began recording for Atlantic in 1992 and exciting audiences in clubs and jazz festivals.

Many women also teach while nurturing their playing careers. The hardiest, most organized and determined women with administrative talents form their own groups and even jazz orchestras for recording or touring, or they work toward those goals. But it's difficult for anyone but the biggest stars—men and women alike—to find enough work to keep a group together. To help earn a living, reeds player and bandleader Carol Sudhalter started her own firm to hire musicians for parties and special events. Women have discovered that entrepreneurship is usually the only way they can showcase themselves and build careers when calls to play with established all-male groups don't arrive. Deuce, a fusion group co-led by saxophonist Jean Fineberg and trumpeter Ellen Seeling, is an excellent case in point. So was the short-lived, traditional, bebop-rooted group that was co-led by two outstanding, experienced musicians, trumpeter Rebecca Coupe Franks and saxophonist Virginia Mayhew until mid-1990.

Using a variety of tactics, a younger generation emerged in force in the 1980s. By the early 1990s, an even more numerous group was coming along, trying its luck in New York, where all the trends for women in jazz are the most evident and intense. On the West Coast, Terri Lyne Carrington and Ann Patterson, leader of Maiden Voyage, and others have noticed a similar emergence of women.

Veteran women musicians enjoyed fresh surges in their careers in the 1980s too, as jazz became more trendy. The veterans had the advantage of having been active and excellent for so long, even if some of their careers went into partial commercial eclipse in the rock era of the 1960s and 1970s. Among them is pianist Marian McPartland, whose fame, for her increasing depth and technique as a jazz pianist and composer over five decades and for her appearances at the glamorous Cafe Carlyle and prestigious concert halls, has been augmented by her National Public Radio show, "Piano Jazz," now in its sixteenth year. She has interviewed many pianists and other musicians, even Roy Eldridge, who played piano in later life when his health prevented him from playing trumpet. Her interview and duet with pianist Hazel Scott playing a Duke Ellington song has etched itself as a lesson into the minds of some people—the intellectually curious pianist John Hicks, for one, who pays attention to all developments and literature concerning music. McPartland has also done historic interviews with Sarah Vaughan, who played piano very well, and pianists Mary Lou Williams and Dorothy Donegan. And Marian has included many young women in her show's guest list. Recently, some of Marian's interviews—Dave Brubeck's first—began to be released on CDs on The Jazz Alliance label.

Donegan is a veteran whose career became particularly renascent in New York City in the 1980s. Her first recording to be released in quite a while, "Dorothy Donegan!" with her trio, on Chiaroscuro Records, was done live on a jazz cruise in 1990. Then came "Dorothy Donegan Live at The Floating Jazz Festival," 1992, with Clark Terry, on Chiaroscuro. Patti Bown also had a high profile for a while again in the well-known club, the Village Gate, in the late 1980s. Donegan appeared often at the Village Vanguard, Michael's Pub, Fortune Garden Pavilion, Carlos I, and concert halls. She and Patti sing and entertain as well as play. Bown can charm audiences with her quick ad libs and turn the potentially sterile experience of a solo concert into an intimate, sophisticated interlude—a quintessential jazz experience. Donegan also has natural rapport with audiences. Donegan and Patti dress in eye-catching ways for down-to-earth reasons. Donegan wears opulent gowns and turbans. Bown has concocted exotic costumes out of a dash of this and that; her straw brimmers and other decorative hats have attracted positive notice from amused music critics.

Free jazz pianist Joanne Brackeen, whose career caught fire with the public particularly in the 1980s, used to wear plain dresses and a lank hairstyle to gigs. But as the 1980s progressed, she dressed with flair and cut her hair in an expensive, asymmetrical style. She discovered that her fees doubled and tripled. And she too often played in international concerts and jazz festivals. In Chicago's jazz festival, her group received standing ovations in 1987 and 1988.

She was hired, she knew, because the Chicago festival promoters wanted a woman group leader as a token of the growing strength of women jazz players. She emerged with honors. Fans telephoned several men in her group to say that it had given the most sparkling and exciting performance in the festival. One *Down Beat* magazine editor, who had never heard of her before, became aware of her playing because of the festival; he turned into an enthusiastic fan. "I got jobs all over the country from that festival," she said later.

To a point, one could say, her career became illustrious in the 1980s. That point was the place where most of New York City's main clubowners still refused to book her with her own group as a headliner for a full week's work, claiming that she and most women leaders could now draw crowds. Then in the early 1990s, Joanne began to get engagements for her larger groups in such clubs as Sweet Basil and Visiones. She and her trio gave an especially successful concert, where the audience cheered, at Columbia University in 1992. At the same time her avant-garde compositions such as "Picasso" on "Where Legends Dwell," her 1992 album of original music, sounded more mellow and acceptable to general audiences than some of her previous work. And her Brazilian albums, "Breath of Brazil" and "Take a Chance," were more accessible too, confirming the brilliance of her playing and composing, as she blended her jazz background—with her own arrangements, and odd, alerting chords—and the Brazilian musical ethos, with its difficult melodies and rhythms.

Clubowners hire the traditional Donegan as a group leader regularly—and would do the same for McPartland if she wanted to work more in clubs. Those women proved in the 1950s that they could draw affluent audiences. Donegan had special backing at the time; her husband, a clubowner on the West Coast, promised to reimburse the owner of the glamorous Upper East Side club, the Embers, if he lost money on Donegan's booking. Of course, he didn't lose. British-born Marian's husband cornetist Jimmy McPartland helped pave the way for her, presenting her with his praise and moral support to everyone he knew. Both women had the *je ne sais quoi* and the gifts to make audiences embrace them.

Most of the relative newcomers lack promotional teams. Clubowners would have to take chances on the lesser known groups, and clubowners usually don't take many chances—they can't afford to—although they know that publicity plus good reviews can work wonders for any group. Some younger women get their chances. Sweet Basil's Horst Liepolt hired Canadian soprano saxophonist Jane Bunnett to lead a group for a week in 1993. "She's a friend of mine, and I like her music," Liepolt explained. Wendy Cunningham hired Renee Rosnes to lead a trio—a rhythm section she had been playing with in Joe Henderson's group—for a week in April 1993. It was Renee's first time as a group leader in an important jazz club in New York. Then came other clubs—the new Down Beat, for one, with her husband Billy Drummond on drums. These bookings classify as breakthroughs.

If women don't always pack the clubs, it's also true that well-known male group leaders can't always draw crowds for reasons having more to do with the economic climate or even the weather than sexual politics. The bias against women group leaders is reminiscent of the generally accepted fairy tale that television news executives espoused in the 1960s. They claimed that women's voices weren't authoritative enough to broadcast the news and would cause audiences to shut off their radios and TV sets. Those claims were based on "official polls," executives said with assuredness—polls long since forgotten, if they ever existed. But there is no affirmative action in jazz. To get booked as leaders, jazz's women make the best of their individual drives, personalities, talents, finesse, drawing power for audiences, and luck.

If they cannot always move upward, they can make lateral moves. So some women regularly cross the line between all the styles of popular music and even play classical and light classical music—going from Broadway and pop concert orchestras to jazz groups—to establish themselves, earn a living, and express the gamut of their feelings. The list of players on the soundtrack album (not a jazz album) for the movie *Malcolm*

X, composed by jazz trumpeter Terence Blanchard, includes some classically trained women—string players and others such as drummer Sue Evans—who cross that line easily. Rachel Z, who plays electric keyboards with Steps Ahead, jumps from keyboards to acoustic piano for her debut album, "Trust The Universe," with Columbia in 1993. Until 1990, Stephanie Fauber, a classically trained French horn player, used to travel from Broadway orchestra pits to the Monday night Village Vanguard jazz band. "You've got to diversify to stay alive. You've got to be a chameleon," says Virginia-born singer and guitarist Kat Dyson, who usually plays the blues but also works in jazz and pop groups in her adopted city, Montreal.

Women of all backgrounds, from classical to jazz, can find work in studios—jobs for which contractors call musicians to play for jingles (the insiders' word for commercials), recordings, television specials, Broadway pit orchestras, symphony orchestras, and chamber groups—all kinds of events. Though studio work has fallen off, and musicians have been increasingly replaced by synthesizers, some women musicians—brass, woodwind, and string players primarily, and a few drummers and percussionists—have continued to find jobs performing, recording, and playing some jazz. The majority don't play jazz however; either they're not comfortable improvising or aren't familiar to people in the jazz world from whom the calls must come.

A jazz musician—man or woman—who wants to play in the studios must not only play but also read music very well and require virtually no rehearsal. Historically, jazz musicians have felt constrained in the studios because there are few, if any, opportunities to improvise. The acclaimed Thad Jones-Mel Lewis Orchestra was founded as a rehearsal band for jazz musicians who worked in studios and wanted a group in which they could stretch out, improvise, and play jazz. They didn't care if they earned very little money in the jazz band, or even no money, because the band played music dear to their hearts. Usually, musicians can't simply move back and forth between the studio, or commercial world, and the jazz world. The commercial world is as cliquey as the jazz world, if not more so; a musician must know somebody who opens a door.

It should be noted that some of the best male jazz musicians—trumpeter Joe Wilder, for example—cross the line between jazz and commercial work regularly to earn their livings. And they find they're not called for certain types of shows. Bassist Ron Carter, one of the most famous teachers and players in jazz clubs and concerts, works a great deal in the studios, but never gets called for beauty pageants. Such jobs are political plums. Ron Carter's encounters with music industry politics cast into bold relief the roadblocks for female newcomers.

The financial rewards of playing commercial music can be great.

There are fees and residuals for jingles, fees for recordings, and excellent weekly paychecks for musicians in the Broadway orchestra pits, plus rehearsal fees. In general, studio musicians earn more than jazz musicians. And commercial and studio musicians avoid the unhealthy smoky night-clubs and late night hours of the jazz world. Naturally competition is stiff in the commercial world, for men as well as women.

Women's progress became palpable in New York, the international capitol of jazz during the 1980s and early 1990s. Almost completely banished are the sad stories of blatant bias or harassment, such as the following incidents and general situations.

Patti Bown recalled her first record date around 1960 for Quincy Jones, whom she had known since her childhood in Seattle. One well-known, African-American big-band musician at the studio said, "Oh, a bitch is going to play."

Jones told her, "Go warm up a little at the piano."

"Afterward everyone in the studio stood up and applauded. I thought someone important had come through the door," she reminisced. But the cheers were for her.

Calls came for record dates from people who thought she was "Pat" or "Patrick" Bown. She would try to cajole them by saying, "I'm not a man, but give me a chance." She concedes that "it was cliquey for men, too" in the 1960s—the "old days" for her—"but it was even harder for women."

Some women made certain they were mistaken for men in the 1960s and before. An obituary notice about trumpeter-pianist Billy Tipton in 1989, a woman who had dressed and posed all her life as a man, implied that she had promoted her charade because it was the only way she could have worked with Jack Teagarden and other musicians' groups. The news shocked women in the jazz world less than it did any other group. Some male musicians felt that Billy Tipton didn't have to pose as a man with a wife and adopt children to get work. But his one-time "wife" referred to an unwritten code of ethics in the jazz world as the unequivocal reason for Tipton's masquerade.

Drummer Dottie Dodgion purposely signed her name as D. Dodgion to get calls for work in earlier days. Once she showed up for a gig at a strippers' club. The management was "upset," she reminisced, strangling a laugh in her throat. "But I said, 'Don't worry. My father was a strip drummer. I can handle it.'" And of course she did.

Scores of women tried their luck as trailblazers as far back as the 1920s, 1930s and 1940s. Few established reputations outside of women's groups. Most were pianists in groups that schools or male relatives had founded. That's how Norma Teagarden, Jack's sister, and Marge Sin-

gleton, sister of a musician and later Zutty Singleton's wife, began playing
professionally. Norma was still playing in a San Francisco club in 1994.
Marge met Zutty when she was playing on a riverboat, and she gave up
her life as a performer to promote and manage Zutty's career. That too was
tradition; though the couple could have used a second income, women
were not expected to compete for—or even share—the limelight, and
Marge always said she preferred the traditional role. It was not until the
1970s that the definition of the traditional role began to change in the
United States.

Before then, as we've already noted, only trombonist-arranger Melba
Liston effectively transcended the prejudice against women horn players
on the bandstands with men in the most illustrious groups. She was
introduced to all-male jazz groups by her former schoolmate Dexter Gordon, and then encouraged by arranger and trumpeter Gerald Wilson.
Even so, Melba appears never to have been able to give herself the same
financial security from playing and arranging as the best women pianists
could. One reason may have been that, as a player, she was never a highly
paid concert artist or a consistently commercial bandleader. She might not
have collected royalties but only fees for some of her arrangements. As a
sideperson on recordings, she picked up her paychecks, not always aware
of the title of the recording she had made; often she recognized the songs
later when she heard them broadcast on radio. She experienced more
prejudice in her earlier years than the women pianists did. The men
resented the "bitch" trombone player, and they didn't calm down until
they saw the arrangements she wrote for them. Her relations with the men
thereafter ranged from that of "little sister," whom they looked after and
with whom they shared coffee, cigarettes, and drinks, to "Mama," who
looked after them, sewed buttons on their clothes, and cut their hair.

Melba was also able to become friendly with the men because she was
"cool." She could "hang out" with them, as they say, and order the same
drinks they did. A handsome, statuesque woman, she could banter with
them too. In short, she had the stamina and demeanor to establish her
autonomy, her independent personality, her musical authority, and get
along in the jazz world, a man's world. Drummer Dottie Dodgion also
knew how to drink Scotch with the men and talk their language, when her
husband, altoist Jerry Dodgion, gave her entrée to the jazz world. (Wom-
en musicians don't have to hang out with the men in the old, hard-
drinking culture that used to be traditional in jazz. There's now less
excessive alcohol use among all jazz musicians in general. Vegetarianism
and other healthful habits are in vogue in the jazz world as well as everyplace else.)

"Very few women jazz musicians, black or white, survived," Melba reflected in the early 1980s. "It was hard for all. The problems were almost unique. Maybe the musicians didn't treat me any worse than they treated their own families. And I was never a problem. I was just a hard-working, patient music person. I carried my own luggage and took care of myself. And I learned to build relationships with the men and the jazz world. It's not something you pick up and understand right away."

If American women jazz musicians had a difficult time finding space for themselves on domestic bandstands, they had an even more frustrating time abroad. The pianists who first established themselves in the United States—McPartland, Dorothy Donegan, Mary Lou Williams, Hazel Scott, and a few others—were again the exceptions. Dottie Dodgion recalled playing with her ex-husband, Jerry, in a small combo in Italy. Afterward, the son of a prominent Italian filmmaker approached Jerry and said, "I'd like to introduce you to a wonderful drummer." Jerry said, "My wife's a drummer." The Italian replied, "No, I mean a real drummer."

Apart from the handful of lucky women whose husbands or instrument (the piano) cleared the way for them, women musicians worked with a modicum of regularity only when they formed their own, sexually segregated groups until the 1980s, whether in Europe or the United States. Some groups were interracial, such as the International Sweethearts of Rhythm coached by Eddie Durham from the Count Basie band and originally founded as a profit-making group to support a school. (It has always been much easier for women to work in racially integrated bands than to find work in sexually integrated groups. That demonstrates how deep sexual prejudice has run in music.) A documentary testifies to the quality of the band's music and the pluckiness of the women. But highly promoted, first-quality records are the primary way to the public's heart and consciousness. Few all-women's groups made any records, so the documentation of their legacy is paltry. Jazz historian Rosetta Reitz's important releases on Rosetta Records include the International Sweethearts of Rhythm.

Nowadays, the surviving veterans and the gifted, educated, driving newcomers are reaping the benefits of their own qualifications plus the new respect for the pioneers and the influence of the women's movement. In the 1980s, Patti Bown served on panels picking the winners for the National Endowment for the Arts grants for jazz. Having lived for decades in New York, by the time she was a panelist in 1988, she was very alert to the change in the scene for the journeywomen players and especially for the youngsters. "So many outstanding women have come out of the woodwork in the 1980s. And it's okay for women to be out here, doing it," she observed. Joanne Brackeen also marveled at the number of emergent women instrumentalists—and at the quality of their playing, though she still rued the lack of parity in opportunities for women. Only a decade earlier she had not been very impressed with the relatively few women players.

Pianist Geri Allen, in her early thirties by 1990 and one of the young musicians, male and female, most acutely aware by inclination and education of the history of women jazz instrumentalists, paid tribute to Patti's generation and the previous pioneers: "We must be thankful to (pianist) Lovey Austin, Mary Lou Williams, and Melba for their help. They made it easier for us now." With the aid of the Smithsonian Institution, Geri respectfully recreated Lovey Austin's work as a pianist accompanying silent films in theatres and presented the project at the Smithsonian Institution in the fall of 1989.

Geri had struggled for over a decade, beginning under the wing of trumpeter Marcus Belgrave in her native Detroit, going on to study at Howard University, then with Kenny Barron on a National Endowment for the Arts grant in New York for a summer. She moved again to get her master's degree in ethnomusicology at the University of Pittsburgh on a scholarship, and returned to New York City to work in a variety of music jobs beginning in 1982. Some male musicians, to whom she had been introduced by Detroiters, were supportive and hired her; other men gossiped behind her back about how well she played. She toured as singer Angela Bofill's accompanist; she played the soulful music in the band of the New York, gospel-based show *Mama, I Want to Sing*. It wasn't until 1988 that a critic mentioned in print that the JVC Festival—formerly the Kool and before that the Newport Jazz Festival—should hire more youngsters and women such as Geri Allen. The JVC people called Geri to play. That quick response wouldn't have happened ten years earlier; the critic never would have even written such an article.

Geri's intensely personal, experimental style, sometimes moody original compositions, and always electrifying technique are typical of her formally educated generation. She has special mastery of composition. And she and her contemporaries have in common a predilection for blending modern, classical European music with jazz traditions, inventing music *sometimes* light years away from jazz's traditional joyousness, assertiveness, or bluesiness; the original swinging, rhythmic underpinnings of the art at times become a trace element. Joyous laments are a memory, as contemporary angst reigns. And if it is difficult for men to find peer acceptance and audience enthusiasm for their original songs, it is even more difficult for most women players to have their compositions taken seriously and played in public. Geri is one of the growing numbers of women composers afforded some chances.

If there is a glass ceiling—and there is—it prevents women from getting enough, or sometimes any, chances to lead their own groups in clubs. Polished and popular young male sidemen used to bump their heads hard against that same ceiling in the early 1980s. Now they're having more success; for one thing, the older, established jazz legends who were the popular leaders have died, and the youngsters are filling a void. It's the rare woman who has been allowed to step in too.

But talented women musicians in their twenties and thirties, who had moved completely and assuredly through the door, and were earning their livings—at various levels—as leaders and sidepeople, were sending a signal. However difficult a life in music was for them in extremely competitive, economically pinched New York, it was immeasurably easier than it would have been only eight years earlier, when radical changes for women jazz players truly began to manifest themselves.

Chapter Three / / / Remembrance of Things Passé: Jill McManus Recalls the Frustrations of the Jazz Sisters in the 1970s

Three wonderful reviews ran in *The New York Times* on January 21 and 25, 1977, and in the *Daily News* on February 17, 1977, about the Jazz Sisters. The first one, headlined "Women Who Make Jazz," told how a sextet of women jazz instrumentalists came together by accident to perform for a special event and encountered such an appreciative audience that they decided to make the group formal. The second story raved about the group's performance in a women's jazz concert featuring two different groups and soloist-pianist Valerie Capers. That headline read "Women Prove They Are Equal to Men in Jazz." The third story focused on a quotation by Jill McManus, the Jazz Sisters' pianist and unofficial spokesperson; the quote was used as a headline to tell the gist of the group's situation: "People Aren't Exactly Lining Up To Hire Us."

It might also be said that, in any era, no matter what sex the players are, few groups have been destined for long weathering unless they have had very strong leaders who can survive many changes of personnel. An extra strike against all women's jazz groups used to be the small pool of players from which leaders could choose. Though women bassists, for instance, are still few and far between, they were once even rarer. Dottie Dodgion recalled playing with Toshiko Akiyoshi as the pianist for an all-women's concert on the West Coast. At the last moment, they realized they didn't have a bassist; each had left it up to the other to call one, because neither of them had known any they could call readily in the area and hoped that the other might. On occasion, the scarcity of women players has led some to be, at best, obnoxious—probably more so than men, who had more competition to be mindful and wary of. Big-band leader Kit McClure and a few other women leaders have noticed that trend. Jill McManus tempers the judgment, saying, from her experience, women can become "a bit overbearing."

Taking into account all the complications of the Jazz Sisters's era, here is the story of their short and interesting life. (Other all-women's groups in the period in New York were the Latin group Latin Fever, Celebration led by singer Evelyn Blakey, and Melba Liston and Company. Jill McManus also recalls a group called Ariel, with Barbara London and Nina Sheldon. Isis was another. Other groups played in other cities.)

From *The New York Times,* January 21, 1977, by Robert Palmer:

"Do I get resistance, being a woman playing jazz?" Jill McManus, a pianist, composer and leader of a group called the Jazz Sisters, considered the question and repeated it again. "You feel bad complaining because it's tough for almost everybody in jazz, but, yes, being a woman has made a difference. The resistance is spoken and unspoken, and it's almost better not to address the problem, to grit your teeth, keep smiling and keep practicing. Having a jazz group that's composed entirely of women does have a certain novelty value; but we don't get a lot of heavy offers for work."

Once they began performing professionally, their sex began to make more of a difference. "The attitudes were typified by what happened to the Jazz Sisters' trumpet player, Jean Davis," said Miss McManus. "She showed up early for a new job and was sitting on the bandstand with her horn case. A few musicians came in and looked at her, and eventually the clubowner came over and asked, 'Where's your old man?' A lot of women become discouraged by that kind of thing and quit playing. Or they marry musicians and end up giving up their careers for their husbands. In fact, I don't know many women who are married and musicians. Most of us are functionally single."

The formation of the Jazz Sisters is characteristic of the sort of situations in which women who play jazz are likely to find themselves. "The New York Jazz Museum runs regular Sunday afternoon concerts," Miss McManus explained wryly, "and one Sunday a year was Ladies Day. The second year they tried it, they got my name, and I suggested some other people. Some names were just picked out of a hat. Anyway, the ones of us who were chosen warmed up—and played. Most of us had never met, but the reaction we got was really warm, and we decided to get together and play some more."

Since then, the Jazz Sisters—Miss McManus on piano, Miss Davis on trumpet, Janice Robinson on trombone, Willene Barton on tenor saxophonist, Lynn Milano on bass, and Paula Hampton, drums, and vocals, have performed at the Village Gate, Storyville, the Five Spot and other clubs in the Metropolitan area and colleges.

The Jazz Sisters are more eclectic. "We'll be playing a couple of my originals and something by our trumpet player," said Miss McManus. "Then we'll do a standard, some blues and some contemporary jazz-rock type things." Valerie Capers, who directed a choir of 100 voices in an original composition as part of Dizzy Gillespie's appearance at the Newport Jazz Festival last summer, will be playing her own music. "It should be interesting," Miss McManus noted. "Most of the offers I've had for the group have been to do top-40 material, go to Las Vegas, wear costumes and do a choreographed thing. People don't seem to want us to just be musicians who go out and play, but that's what we're going to do."

From *The New York Times,* January 25, 1977, by Robert Palmer:

Le Jazz des Femmes, a concert featuring women in jazz that took place at Town Hall Sunday evening, offered proof that some well-known critical cliches are in need of revision. First there is the use of the adjective "masculine" to describe a firm touch on the piano, a big tone on the saxophone, or an aggressive sense of swing on the drums. The first group on the program, the Jazz Sisters, demonstrated that these qualities are not male prerogatives.

Jill McManus, the Sisters' musical director, displayed a driving right hand and a more energetic version of Bill Evans's style of chording on the piano. Willene Barton played the tenor in the gruffly rhapsodic manner of an Eddie "Lockjaw" Davis; her ballad feature, "Come Rain or Come Shine," brought down the house. Paula Hampton on drums and Lynn Milano on bass drove the group with a springy pulse. The other soloists were Janice Robinson, a trombonist with a wonderfully assertive sound, and Jean Davis on trumpet.

Donna Summers's group, the Peace Makers, featured a declamatory Sandi Hewitt on vocals. The rest of the players were men, and one of them, Bill Saxton, presented an unwitting parody of macho as he roared through a tough tenor solo, with energy to spare but without a trace of the bluesy elegance Miss Barton brought to the instrument. The highlights of the set were Miss Summers's melodious compositions.

The highlight of the evening was the performance by (Juilliard graduate) Valerie Capers, a blind pianist who has put an exemplary classical technique at the service of jazz improvisaton and come up with a commanding style all her own. There are echoes of Fats Waller, Oscar Peterson and others, but the bristling density of Miss Capers's chordal passages and her habit of materializing melody lines out of lush tremolos are notably original. Her ballad playing, especially on a deliberate "I'll Remember April," was remarkable for its control of dynamics and depth of feeling.

From the *Daily News,* February 17, 1977, by Ricki Fulman:

Sounds of Duke Ellington swung through the room. Five of the Jazz Sisters closed their eyes, tapped their feet, dug the music.

They were listening to the tape of their concert at Town Hall a few nights before.

It was something of a milestone in jazz circles. It was probably the first concert which featured women musicians, and did not rely on a male "name" to sell tickets.

"Mmm," smiled Paula Hampton, the group's drummer and vocalist. "We really sound good there. If we could only play together more often, we'd really get our act together."

"Yeah," sighed Jill McManus, the pianist and group leader. "If only . . ."

. . . Officially there are six Jazz Sisters, but getting everyone together at once can be tricky so they play even when only four or five of them are available.

"We're all busy working at other things to make enough money to support ourselves," explained Jill.

Of the six, only trombonist Janice Robinson is a full-time professional musician. She plays these nights with the orchestra for the Broadway musical, "Guys and Dolls."

Pianist Jill McManus and bassist Lynn Milano teach piano and bass respectively.

Jean Davis, the trumpet player, supports herself doing interviews for a city agency. Paula Hampton, whose cousin is Lionel Hampton and whose uncle is Slide Hampton, works as a clerk about six hours a day. Tenor saxophonist Willene Barton is a full-time messenger for Hertz Rent-a-Car. [*Author's note:* Paula Hampton's mother and Slide Hampton are brother and sister; the family relationship is warm, but Paula's cousin Lionel, an influential bandleader, has stayed remote from her personally and professionally.]

All work nights and weekends as freelance musicians, which means they will fill in when a group needs a pianist, drummer, whatever.

Jill has found that women are usually the last to get called when a group needs someone to substitute.

The Sisters got together a couple of years ago after a Ladies Day concert held at the Jazz Museum. "The Museum invited a few women to come and play," recalled Jill. "Some of us did, and we found we liked playing together and decided to try it."

Now they average about one booking a month and rehearse two or three times a month.

In addition to their recent Town Hall concert (one segment of a night devoted to women jazz musicians), they have given performances at colleges, as well as at the Village Gate, Storyville and Shepheards. Their reviews have been good.

"Different things come up," noted Jill, who, as group leader, handles publicity and bookings. "But people aren't exactly lining up to hire us. Often they come and talk to us at a concert and say they'd like to book us, but frequently they don't follow through."

The audiences are more supportive and appreciative than the booking agents, she continued. "Audiences listen, and if the music is good, they're satisfied. But club owners and booking agents tend to see us as a novelty act, which is the last thing we want."

They would like to be taken seriously as professional musicians. "What we wear, for example, has nothing to do with anything, but agents talk about us playing cocktail music and wearing tight, low-cut dresses."

Paula Hampton interrupted at that point, and told how she was supposed to sing with trumpet player Howard McGhee's group. "The first thing he says is get yourself a nice lowcut gown," she recalled.

"I refused and quit," she said angrily. "I'm not going to sell myself. I'm a musician. I'm thinking about giving up my false eyelashes. I get sick of everyone saying how I'm the sexiest looking drummer they've ever seen." [*Author's note:* Paula looks chic in men's formal clothes, which she sometimes wears to work, in the style started by Marlene Dietrich.]

McGhee, meanwhile, just laughed when asked in a telephone interview why Paula is not playing with his group. "I don't know," he reflected. "It just didn't work out. But you know," he added, "a woman does represent problems if she's part of a male group. Someone could come up and start messing with her, and that just puts a pressure on all the men. We are put in the position of having to protect the women who play with us.

"If it's all men in a group, they just watch out for themselves. When a woman is on the scene, it's different. Even with the grandmother of all the lady musicians, jazz pianist Mary Lou Williams, you really have to be extra respectful."

"She expects it. So if you hire women, it's just going to mean hassles."

Several other male musicians were interviewed about the scarcity of women in jazz. Bassist Ron Carter pointed out that the heavy equipment is difficult enough for men to move around. "For women, it's extra rough," he said.

And another male musician observed: "There is a difference between men and women in everything they do, if you think about it. Like, look at how a woman washes a floor, compared to the way a man does it. Somehow, the woman is more dainty. Same with music. Men just have more guts when they play. I don't know why, they just do. Rock is easier, which is why you find more women playing it."

One point the Jazz Sisters stressed is that for a woman to make it in jazz, she has to be serious and dedicated. All insisted that they are.

Born in New Jersey, Jill had moved with her family to New York City when she had been a year old, then to Connecticut five years later. She lived there until she went to Wellesley College, where she majored in English. From the age of seven, she had been playing piano and noticing all along: "It feels really good to play. It's really fun."

After college, she worked as a researcher for *Time* magazine in New York City. And she began her piano studies with John Mehegan, who had earlier constituted the jazz department, or what had passed for it for a while, at Juilliard. He had also taught at Columbia University in Teachers' College in the late 1950s and later lectured at Yale University. "It took me a long time to get used to (Mehegan's) manner," she recalls. "But he was also very affectionate in his curmudgeonly way. And he really got me started in playing."

She married a journalist, Jason McManus, who would rise to become editor-in-chief of *Time,* Inc. As youngsters, the couple went to jazz clubs, primarily Slug's on the Lower East Side. "We would park the car. Street gangs would throw lighted matches at us and run away. Physically, Slug's was a funky place," says Jill. "As you walked in, you faced the bandstand, and there were banquettes around the room. The music sounded far out to me, but it was engrossing. Records didn't strike me as strongly as live performances by McCoy Tyner, Curtis Fuller, Pharoah Sanders doing that chart 'The Creator Has a Master Plan'. Everybody played there: Ornette Coleman, maybe Don Cherry, Lee Morgan, Cedar Walton, Sam Jones, Wayne Shorter, and Art Blakey and the people in his band."

The more she played the piano, the more little gigs she found, and the further away from each other she and her husband drifted. Eventually they divorced. She lived alone in a comfortable apartment on the Upper East Side of Manhattan where the rent was reasonable. From that base, she was able to support herself by playing occasionally and teaching throughout the 1970s into the 1990s.

Her first gig had been at a Lexington Avenue bar in 1971, she recalls, at a time when jazz was very much out of popular favor. "We were working seven hours a night for $15. Bobby Jones and even Gerry Mulligan played in this strange place just to keep their chops up. I was learning changes. They would call a tune in an unfamiliar key, and it would devastate me. I worked there and a few other places."

Later on, Jill worked at the Village Corner, sometime between 1975 and 1977. "Joanne Brackeen worked at the Surf Maid in the Village. Nina Sheldon, the pianist and singer, was playing nearby at the Village Gate. After work, we would meet and go to hear music. I also played gigs in psychiatric hospitals. I've done some things that were not all just joyous. But I thought: 'At least I'm getting a little start'. I didn't realize that those were some of the busiest times in my playing career," she reflected with a wry smile.

The Jazz Sisters came into being in 1974. "Sometimes Ellen Seeling or Jean Fineberg subbed for Jean Davis and Willene Barton, as time went on, if we needed a sub for a night. And we hashed over the names. We didn't want anything for the group that would sound too sweet. We picked the Jazz Sisters."

"We played in parks, at Hunter College, at the Brooklyn Museum, at Shepheards' Jazz at Noon, which was televised. We were featured on CBS News. We played at Storyville, the Five Spot, the Ramapo Jazz Festival, and at Glassboro College, Rutgers University, and Riverside Church, the Cathedral Church of St. John the Divine, and Stony Brook University. We were hot for a minute there."

"We played opposite Charlie Mingus at the Village Gate. He was pissed that we had six players, while he had five. But he was sweet. I never saw his bad side. He did . . . strange things. But I never witnessed such events.

"Playing with the Jazz Sisters was a heady experience. We were a surly, odd, mismatched lot, a token female group, a novelty, and all of us really favored different styles of music. Some were into Swing and early bop. I was into the newer harmonics and complex tunes. But we sounded good. We played 'Nica's Dream', standards, my tunes. I did most of the arranging. I took Freddie Hubbard's 'Sky Dive' off a record and voiced it a little differently. The group began as a cooperative, but I was the one who was sending out press releases and making most calls. I told them that I was feeling as if I were the bandleader, paying all the expenses for getting the gigs myself. And I was certainly one of the least experienced members in the band. Jean and Paula and Willene had played for years. But they had day jobs and didn't want full-time playing jobs by then. Security was involved for them.

"We worked sporadically and had a lot of fun at the beginning. That is, we enjoyed the chance to do some regular playing. As with any band, it can get a little funny after a while. We had different priorities, different tastes, very different lifestyles. Often, to make the music commercial, appealing, we would put in 'Mr. Magic'. And the group didn't want to do my original, arcane tunes; they were difficult to play on.

"Another problem was finding women who could play all the styles and improvise if we needed a substitute. Really, there was almost no one to call. We got into a hassle once in a place in New Jersey. Paula was sick, and so we lined up Al Harewood, the drummer, who worked in that club quite often. And the owner was annoyed that we didn't show up as an all-girl group. So the owner slipped away without paying the drummer. And I gave Al my pay. We were playing for eight shows a week for $275 in that place. It wasn't worth it, really.

"Soon after we got started, Lynn Milano joined us as the bass player. She had back trouble, and guys would say to her, 'Poor little thing, how can you carry that big bass?' The attitudes were really so—macho. But in those dark, smoky places, with junkies around, we were such a novelty, playing all the heavy tunes, that people loved us and looked out for us. Not the owners, who were sometimes very tough, but the customers were good to us. Sometimes we played in places with bad pianos, bad mikes. And people wondered why the band wasn't playing perfectly in tune. We were pretty together, though, as good as good working bands. The Jazz Sisters was close to being a real, viable band. I think we could have done quite well if we had had more unity of purpose, and if clubowners had been more receptive. A few thought we were cute, but others didn't even want to hear about us.

"Some of my memories are wonderful. Willene was great. She would come to the gig with her proper little dress and her horn case. And she would have a bottle of vodka in the case. She's a very swaggering player with a big sound like Gene Ammons. And she played all these pretty ballads.

"Jean Davis was born in New Orleans, studied with Doc Cheatham, and played with many groups. Willene Barton has played with top groups. So has Paula Hampton. Lynn Milano has a music degree from the Eastman School of Music, a master's from the state University of New York at Stony Brook, and a teaching certificate. She plays upright and Fender (electric) bass; she has played with the New Orleans Philharmonic, the Canadian Opera Company, the Boston Pops Orchestra under Arthur Fiedler, and other professional orchestras and chamber groups in the United States and Europe, and with such jazz people as (pianist) Duke Jordan, (trumpeter) Charlie Shavers, and (trumpeter) Jimmy Nottingham. And we never got a record out, just some odd tapes that weren't done in a controlled way, only in live concerts.

"The group broke up in 1977. I saw Jean and Willene at St. Peter's Lutheran Church several years after that. And it was nice to see each other . . . . Jean had good ideas, a feisty sound, and bright moments. And we had all played in the group, despite our diversities, because we wanted to play. I don't know why something big didn't happen, damn it, for any of us, except for Janice getting the job with the Thad Jones-Mel Lewis Orchestra. I remember the way we played 'A Night in Tunisia' was as good as anybody's. Roy Haynes showed up. He said, 'Man, I heard you guys being broadcast. I heard someone playing one of my licks, and I knew it was you, Paula, so I had to come down and hear you in person'.

"We needed to make a record. And we made a demo with a male singer. The jazz record companies said, 'We don't get the concept. You've got an all-girl band with a male singer. The group is nice; everyone is good. But what can we do with an all-girl band with a male singer?'"

"I said, 'Well, you've done pretty well the other way around.'"

"But they didn't go for it. We never got a chance to record! It was like running into a wall. Now . . . so many years have gone by."

Jill McManus, who had taken Bill Evans as her role model, kept composing and working at occasional gigs in clubs and restaurants, making tours in Europe, and teaching in the Mannes College of Music. She enjoyed the sense of belonging to the jazz community. She played in One Fifth Avenue, Fortune Garden Pavilion, Birdland, and Garvin's, among other New York places, and the Pizza Express in London, and in the

Birmingham, England, Jazz Festival in the 1980s and 1990s. She received commissions to compose. But she was basically dispirited throughout the decade. She summoned up a yeoman's share of eloquence in reflecting on her situation and outlook. Rarely did a male leader call her to play piano with his group. Any job she found playing in public was totally up to her as a leader or soloist. Once she was called for a group by an eminent musician who really wanted a swing-oriented pianist with the ability to play orchestral backup riffs. Jill didn't fit comfortably into the job. "I knew a lot of the repertoire, but not the characteristic intros, riffs, etcetera, from their earlier incarnations." She apologized several times for these deficiencies to the leader.

One high point would come when she led the all-star group at the Kansas City Women's Jazz Festival in 1980, and the band, playing some of her original tunes, was well received. When she hung out in jazz clubs, she would be friendly with the male musicians and appreciative and knowledgeable about their work. They, in turn, occasionally encouraged her. Pianist Sir Roland Hanna, who was a loyal critic, mentor, and adviser, sometimes called her to substitute for him, and Dick Wellstood helped her get work at the Upper East Side club, Hanratty's. But she was not playing in public as much as she wanted to.

Among her credits, Jill McManus recorded a duet with bassist Richard Davis, "As One," on Muse, 1977. Her song "Cloud People" became the title tune of the Rein de Graaff/Dick Vennik Quartet Record, Timeless, Holland, 1984. The album was voted best jazz album of 1984 in Holland. She also composed and arranged the music and led a group that included Native American drummer Louis Mofsie on "Symbols of Hopi," on the Concord label, 1984. The project was a collaborative effort with two composers of the Hopi Tribe of Arizona, and it blended their chant melodies with jazz. The cross-cultural venture received five stars in *Down Beat* magazine. Her piece, "Women Jazz Composers and Arrangers," was included in *The Musical Woman,* Greenwood Press, Vol. 1, 1984.

Chapter Four / / / Several Successful Contemporary Young Women Musicians Talk About Their Inspiration and Commitment

They are soignée and serene. They are articulate when they talk about the spiritual force and drive they feel all the time about their careers in music, as they go about their lives. Some are wives and mothers. They often reflect on the mentors who encouraged them to practice and stretch their imaginations and capabilities. Music gives them a sense of continuity, no matter where they travel to play. And it doesn't hurt their images at all, on the world's most illustrious concert stages and jazz club bandstands, that they're very attractive women, with great style in their clothes and natural-ness in their demeanor; their aplomb radiates charisma as soon as they step on stage.

In 1989, Geri Allen arrived at the piano for a Lincoln Center concert, with her hair, worn in short Rastafarian curls at that time, piled on top of her head; the soft folds of her long black gown with its low neckline emphasized her femininity. Sumi Tonooka kept the stage lights low in the Henry Street Settlement House's Playhouse; the gleam of her beaded shirt was all you could see, adding mystery to the already mysterious power of music and especially to her intense style and unusual harmonies. She used a similar aesthetic ideal for lighting when she led a concert of her own music at the Ethical Culture Society. Although it's not the setting she is best known for to the public now, Patrice Rushen played electric key-boards near brightly lit centerstage in a prestigious New York concert hall; her whole body leaned toward the instrument, completely engaged in playing the highly charged music of the George Santana/Wayne Shorter group. Petite Diane Monroe and statuesque Maxine Roach in their black, formal stage costumes looked calm and almost demure, until they lifted their violin and viola respectively to play a repertoire they love at a concert by the innovative Uptown String Quartet at the 92nd Street YM/YWHA in 1990. The quartet interprets music from the African-American culture in a chamber music setting.

The unself-conscious movements of all these women in performance always become purposeful and packed with force. All of them spent years perfecting their techniques so they could express the passions of their secret, conscious lives and experiences. These years of work have given them the confidence and mastery to rank high among the best musicians on the contemporary jazz scene. Geri has been one of the few women to lead a group at the Village Vanguard. They have achieved some commercial parity with their male contemporaries; the women can draw audiences, which are enthusiastic and respectful.

Geri Allen, who was born in Detroit on July 12, 1957, became a darling of the jazz critics in 1988, when she was called to play in the biggest, most glamorous U.S. jazz festival, the JVC in New York. The impetus for her to play the piano has always been to see "what it feels like to be creative," she says. Critics were charmed by her soothing, introspective playing on albums such as "Etudes." Even more astonishing was her artful blending of classical and jazz techniques and feeling in her compositions. She has an exquisite touch and a thorough mastery of the piano's capacities. With lightning speed, she interweaves the influences of contemporary European classical music with the jazz tradition. She has an attitude as well as an adroitness born of years of committed study.

When JMT, for which she was recording at that time, discussed plans for one of her albums in the late 1980s, she said she would play her own compositions as usual. "I feel bad," she confided to a friend, "because I've upset the man at the label. But I've insisted on doing what I believe in." Seconds later, her phone rang. The label's man said she could do what she wanted. So she created the album, "Twylight," distributed by Verve, playing a synthesizer herself and hiring a musician who played folk percussion for special effects.

An important critic was distressed; he wanted to hear her usual touch and clarity on acoustic piano, not her exciting, volatile stylings on an electric instrument. Geri was upset by the critic for a while. Then she faced it: "Everybody has opinions," she said. "I did the best I could do at the moment. I didn't have to cringe. I was honest. I plan to continue to do the best I can do from project to project and to dig in deep. I think that's the major challenge for artists today—to stick to what they believe in and go for it."

She wished there were more government funding of the arts to help young people build their craft, so they wouldn't have to try to pigeonhole themselves in categories for commercial purposes. Playing in a variety of styles is of paramount importance. "You can't just eat one thing," she says. "You have to eat vegetables, and veal, and ice cream, and chocolate cake."

"What moves me most is something like what I saw on television. A young blind dancer from Africa came to a point where he was dancing in a sighted class. The sensitivity that this man must have to move with the other dancers! The ability of the human spirit to transcend excites me in life and in music. That's what inspires me to a standard of excellence that I strive for."

So she went back to work on new compositions and eventually released two more albums with her original compositions, "The Nurturer" in 1991 and then "Maroons" in 1992, both on Blue Note. In the same period, she became a mother. And she kept playing concert and club dates and teaching classes at the New England Conservatory of Music in Boston, then at her alma mater, Howard University, in Washington, D.C., where she felt even more comfortable, in touch with her roots, fortified by her belief in variety, experimentation, and the majesty of the human spirit.

Imbibing inspiration had become a habit with Geri by then. As a child, she had gone to the ballet and concerts with her parents often, because they hoped she would come to love the arts. "And I became curious to find out what it felt like to create." So she asked her parents to buy a piano. They shocked her by obliging. Her father, a schoolteacher, "became adamant that I practice," Geri said. Her classical teacher appreciated the richness of her African-American musical heritage and didn't discourage her instinct to improvise on her own time. Her father played his bebop records for her, and she was surrounded by Motown music.

Later on, jazz trumpeter Marcus Belgrave, her high school's artist-in-residence, took her under his wing. Their friendship would endure, and they would record together on their 1992 albums. Marcus's was called "Walking Together," co-led with drummer Lawrence Williams, on the Detroit Jazz Co-op Productions label. "Because of Marcus, a mentor became important to me," Geri has recalled of her teen years. He introduced her to professionals in Detroit. In common with every other contemporary woman musician, Geri feels that the most important events in her life were having her talent noticed, her imagination nurtured, and her drive praised. Music, she soon felt, was her responsibility and her mission—an engulfing, beautiful job.

She could count on one hand the few times she has wavered. Once a disagreement with a friend depressed her so much that she stopped playing for months. But her instincts, cultivated from childhood, directed her to play again. The malaise lifted. "As long as I'm doing something, I'm healthy," she reflected on her commitment to listen to her inner songs and not to the quirky criticism that can function as competition.

Geri released "Maroons," an album in memory of the Maroons,

African-Americans who broke away from slavery at the turn of the nine-
teenth century and set up their own community. African-American history
is a recurring theme in Geri's work. Virtually in ferment from all her
concerns and influences, Geri illustrates her reach on this album. It begins
with "Feed the Fire" with a flurry of Afro-Latin percussion that leads to a
bravura solo contrived from a few notes. Bright, beautiful, and even replete with boogie woogie, which is woven into the whole with amazing
sleight of hand and taste, this joyful theme recurs on the eighth track and
crowns her avant-garde album. It also serves as home base, a comfortable
campfire, for other tracks of quixotic, adventurous music rife with ideas
and asides, ranging from a weird bass solo on the seventh track to Geri's
Monk-like, angular style on "And They Parted," to a blistering performance by the haunting trumpeter Wallace Roney on "Mad Money," while
Geri plays with him dazzlingly. With reverence for the piano's resources
and expressiveness, and with great discipline, civility, and consideration
for listeners, she nevertheless clearly demonstrated her feeling of responsibility for being a rebel.

Some of Geri's other albums are "In The Year of the Dragon" and "In
The Middle," on Verve; "Live at the Village Vanguard" and "Segments,"
DIW label; and "The Printmakers," Minor Music.

For Sumi Tonooka, a mysterious love for the jazz she often heard in her
Philadelphia home increasingly became a commitment for her to play jazz
as a career. "Something drew me to jazz instinctively," she says. "It makes
you examine and go inward as well as onward." She was frequently in the
company of creative people. Her father, who was African-American, and
her Japanese-American mother met because they were part of a radical
political milieu in Philadelphia, and most of their friends were creative or
interested in the arts and politics. Sumi's father was actually a member of
the Communist Party during the McCarthy witch-hunting era. For her
thirteenth birthday, her parents took her to hear the moody jazz pianist
Thelonious Monk in a Philadelphia club. "It wasn't an odd present for me.
I was a Monk fan," she reminisces. "I thought that night that I wanted to
become a musician. Monk turned my head around."

Graduating from high school at age fifteen, she sought musical mentors. In Boston it was jazz saxophonist Serge Chaloff's mother, Madame
Margaret Chaloff, a classical pianist, who taught Sumi to pretend that she
was breathing through her fingertips and singing into the piano. In Detroit, Marcus Belgrave, trumpeter and mentor-about-town, met Sumi,
who was going through an itinerant searching phase, and recorded one of
her compositions. "Composition was always important for me," says Sumi,
who was born on October 3, 1956.

She wrote the score for an Oscar-nominated documentary, *Family Gathering,* in the mid-1980s. Her first album, "With an Open Heart," on the Radiant label, 1986, presented her own modernistic compositions. She also wrote a concert piece, called "Out from the Silence," which wove traditional Japanese instruments—koto, a string instrument, and shakuhachi, a bamboo flute—into a jazz ensemble. It had its premiere at International House in Philadelphia in 1988; then she performed it at New York's Ethical Culture Society, and went on to play it at several college campuses. The music was inspired by her mother's experience in a World War II concentration camp for Japanese nationals and Japanese-Americans. Later on, a film named *Susumu* was made—a half-hour documentary about how the piece was composed, with interviews with Sumi and her mother and excerpts from the music.

Mary Lou Williams was one of Sumi's most important role models. Sumi found Mary Lou's telephone number in a musicians' union book and called to ask for lessons. Then living in New York, Mary Lou welcomed Sumi. "She kept telling me that she didn't think I needed lessons," Sumi recalled with a smile. She was working toward her music degree from the College of the Performing Arts in Philadelphia by then. "She told me to get out there and play. She thought that I had the facility and the ears to take it from there. But I wanted to hang around, because I thought there was a lot she could show me, which she ended up doing. We took turns playing. When she played, I would learn from just watching her. I learned a lot about the blues from her. She would say, 'Listen, listen,' and then she demonstrated. She was one of the most inspiring people I've been around, because of what she taught and because of what she was. She had so much history in her playing. It was kind of intimidating for me, because Bud Powell and Monk had been in that room and played on that same piano." Sumi would eventually write a driving and dramatic piece, "One For Mary Lou."

Sumi earned a college degree in music and decided to live in New York, where "the dynamism slaps you in the face," as Geri Allen aptly observed. New York is no city for a creative person to relax—you must grow or perish. It was difficult at first for Sumi to find places to showcase herself. But she worked with good, well-known musicians through the years, beginning with drummer Philly Joe Jones in Philadelphia. Cobi Narita's Urban Jazz Coalition, a teaching forum and performance space in the 1970s and 1980s, gave Sumi some public exposure. In the late 1980s, she began touring with violinist John Blake, formerly with McCoy Tyner. In 1989, Blake and Sumi made a record, "A New Beginning" on the Gramavision label, on which Blake, the leader, included one of her tunes, "Yours and Mine."

In an ideal world, Sumi would sit home and write scores, she has said, perfect them, and deliver them to producers. But she works in clubs too; she even played for the 1990 JVC Jazz Festival's opening party just a few days before she gave birth to her first child, Kai, a son. She was working hard to establish herself as a performer and composer.

Kai cried audibly in the audience when she produced "Out from the Silence." He was two years old when Sumi performed in a solo concert as part of the JVC in 1992. By then she had recorded two albums, "Here Comes Kai," and "Taking Time," which were released by the Candid label, and she was waiting for another album, "Secret Places," to come out. Kenny Barron admired her playing so much that, when he contemplated starting his own label, he asked her to tape that recording. She had no resentment about the years of hard work before she began to get public exposure in important places.

"I write what I've felt or wanted to feel. You always have to be working on something and trust that it will turn out well," she says. "Sometimes I'm not sure why I do it. It's a love of music. That's what keeps me going. I can't consider life without it."

In December 1992, her second child, a daughter Nami, was born; for about three months Sumi didn't travel, devoting herself to motherhood. She and her husband, Harry Bates, a commercial artist, decided to buy a house in Woodstock, New York, and moved there in late 1993. Both Sumi and her husband have studios. During the summer of 1993, she performed in public again—for a solo concert at the National Museum of American History in Washington, D.C., at the Clifford Brown Jazz Festival in Wilmington, Delaware, then at One Step Down, a club in Washington. She gave a concert with bassist Rufus Reid and drummer Ben Riley at the Monterey Jazz Festival.

She received a commission through Meet The Composer to write an extended work using Japanese drums, called *taiko,* and she performed her work with a five-piece jazz group and two *taiko* drummers in December 1993. At the same concert, she presented "Out from the Silence" again, a performance for which she had gotten a grant from the National Endowment for the Arts.

All her life, Patrice Rushen was called on to play music by her teachers. A shy child, she became a vivacious little singer and dancer as soon as the music started. When she was fifteen, in the University of Southern California's school for gifted children, she realized it was time to work hard at music. Until then, she had played music because other people had recognized her talent, and they had placed her in a school where she was required to play, though not necessarily to commit herself. But in her teens, she became more aware of her position. "I saw the power of music and the pleasure it gave to other people when I played, and I became driven to take responsibility for the privilege of being talented," she says. The urge to play more complicated music, especially jazz, took hold. A teacher convinced her to enter a Monterey Jazz Festival competition, where she made a big hit. After that, Patrice's phone started ringing with calls for jobs in Los Angeles.

"I never had a hard time. I got turned on by word of mouth. I came up at a time when we were allowed to discover all the music styles. We didn't have to fit into a category. And when I found myself being typecast as a studio jazz pianist, I branched out to show I had skills for pop and rhythm and blues," she says. Finding her way through the politics of music industry circles, she recorded and played her own songs. Elektra signed her to a recording contract and, beginning in 1978, ten of her songs rose to the top of the pop music charts.

She had always secretly yearned to write music for films. Though she was in the perfect city to make her dream come true, she had heard of only one woman film scorer—and didn't know her. Through friendships in music circles, Patrice met Robert Townsend, who asked her to score his brave, independent venture, *Hollywood Shuffle*. It would begin an enduring professional relationship.

She had studied scoring, and she was ready for the moment. She knew her obligation was to heighten the emotional content of a film, which is usually someone else's emotional expression. She felt that this was a challenge, not a straitjacket. *Hollywood Shuffle* led to *Without You, I'm Nothing* with Sandra Bernhard, released in 1990, and then to a video for kids and other projects, including scoring television shows for Robert Townsend. Film-scoring projects kept coming slowly to hand. "You end up fighting to keep people from putting you in a bag. Just because I wear jeans one day doesn't mean that I don't have anything else in my closet," Patrice explained, echoing the message of Geri Allen's varied diet theory. As a performer, Patrice didn't want to confine herself to pop, or rhythm and blues, or jazz. "I'm looking for a recording company which doesn't view my versatility as a handicap," she said just before signing for her last album. See the Appendix for the recent developments on her prominent career in the 1990s.

Practice, patience, and planning gave direction to Patrice's drive. Born on September 30, 1954, she became a pop star at such a young age, when few women instrumentalists could find any work in the limelight, that other musicians—Geri Allen for one—regarded her as a role model. When Patrice met Geri and other younger musicians, she encouraged them, inspired by their efforts within the community of musicians.

The Uptown String Quartet, an all-women's chamber music group, had its raison d'être handed it by the redoubtable drummer Max Roach, who helped develop bebop with Dizzy Gillespie at Minton's Playhouse in Harlem and on 52nd Street in the 1940s. Max's talented, classically trained daughter, Maxine, a viola player, collaborated with him on his idea. She invited three women, all classically trained string players, to perform a new repertoire—blues, rags, spirituals, and jazz. The women transcribed them into contemporary arrangements for strings. Playing music in such a fresh way motivated all the women more than they had dreamed possible.

"Even before I sat down to play that music, I was akin to it," said Diane Monroe, the first violinist in the quartet, soon after its performance debut with its current personnel in 1990. Many of her relatives were jazz and church musicians, who encouraged her from the time she was two years old. She began by playing her late grandfather's guitar. Her grandmother gasped with appreciation and joy. "I felt the vibrations right away," Diane recalled. She was given classical piano lessons and, at the suggestion of a teacher, switched to the violin. Her entire focus was the classical world, where she found guidance and praise. Charles Castleman, an influential violinist, encouraged her. Eventually she realized the dream of being invited to play at the prestigious Marlborough Chamber Music Festival in Vermont.

"I was in awe of the stars that played there. I told myself, 'I have arrived! But I haven't, because I really can't play!' But the whole ethic and love for chamber music has a chance to grow there. And you learn from within. It's a fabulous, hands-on experience, with the sounds and sense and talk about music," she said.

When Maxine Roach called her to join the Uptown String Quartet, Diane was delighted. She had played second violin in a forerunner of the current quartet, as Max Roach's concept for an all-women's quartet kept developing in the 1980s. (At least two other jazz string quartets preceded the Uptown String Quartet. One was the Black Swan, in which Eileen Folson had been the only woman, and another was the Quartette Indigo. Violinist Gayle Dixon and her sister Akua Dixon Turre, a cellist and composer, had played in the Quartette Indigo, and so had Maxine Roach and violinist John Blake. In the 1980s, there was some overlapping of personnel in the Quartette Indigo and the Uptown String Quartet, until the current U.S.Q. emerged with its all-women personnel, and the Quartette Indigo went its independent way, keeping John Blake and finding a violist to replace Maxine.) As first violinist in that quartet, Diane Monroe thrived under Max's authority. "It's all chamber music to me," she said. "I've found my niche. I look at everything else I'm doing as an offshoot. I can integrate my classical training with jazz. And improvising jazz frees me so much that it catapults me to another level of playing."

Diane has taught at the prestigious Oberlin Conservatory and at

Swarthmore College. A performer in solo recitals and a soloist with major American symphony orchestras, she won the Pro Musica Foundation Award. Lesa Terry, the quartet's second violinist, played most nights in *Black and Blue* on Broadway during the run of that show. She was given the Outstanding Young Women of America Award in 1985, when she was playing with the Atlanta Symphony Orchestra. Aside from her many accomplishments as a violinist and teacher in the classical music world, she has played with saxophonist Yusef Lateef, trumpeter and flugelhornist Clark Terry, pianist Sir Roland Hanna, bassist Rufus Reid, and guitarist Kenny Burrell, all leading jazz players. Cellist Eileen Folson is a busy freelancer, who played with the New York Philharmonic under the direction of Zubin Mehta, among her many prestigious credits. She has also played on the sound tracks of a handful of Spike Lee films and in many Broadway show orchestras. All the quartet members shared in the inspiration of the new repertoire, which required them to develop new skills.

Maxine Roach's love for the quartet's work led her to transpose one of her father's famous drum solos from "Billy The Kid" into a composition called "Extensions." She wrote a part for each string instrument based on what her father played on each piece of his drumset. The oddly whirling piece rose to become a Grammy nominee for 1989. Though it didn't win, it symbolized the communication that musicians have with each other as mentors, colleagues, and students. In the end, communication is the greatest motivator for them all.

The Uptown String Quartet kept the excitement going among its members by speaking on the telephone about their quartet often, no matter what other playing jobs they had. A Philips label contract for the quartet's first album, "Max Roach Presents the Uptown String Quartet," plus critical praise after the January 1990 concert at the 92nd Street YM/YWHA in New York gave them an even more enraptured outlook. The quartet also was playing with Max's double quartet, a jazz group combined with the chamber group. The women made a second album, "Just Wait a Minute," produced by Max and released by Mesa Blue Moon in 1992.

Maxine Roach, who was born on May 12, 1950, had always been extremely influenced by her father, his milieu, and his music. Dizzy Gillespie and Charlie "Bird" Parker were visitors in her house when she was young. In public school, she had been tested for string-playing talent and walked directly to the viola. The best teachers trained and encouraged her. After attending Oberlin College on a scholarship and studying in Switzerland, she returned to New York with the idea that she wanted to freelance, not work in an orchestra full-time. And she loved the innovative premise of the Uptown String Quartet, a group that transcended the demarcation between American jazz springing from the African-American culture and European classical music. She enjoyed her father's guidance for the quartet, and also liked working in his double-quartet combining his jazz group and the jazz chamber group, the classical players. Her father's ideas for treatment of the music by a string quartet was an interesting development of the post-bebop era—another example of Dizzy Gillespie's premise that all post-bebop innovations emanated from his invention.

All these women—Geri, Sumi, Patrice, and the quartet players—reflect that they fell in love with perfecting their art and learned to believe in themselves when older male and female musicians, communing with them, opened doors—the inner doors to personal musicality and the outer doors that led to performances. Gender had nothing to do with their mentors' decisions and efforts to reach out and guide them. "The power to draw someone in and communicate experiences—for we're all experiencing growth and pain on a day-to-day basis—that's the important thing," says Geri Allen. "It's a nutritious experience. Music shows us ourselves."

The development of these women, nurtured primarily by men, underscores once again an important reason for lingering discrimination against qualified, contemporary female players: the profit motive. Once women leave the classrooms and enter the playing arena, they compete with men for the fees.

Chapter Five / / / Pianists Renee Rosnes and Rachel Z, Rising to the Top in the 1990s, Ruminate About Their Worlds

One of the women who managed not only to arrive in New York in 1985 but also achieve career high points by 1994 is the Canadian-born pianist Renee Rosnes. Blue Note released her first record as leader for that label, "Renee Rosnes," on January 1, 1990, then "For the Moment." On her last CD, "Without Words" in 1993, Renee led bassist Buster Williams, her husband Billy Drummond, a drummer, and twelve studio string players. It is her most fully realized recorded work as leader, with a splendid collection of varied pieces by composers Fats Waller, Duke Ellington, Erroll Garner, Miles Davis, Cole Porter, Schwartz-Dietz, Martino-Brighetti, Bobby Hutcherson, and Stan Getz. When one finishes complimenting her command of the piano, her flowing style, her smoothness, her touch, her obvious love for beautiful melodies, and her versatility, the last thing to be said must be that her performances are completely enjoyable.

She has played on sixteen more albums, leading one herself—a trio recording "Face to Face" for Toshiba/EMI, a Japanese label; she worked as a sideperson on the others—as impressive a collection as any young player has compiled, led by such stars as J. J. Johnson and Jon Faddis.

She arrived in town with a small Canadian Arts Council grant to study with pianists Cedar Walton, Jim McNeeley, James Williams, Mulgrew Miller, and Barry Harris. Her money went fast. She sat in everyplace, hoping to be called for work. Everyone noticed that the slender pianist added power, intensity, flowing lyricism and swing—in short, beauty, spirit, and energy—to groups. Drummer Terri Lyne Carrington recommended Renee (pronounced Ree Nee, a diminutive of Irene) to Joe Henderson. Then she caught the attention of OTB, with whom she played in Japan in 1987 and 1988. She met Herbie Hancock there, and they "fooled around" at the piano, she recalled. He recommended her to Wayne Shorter's group, including Terri Lyne. In one week Renee learned to play Shorter's complex music on synthesizer. Since then, she has won acclaim as one of the talented, educated modernists who emerged during the 1980s. She wends her way with ease and strength in and out of many groups, playing in 1993 with Buster Williams and Joe Henderson. Tours with J. J. Johnson, with whom she recorded as sideperson for his 1993 album, "Let's Hang Out," were lined up for that summer, when she would make the rounds of the European jazz festivals. She continued touring with him in 1994.

Renee inspired Rachel Z to come to New York. Manhattan-born Rachel, who had studied at the New England Conservatory, was playing contemporary, post-bebop with a group in a Boston lounge. On a side trip to New York, Rachel heard Renee play with Shorter at the Blue Note. "See what can happen," said a friend. Rachel came home.

Rachel was first convinced to become a jazz pianist by listening to the post beboppers—Miles Davis, for one, and the avant-gardist Joanne Brackeen among them. Rachel's compositions show their influence. Renee, now thirty-one, began playing at age three. The child of East Indian Asians, adopted by Canadians of Norwegian and British heritage, none of them musicians, she was encouraged to play piano by her adoptive parents, who loved music. She fell in love with a master of mainstream and technique, Oscar Peterson, and she has always emphasized blazing technique. As a young professional pianist with a regular gig in Vancouver, she took the good advice to learn as many songs as she possibly could so that she could become a successful rhythm section pianist. She absorbed the standards and added countless songs from all the jazz players through history—Cedar Walton, Lee Morgan, Wayne Shorter, Art Blakey. "I learned when I was young," she says. She also listened to Ella Fitzgerald, Sarah Vaughan, Frank Sinatra, and Billie Holiday, memorizing the lyrics to immerse herself even more thoroughly in songs for a vast repertoire. Rachel Z has also concentrated on technique and in common with Renee has an exceptional versatility. Both can play at breathtaking tempos. And their drive is evident in their styles.

Renee, who has yet to record some of the beautiful melodies she plays and obviously loves—"The Peacock" by Jimmy Rowles, for example, and many by Thelonious Monk—has primarily traveled in acoustic circles. It usually takes one brief hearing for an established star to hire Renee. J. J. Johnson hired her after she played at an impromptu special session in the Village Vanguard. Blue Note got the message around that time.

Her admirers and nurturers Herbie Hancock and Wayne Shorter plus

Branford Marsalis played on her first recording, on which she interspersed her own compositions with some by Monk, Shorter, Henderson, and pianist Donald Brown. Though she had no professional connections to begin with, in five years she built a career and a life; in 1990 she married OTB's drummer Billy Drummond.

Rachel Z, still in her twenties in 1993, stressed her own compositions on her debut album, "Trust the Universe" (Columbia), including keyboards and electric bass on six of the CD's twelve songs. A few years ago, she was the second woman ever hired by Mike Mainieri for Steps Ahead. (The first was the pretty, accomplished Brazilian Eliane Elias.) Mainieri shortened Rachel's last name from Nicolazzo to Z because he didn't want her to waste time spelling her name for people the way he had always had to. She recorded an album with Steps Ahead and traveled with Al DiMeola, performing "fusion extravaganzas," she said, promoting his album, "Kiss My Ax," in 1993, on which she plays. She began talking with Wayne Shorter about making an album with him. "If it happens, it will be another life goal," she said. "I really want to have that knowledge of what he's about." It did happen. And she made her debut as leader in a club, B. Smith's, to promote her first album, switching from acoustic piano to electric keyboards with her own characteristic touch of fusion extravaganza. (She would record her second album for release in 1994.)

Exercising her "major animalistic skills," as she has called her instincts toward survival of the fittest, she was playing keyboards in a little club, the Bond Street Cafe, on a dark sidestreet in Manhattan a couple of years ago. Milan Simich, a European jazz promoter whom she met through Mainieri, brought George Butler, a Columbia vice president in charge of jazz and new music, to hear her. Around that time, Ron Helman, a manager who had already signed a group with Columbia, said to her in the club, "I'm gonna make you a star." It took a year of anxious waiting, but Helman settled the deal for Rachel with Columbia. He and Rachel became engaged and married in December 1993.

At first Rachel thought she would make a record with drummer, composer, leader, Muse label artist Cindy Blackman, who works a great deal, and Kim Clarke, who plays both acoustic and electric bass and used to travel with DeFunkt. In the end, Rachel led her own album with established male players, among them bassist Charnett Moffet and saxophonist David Sanchez. She wanted to produce an all-women's record for her friend Sarah Cion, who has played piano in Kit McClure's band and in Diva. The all-women's group was a very good launching pad, Rachel believed, in some cases.

It was natural for that thought to occur to her. Women must spend time thinking hard about sexism in jazz, if only to fortify themselves against the sadness of being bypassed because of gender. Then they put aside their musings and frustrations and keep trying to get ahead. Renee Rosnes likes to spend as little time as possible thinking about discrimination. Her mind constantly goes to her music. She always feels pressured to play at the highest possible level. There were times when she contemplated the dearth of chances she has had to lead her own group in New York jazz clubs. A popular sidewoman called often by men, she led her own group in a club—Bradley's—for the first time in April 1993. Renee noticed that she had been called only twice to substitute for men players in groups in the eight years she played in New York. She thought it was because she didn't belong to a clique. But she was called; her gender appeared not to have worked against her.

Rachel Z, far more than Renee, has enjoyed reading about and analyzing the gender-benders that jazz women have lived through. She found inspiration for her compositions in her political concerns. "You have to understand yourself psychologically and the political structure of the world, and that includes feminism, sexism, and racism. I want to change the world, so I have to understand what is going on," Rachel said.

"Renee and I are exceptions. She has had major gigs with players throughout her career that have nurtured her growth. And Tracy Wormworth [an electric bassist, daughter of bebop drummer Jimmy Wormworth, Sr., and a girlfriend of pianist Kenny Kirkland] has had that." A combination of diligence, talent, and networking with musician friends brought Tracy success, primarily in the pop field. But in 1992 Tracy played with her friend, critically acclaimed pianist Geri Allen, in a jazz gig at the Village Vanguard. That was done for pleasure. Most women cross the line from pop to jazz and sometimes even to classical music for economic reasons.

"But other women," Rachel continued, "have lost confidence because of put-downs in their adolescence and early twenties when you usually try to develop your confidence. Women have a really hard time." She worried about some friends of hers in New York who were going through crises of confidence because they weren't having the encouragement. "I identified with men and totally disavowed my femaleness so that I could develop . . . I've been really blessed because of the sweet people that hire me, but I think . . . I feel pressured to have a big career to have political power to help other women."

Women usually feel that it's not a stepping-stone to success in jazz for them to stress feminism. Men don't like to talk about it. Furthermore, many men had become quick to pass along the word about good women players. It's solely the playing mystique that is bringing success to women. Renee's artistry brought her invitations to tour with James Moody, to play with Hank Jones and other stars in a JVC tribute to Marian McPartland, and to visit with Marian on her "Piano Jazz" show. In 1992, Renee was invited to play with the Carnegie Hall Jazz Band led by Jon Faddis to honor Miles Davis. "I was thrilled because Ron Carter was playing bass. He had played all that original music," Renee says. (He also played on her first Blue Note album.) She named other stars—all men—at that concert who helped to make it a highlight of her life.

Renee and Rachel belong to a relatively small group of women players who counted among the top jazz artists of their generation, and they divined that, even for them, there was still a glass ceiling. Clubowners cited commercial considerations for resisting women leaders. The problem could disappear, Rachel Z thought, if women leaders in clubs become commonplace.

Rachel Z learned from *Stormy Weather,* Linda Dahl's book, that women musicians have existed from the beginning of jazz. "It's something people don't really highlight," she said. "They want us to be anomalies, exceptions. They still want to prove that women can't do it. But now it's all subtle, because now it's not cool to be sexist or racist. It's all under the table." She worried about exceptional musicians such as bassist Melissa Slocum, who not only played in Diva and Unpredictable Nature for a while but had worked regularly at Arthur's Tavern in the Village throughout most of the 1980s until 1993—and bassist Kim Clarke, who has worked with popular fusion and pop groups as well as in jazz gigs. They have to play better than men and also cope with the demands of motherhood as they plan their careers. All sorts of problems beset them, particularly the proud, daring, and outspoken Melissa. "They really have it tough," Rachel mused.

Searching for the final solution—the one beyond the recording contract—Rachel focused on the lack of women innovators and superstars. "There are no women Coltranes . . . I think it's because people don't get enough playing experiences. . . . If a woman plays with strength, she should aim to be as great as Tony Williams, to be an innovator. . . . It's not about just making it. I want to see women at the forefront," she said.

Chapter Six /// A View from the Business Women

In New York City in the 1980s, Max Gordon, founder of the famed Village Vanguard, died. His widow Lorraine, who had been running it with him for years, continued on her own. In the 1940s, she had been married, at age nineteen, to Alfred Lion of Blue Note records; she was active in the early recording sessions of Sidney Bechet, Thelonious Monk, and Vic Dickenson. On first meeting Max, she convinced him to book Monk into the Vanguard. After Max died, the Vanguard continued at full power, because of Lorraine's musical taste and business judgments. If some weeks she booked a musician whose work she liked but who was little known in New York City, she made up for it by booking Kenny Barron for three weeks in a row, and Terence Blanchard, and Roy Hargrove, and Harry Connick, Jr., all of whom packed the place with their fans.

Also in the 1980s, Wendy Cunningham inherited her husband's legendary jazz piano club, Bradley's; though inexperienced, she placed herself at the helm, holding court in person at night, involving herself in management, booking—everything. She changed Bradley's extraordinary vision of a club for piano-bass duos into a showcase for small groups, usually made up of young, emergent musicians, often featuring horns. These women wielded enormous influence, deciding who would appear before the public.

In Los Angeles, at the end of the 1980s, a trendy club named Linda, which lasted a while, was owned by a singer who featured herself with jazz groups. In New York in the early 1990s, a small East Village club, Deanna's, gave the young owner a chance to sing with groups. Sarah Czercowski, owner of La Cave on First, formerly ran Memphis Melody in Paris. It's not such a novelty now for a woman to own a club as it was when Bricktop held court in her club patronized by Cole Porter in Paris in the Jazz Age.

48

Furthermore, several women have moved into positions of high visibility on staffs of recording companies, particularly in the art, publicity, and legal departments, and as agents and artists' managers. Women photographers have specialized in jazz journalism—Lona Foote was one. She unfortunately died at a young age in 1993. Women have produced books of jazz photos. Women writers began writing in greater numbers for magazines and books about jazz; then record companies hired them to do liner notes for albums or prepare publicity kits. Flautist Sherry Winston has worked as an executive in marketing for such companies as Columbia Records. However, it's the rare woman who produces records or sits in the first engineer's chair in recording studios or guides the artist and repertoire department with enough influence to say: "We'll sign this artist." Although the record companies have many titles within their corporate structures, and women's names may frequently appear, women still don't have much power. None have become executives in the upper echelons of the corporate structure, where the important financial decisions are made.

As publicists with their own firms, women find they can influence the public, and the better they do that, the more respect they can get in the industry. Carolyn McClair, now in her forties, had her own publicity firm for six years in the early 1990s. She began in publicity at age twenty-one, working for Alcoa, then Westinghouse Broadcasting. Her work for special events brought her in touch with George Wein. He hired her to do publicity for his jazz festival company, Festival Productions. Her prestigious contacts began—first with saxophonist Donald Harrison, then trumpeter Jon Faddis and Dizzy Gillespie's United Nation Orchestra. The list of her clients grew to include soprano saxophonist Courtney Pine, trumpeters Arturo Sandoval and Claudio Roditi, trombonist Steve Turre, saxophonist Paquito D'Rivera, and singer Nnenna Freelon.

Blues lover Rosetta Reitz made it her mission to produce recordings by old blues singers, all women; she branched out to become a writer, concert producer, teacher, and lecturer, and she also produced recordings by the wartime big band, the International Sweethearts of Rhythm. Some women have gone into broadcast; Dorthaan Kirk, widow of musician Rahsaan Roland Kirk, exerts her influence as music coordinator and special assistant to the general manager at WBGO-FM, which broadcasts in New Jersey and the New York metropolitan area. Other women have become disc jockeys there and at other stations, selecting the music played for the public.

Individual musical artists have sometimes had the savvy to control at least their own careers. Singer Susannah McCorkle retained ownership of her own recordings from the beginning of her career; when young singers have asked her how she managed to become well known, she advised them to pay close attention to the business side of their art and stand up for their right to earn a living. It's the rare artist who retains ownership of his or her own recordings—ownership that can make an enormous difference for artists. As an example, Nat King Cole's manager had the foresight to make sure Nat owned his own masters, which helped make the singer a very wealthy man and have an influential voice in his relationship with Capitol Records. Guitarist Peter Leitch's wife Sylvia Levine was managing her husband's career, keeping the reins in the family. But women involved in the business side of the recording industry have little autonomy or involvement in financial decisions.

Women in any part of the music industry rarely give much public indication that they think about their lack of influence. The co-leaders of the jazz fusion group Deuce, Ellen Seeling and Jean Fineberg, have been outspoken. They have resented picking up music magazines and seeing all the stories and advertisements about men's performances and recordings. They also have noticed the dearth of women in top jobs in recording companies. (On the bright side, they love finding themselves in the position of role models when they have done clinics in schools and inspired girls, who would like to play wind instruments, to approach them. Deuce hopes that they themselves will be a catalyst for change.) Other women just seem to live with "the conditions that prevail," as comedian Jimmy Durante used to sum up his philosophy of the human condition, "surrounded," as he often said, "by assassins" and beleaguered by "revolting developments."

Helen Keane, however, has a rather unique view of woman's fate in music. She began her rise, from secretary to talent scout, artists' manager, and record producer, learning every facet of the music business on the job, in the 1950s. She thinks that, overall, women have done as well as they have tried to do.

"Women have to fight harder," she says.

After nearly four decades in the music business, she has found herself regarded as an authority. She shows up at feminist meetings to tell women, "I'm here because of men," a concept, she chuckles, that may not have endeared her to people who would prefer her to grind an ax. However, it has been true that men opened doors for her at a time when there were no women to open them. And her position as a pioneer makes her views invaluable. As she was earning her promotions, she was always conscious of being the first woman this, the first woman that, and attributed her success to luck, ability, talent—and support and respect from male colleagues, friends, and musicians. More than twenty years later, Linda Goldstein, Bobby McFerrin's manager since 1980, rarely gave her gender a thought as she guided herself through the shoals and politics of the music business. Nobody makes an issues of her sex, and she is the embodiment of Helen Keane's thesis that today women can become artistically and financially influential, as long as they decide they would like to take charge.

There are other artists' managers among women in the jazz and pop fields. Joanne Klein has been managing aspects of pianist Kenny Barron's career since the 1970s, and occasionally takes on work for other clients. Mary Ann Topper has managed scores of important jazz artists. Among Helene Greece's clients is pianist Barbara Carroll. Christine Martin has managed Steps Ahead and pianist Eliane Elias, whose jazz albums have gone to the top of the radio popularity charts. Youthful Robin Burgess has the confidence of her client, trumpeter Terence Blanchard, who scores and plays for Spike Lee films, plays in concerts, and fills the Village Vanguard. Maxine Gordon was saxophonist Dexter Gordon's manager before she married him. In the 1990s, she was managing organist, pianist, teacher, and composer Shirley Scott. Sue Mingus, bassist Charlie Mingus's widow, has stayed in charge of her husband's legacy. In the early 1990s, under her aegis, a big band played his music every Thursday night in the loose atmosphere on the basement level at Manhattan's trendy Time Cafe, where a gaudy gold curtain served as the bandstand's backdrop, perhaps helping to elicit exciting, voluptuous performances from such respected players as pianist John Hicks. Marcia Glaser managed Erroll Garner with intense devotion. Lorraine Gordon used to steer Jabbo Smith's career and life with loving care. Wendy Cunningham has nurtured the careers of some of her favorite musicians—young trumpeter Roy Hargrove for one. And Cobi Narita has functioned as an artist's manager, educator, and concert and festival producer, depending on public and private grants and fund-raisers.

The stories of Helen Keane and Linda Goldstein demonstrate the dedication of full-time artists' managers and the differences between their eras. Helen was a novelty as an agent beginning in the 1950s and then later as an artists' manager/record producer. Linda was a naif when she started out as a booker, then developed into a manager/record producer simultaneously. What they have in common is that they taught themselves everything they know. They had a burning desire to gamble on their tastes and talents. They had specific clients in mind when they decided to become artists' managers and record producers. And both fell in love with the music as well as the business side of the music industry and wanted to make an impact on the country's creative, popular music.

A. Helen Keane

At age eighteen, Helen arrived in New York from a secretarial school in New Jersey to visit her aunt, an actress who had one of the leads in *The*

Women on Broadway. Immediately fascinated by show business, Helen decided to put her secretarial skills to use by finding a job with a music industry firm; it turned out to be the Music Corporation of America (MCA). The first man she worked for said, "You've got talent, kid. I'm going to train you." And he did.

After two years, she was promoted to become the first woman agent to hire talent for musical variety shows under the aegis of MCA. It hadn't been a smooth rise. MCA hired her as an agent only after it learned that another company wanted her. But then she was off and running with a prestigious company, doing the brightest work she could imagine, going to clubs every night and spotting talent. "I discovered Harry Belafonte," she says. "That was my big coup. I became the darling of MCA because he became a star."

Dedicated to the job, even when she got married and became pregnant, she kept working—not a usual decision for a woman to make in the 1950s. But after she had her first son, she no longer wanted to go out every night. So she moved to CBS as a daytime director of variety casting. Auditioning people, she discovered Jonathan Winters. By the mid-1960s, she decided to try doing her job on her own, without the protection of a major corporation. She was in the throes of a second divorce by then— 1967—and in love with Gene Lees, a noted jazz writer. Lees said to her, "You should manage Bill Evans."

"And that's how I began managing Bill Evans," she recalls. Until Evans died in the early 1980s, Helen managed the innovative pianist's career while he won seven Grammys and traveled the world. Bill also wanted Helen to become his record producer. "So the door opened for me to produce other people's records too," she says. "Creed Taylor was then head of jazz for Verve records; he became my mentor. Between Creed and Bill, I became a record producer. Certainly it was easier for me than for most women. I had credentials, because it was Bill Evans. But if I hadn't been able to do the job, I wouldn't have lasted."

She discovered that she had the talent for it. "My extra set of ears is the gift," she says. "You can develop, but you can't acquire that."

On Broadway or for films, a producer may operate as the money person. But in recording, a producer is a director. Helen begins by choosing the musicians as well as the tunes. The recording sessions are usually done in two or three days, "because I work with jazz giants," she says, who can work that quickly. Another reason for working fast is that the budgets for jazz recording are much smaller than those for pop albums. Then the recording mixing and editing begins, followed by the sequencing and time spreads between each tune and the levels. "The sequencing and levels are subtle matters and have a lot to do with the public's acceptance of the recording. Then there's mastering—going from tape to disk so that metal parts can be cut. I must approve that. Then comes the test pressing. And then you work with the art director and on the cover. And then you have to hire a person to write liner notes. So the process takes about three months, and not every day, and sometimes not even consecutive months."

In 1989, she scheduled about a dozen records to produce—"too much," she summed up. Because of her background as an artists' manager, she got involved in every step of a recording's journey from planning to record stores sales. She gets ideas for publicity and talks to the publicity department. Though she technically managed only trumpeter and flugelhornist Art Farmer and guitarist Kenny Burrell in the late 1980s, she planned singer Carol Sloane's date for a week in the Blue Note in New York. She also shepherded singer Chris Connor's career when records came out. In the 1990s, she would produce her second recording for Joanne Brackeen, involve herself in the presentation of a concert by Joanne at Columbia University, and undertake production of Sue Terry's first album as leader.

"I help with career moves because they help with record sales. Not everybody does what I do. But not everybody has my background as an artists' manager, and that's part of who I am as a creative person. It's a lot of work, but it pays off—not necessarily in dollars but in spiritual reward."

Carol Sloane's 1989 recording, which was a superb example of her jazz singing, was called a masterpiece by critics. For the cover, a photograph of Carol, Helen worked with Phil Carrol, with whom she had collaborated on many covers since 1974.

When the whole package is praised, Helen basks in the glory with the artists and all the other people who have worked on the album. "I'm lucky to do what I love," said the attractive, blonde-haired woman with dramatically large, bright red framed eyeglasses, as she sat in her Manhattan office. Its walls are covered with scores of record album covers whose production she has been involved in. She loves the ego-bolstering of a job well done, and enjoys being written about. "It's not the most important thing, but I like it," she said. She also likes the respect that she suddenly discovered in the late 1970s, at festival and concert producer Cobi Narita's daytime jazz panels during the women's annual jazz festivals in New York City. Helen noticed that people were hungry for her information about the business side of the music industry.

She has sometimes traveled to speak at the University of California at Berkeley, San Francisco State, Northwestern, or simply to Greenwich Village to the New School's jazz faculty, and she has given insights to women who want to get into the music business as performers, producers, managers, and agents. Her impression during a talk at the New School in

1989 was that more women were on hand, hoping to become managers—
mostly in pop, not jazz. She was disappointed to see how few women
entertained the idea of becoming record producers for pop or jazz. Legend
says one can't make a good living in jazz record production. But Helen
knows it isn't true.

An amusing story came to her about the differences between producing rock and jazz recordings. Waiting for Herb Pomeroy's twelve-piece
jazz band for a recording date in Boston at the Newbury Recording Studio
in 1989, she noticed how dark the studio was. A rock group had recorded
there last. The track lights were covered with red gels. In the isolation
booths hung 40-watt bulbs. "There was no way you could read charts by
those lights. I had to get the gels off and use clip lights in the isolation
booths," she said. When the jazz musicians arrived and couldn't see to
read, she told them, "Don't worry, guys. I'm fixing it." The rock group
hadn't needed to read music. "You see it, but you don't believe you're
seeing it—because you can't see it," she joked. "Many pop stars of course
can read music; the ones at the top who stay at the top develop themselves
and work hard."

Never once has she had trouble with a recording engineer. "Nobody
ever wondered what I was doing there," she said. She has noticed a few
women working during the past ten years as the second engineer, essentially the first engineer's assistant, who sets up, assists with tapes, and does
whatever the first engineer needs. Adam Makovicz, the jazz piano star,
helped a woman rise as an engineer, from a "gopher" (a person going for
coffee) in a studio to a second engineer. And Helen was astounded when a
tiny second engineer in Boston, at Newbury, did the whole job of recording the twelve-piece band's album herself. In California, a woman did the
second engineer's job splendidly too at the start of the 1980s.

Women can find acceptance in the recording studios as producers and
engineers, "if they would fight a little harder," she said. She had the same
view of the scene for women instrumentalists. Women essentially have
their foot in the door, she believes. Like the women players, women on the
business side have to demonstrate great ability and more drive than men
players. Women have an advantage in music because they often have a
touch of the nurturer—virtually a *sine qua non* for building good relationships with creative artists. With those qualities, sooner or later, if a woman
is in the right place at the right time and meets the right people who like
her, she can transcend the remaining prejudice.

In Linda Goldstein's era, it was socially acceptable for a woman to become
an entrepreneur and learn the ropes totally on her own. Linda never had to
consider taking a job as a secretary and rising through the ranks, shepherded by men. She played it the company way only in her own company

from her early twenties in the 1970s, at a time when the independent woman business owner was becoming fashionable and even sometimes formidable, because of her pioneering spirit and youthful enthusiasm, bolstered by the women's movement. If the movement was controversial, at least everybody was being affected by it. And Linda began without self-consciousness.

B. Linda Goldstein

An ancient French farmer sat down on an ovoid object one day. When it broke under him, he said "Ooof," which in French sounds like "oeuf," and that became the word for egg. It still doesn't answer the question of which came first, Bobby McFerrin or Linda Goldstein, his manager. They are nearly the same age, Linda born in 1952, Bobby in 1950; they believe in each other, and they became wealthy and successful by putting their destinies in each other's hands. Their life stories, in which their sexes don't matter a whit, are inseparable.

As Linda drifted away from her own singing career to manage jazz musicians in the late 1970s, she didn't once feel that her sex handicapped her from becoming successful in the macho pop and jazz music worlds. "Most of the time, if you're a professional, I think it's an advantage to be a woman, because you can ask a lot more questions," she said in her bell-clear voice several years ago, reclining regally on a couch in the office in the Upper West Side Manhattan brownstone she owned for a while. Now she lives in a duplex in Greenwich Village. "And it just boils down to whether you can cut it, I think."

Most women in the music business were telling her that she was wrong; most of them were still in publicity. But then most people told her she was wrong to believe that Bobby McFerrin's idiosyncratic, scat-based art song was going to be a commercial windfall. So a part of Linda's outlook may always have been as blithe as the sound of her trained singer's voice.

At age eighteen, she moved from Los Angeles to San Francisco, where she worked professionally as a singer and attended the University of California at Berkeley, on scholarship, studying languages and philosophy. On Monday nights, she sang with a big band "made up of the best players in town," she says. They worked at the Keystone Korner and the Great American Music Hall—well-known places in the jazz culture. She also led a band including pianist Mark Levine, who worked with the saxophonist Joe Henderson and vibrist Cal Tjader, and percussionist Mongo Santamaria.

Because Linda was in love with all kinds of jazz and wanted to be

taken seriously as a jazz singer, she felt a little chagrined at singing "I Left
My Heart in San Francisco"—"for the tourists from Omaha," she says.
They went to her top-40 gig in Henry's room on top of the San Francisco
Hotel five nights a week. It was a living, she thought, as she struggled
around in her evening gowns. She also got a National Endowment for the
Arts grant to write her own lyrics for jazz instrumentals, and she won a
Best Vocalist award in a college competition in 1976 on a night when Joe
Henderson played there. Becoming friends with Joe, she started writing
lyrics for his tunes such as "Inner Urge."

"And I began to ask a lot of questions about where his career was
going. I was a jazz freak, a bebop fanatic, while others were listening to
pop. I was obsessed with jazz, jazz history; I listened to John Coltrane,
Louis Armstrong, and everyone in the Blue Note [record label] era of the
1960s, and CTI [label] music, and Herbie Hancock in his 'Maiden Voyage' period, and trumpeter Freddie Hubbard. Joe Henderson was one of
my idols. I was becoming consumed with Joe Henderson's career—or lack
thereof. It was astounding how much work there was to be done by an
agent. Most of the time he survived on phone calls that came in. There was
never a real agent, no order, no tour put together. Though he had made
close to 100 albums, his career was haphazard, based on chance" [at that
time].

She spoke to Joe about his lack of planning. "Joe took out the map of
the United States and said: 'You book a tour. Here's Philadelphia, Boston,
New York. Connect the dots'."

Gee, that sounds easy and fun, Linda told herself.

"So I got on the phone, called the clubs he had told me to call, and
put together a tour. And it bore much fruit. I was naive, I must admit. The
first club that I called was the Village Vanguard, and I got Max Gordon.
'Oh, sure, Joe Henderson, love to have him,' Max said. 'When are we
talking about?' I looked at my map and said to myself: 'Boston to New
York'. I gave Max a date. 'Okay,' he said." but when Linda asked him for
$10,000, which Joe Henderson had told her to request, Max thought it
was "outrageous," Linda recalls. "So all his politeness went into a New
York routine. 'What do you mean? I wouldn't pay Miles Davis $10,000 a
week. You goddam stupid——!' The normal fee was probably $3,500 a
week at that time," Linda surmised.

"So we hung up the phone. I was shaken. Max and I became great
friends afterward," she recalls. She sat down with a pencil and paper and
figured out that if the Vanguard held about 92 people, and there were two
shows a night, with a $5.00 admission charge per person at that time, then
even if the club sold out every seat for every show, the total take came to
perhaps $6,000 for the week. Joe said that the club made all its money on

drinks. But Linda figured out that each person would have to spend $200 on drinks per set—something like that—to make the engagement worthwhile for the Vanguard. Eventually she worked out a reasonable fee.

"I began to take a great pride in the logistics. The longer the tour, the more profitable it would be. So we went to Indianapolis, Chicago, Detroit, and other places on the way back to San Francisco. I loved doing the calculations, the budgets. Joanne Brackeen was playing with Joe at the time. She was just beginning to be managed by Helen Keane. I began a thorough appraisal of the jazz scene around the world. I set out to find where every club, promoter, festival, etcetera, was. I developed an extensive card file. After a year I called it 'the morgue', because a lot of numbers were disconnected all the time. People (in jazz) go in and out of business, mostly out.

"Then Helen Keane said, 'Can you get a few things in California for Bill Evans?' So I did. I got jazz societies, not places that would normally be booked. And the whole thing escalated.

"I was still singing, but I got to the point where I really wanted to make the world safe for bebop, and I would proudly and definitively talk about America's Only Indigenous Art Form, this wonderful music which it was an honor to represent. And I thought the artists who were being forced to peddle their art commercially deserved a much more honored place in our culture. The small-time jazz club owners were always fanatics about jazz, but they were also slimy [about the money]. Give me a blatantly cutthroat, ruthless business guy to deal with rather than an altruistic fanatic."

She learned all this as she booked single dates and tours for Chet Baker, Joe Farrell, Astrud Gilberto, Illinois Jacquet, Benny Carter, Zoot Sims, Al Cohn, and Shelly Manne. She lost $700, which amounted to her shirt in those days, when she backed a wonderful, obscure Brazilian musician named Moacar Santos. Then pianist-arranger Dave Frishberg, who has written such memorable boite-jazz songs as "My Attorney, Bernie," introduced her to the concept of artist management. For a while, she steered his career—his bookings, his record deals, his publicity. She was still so naive in this period that she went to the Harry Fox Agency, which keeps track of record royalties, and asked to see Mr. Fox, who had been dead for many years. While managing David Frishberg, she became more savvy about the entire business apparatus of popular music.

A bass player whom she had once worked with told a young singer named Bobby McFerrin to call her in San Francisco. "By that time I was getting known as the new sucker who could get gigs for people," she reminisces about the reputation of her little one-phone, no-office, no-staff operation. Another woman with a $100,000 office investment couldn't get gigs for people; Linda was the person to speak to. But Linda wasn't impressed with Bobby because he was singing a well-worn, ornate bebop cliché, she thought—the gorgeous old music that Miles Davis, in his fusion phase late in his career, said bored him to think about rehashing. Then Linda moved to New York City to live in the midst of the jazz action. There she heard Bobby again; he was singing with the Jon Hendricks family group at Sweet Basil. The Hendricks family normally put lyrics to the great bebop and Swing era, improvised horn solos. "Bobby did one solo, a cappella—'Opportunity' by Joan Armatrading. It was the most extraordinary thing I ever heard," Linda recalls.

Alerted, she asked him, "What do you want to do?"

He said, "I picture myself alone on stage, improvising vocally like a Keith Jarrett concert. I don't know how I'll do it or what I'll sing."

Linda said, "I'm with you."

She went to work to get him his first record deal and produced it for Elektra. He had a band then; the record had a rock feeling. "It was my strategy to develop him, get him known first, and find him safe places to experiment. It's a radical leap from one song to one-man, one-voice alone on stage," Linda says.

She booked him as the solo singing act opening at festivals. The bookings were based on her telling producers: "Trust me. This guy will go over great." Bobby began to get more experience and ideas. Linda booked a European tour for him with his band. But then Bobby decided he was ready to do the whole show a cappella and alone. When the promoters found out what he was going to do, half of them cancelled. "But the ones that didn't cancel were triumphant," Linda says. She taped fourteen hours of the concerts on a Sony two-track digital machine, edited them down to album size, and tried to persuade Bruce Lundvall, then the head of Elektra Records (later of Blue Note) in New York, to release that very inexpensive solo voice album. It was called "The Voice."

At first Lundvall was reluctant. Nesuhi Ertegun, whose brother Ahmet had founded Atlantic Records, didn't believe in "The Voice" either. Though Nesuhi thought Bobby was a fine singer, Nesuhi told Linda, "You can't release that solo record. You'll ruin his career."

But Linda loved the record. Bobby was also distinguishing himself in jazz gigs with pianist Stanley Cowell, bassist Cecil McBee, drummer Idris Muhammed, and reeds player Chico Freeman. But Linda felt that Bobby was or should be label-less: "One of the greatest, most original virtuosos, one of the finest entertainers of the twentieth century: has been her vision of Bobby. She doesn't know what would have become of him or her, if she hadn't persisted in pursuing the vision that she and Bobby had brainstormed together for his future. She kept him out of "sleazy clubs," she says. "I was very clear. I saw him on the stages of the finest halls in the world. I saw him being taken seriously in another kind of way. And at the same time, I helped pave the way for him to gain tremendous commercial success without any compromise whatsoever. I set up the advantages. Then Bobby McFerrin had a terrific impact."

He began winning Grammys for singing and also for arranging in 1986, then for singing "Round Midnight" from the 1987 film starring Dexter Gordon. In 1988 Linda encouraged him to write a catchy song for his album "Simple Pleasures," which sold three million copies, while the song in a variety of single formats, "Don't Worry, Be Happy," sold over 13 million copies. Less well known was his *tour de force* performance on a recording of Rudyard Kipling's children's classic, "The Elephant's Child," replete with animal voices and jungle sounds. And everyone was at least dimly aware of Bobby's voice ricocheting around the octaves on television commercials. But most of all, the great success of "Don't Worry, Be Happy" put Linda into the category of one of the top pop music managers/record producers.

Married to David Plattner, an entrepreneur and musician, and pregnant with their first child, Daniela, born in 1989, Linda went to the Grammys with Bobby and won an award as the producer of the record of the year for "Don't Worry, Be Happy." The next week, Bobby took out a full-page ad in *Billboard:* "To Linda Goldstein, manager and producer extraordinaire."

"Bobby and I have always been mutually supportive and can communicate in a kind of shorthand. I usually understand what he wants to do, and I can guide and protect his freedom. So he leaves his career up to me. I'm the manager, and he's the artist. And that's it."

Their roaring commercial success seemed to have happened fast, though actually Linda struggled along for years. "There were times when I lived in fear of phone disconnections and apartment evictions. I screwed up my credit, because I knew there were things that had to be done. Like I knew the (McFerrin) band had to do a European tour. And no record company would support it. So I put the plane tickets on my credit card, and then I couldn't pay it off. I destroyed my credit."

"Bobby and his wife had a child in those days" (a son ten years old in 1990), "and I felt that they needed money more than I did; so for years I deferred any commission. I got by because I was booking others. It's very expensive to develop a band, and I never had any capital. George Avakian, the record producer, believed in what I was doing, and he gave me a loan. It took me seven years to pay it back."

Once, getting herself involved in a deal that would have brought her a $250 commission, she instead became embroiled in a lawsuit with

$15,000 of legal fees. She also briefly went into partnership with someone; that too ended in legal wrangling.

"It has always been my intuition, my judgments, and my strategy that were employed," she summed up the essence of her success with Bobby's career management, exhibiting the firmness of purpose and self-assuredness that Helen Keane defined as the secret of success for women in the music business.

Linda has become a manager for several artists in addition to Bobby. And it seems natural that one of them has been the uncategorizable, almost indescribably abstract performance artist Laurie Anderson, as well as David Byrne. For the foundation of Linda's professional vision is her faith in the ineffable.

C. Cobi Narita

Cobi Narita invented a unique position for herself in the jazz world, when she founded a nonprofit educational group called the Universal Jazz Coalition in the late 1970s. It was her idea to help musicians manage their own business affairs when they lacked managers and bookers. Her premise grew so that she became a concert promoter and producer. And she hired well-known musicians to teach workshops for newcomers. She soon noticed that women were having even more difficulty than young, struggling men in jazz; so she founded a women's jazz festival in New York to give women a chance to play in public with a great deal of fanfare and catch media attention.

Cobi herself didn't play an instrument; she began singing in public only at some of her birthday parties, beginning with her sixtieth in 1986. But she has led a life that rivals the odysseys of many jazz musicians. No instrumentalist or business person has gone against the odds of succeeding in jazz with more fervor, optimism, self-assurance, and determination— character traits that Cobi shares with Helen Keane and Linda Goldstein. A Japanese-American born in California, Cobi learned to love jazz from the radio. An enthusiast of Duke Ellington's music, and an inveterate club-joiner when she was in high school, she was molding her character while leading the life of an ordinary American child.

One day, at age fifteen, in 1941, she was sitting in her tenth-grade classroom when the U.S. Military Police picked her up out of her chair, brought her to Tulare racetrack, and sent her to the Gila River detention camp in Arizona for the duration of World War II. There she lived with her parents, two brothers, and two sisters in a room about 20 by 20 feet. One brother volunteered to fight the war in Europe.

Instead of becoming withdrawn and bitter, Cobi ardently believed in her mother's encouragement. Cobi could do anything she wanted to if she would work hard and not complain about adversity, her mother urged. Cobi spent her time organizing clubs in camp: a jazz group, a debating society, a theatrical company, even a camp newsletter. She took charge of all these projects herself. She thinks that it might have been her Japanese cultural background, with its admonition never to complain, that gave her strong ambition and a buoyant spirit in spite of her adverse circumstances.

Two years later, when she was freed, she finished high school and spent a year on scholarship in Gettysburg College in Pennsylvania. She studied theatre, English, and eclectic cultural courses. One night, she went to a dance with friends, met a serviceman, and fell in love. Quickly she decided to marry and drop out of college. She and her husband began to have children—seven of them, one after the other, right away. She had all her children by the time she was twenty-eight, because neither she nor her husband knew anything about birth control in those postwar days. Later she would consider her children the main blessings of her marriage. She was so unhappily married that she did something revolutionary for a Japanese-American woman in the 1950s. She decided to get a divorce. "It was just something I had to do. I didn't know what I would be facing. But I knew I could handle it all. I just knew!"

At first she took three jobs to make sure that the children had vitamins, bicycles, a house, and a family car. Her ex-husband didn't feel obliged to help at all. She worked in an office by day, a restaurant by night, and a printing plant on weekends, paying a full-time babysitter "to warm up the macaroni and Campbell soup," she recalls. When financial pressures eased, she volunteered to do bookkeeping at a California jazz club. Eventually she worked her way into a weekday job in marketing with The International Council of Shopping Centers, which supported her and her entire family and sent them to live in New York City.

On her first weekend in town in 1966, she took a walk in Central Park where she heard some jazz musicians playing. She began to talk to them and they advised her to go to St. Peter's Lutheran Church, where the associate pastor known as the jazz pastor, Reverend John Garcia Gensel, would be able to guide her to volunteer work for jazz musicians. Connecting with the jazz world through St. Peters's, Cobi worked as the executive director of Collective Black Artists, with an office on Fifth Avenue. A slender, very youthful-looking woman, she had enough energy to work all day, stay up late with jazz musicians, and go to work the next day.

She was booking a few jazz musicians. In the early 1970s, she won a scholarship to study new community activism techniques at the Massachusetts Institute of Technology. When she returned to New York, she put her education to work by organizing a jazz festival on a Fourth of July weekend. So many people were out of town that she didn't know if she could attract an audience and make money. In partnership with her friend, Paul Ash, of Sam Ash Music Stores, whom she would work with for the next few decades, she showed a profit.

Encouraged by success, she founded the Universal Jazz Coalition, an educational group supported by grants from the National Endowment for the Arts, the New York State Council on the Arts, private donations, and low fees for performances and workshops. It was headquartered in a Fifth Avenue office. She mobilized such illustrious musicians as Dizzy Gillespie, Ahmad Jamal, and singer Betty Carter to serve as the group's board of directors.

By 1977, under the UJC's auspices, she was advising fledgling musicians about self-promotion; she was also providing courses for neophytes taught by nationally established players. Trumpeter Jimmy Owens, for example, gave lectures on business practices in the music industry. And Jamil Nasser, the bassist, Harold Mabern, the pianist, and drummer Frank Gant became her "house" rhythm section, with such duties as accompanying singers' workshops and giving constructive criticism to the young singers. One of Cobi's children became friendly with sculptor John Spaulding, brother of jazz saxophonist James Spaulding; the sculptor, who had a West 19th Street art gallery called the Jazz Gallery, offered space for Cobi to use for jazz performances and workshops.

Disturbed by the trouble that young women jazz musicians were having when they tried to establish themselves, Cobi founded the first women's jazz festival in New York. She called it a "Salute to Women in Jazz."

"I think women might never have had a chance if it hadn't been for Cobi. She started the whole thing," says reeds player Carol Sudhalter. (Cobi was particularly intrigued to hear Carol play a baritone saxophone as one of her instruments.) "It's a tremendous thing that Cobi did, a pioneering thing that gave women a chance for the exposure they needed, deserved, and might not otherwise have gotten."

That first year, however, the "Salute" nearly foundered. Cobi rented a midtown club, Casablanca, which had formerly housed the famed Birdland. In short order, the management rescinded its permission for the festival to continue because audiences were too small. Raymond Ross, a jazz photographer on the scene, thought that not enough liquor was being sold. The festival was sent packing into the street. Paul Ash talked to the management of the parking garage next door, and the garage let the festival run cables there for the sound equipment. The women played music in the street. Then jazz festival producer George Wein heard about their plight. He rented Carnegie Hall Recital Hall, now called Weill Recital Hall, for the last night of the "Salute." Cobi's imaginative venture survived.

The next year, in 1978, when she sponsored the "Salute" at the Top of the Gate in the Village Gate, a handful of women singers with gorgeous voices, including sopranos Jay Clayton and Janet Lawson, and bassist Carline Ray, also noted as a contralto singer, experimented with an improvised jam, scatting jazz and new, experimental music. It was an exotic musical adventure that few audiences have ever experienced. Tall and statuesque Melba Liston, with her heart-shaped face, dressed in a strapless white gown, led a swinging band with her authoritative, sweet trombone.

By 1980, the "Salute" was being called the Annual Women's Jazz Festival. It was held in the 19th Street Jazz Gallery owned by John Spaulding. Cobi asked pianist Tommy Flanagan to present singer Sheila Jordan with an award during an evening concert. Established musicians led afternoon workshops for students who arrived from Boston and other northeastern cities. Pianist Joanne Brackeen mesmerized young musicians with her articulate, swinging, rhythmically intense and controlled avant-garde compositions one afternoon. The students gave her a standing ovation and demanded encores.

And Cobi saw that it was good. She expanded, staging opening concerts for the women's festivals in Damrosch Park at Lincoln Center. A typical Damrosch Park concert was coordinated by Carol Sudhalter, who also led her own group that had as a member Hiroko Kokubu, a young woman jazz pianist from Japan, and several men who played in New York City nightclubs. A trio, Jazz Babies, including Judy Niemack, sang close-voiced harmony on 1930s and 1940s Boswell Sisters arrangements and Duke Ellington, Cole Porter, and Billy Taylor songs. Judy at the time was attracting a modicum of attention from such critics as *The New York Times*'s John S. Wilson. By the late 1980s, she began appearing in glamorous supper clubs, and later she would record as leader on CDs and work with Peter Duchin, the bandleader, for his society parties. The funk-rock/contemporary jazz contingent, Ellen Seeling, the trumpeter and flugelhorn player, and her partner, tenor saxophonist Jean Fineberg, led their Deuce. Tina Pratt tapdanced. And Cobi's creation, the Big Apple Jazzwomen, an all-women's jazz orchestra, with Willene Barton on tenor saxophone, Bertha Hope on piano, Melissa Slocum on bass, and other women who had played during the day, ended the festival's opening concert. The personnel in the Big Apple Jazzwomen kept changing. Sometimes Sarah McLawler played organ for the group.

Usually singer Dakota Staton or Abbey Lincoln or both sang during the festivals because it was always Cobi's idea to hire established stars to lure audiences to see and hear the young or lesser-known hopefuls. By 1984, Cobi could afford the space to produce a whole festival in one place: a huge loft that she used as a permanent home for the Universal Jazz Coalition.

She explained her attitude toward her ventures. "I just did them. And I did them with good spirits. I was always that way. My mother was strong and positive. She never did anything wrong in her life. That's a child talking. But she taught me that if there's something to be done, go ahead."

The loft was on the third floor of 380 Lafayette Street, about 8000 square feet for $4000 a month. She called it the Jazz Center of New York and supported it with fund-raisers, grants, and myriad festivals. In the first year of the loft's existence, Cobi launched an annual Asian-American jazz festival for the third weekend in October. She also started a Latin jazz festival and a Cherry Blossom festival featuring Asians and Asian-Americans in all the arts. And she produced weekend jazz shows year-round with famous musicians. Pianist George Russell and trombonist Benny Powell brought orchestras to play in the loft.

Cobi advertised her events through a regular newsletter she sent by mail, as she juggled funds, planned, bargained, promoted, and, when money ran short, which happened often, joked and kept her chin up. "Since I started the Universal Jazz Coalition, I've really had no full-time paying job!" she laughed, realizing that she had said that she worked essentially without pay.

The women's festival took place every year in June until 1987. By the next summer, she was forced to shut the doors of her enterprise because the landlord was doubling the rent. Cobi, still slender, with long, cascading dark hair and oversized, tinted glasses, went to live quietly in Hicksville, New York—a town as remote from New York's jazz scene as its name suggests. She took courses in a nearby college and maintained a quiet household with Paul Ash. Of course, even as she was resting, she had an idea that she would do something in jazz in New York again; exactly what, she didn't know. Paul was concerned because Cobi was unhappy without a job in jazz.

In addition to the hundreds of men who had played at the Jazz Center of New York, scores of women remembered the refuge the Universal Jazz Coalition had offered. Marimba player Valerie Naranjo recalled how she was playing in the street one day when Cobi heard her and hired her to play. Deuce and Carol Sudhalter and Sumi Tonooka and so many others performed there. When a women's jazz festival had been produced upstate, Cobi supplied the groups. Carline Ray, with one of her National Endowment for the Arts grants in the 1980s, had created three choral group concerts and produced them at Cobi's center. "Cobi did this for me . . . " and "Cobi did that for me . . . " one often heard, traveling around the town's jazz scenes.

In 1990, the "rest period" ended. Cobi and Paul Ash married. The Universal Jazz Coalition's newsletter, a chatty document with news of performances and the personal activities of musicians and Cobi's talented children in the arts, started circulating again. Cobi began producing performances in various clubs and restaurants in New York in her late sixties. She reactivated the women's jazz festival on a small scale in Manhattan. The romance was on again.

Chapter Seven / / / The Instrument Is the Image

Helen Keane first noticed the improvement for women in 1980, when she produced a record in San Francisco for the all-women's group, Alive!, with Carolyn Brandy as percussionist. She had already been recognized as an excellent *conguero* for about five years. By 1980, many women had started playing percussion and bucking the traditional prejudice, Helen learned from Carolyn. It wasn't Carolyn, however, who made it acceptable for women to play hand drums and the traditional drumset. As already mentioned, the credit goes to Sheila E, the daughter of Oakland, California-based musician Pete Escovedo; she worked with Marvin Gaye and then very prominently with Prince in rock music.

Before then, all women percussionists had been accused of destroying their feminine image when they played their instruments. Women horn players suffered the same insult and occasionally even physical attacks. Helen Keane, who has always thought that women looked very good playing their drums or horns or any instrument, has speculated that prejudice might have stemmed, in part, from the days when jazz clubs were traditionally in the "wrong" parts of town, the dangerous and economically depressed areas.

"Guys would go without their wives or girlfriends with few exceptions, when the music started to become popular," she recalls, "and there was an invisible barrier for women. The barrier announced, 'It's not lady-like' to play jazz. And there was always the suggestion that women could never play as well as the men. I think that women were afraid to assert themselves, to get in there and really play, and fight their way through. Only the piano players were the exceptions." Pianist Emme Kemp agrees with Helen's perception that uninviting neighborhoods discouraged women from playing. Emme, for one, always refused to play in depressing rooms or areas. And women needed to play in some of those places, so that their abilities could improve and they could fraternize with the men in a position to hire them.

But now jazz has become a feature of the grandest neighborhoods. Women go everywhere to play. Everyone involved with jazz has become aware of the growing number of excellent women pianists. Women playing other instruments are still far less numerous, although by the 1990s enough existed that never again would male musicians think there simply weren't any.

As recently as 1988, a well-known musician and concert producer was asked if he ever thought about hiring a woman saxophonist. He replied, "There's only one tenor player. What's her name? She plays with Charli Persip."

"Sue Terry," came the answer.

The musician said, "Yes, that's the one."

Actually Sue plays alto as her main instrument, and only occasionally has she played tenor in gigs.

"I can name a dozen others off the top of my head," he was told.

"Mmmmm, I don't know any," he said.

That sort of attitude was so prevalent until the late 1980s that none of the tenacious women musicians were surprised that some gifted colleagues simply dropped out of the playing scene.

In the 1980s, saxophonist Jean Fineberg and trumpeter Ellen Seeling played in New York and toured the country, but in bebop-happy New York City, their fusion group had difficulty attracting audiences. That was one reason they decided to move to the West Coast in the late 1980s. (They also felt that New York was a risky environment.) Throughout their entire career together, whether playing in acoustic or fusion groups, Ellen always suffered from the prejudice against women trumpet players. There was something about a woman trumpet player, she said, that attracted the most criticism from men; other women horn players have concurred.

Ingrid Jensen, flugelhornist and trumpeter, chose to teach in Europe in the 1990s rather than brave the prejudice on the U.S. playing scene. She had good friends among American men musicians, who invited her to sit in with their groups when she visited the United States, but sitting in didn't constitute a career. She established herself in Europe before returning to the United States. Men musicians hoping for stability in a music career also teach as a viable alternative.

The extremely attractive and gifted saxophonist Erica Lindsay arrived in New York with high hopes for a career and tried to get the work due her abilities in the late 1970s. At first she played in Melba Liston's all-women's group. That disbanded in the early 1980s, and because Melba became ill, the group never reconvened. There still wasn't a great deal of room for newcomers of either sex in jazz in the early 1980s. Competition compounded by sexual prejudice hampered Erica, and she eventually moved to Woodstock. So did her friend, pianist Francesca Tankesley. The women had grown up in an American community and played together in Germany. Several years passed before Erica recorded her first album as leader; it was her first commercially recorded performance. Francesca became the pianist in Billy Harper's quintet in 1983.

In truth, the current playing scene is still about as secure as a swamp for most women trying to get their footing. Even the best women players, especially trumpeters and saxophonists, feel the affront of lingering prejudice when men don't call them for jobs, and the women must always be active and self-starting to pursue their careers, leaving nothing to the chance that the phone might ring with a call to work. Jane Ira Bloom, who garnered wonderful reviews in the 1970s when she was still a graduate student at Yale University producing her own records, spent years waiting for her telephone to ring. Those calls never came, not even when she started recording for CBS in the 1980s. "And they should have come," she reflected, echoing French horn player Stephanie Fauber. (On the other hand, trombonist Lolly Bienenfeld, who could be typified as a lead player and an accomplished reader rather than strictly a jazz player, and who stopped playing professionally for a few years, received many calls at the level she liked; her situation was obviously not the norm.)

Despite the obvious hardships that women horn players have continued to endure, by 1989 and 1990 there were notable breakthroughs. And all the players have two things in common: no matter what their private lives and musical interests, each player's personality blends a protective toughness with a professional, unself-conscious charm. And each has been playing professionally for years.

The short-lived team of saxophonist Virginia Mayhew and trumpeter Rebecca Franks began leading a group. For a while, there was strength in their buddy system that presented audiences with the sight of two attractive young women who could play so well that they transcended the gender barrier. They are treated in Chapter Eleven about horn players.

All the horn players in Diva, for which Virginia and Rebecca auditioned separately and successfully, represented a breakthrough with their collective excellence in 1993. Kit McClure, who plays many horns, spent the 1980s honing an admirable all-women's big band. Exceptional players have passed through its ranks, among them Rebecca Franks. It has endured as a refuge, showcase, and launching pad for many women.

Saxophonist Sue Terry has been the player most men have mentioned when they try to think of an excellent woman reeds player. But they don't often call her for gigs. Some men are biased; more simply forget when it comes time to dial the phone. For drummer Charli Persip, however, she has been a brilliant voice in front of his small groups and his big band; in that featured position, she has furthered her reputation in jazz circles.

Flutist Ali Ryerson, who inspired a following in New York clubs, went to Belgium in the early 1980s and allied herself with a group rather than struggle in New York City. Catching the attention of France's great jazz violinist Stephane Grappelli, she started playing in concerts with him in Europe. At Carnegie Hall, in a Grappelli concert, she impressed producer Bob Thiele so much that he offered her a recording contract in the early 1990s.

Though the flute is still not technically regarded as a jazz instrument, many of the women playing wind instruments have flute as their main instrument, or they can double on flute. To Carol Sudhalter's father, the flute was ideal for a daughter to play. It wasn't until he died that she began playing saxophones. She also uses multiple approaches to earn her living as a professional musician; she leads small groups, works as a sideperson, runs a booking agency for other musicians, and has founded a big band in Queens. She uses the flute strictly to double.

Playing the flute as the main instrument can be a two-edged sword for women. Though they are more readily expected to play flute than saxophones, and more accepted as flute players, there has been uneven acceptance for the flute in jazz groups except as a doubler's instrument. Elise Wood worked for years to reach the point where she released "Luminous," her first and universally praised album as leader, with the especially sensitive, open-minded support of her partner and friend, pianist John Hicks. Of the flutes she uses, the lower-voiced alto flute seems to have the greatest impact for jazz. There have been times when she has been bypassed for jobs because her instrument is flute, not saxophone. Flautist Jamie Baum decided to lead her own group because the flute was so rarely used in other people's jazz groups.

Women who play acoustic bass are rare, perhaps only in part because the instrument is unwieldy. Those who have successfully bucked the prejudice and avoided the teasing usually play electric bass; veteran Carline Ray, who plays acoustic and electric basses, and relative newcomer Tracy Wormworth have had wonderful bookings in the 1980s and 1990s. Carline has played for singer Ruth Brown, and Tracy, who plays only electric, has worked in studio bands for such people as Bill Cosby. She has also played with Sting and other very popular groups. Both women were the daughters of musicians and found their way around the playing scene through family and friends. A few bassists have built reputations on the

West Coast and Chicago and other areas outside New York, and they rarely come to town.

Women guitarists are even rarer than bassists. In recent years, remarkable Emily Remler, whose career spanned the 1980s, built the beginnings of a sparkling career for herself in the tradition of her idol, Wes Montgomery. She left a rich legacy of recordings for Concord. Even Emily had some difficulty drawing crowds when she headlined alone in a club. Her commercial appeal improved when she teamed up in a duo with Larry Coryell.

As already mentioned, few women play jazz guitar because it takes such strength to play the complicated music on the instrument. Jazz is not folk or rock music. And so prejudice against women playing jazz guitar follows as the night follows day. It took guitarist Mike Stern's wife, Leni, herself a guitarist and friend of Emily's, a long time to get chances to record. "The guitar is thought of as a man's instrument," she says. Mimi Fox in San Francisco encouraged herself for years. Emerging in the 1990s, Sheryl Bailey based in Baltimore plays in a newly welcoming climate. Both have begun to get recognition in some of the best known music magazines. Gia Arnett in the Midwest impressed Diva's musicians when she was considered for that band; unfortunately, there was no budget for a guitarist.

Women who play organ, oboe, violin, viola, cello, bassoon, marimba, French horn, or any instrument usually associated with classical music occasionally cross the line from classical to dabble in jazz and pop music. In some instances, they decide to play all kinds of music strictly to make a living; there are also women extremely intrigued by jazz and the opportunities it affords improvisers. Notable among classical musicians who also play jazz are Akua Dixon Turre, the composer and cellist whose husband is jazz and Latin trombonist Steve Turre, and her sister, Gayle, a classical violinist. Violist Maxine Roach, drummer Max's daughter, plays in his creations—the Double Quartet with his jazz group combined with the Uptown String Quartet, and the quartet performing as a separate entity. Prestigious and interesting as the Uptown String Quartet is, the extremely unusual group has not yet achieved commercial success on its own.

Kathy Halvorson, whose principle instrument is oboe, and who doubles on baritone saxophone and dabbles with flute, has always played both jazz and classical music for satisfaction and remuneration. She has had success in recent years as a crossover player, touring Europe with the orchestra performing Charles Mingus's "Epitaph" in 1991 and with George Russell's orchestra at Wolf Trap in 1992.

For years Stephanie Fauber, a classically trained French horn player, undertook an interesting odyssey. When she was married to the Village Vanguard band's lead trumpeter, he taught her how to play jazz for the Vanguard gig on Monday nights. So Stephanie left the Broadway orchestra pits and got to the Vanguard in time for the second set on Monday nights. The late drummer, Mel Lewis, kept the band going after his partner Thad Jones left. Lewis never thought that French horns were actually able to swing. But Thad Jones, a great flugelhornist and trumpeter, arranger, and composer, wrote music for French horns. And Mel liked Stephanie's playing very much. After he died in February 1990, Stephanie decided to leave the band and move to Santa Fe. "I had come here on a vacation seven years ago," she reminisced in 1993. "I fell in love with the land, the mountains. Four years ago, my marriage broke up. Then, after Mel died, nothing was holding me in New York. I still miss Mel Lewis. So I moved on July 8, 1990."

It was difficult to earn a living as a musician in Santa Fe. She was teaching French horn, trumpet, and piano lessons; she was also studying accounting and setting up a records system for the Santa Fe Symphony. "They're starting a jazz concert series with a local radio station this year. It's not like I'm totally out of the music scene, though I'm not actually playing much."

On alternate Monday nights, she was playing in a band in a club— "not a great band, but we're working on it," she said. She was surprised to find women instrumentalists in Santa Fe, including one trumpeter and two trombonists in the band. People have asked her how she felt about "putting the horn in the case"—not playing the way she used to. When she lived in New York, she had often fled the city to a country retreat. Her husband had loved the city. "Life is a lot easier, the weather is better, the people are nicer," she mused about Santa Fe. "Music gave me a lot, but it's so nice to be here that it almost doesn't matter what I'm doing."

"And I took a lot of hard knocks," she reflected about her experiences in the music business in New York. "I had mixed feelings, so it doesn't bother me to put the horn in the case for a while." She was never actually insulted about playing the horn after she left Philadelphia in the early days of her career. At that time, when she graduated school, the Philadelphia Orchestra had three women violinists, "and that was it. There was a lot of prejudice against women musicians in those days," she recalled. In New Mexico, as in New York, discrimination is covert. "I'd say I had the standard amount of prejudice. You just don't get called for the real high-paying jobs. Any guy who had been in my position would have."

In New Mexico, the charts for the band playing on alternate Monday nights surprised her. They had French horn parts—a notable departure from the tradition. The leader told her, "See what you've done," referring to the development, suggesting she caused it. Whatever the reason, Thad Jones's influences on writing courses for jazz arrangers and composers in music schools has been strong. His band used excellent French horn players.

Normally in the jazz world, no one ever thinks of calling French horn players for a small jazz group, and they must double or crossover from classical music if they want to play jazz. It's impossible to earn a living strictly as a French horn player in the jazz world. An oboe player is even more exotic and finds only the odd job in jazz—usually only in a recording studio or in an experimenting group, if at all. Small jazz groups rarely include offbeat instruments. A woman—or man—who switches from classical to jazz with a cello, for example, has a very small role to play in jazz. Jazz bassists, who occasionally play cellos on the side, get the chance to expose their cello playing as a novelty in the course of their usual gigs.

Faced with such realities, women who play instruments other than piano and prospect for careers in jazz have found that their future rests on the amount of fight they are willing to put up. By the early 1990s, it was clear that many women were equal to the challenge. They had committed themselves to overcoming prejudice by "hanging out," looking for jobs as sidepeople, leading groups, making their own albums, and convincing recording companies to sign them. Many had more opportunities to record. And the sheer force of their numbers and abilities was helping them to make headway.

Helen Keane has said, "I look forward to the day when the notion of women in jazz could become a relic of the past, and they will be regarded simply as people in jazz."

Every woman player was hoping to live to see that day. Some had intimations that it might have even started to arrive. Reeds player Carol Sudhalter knew that the playing situation was better for her. Prejudice had definitely diminished, she said. Then she joked, "Sometimes I think I might just be imagining it. Then I realize that I'm not."

Introduction to the Profiles

It's impossible to say that one woman's life mirrors another's; however, a few things are true about all the women who are progressing and succeeding. Each is an individualist, who has led a unique life in a subculture with no set route to take. Each one lives life immersed in music, and the difficulties of putting music first usually seem worth the pain because of how much each woman loves music. With experience, the women develop stamina, thick skin, resourcefulness, and some business acumen.

If many have had similar histories—for example, parental disapproval of their playing jazz—they have handled their situations differently. Laurie Frink committed herself to playing trumpet in established groups and orchestras and, taking her inspiration from a trumpeter whom she admired very much, became a sought-after teacher. Fledgling musicians have called her from England and Korea to take lessons by telephone.

At first, bassist Melissa Slocum's parents were livid that she was playing jazz professionally. Carline Ray, whose father was a Juilliard graduate, and in whose footsteps she followed, felt sympathy when she heard about Melissa's family situation. The hardships for Melissa have been extraordinary, but she has learned to persist with feisty spirit and courage against the odds on the playing scene. For about eight years, until 1993, she played in a house band at Arthur's Tavern in Greenwich Village, hoping, among other things, to lead a group on a recording. "Geri Allen told me that I have to make my own album, nobody is going to do it for me," Melissa reflected several years ago, "and so that's what I want to do." By the early 1990s she was attending music school for a degree, raising a daughter, and running from gig to gig. The good news was that she had acquired a track record, had played on several albums, and for a while was the bassist in Diva.

Kit McClure decided to found a big band, take it around the world, and make recordings. Her parents only began going to her performances once she was in early middle age. For most of her career, she had worked without their approval. Because Kit's band has touched the lives of so many women musi-

cians, her profile comes first. Her story picks up where the Jazz Sisters left off in time and spirit. Unlike the International Sweethearts of Rhythm, which was conceived of as a fund-raising enterprise by a school, and whose musical director was a man, Kit McClure's band was created, led, and administered by Kit alone.

Following her story come others that demonstrate the drama of life as a woman jazz musician.

■ ■ ■ ■ ■ ■ ■ ■ ■ ■

Chapter Eight / / / Kit McClure, Big-Band Leader: "You Did the Right Thing"

■ ■ ■ ■ ■ ■ ■ ■ ■ ■

In a display of extraordinary determination, Kit McClure, who plays all the reeds, founded a successful, sixteen-piece, all-women's big jazz band. It specializes in Swing Era music, and the repertoire is bountifully endowed with Duke Ellington's songs. The band book also includes many rock and fusion pieces, because Kit appreciates these styles and wants to appeal to a wide audience. She has established, in effect, a swinging society and jazz band in New York City, playing at the Bottom Line, Cafe Society, The Red Blazer, at trendy annual parties for such companies as *Spy* magazine, for Brooke Shields's birthday parties, on the Riviera, in concert halls in Japan, and at New York's Tavern on the Green. In New York, she also plays in parks as part of the city's summer cultural program.

"We went to Tokyo and played in concerts. Then we got on the bullet train and went toward China. We turned around and headed south on the bullet train to Osaka and several other cities. The next year, we went back for double the money," she said with satisfaction in 1989.

The band grossed $160,000 in 1988. but Kit still didn't pay taxes. "I paid $100,000 in salaries, $45,000 for studio rehearsal time, and $15,000 for publicity. That doesn't leave me much," she said. "But I go for a bank loan for equipment. And they say, 'Oh you grossed $160,000, come right in, we'll roll out the red carpet for you.' But the truth is I'm at the poverty line: I'm way in debt to keep the band going. And the only way to get ahead is to make a record. So I'm talking with a very big company about a record deal." Eventually she made two records herself. The first was "Some Like It Hot" on her own Red Hot Records label. The second was in production in 1994.

She always had the pluck to organize and lead a band with all the business and social problems and risks that the world can heap on an all-women's group—or any group—in jazz. Enduring the "vicissitudes," as another big-band leader, Dizzy Gillespie, called some of life's routines, Kit, in performance, with cascades of curly red hair and wearing a bright uniform—a white one in 1989, a gold gown in 1993—looks and feels like the epitome of glamour and success. Her band has developed a clean, swinging sound. The few best-known, all-women's bands in the past—Ina Rae Hutton's and the International Sweethearts of Rhythm—didn't record enough to attest to their quality. Other women's small groups have come and gone, mostly without making any records. Since Kit developed as a multi-instruments player herself throughout the 1980s and set high standards for the accomplished women players she finds in New York, she kept increasing her chances to improve her commercial success with recordings.

She had no competition of any kind on the East Coast until Diva was founded, and Diva is strictly a jazz concert band, never a dance band. Leading a band is an enterprise so enormous, requiring a resourceful leader of such extraordinary pluck and financial management abilities, that not many people would want the job even if they could do it. (Toshiko Akiyoshi's award-winning band comes to mind as a great enterprise, but Toshiko is the only woman in it. Possibly bound for commercial success in the long run as well as its immediate artistic success as this book was being written, was Straight Ahead, a small, contemporary all-women's jazz and fusion group.)

Women know they can audition for Kit's band and, if they're good enough and behave themselves, they can get in and keep the job. There are so few jobs tailored especially to women that some of the best players think they can take advantage of the shortage of personnel candidates, Kit says. They try to test her mettle. But her standards for their behavior as well as their music prevail.

A slender woman with a savvy smile just beginning to etch a permanently knowing expression onto her face, Kit first learned the meaning of true grit in her hometown. Born on March 18, 1951, in Little Falls, New Jersey, she started playing the piano at age seven. A remarkable teacher gave her lessons in the classical literature.

"She taught me music theory right away. 'This is by Mozart,' she would say. 'And this is why he wrote this, and why he plays two or three notes at the same time, and this is their relationship to the next notes.' It still amazes me that a teacher could teach a child music theory. That understanding plus my ear gave me a great background for improvisation. The more theory you know, the more options you can show yourself. She taught me to play the piano, which was useful in composing. And her music theory lessons made it easy for me to understand jazz."

Kit improved her playing on the classical assignments, until her accomplishments caught her parents' attention when she was ten. They decided that she wouldn't be allowed to play the piano anymore. Her only explanation, in retrospect, is that they had emotional problems. To this day, "they don't like this music business," she sums up. They decided she could learn another instrument, and the trombone looked rather appealing to her. "No," they said, "it's not ladylike." They insisted on either the flute or the clarinet. "I saw what I was up against. In my case, male chauvinism started in the home, from both my parents," she reminisced. "I could see myself liking the saxophone, so I chose the clarinet, because it looked sort of like a saxophone," she recalled. But she hated the clarinet in those days. "Even if I had liked it, I wouldn't have liked it, because I was being forced to play it."

Then something horrible happened in her high school—a quiet, middle-class school. Of the two fourteen-year-old trombonists in the school band, one killed the other. The killer went to reform school. "That decimated the trombone section," Kit says. So she talked to the teacher in charge of the band and begged him to let her play trombone. In return for his permission, she would help him out the whole season for football games and anything else he wanted her to play for. "I'd teach myself, I told him, if he would give me a little coaching. I would stay after school and practice myself until I got it right. The only stipulation was that he couldn't tell my parents."

He agreed to her deal. Kit made up stories to keep her parents from knowing what she was doing. She learned to play so well that she was selected to audition for the county band competition. It seemed likely that she would win, and she did; so she and the band director agreed that he should tell her parents. When he talked to them, he added that the school would continue to let her play the school's trombone on loan. "Why don't you give her lessons, for Christ's sake?" he added.

Her parents found her a fine trombone teacher but all the while tried to discourage her. "No one will marry you. Your lips will be so strong that you'll kiss a boy and knock his teeth out." So Kit did what she could to avoid them. "I ate in a separate room," she recalls.

When youngsters around the country were forming rock bands, and Blood Sweat and Tears and Chicago were the role models for jazz influence in the kids' groups, Kit tried to join another band in her high school. The leader explained that the guys thought it would look weird to have a girl in the band. They vetoed her, he said, and he was forced to audition several boys. But the leader was blind; he could only hear, and he told her she had the trombone seat because she was the only one who could play the instrument. The band insisted she wear a dress on the bandstand—probably to emphasize the novelty of a woman rather than disguise it.

In rehearsals, she learned to play all the instruments, as kids often do in youthful bands. "You go through putting music together step by step; you learn how to be a band leader," she says. She learned to play guitar, bass, drums, and, again, the piano; she liked involvement with the band's whole organization. The boys came to accept her fully. Then for her first gig, which was on the fifth floor of Essex Catholic High School in Newark, New Jersey, she ran into a new roadblock.

Wearing her dress and carrying her trombone and music stand, she tried to take the elevator up to the gig. The elevator operator said, "Girls can't go on the elevator. This is only for musicians."

"I stood there and waited," she recalled. The bass player, who stood six feet six inches tall, came along; he put his foot in the door and told the elevator operator he had to transport Kit.

She went on to Yale in 1969, the first year it admitted about 400 women to join many thousands of men on campus. A strong women's movement existed on campus and in New Haven then, so Kit organized an all-girl band made up completely of politically oriented women, not one of them more than an amateur musician as a side venture.

"I taught each woman to play. I made a bass player out of a girl who had played cello for six years. I made a leader guitarist out of a folk guitarist. And we made a record for Rounder Records in the early days. They took us up to their Massachusetts studio. On one side of the album, we played, and on the other side, a women's movement band from Chicago played. We played rock, jazz, fusion. Our lyrics were in support of feminism. And it seems as if everybody loved us."

"I wanted to be in the Yale Marching Band. I was already in Yale's classical concert band as a trombonist. 'But, oh, no, there are no women in the marching band,' I was told. I had to make them integrate the marching band. After the band fought it, then accepted me, Brown University and Yale played a football game. And the Brown Bear picked me up during the game and started running with me down the field. Can you imagine that? There was never a moment when I was allowed to forget that I was doing something I wasn't supposed to do."

In private, she was listening to saxophonist Sonny Rollins's new records in 1969, 1970, and 1971, trying to emulate him on her trombone. She even transcribed his solos. Finally she realized that she couldn't sound anything like him, because the saxophone was a very different instrument. She liked it so much that she borrowed a tenor saxophone from the woman drummer in the town's feminist band.

"And by then I was able to teach myself to play an instrument," Kit recalls. "You figure out how it works and what sound you want, and you work on it and figure out which muscles it's going to tax, and you work on those muscles every day. I played the sax four hours a day for the muscle development in addition to keeping up the trombone."

It took her until 1975 to graduate. She spent time working in a band; she spent more time working as a school bus driver. She finally told her parents that she had switched from pre-med to a music major. Then she auditioned for the Manhattan School of Music, was accepted as a saxophone student, but became too busy performing to finish even one course and never graduated.

Instead, to support herself, she answered ads in the papers, before the Reagan Administration cut grants for schools, and she taught in private high schools—three different schools on different days, giving lessons in everything she had learned by experience in her own high school, in bands, and in college work. "I taught them how to put together a band, what the theory is behind it, how you write out charts, how you write tunes, how you play tunes. And I taught them how to have jam sessions and to support each other in groups."

"The gig scene was not bad, either. I played for one month straight at the Rainbow Room for a singer, with Kirk Lightsey as the conductor. We had a great time. Then Barry White came to town and did a week at Radio City with a 63-piece, all-women orchestra." He included many violinists and classical players, as well as some jazz musicians. "Everyone was in it," Kit recalls. "Sue Evans [the drummer] was in it. I was the sax soloist in a white dress doing an improvised, a cappella jazz solo for five minutes. And after that, I got a call to play in a women's jazz festival in Italy in 1979. I auditioned for Stephanie Chapman, a drummer and songwriter who would lead the quartet. And I got the gig. It was only for one day in Rome supposedly, but we were held over and toured Italy for another eight weeks."

"It was so wonderful to me to be making a living and living in Italy, playing jazz. It was a dream come true. We played bebop, some fusion, a little rhythm and blues, and some Herbie Hancock and post bebop-type standards. I got a thrill when Dexter Gordon complimented me on my rendition of Charlie Parker's 'Confirmation'. I was devastated when the tour ended and I was back in New York. I wanted to find a way to go to Italy and make that life last forever."

In New York, she went to the men players and asked them, "How do I get a steady gig? I don't want to teach anymore." It was the same question that many of them usually asked themselves. But they tried to be helpful, sending her to various people for auditions. She even called Thad Jones, who then co-led the Village Vanguard band with Mel Lewis. With a saxophone she played a set with the band as her audition, but didn't get that band job. [The band played, and still plays, some of the most difficult music in jazz, "as Mahler is more difficult than Haydn," says Stephanie Fauber, who had to struggle to fit in with the band in the Vanguard in the 1980s.]

A saxophonist told Kit that she could probably find a gig with Sam and Dave, a rhythm and blues band from the 1960s. She tried out one night at the Lone Star, a blues club in Greenwich Village, where the audience stood up and cheered for her. So she got the job with the all-black, ten-piece band as its only woman player; she earned $60 a night if the band worked. It toured the South in a station wagon pulling a trailer with the band's equipment. A separate Cadillac took the leaders, Sam and Dave, and the business manager, who wanted her to ride with them. But after a short time, she decided to ride with the men in the station wagon. The men appreciated her gesture and befriended her. During three years with them, she went for a European trip and appeared on *Saturday Night Live*. The road life was rigorous.

"And then I had too much of it," she recalls. Alighting in Manhattan, she approached several booking agents whom she had made contacts with through friends. She said, "I have a jazz quartet. We'll be great in Italy. We'll be great everywhere. Everyone will love us. Why don't you just book me?" She got "no" after "no." But she knew an all-female quartet would sell. Finally one agent said, "Why don't you put together a Swing band? I can try to sell it."

She signed a contract with him, saying that he owned everything that came of the band. If there were any records, he would take all the royalties. And he would own everything she wrote, in exchange for which he would underwrite the production of the band. "It seemed like a good idea to me," Kit reflects, "because I didn't have any money at all, and I wanted to work." But soon after she organized the band, in 1981, he stopped paying for rehearsals. She broke relations with him; in return, he sued her. She had a few gigs within a few months period and had to go to the Volunteer Lawyers for the Arts for help. But her lawyer didn't know what he was doing, she says, he never cleared up matters. She held the situation at bay until she could afford to pay for a lawyer; he then sued her V.L.A. lawyer, won some money, and also freed her from the contract with the agent.

The legal troubles never deterred her from pressing on with the band. While gigging around town and teaching students, she spent a great deal of time—often eight hours a day—on the telephone. She called banks, special events departments, corporations, the parks department, magazines, "begging for work," she recalls. "And I got work, then more and more work. In the last few years, I've pretty much stopped calling people. And they call me."

She took the band into Joanna's restaurant in New York City in the mid-1980s. Right after her series of Monday nights finished, they went for a spring season to a casino in Monte Carlo. The rock star, Robert Palmer, heard the band and liked it. He made sure that it was on salary with him at Island Records in 1984. Several years later, she played as the featured saxophonist on a world tour with the Robert Palmer group for five months. Wherever he went, she performed, then flew home for a day or two to rehearse her big band. The salary with his group allowed her such a luxury.

That year gave her added income, status, and confidence. She credited some of the rise in her band's fortunes to the late Mel Lewis, talking about him shortly before he died of cancer.

"He's like a father to me," she said. "At the beginning, I'd have financial and personnel problems. I didn't know what to play or where to play. I called Mel. 'Help, I can't make this arrangement work!' And he would be there at rehearsal; he would advise me how to do it. He'd also tell me to fire a musician if she were nasty. That happens. Women can be nasty to each other. If I fired a musician, even if she were a good player, Mel would hear the next girl I hired, and he would tell me, 'You did the right thing. She's better than the last one.' He has helped me a lot, telling me, 'You did the right thing.'

"Maybe men are nasty, too, but they have more competition for the all-male jobs. They might be on better behavior, because there are 100 men lined up for every job. And there are fewer women lined up for the women's jobs. So I've had to work out a lot of personnel problems. I put a lot of effort into it.

"I want a racially mixed band. And I've had some racial problems, mainly because a few white musicians have been nasty to the blacks. In Monte Carlo, I had a new musician along, and she was harassing a black musician. Finally, just before a performance, the black musician put her up against the wall and told her to cut it out. The white musician started crying, but I just ignored it and said, 'Let's get on stage.' On the plane home, the black musician told me that she didn't know if she could play in a band where she had to take that harassment. And I told her that she didn't have to, because she would never see that white musician in my band again.

"In Tokyo, I heard about some trouble, and then it was settled among the women. But nobody has to take any harassment of that type in my band. There's no name calling.

"There's no smoking, either. Whenever they're in an enclosed space with me, in a club or a bus, the women can't smoke. And the women can't drink until after the gig is completely over. I'm acquainted with the women in the band. I have a working relationship with the members usually. I'm the leader, and we need to know what to expect from each other." Kit has felt close to Kim Clarke, the bassist, who played with the band and then with Kit's small group, Bernice Brooks, the drummer, Anita Johnson, the trombonist, and some others, she says. "We hang out together."

"I pay what the union requires, though old-timers get a little more.

Every night it's about $185. If a musician needs a car to transport an instrument, I pay an extra $10," Kit said in 1993.

She had four trumpets, three trombones, four saxes including her own, one singer and a piano, a bass, drums, and a guitar. While Kit got to wear the bright gold gown, the other women wore tuxedos with black spandex pants or tight-fitting black, shimmering dresses. Kit plays lead alto with the band, but she regards the tenor as her main instrument. She also plays bass clarinet, the most recent addition to her repertoire, since she got a nice one during her travels with Robert Palmer. She has been working that, plus an alto flute for reggae and jazz, into the band. She also uses clarinet a lot, because of its special sound; her early aversion to it has passed, now that she can choose to play it freely. And she does section work on a flute, though she doesn't use it as a solo instrument. Her voice softens, and her eyes take on a dreamy look, as she talks about the instruments she plays.

Many women in the band are married and have children. She has never had a family, although she would like a child. Because of her commitment to music, Kit says, her relations with her own parents were strained for a long time. "Actually we have no relations," she said softly as late as 1989. But right afterward, her parents came to some of her performances and became reconciled and proud of her career, when they realized they had a successful daughter.

Introduction to the String Players

In New York City, among the few, best-known, most active women jazz bassists, whether on acoustic or electric basses, have been Lucille Dixon, Carline Ray, Melissa Slocum, Kim Clarke, and Tracy Wormworth. Carline played with the Sweethearts of Rhythm in the 1940s and was still very busy in the 1990s. Karen Korsmeyer replaced Kim Clarke as the regular bassist in Kit McClure's band. Sue Williams also plays electric and acoustic bass with jazz and pop groups in the New York area. Lynn Milano teaches, plays, and writes music on Long Island. And Marion Hayden-Banfield was playing and recording, with a strong style, with an exciting new all-women's group, Straight Ahead, from Detroit. Nedra Wheeler and Mary Ann McSweeney have distinguished themselves with California as their base. Nedra Wheeler had scholarships to encourage her from half a dozen sources for her schooling, when she was a student of bass. Californian Leslie Baker has a collection of very good reviews of her performances. Recently Mary Ann moved to New York to play in Diva and other groups. Several women are very active and financially successful playing acoustic bass in the studios and in commercial settings such as Broadway orchestra pits, but that is a world apart from the jazz scene. (The chapter on percussionist Carol Steele and the Appendix at the end of the book with its entry on drummer and percussionist Sue Evans will shed some light on studio players.) There still aren't very many bassists compared to the pianists or even the varied horn players.

The legend has been that the acoustic bass is too big and awkward for women to carry around, and its size discouraged women from taking up the instrument. The smaller Fender (electric) bass has become the preferred instrument, particularly for women in pop music groups. However, like the men, the women bassists playing jazz have usually learned to play both acoustic and electric bass. And the acoustic bassists are often more attracted to playing cello than electric bass as a second instrument.

Tracy Wormworth, who plays only the electric bass, thought her instrument would allow her more opportunities to work in young, rock- and funk-oriented popular bands. Not only were they more numerous, but they had a more relaxed attitude toward hiring women. In pop music, groups preferred to have a woman on stage to attract attention. And there are quite a few women playing electric bass in pop groups these days.

The women who play acoustic bass never complain about the difficulty of moving it around. Bassist Lyle Atkinson's classically trained, bass-playing wife Karen has surprised men by assuring them that she doesn't need help getting her bass down the street. She herself was surprised to discover that men have thought the bass's size might bother her.

So perhaps the bulk of the instrument has not been very crucial for the perpetuation of a traditional bias against women players. As already mentioned in Chapter Seven, women guitarists in jazz have never found acceptance easy either, though their instrument is small. Mary Osborne was an exception—a prominent guitarist in the studios and on radio in the 1950s—who virtually abandoned her career, though she kept playing, when she moved to Bakerfield, California, to raise her sons. She returned to play in New York's Village Vanguard in recent years but died soon afterward. Because of the complexity of jazz guitar and the physical stamina it requires, men—and even women—have tended to accept the idea that, in jazz, the guitar is a male province.

Guitarist Leni's marriage to Mike Stern, at one time the guitarist in Miles Davis's group, didn't clear the way for her to find work. She played in East Village coffee shops with electric bassist Lincoln Goines and in other small clubs. It was a rare occurrence for her to play at Sweet Basil. Gradually, in the 1980s, Leni began to surface in clubs more often, and started leading groups on records. By 1994, she was leading groups in high-profile clubs such as Zanzibar. Sue Terwilliger, less known in jazz circles than Leni, has played in jazz groups in New York too. Jane Getter was recently playing in clubs in New York—Hudson Bar and Books, and Zanzibar for example. Guitarist Emily Remler became the most famous women jazz guitarist in the 1980s; she liked to tell people about her friend Leni's playing long before Leni started to record. Even Emily, who would leave a valuable legacy of records in the Wes Montgomery tradition on the Concord label, experienced, in small measure, the enduring bias against women jazz guitarists. At the Monterey Jazz Festival in California, she was carrying her guitar on her way to play a concert when she was stopped by a festival employee. He asked whom she was carrying the guitar for, and was prepared to block her way to the stage.

As Jane Getter, who plays a "a lot of electric jazz funk guitar," and tradition-rooted jazz guitar, described her world, in which she survived in part because of her versatility, "It's a little bit better for women now. There's still prejudice. Some men still won't hire women for various reasons. Some don't think that women should play guitar, and they won't check a woman out. There aren't a lot of women playing strong, electric, screaming guitar [in the jazz funk idiom]. And there's economic competition; it's slow for everyone right now, with fewer festivals in Europe. Some were canceled, or postponed, or cut back in 1993, or else the festivals are paying less." Jane finds opportunities because she leads her own groups, and composes on her own—she won a ASCAP Gershwin Award for writing music for a dance piece in 1991—and as a collaborator with drummer Lenny White. She also co-leads a group called No Soap Radio with her husband Adam Holzman, who was Miles Davis's keyboardist for a long time. They hire sidemen from well-known pop groups. And Holzman included one of his wife's songs, "Road Town", on his album "In a Loud Way" in 1993.

Though many women now play violin in studio bands, and the Uptown String Quartet has become a viable group (in large part thanks to the support of drummer Max Roach), and another chamber jazz, string quartet, the Quartette Indigo, with well-known classically trained, versatile players, finds opportunities to play and record, few women have played violin or viola as their main instrument in jazz. Audrey Hall Petroff, who also played reeds and piano, played violin on the side in the 1920s. So did Valaida Snow, primarily known as a trumpeter, who became quite a popular star in the 1930s.

Male violinists often switched to bass for jazz work, once the violin lost its cachet at the end of the era when bands played for silent films. The bass, aided by new amplification techniques, replaced the slower-moving tuba in jazz groups. So even male jazz violinists were a rarity; only a few have distinguished themselves, and one of the greatest, cornetist Ray Nance, was a doubler.

A notable exception to any generality about women playing violins as their first instrument and concentrating on jazz is Regina Carter. She became a jazz player because a teacher in Detroit in the 1970s advised her she would have more opportunities, as an African-American, to play professionally as a jazz musician. She became a member of the exciting new all-women's group, Straight Ahead, that now has two albums out—the latest, "Body and Soul," on Atlantic Jazz in 1993. The first album, "Look Straight Ahead," put the Detroit-nurtured group, whose members all sing as well as play instruments, on the jazz popularity charts and smoothed the way for their performances in festivals and clubs around the world, with due acclaim. The group has been getting standing ovations in clubs and theatres since it played at the Montreux Jazz Festival in Switzerland in 1992. Off and on, it has been touring since then.

Chapter Nine / / / Tracy Wormworth, Bassist: "Doors Just Opened"

Tracy Wormworth remembers exactly the day when she dropped out of the workaday world to which she tenuously belonged as a temporary secretary. On Wednesday, November 5, 1980, she was, as usual, late getting to work from Cambria Heights, Queens, because she had stayed out late the previous night to play her electric bass, jamming and auditioning. She was especially dejected that day because Ronald Reagan had won the Presidential election the night before. It had been the first election in which Tracy, born December 15, 1958, had been old enough to vote. And she wanted to play her bass and cheer herself up.

"I was supposed to be at work by 9:45 A.M. I was standing outside the CBS building at 10:20 A.M. and I got depressed. I called from outside the building and said, 'Look, I'm late, and I can't come anymore'."

Tracy had had a short-lived spat with her protective father, Jimmy Wormworth, Sr., the drummer with a "bebop vibe," as Tracy calls it. So she was living temporarily with a girlfriend and her mother in Queens. They were dismayed when Tracy quit her job, because she was contributing $50 a week to household expenses. But Tracy, a vivacious, twenty-one year old, had become so attached to her electric bass that she even carried it to her day jobs so she could practice at lunchtime. She recalls gleefully how she would show up for a new job a few days without the bass, make a good impression, and then bring it along. Her co-workers always did a double-take. But playing the bass stayed uppermost in her mind, no matter how she had to earn a living.

As luck would have it, a funny thing happened to the charming, very beautiful young woman. "I was walking down the street with my bass. I was always getting stopped on the street and being invited to audition anyway. And I was always auditioning, because I wanted to be a musician. Sometimes I auditioned until 4 A.M., and then I traveled two hours back to

Cambria Heights. I went to sleep for a few minutes, and I had to get up and go to work. That's why I was always late.

"This time a man stopped me and said he knew of a band looking for a bass player to tour. He said it was 'new wave'. I said, 'What's that? I'll check it out.'" It turned out to be the group, The Waitresses, which had already recorded a campy hit, "I Know What Boys Like." The group sang it flat to the enormous delight of a cult of fans primarily in New York and California. Suddenly Tracy was traveling by van and immersed in a new lifestyle with The Waitresses.

"I was always falling asleep on the tables after the gigs," she recalls. "I wasn't used to it. But I just kept going. It wasn't like: wow, look what I'm doing. My whole life has changed." No, she simply muddled through, without thinking about her trendy new status. She made two albums and one extended play record with The Waitresses, which broke up after a few years because of "internal dissension," she says. Tracy was poor again. Though she had been making $100 to $200 per gig with the band, she had also begun paying $325 a month for half the rent for an apartment in Queens plus half of the rest of the bills with her new roommate.

And who might that be? It was Kenny Kirkland, one of the best jazz pianists of his generation. He had worked with Wynton Marsalis's group for several years, recording and composing for Wynton's first album. Then Kenny began to work with Sting, which many fans of the group call fusion jazz. Though also a fan, Tracy calls it rock. Through Kenny's introduction to Sting, Tracy would be invited to audition and play for the group. One connection would continually lead to another for her.

Tracy was born in Women's Hospital in Manhattan and then went home to Bedford-Stuyvesant, where, she recalls, in the 1960s, musicians who lived in the Brooklyn neighborhood were always dropping by the house to visit her father, a busy drummer.

Jimmy Wormworth set Tracy and her brothers and sisters to studying piano. Tracy also studied clarinet; a brother studied trumpet; a sister played violin for a little while. "And we heard quality music every day, every night, WQXR and WNCN for classical music in those days, and organ music on Sundays. I heard Edgar Varese and Tchaikowsky. I loved 'La Gaite Parisienne', the ballet," she recalls. "And we heard Clifford Brown, Max Roach, Miles Davis, Bird, Dizzy, 'Trane—my father's records. In the street we heard James Brown, Sly and the Family Stone, and Motown on WWRL. We heard everything. My father always had the radio or the records on. He was continually working and involved in the community. The seed was planted when I was really young.

"But from the age of five, I wanted to be a ballerina and pursued it into my freshman year at the State University of New York at Rockport. I took three dance courses a day and some required courses. Finally I said to myself—what am I doing, spending all this money? If I want to be a dancer, I can get the best teachers right in New York."

So she took a leave of absence from school at the end of her sophomore year and started going to gigs with her father at the Tin Palace and the Ladies Fort—Greenwich Village clubs—in 1979. She had always gone to gigs with her father, but now she was doing it often and listening with rapt attention to the music. In one club, she met an electric bass player who became her boyfriend.

He took her to Kenny Kirkland's loft on 30th Street in Manhattan. So many musicians went there that it was an informal jazz scene. Someone brought Branford Marsalis to the loft too. He was so impressed with Kenny's playing that he advised his brother Wynton to hire Kenny. Violinist Michel Urbaniak and his wife, singer Ursula Dudziak, also used to go there.

Tracy was thoroughly at home on the scene. Her sister had decided to study singing at the Berklee School of Music in Boston, Branford Marsalis's alma mater. Tracy had met him and many other young musicians there before she met Kenny. She knew scores of musicians who would rise in the music business. Musicians were her milieu.

"Six months into our relationship," she said about the electric bass player, "he bought me a bass; he had been taking me to gigs and record sessions, and I had been bombarded by the music and his sound. I would pick up his bass and try to learn. I didn't think about it, but it was happening."

He told her, "Don't put that bass in the corner. Don't let it collect dust and show it off only as a gift." He didn't have to remonstrate with Tracy. "I started playing it all the time," she recalls. "I slept with it, and when I woke up with it in my arms, I played it. I started working family gigs, with a sister who sings and a brother who plays drums [Jimmy Wormworth, Jr.] and Bryan Carrott, a vibraphonist. He too was instrumental in my development. He taught me harmony; he told me what to listen to. Those were my formative days and constituted my growth as a musician to get to where I am now, wherever that is," she says.

When Tracy began playing bass, Kenny Kirkland may have been a little surprised, she thought. He had known her at first as someone who listened. Her love affair with her bass far outlasted her relationship with the bass player. She and Kenny began living together.

Once The Waitresses broke up, she went back to the routine of playing once in a while for pay. In a stable household with Kenny in 1983, she found a job playing with Phyllis Hyman, the singer, and stayed with the group for three years. Tracy played at the Blue Note, Fat Tuesday's in New York, Blues Alley in Washington—all around the country, and in George Wein's Kool Jazz Festival. Though Hyman was singing rhythm and blues, for festivals she did her material from the Broadway show, *Sophisticated Ladies,* and from her record with McCoy Tyner in the mid-1980s—a record Tracy didn't play for.

Then Tracy made a record of songs and incidental music from Bill Cosby's popular TV show. And she met Sting when he was recording his second album in May 1987. "Until then, I had been the elusive one. Sting had met all the other girlfriends and wives of the guys in his group, but he had never met me, because I was always traveling, working. The group did a second album on Montserrat, the Caribbean island. I went to the studio with Kenny that time. I picked up Sting's bass. And he saw I could move my fingers up and down the neck. That fall he called me to audition. He was set on having me, because Kenny had told him I could cut the cake."

"I played with Brook Benton too. I don't get called for any jazz gigs. Kim Clarke, who plays acoustic bass primarily, gets the jazz jobs. I've been called by various women's festivals. Deuce called me. They had a man bass player, but when they had to play all-women situations and had to have only women in the band, I played. I'm open-minded, but sometimes it was emotionally draining for me. I'm sympathetic to feminism—to a point. But there are women who don't want to play with anyone but women. The mainstream has never heard of them. All you see is women at these festivals, not a man in sight." And some of the women—*absolutely not Deuce*—she emphasized, concentrated on politics and ignored the sound of their instruments which needed to be tuned up. She herself had no political ax to grind.

"I never had any flak," she explained. "The way it unfolded for me as a musician was a miracle. I found what I wanted to do in life. And the doors just opened for me. After floundering around, it was like being touched by God. Maybe it was difficult, but I never felt that it was. I never felt that I was paying dues, never dwelled on my apprenticeship. It just flowed. I wish I had started playing earlier, but things happened, perhaps, because I was older and more mature. As a kid, I hadn't thought that I would play and make thousands of dollars. I was older and formed when I started. And I was always encouraged."

"Maybe it would have been different in traditional jazz. I have never been on that scene because of my instrument—electric bass. The acoustic bass is for traditional jazz. Bob Cranshaw may play electric bass on that circuit, but Bob Cranshaw is Bob Cranshaw. Everybody knows what he can do, so he can play electric bass and get no flak. But if I or a young guy tried it, oh, no. Now, if I got there and just burned, maybe they'd be civil."

"At first when my father heard me playing electric bass, he thought that it was foolish for me to copy my boyfriend. But then he became my number one supporter and fan. He follows every detail of what I do."

"Normally a woman used to be a person who would go to the front of the bandstand and flirt. The men would fight over who would take her home. But I've had good support. Rodney Jones, the guitarist, recommended me for jobs, because he liked the way I played. He didn't see sex," she says.

Jones, in his mid-thirties, by 1992, said he couldn't overstate what a good player Tracy is. He has hired her for his own group, recommended her to Charles Aznavour and Brook Benton, who were very happy with her playing, and sent her to Lisa Bonet for the TV show *Different World* on NBC, where Tracy became the show's staff bassist. Jones even sent her to Cosby. "She's very sensitive and has extremely good feeling," says Jones. "It has been a feather in my cap with whomever I've recommended her to." When she had to audition for Sting, she told Jones, "I'm not ready." But Jones insisted she was. Each time she was reluctant to try for a job, Jones insisted: "It's my behind on the line. And you're ready." He has played with the best, he says; Tracy is still his choice.

"Kenny just hears music too," Tracy says. "I've had support. Those older guys were different when they were ruling. But they're old. There's new talent around. Time is marching on now. Younger guys are carrying the torch . . . It's almost actually trendy to hire women, especially in the pop world. Everyone wants to have a woman in the band. Of course, my story is so electric."

Tracy has made at least four albums—two with The Waitresses, "Bill Cosby Presents Music from the Cosby Show," and "Good Stuff," with the B52s, whom she was working with in 1992. She has recorded in live performance with Sting. Among her many other credits, she played at the Montreux Jazz Festival in Switzerland in 1990 with Wayne Shorter's group.

Chapter Ten / / / Emily Remler and the Guitarists

Emily Remler died while touring Australia in 1990. The cause of her death, newspapers said, was heart failure. She had been daring and full of life, well liked and respected. She was so modest about her inordinate gift that she remained vulnerable and childlike when she talked about her role in the music world. She could trust her ears so completely that she constantly guessed right in a "Before and After" test given to her by Leonard Feather for an article in *Jazz Times* published in June 1989. But she felt apologetic about criticizing anybody's work. "I gotta say that the time is funny. I don't know what's so truthful about me lately," she said while analyzing a recording. "Who's playing bass? He must be the problem." She worried whether the musicians on the recording would speak to her again.

In the recording studios, however, she knew exactly what she wanted, she said, and learned to stand up for her ideas.

With all the globe-trotting she began to do in her early twenties, she never had a chance to establish any personal stability. She wanted to play. Life in the fast lane at the top took its toll on the girlish *wunderkind*. Part of this chapter was written about her before she died; she was at a point where she was very concerned about developing healthful habits and struggling to leave her dalliance with drugs behind her. But she failed.

Ever since 1981 when Emily Remler assumed her place among the best jazz guitarists, she began saying that John Coltrane's music inspired her. In the liner notes for her 1988 album, featuring "Dahoud," written by Clifford Brown, she said that she also identified with the trumpet's lyricism. At that time, she hadn't yet mentioned how much the pianists—or Wes Montgomery—influenced her.

"Pianists have had the biggest influence on me. Bill Evans, McCoy Tyner," said the vivacious, auburn-haired young woman in 1988, with her green eyes wide open, as she prepared for a week-long engagement in Greenwich Village's Blue Note.

Anyone who listened to the 1988 record, "East to Wes," on the Concord label, with pianist Hank Jones, noticed instantly how her playing had become as articulate as Jones's. She sounded as if his style had been part of the aesthetic goal she had been working toward all along. Actually, guitarist Wes Montgomery had the most easily discernible influence on her style and development.

"Hank is my absolute favorite pianist," she said. As a great accompanist, he could put aside his ego and aim to complement her, she added. "Even when he does his solos, he's doing something I just did. It's as if he gave you a little present, then another, and another. He answers you perfectly. Smitty and Buster" [drummer Marvin "Smitty" Smith and bassist Buster Williams, also on the recording] do that too. They complement you."

Anyone curious about how articulate Remler became in the 1980s, when she emerged as *the* woman guitarist, as well as one of the best jazz guitarists, should refer to her first album, "Firefly," also made with Jones on Concord in 1981. However fine her work sounded when she first became nationally known, her mellow, flowing work was more muted and dreamier, without her later astounding clarity. She attributed her development to years of working constantly with wonderful musicians, including pianist Monty Alexander's group and a duo with Larry Coryell.

"I've wanted to sound like a pianist. I'm taking composition lessons from a pianist, Aydin Esen, a stone genius. I'm a good listener and imitator. That's how I learn," she said. "And I've copied pianists forever."

In the early 1980s, soon after her career was launched by her popular records and personal appearances that attracted young audiences, Monty Alexander hired her to play guitar. "His articulateness attracted me to his music," she recalls. "Perhaps I'm a true Virgo. I like things very clear." She and Alexander married, and for two-and-a-half years, they traveled, sometimes together, sometimes separately for long stretches. "I'll meet you in Paris" was a usual gambit between them, she said. "It was hard to be married and on the road. We had haphazard meetings. We had to get used to each other again." Her personal problems and their effect on the marriage overwhelmed the couple's efforts. Divorced in 1984, they remained friends, she said. His musical strengths left their mark on her, she thought. (Though he married again and rebuilt his life, he would be shaken and saddened by her death.)

Her twenties were a decade of turmoil. "I was introverted, because I was young, eager to please, and scared. I've been through a lot of experiences now. And each year I've become more sure that I belong on the stage. And I play with more conviction and no apologies. I love audiences and musicians, so I can relax. I'm very assertive in the studio now. A record is a product that will show where you're at. And I have to stand up for what I think will sound good."

Her late 1980s albums with Larry Coryell and Hank Jones were probably her best. Excellent jazz critics cherish other favorites by her. The next to last, "Together," with Coryell, was so different from "East to Wes" that they almost defy comparison. But on "East to Wes" she was the leader, not the partner, and the only guitar voice. So you can easily hear how clearly and subtly she asserted her mastery. She and Jones emanated from each other's lines, a collaboration that few musicians in groups ever achieve, unless they play together for years.

As she began her thirties, the decade when, as she figured it, you find out what you want to do, she put aside an earlier dream to compose film scores. She was studying composition, but she didn't have time to stop performing and look for a film project that would keep her sitting still at home. And she didn't want to do that, because she loved to perform. "I'm at the point in my career where all I need is an airport," she quipped.

To counteract the rigors of frequent traveling, she decided in 1988 to live in Sheepshead Bay, Brooklyn, a fishing village—a rarity in New York City. "I have a big safe place on the water. The air smells like the sea," she said. The ambience helped her maintain her equilibrium, a personal priority. She was trying to keep herself away from the fast lane. During her early years of stardom on the road, she ate too much and became addicted to food—and to drugs. She then shed twenty pounds by developing sensible eating habits, swimming every day, and eschewing all drugs. Some of her cues came from Larry Coryell. As they traveled around the globe, including ten European tours a year, she noticed that he swallowed a fistful of vitamins and jogged every day. "The jazz musician in the dark bar—that image is gone," she said. She became very proud of her healthiness, which surfaced at that time in her fresh, good looks.

She had been born on September 19, 1957, and began playing her guitar when she was sixteen. She was the first in her family to become a professional musician. Before she began playing, she had not been interested in anything; she had no plans for a career, and had thought that she might drift through life. Her father was a businessman, her mother a housewife; her brother would become a diplomat in Washington, D.C., and her sister a lawyer and language teacher in New York.

Emily's brother played guitar as an amateur. Emily taught herself to play on his Gibson ES 330. She used it throughout her career, though not exclusively. From her hometown, Englewood Cliffs, New Jersey, a quiet suburb, or as quiet as a suburb so close to New York can be, Emily had to

find her way in unchartered territory—the music world—build her playing career and shore up her own confidence. She loved music so much, and
was so good at it, that she sloughed off all her youthful bewilderment
when she was playing.

Emily took two years to complete a four-year course at the Berklee
College of Music. At eighteen, she went home and played about eight bars
of a very difficult song for her mother. Naive about Emily's fledgling
mastery, her mother said, "When are you going to sing? Where are the
words?"

With tapes and a metronome, Emily repaired to a room in Long
Beach Island, New Jersey, for the summer and spent all her time teaching
herself to play better and better. Then she headed to New Orleans, where
her guitarist boyfriend lived. She kept working and improving, playing
with a rhythm and blues group, and launching her career despite the self-
criticism she was prone to. She had enough confidence to call Herb Ellis
one day when he was performing in town. She asked for a lesson. It turned
out to be a jam session. "I'm going to make you a star," he told her. Within
a month, she was playing at the Concord Jazz Festival with Ellis, Charlie
Byrd, Tal Farlow, and Barney Kessel for colleagues. Afterward she kept
gigging. Soon Ellis helped her get a recording contract with Concord,
which encouraged and recorded her ever afterward.

The word about her smooth, fluid, soothing playing spread quickly.
The haunting feeling of "A Taste of Honey," the happy assuredness of
"Inception," and the mellowness of "In a Sentimental Mood" were rivet-
ing on her first record. With each succeeding record, her abilities ripened.
And the fleetness and rich, round tones of her early work seem almost a
blurry understatement compared with her later lean articulateness and
improvisational ease. Her own compositions often bore the hallmarks of
her generations' intensity. But she pursued a course in the mainstream.
Her tribute to Wes Montgomery on her "East to Wes" album showed her
devotion to the soulful, improvisational genius at the heart of contemporary jazz guitar playing. And she deepened her playing instead of diversifying or experimenting with styles and technology. She loved it when
reviewers called her "smooth." "Remler was subtle but strong": that review of her late 1980s appearance at the Monterey Jazz Festival was her
favorite for a while.

She felt that she was living the good life. She had left Pittsburgh,
surprisingly her residence for a year and a half after her Manhattan apartment became a cooperative. She had friends in Pittsburgh, "a pretty city,"
she said of that mysterious choice. Friends in the music world thought it
was a place she had gone to get her system cleansed of drugs and learn to
live in a healthy style. She had missed New York City's Museum of Mod-

ern Art, she said. That was a serious lack in the life of a woman who wore a Calder T-shirt and had enough talent to consider a painter's career at one time. Furthermore, in Pittsburgh, she couldn't easily put together a group of wonderful musicians. So she had moved to Sheepshead Bay. For a date at the Blue Note in the late 1980s, she was able to arrange to lead pianist Fred Hersch, the engaging bassist Lyn Seaton, who can sing in unison, and drummer Terry Clarke, with whom she recorded. She was able to organize a group with Lincoln Goines on electric bass and Jeff Hirschfield on drums in New York—"the only place where so many good musicians live a few blocks from each other."

She had the company of a best friend, trombonist Jay Ashby, for a few years. A little while before she died, she had gone on to another boyfriend. And she bought a new Volkswagon Fox. Practical enough to feel proud of that and distressed about the theft of a $300 stereo system from her car, she was not particularly dazzled by the financial rewards of her career. They varied from year to year anyway, she said. She had to keep working as much as she could; she was not a superstar. She was committed to the bebop tradition. You had to love soothing, soft, sophisticated music to love Emily's playing.

"If someone like drummer Elvin Jones asked me to play with him, I'd be very happy even if he didn't pay me very much," she said. "I'm totally happy when I'm learning from a good musician. I want to get better myself. I don't think you ever reach the point where you say 'I'm here' and stop trying to get better. I suppose I could call Elvin Jones and say, 'Hey, I know your brother'."

Her last records were "This Is Me" on Justice Records as leader and as an accompanist for singer Susannah McCorkle on the Concord album, "Sabia."

Introduction to the Horn Players

Without any doubt, women horn players have faced the greatest bias. But they are beginning to overcome the lingering antipathy that many men feel for the sight of women with trumpets, trombones, saxophones and even French horns and clarinets in their mouths.

Chapter Eleven / / / Focusing on Trumpeter Rebecca Coupe Franks, Alto Saxophonists Virginia Mayhew, Carol Chaikin, and Sue Terry, French Horn Player Stephanie Fauber, Oboist Kathy Halvorson, and Saxophonists Laura Dreyer and Paula Atherton

When trumpeter Rebecca Coupe Franks joined a group led by Sherrie Maricle for a concert in Washington Square Park in 1989, Rebecca's brilliant tone and technical virtuosity captivated the audience and people cheered. They do the same thing when she plays with Kit McClure's band—or with anybody.

A similar reaction greeted alto saxophonist Carol Chaikin, whose exquisite ballad playing won over an audience at the Blue Note, where she played in front of the cooperative quartet Unpredictable Nature for a Monday night showcase in 1993. Sue Terry gets wild applause when she performs as the soloist in front of Charli Persip's small group in clubs. The women in Diva, dressed in uniforms with slacks, played so well that they diverted anyone's attention from their gender. Ingrid Jensen, playing jazz trumpet and flugelhorn, and Britta Langsjoen, jazz trombonist, established themselves as spellbinding players.

Virginia Mayhew, whose main instrument is alto saxophone though she plays tenor in Diva, showed up to lead her own group in The Squire for a Saturday night; her playing was so smooth, strong, and emotional that she could wear a black miniskirt, black vest with a red silk back panel, and high heels, and not for one second did her exceptionally attractive appearance distract her listeners. She can outplay many of the young men now starring as saxophonists.

Yet she had to plan all by herself to take part of her group for a summer tour of Alaska in June 1993. After that, she went to play in some well-known clubs on the West Coast. "So, it's a good month," she said. The long-range plan for Virginia and most women horn players is simply to keep playing as much as possible. They must live by their own wits and enterprise, because the phones still ring only occasionally for them to work with men's groups.

Rebecca Coupe Franks was moving ahead of the pack by the early 1990s. She had two albums out on the Justice label, "Suit of Armor" and "All of a Sudden," and she was going to make a new album—one of her brightest plans for her future, because she wanted to work on her writing. She saw ads for her albums in music periodicals. She surfaced in groups led by famous male jazz musicians in clubs and concerts. And she has a manager. Rare is the woman horn player who has inspired a manager with a long career in managing male jazz instrumentalists to believe in her work and become involved in her destiny. Victor O'Gilvie, the manager, took on the promotion of Rebecca's career in 1992.

She had been recommended to him, so he listened to a tape and liked it. He invited her to the Pori Jazz Festival party at the Village Gate to see how she came across in a club performance. "She came in quietly and modestly. I asked the producer if she could sit in, and within the first chorus, I knew she had that talent as a trumpeter and a jazz player," O'Gilvie recalls. "I made a contract that night for her to go to Pori that summer." Then she worked with pick-up bands in Europe.

When she came back to New York, O'Gilvie began promoting her in various ways, booking her to play with Lou Donaldson's group in Fat Tuesday's in spring 1993. "Donaldson hadn't heard of me," Rebecca reflected halfway through the week, "but he's been a trooper." For Donaldson, she played obbligato—punctuation, grammar, and editorial comment, behind his blues. "I took the front door in, But I had to take the back door out," he sang, while Rebecca was wailing and telling the same story on her horn, bleating and fitting in. If Donaldson was a trooper, he was a lucky trooper.

She gave the impression that she had become a well-known, busy performer. Yet she was actually working less often than it seemed, she said. "And the men always look at me and say, 'She's a woman'," she reflected. "It's always a little bit like that. They don't know if you can play. I always feel that they're regarding me that way. It hasn't changed."

O'Gilvie also managed pianist Lynne Arriale and singer/pianist Kysia Bostic, Earl Bostic's grandniece, as well as such male clients as Jay Hoggard and Dan Brubeck, Dave's son. O'Gilvie also handled overseas bookings for Kenny Burrell, in conjunction with Burrell's son, David. Both Lynne and Kysia play the piano and so they don't present O'Gilvie with the traditional problems associated with women horn players. However, O'Gilvie says there's no difference in the reception that any of the women get when he tries to book them; the only thing producers and clubowners want to know is if the women can play. So perhaps the most important boost for a woman horn player is to have a professional manager— or a mentor of some type—working on her behalf.

Virginia Mayhew and Rebecca Coupe Franks, for a brief, shining moment, co-led a group in New York in the 1980s. Their buddy system, which survived long enough for them to release one recording, "It's Time for the Rebecca Franks/Virginia Mayhew Quintet," on the Italian Philology label, was a good way for them to try to get attention. By convincing clubowners to hire them, and showcasing themselves together even before the album came out, they were able to impress other musicians, fans, and critics to hire them in Manhattan, the Catskills, and on Long Island. Stuart Troup, then a jazz critic at *Newsday,* became an influential booster in his reviews of the talented women for the New York audience. They did Monday nights at the Blue Note. They also took their group on tours of their native California in the summers, where the critics loved them because the women were playing so brilliantly in the jazz tradition. By the time they decided to go their separate ways, their ploy had given them a boost. The timing had been right for the collaboration too. Men were just beginning to open their minds and realize that there were a number of excellent women horn players around.

Virginia arranged five songs on their CD, and Rebecca wrote a blues called "Honeydew." Rebecca was hired to play in a concert with Milt Hinton and from that exposure was invited to make an album with Bill Cosby. Her subsequent recording contract with the Justice Label in Texas was "a dream come true," as Virginia assessed Rebecca's break a few years later.

Virginia had arrived in New York to study with the Zoot Sims Memorial Scholarship at the New School's jazz faculty and she convinced Rebecca to follow. Rebecca also got a scholarship.

Rebecca was born in San Jose on November 27, 1961, and raised in Aptos, California, near Santa Cruz. She wanted to play the trumpet as soon as she heard her brother doing it. "I loved the sound," she recalls. Other men in her family had played trumpet too. After six months of playing in the fifth grade, she performed "Carnival of Venice," a classical cornet piece, in a recital. Her mother, who had at first wanted Rebecca to play flute, readily agreed to give her private trumpet lessons.

By ninth grade, she was playing in a nearby college's jazz band. Her private trumpet teacher introduced her to Clifford Brown records. "I couldn't stop listening to him day and night. I couldn't wait to get home to listen to him," she recalls. Miles Davis became her other most important inspiration. At age fifteen, she was playing standards five nights a week with middle-aged men in a local restaurant. During high school, she worked in at least three all-state bands. One year she played in the Monterey Jazz Festival. After high school, she had the adventure of a call to play for a year with a woman-led meringue band in a city 60 miles outside Caracas, Venezuela, with salary, room, and board.

Then she headed to San Francisco, where she joined the (nearly) all-women's band, Chevere. Altoist Virginia Mayhew was playing in it, but then she moved to New York because she felt she had gone as far as she could go in California and wanted the challenge of the New York playing scene. Rebecca joined the circus in California, while Virginia began to make friends at school and take advantage of jamming situations.

Born in Redwood City, California, on May 14, 1959, Virginia studied jazz alto saxophone and classical clarinet throughout high school. She couldn't make up her mind between jazz and classical music for a while. She played clarinet in the Oakland Ballet Orchestra and the Marin Symphony Orchestra and first clarinet in the Golden Gate Park Band on Sundays. Sometimes she stopped playing clarinet, but she could never bear to leave the alto alone. She let the instrument lead her.

"I was lucky. I met Johnny Coppola, who had played lead trumpet with Woody Herman and Stan Kenton. He took me under his wing, got me jobs, and introduced me to my sax teacher, Kirt Bradford, who had played lead alto with Jimmy Lunceford after Willie Smith did. Kirt also gave me the chance to play in a band with transcribed Lunceford music. I learned to play lead alto by sitting next to Kirt and listening to him.

"In San Francisco, I was hired to play with the all-women's Latin group, Chevere, which means 'right on' or 'groovy', and I brought in two men, so it was a mixed group with four women including Rebecca."

In New York, Virginia met Sahib Shihab, who had played baritone and all the reeds with the wonderful Kenny Clarke-Francy Boland band in Europe. For a few years, he tried to get his own big band off the ground. Virginia played lead alto, Rebecca lead trumpet for him.

"I've been really lucky," Virginia has said. "All my mentors have been men." They have offset others who have told her, and Rebecca too, that they can't be hired because they're women.

"There are good and bad days," summed up Rebecca in the period when she was studying with trumpeter Laurie Frink and before the better gigs began, such as the two-day recording date with Cosby in 1990. "If I'm having a good day, it's because I'm with somebody's group."

Virginia put her situation into perspective one night in 1989 when she was playing at the Blue Note. During a break between sets, she and a coterie of women jazz musicians, singers, and writers went to the upstairs dressing room, where hundreds of famous male musicians have held court. Virginia looked in the mirror and combed her thick, shiny hair with red highlights. It bristled with electricity. She said, "When is the last time you ever saw this room filled with women like this?" Everyone laughed. Someone said, "I was thinking the same thing." "It may never have happened before," said Virginia thoughtfully.

Virginia began getting more calls to play with men, and she led her own groups in clubs. She played on Al Grey's album, "Fab," on the Capri label in 1992, in the company of such established jazz stars as pianist Norman Simmons, long an admirer of her playing, and with Clark Terry, singer Jon Hendricks, guitarist Joe Cohn, drummer Bobby Durham, and bassist J. J. Wiggins. In 1993, she was hostess of the Monday night jam sessions at the Squire, a small jazz club surviving in an uncertain economy. And in Diva, she added the tenor saxophone to her repertoire.

In 1993, Sue Terry, whose primary instrument is the alto saxophone, made the master for her first album as leader, produced by Helen Keane. Sue included a mixture of seven of her originals, a song by Clark Terry, a guest on the recording, and two standards. A veteran of the 1980s in New York, where she came to live after studying at the Hartt School of Music in Hartford, Connecticut, she thought, by the early 1990s, "It's opening up a little bit more. There are a lot of men out there who are in positions of power, and they'll be helping us. Charli Persip for one, as a player and a bandleader. Clifford Jordan supported us. Jackie McLean does now." And Sue was earning a living playing with various groups, writing, and teaching.

She has played on the following albums: "Down Through The Years," with Clifford Jordan's big band, recorded live at Condon's, (not to be confused with Eddie Condon's), on the Milestone label, 1992; "No Dummies Allowed," with Charli Persip and Superband, on Soul Note, 1987; "Jaki Byard and the Apollo Stompers Phantasies II," on Soul Note. With singers Marion Cowings and Kim Kalesty, she performed on a CD not yet released by 1994 but she was playing with them in live performances, some scheduled for Lincoln Center that year.

She played for many recordings of Haitian bands in New York, among them "Change le Beat," with the Mini All Stars, playing Haitian compas music, Mini Records, 1993, and "Change Encore le Beat," same group, same label, 1984. For both Haitian recordings, she wrote arrangements. (Latin groups are accommodating about hiring women horn players.) She has played in jazz festivals in Montreux, Switzerland; Pori, Finland; Ottawa, Canada; the North Sea Festival at La Hague, Holland; and La Grande Parade du Jazz in Nice, France.

Carol Chaikin, an alto saxophonist who doubles on soprano sax and flute, and plays in Diva, leads an album, "Carol Chaikin," consisting of original songs, done on the Gold Castle label in 1991. Her most recent recording was "Unpredictable Nature" in 1992. She has also written scores for industrial films.

In her native California she played with Maiden Voyage. In New York City, for her own groups, she often hires drummer Barbara Merjan and works constantly, earning a living as a player, traveling often. In June 1993, she led her group in The Squire in Manhattan, flew to play in the Syracuse, New York, Jazz Festival, and then in four concerts in Key West, Florida.

Classical oboe player Kathy Halvorson, mentioned in Chapter Seven, keeps crossing over to play jazz and improvised music. In July 1993, she played music by Mingus at the International Double Reed Society Convention in Minneapolis. She still finds the jazz world in Boston, where she lives, a man's world. However, in her view, the onus of responsibility for changing the world now rests with the women. "Usually men will accept you if you can play and if you're a strong person. Then you may be able to go as far as you want to," she says.

Obviously a number of women have found the world a better place for jazz horn players than their predecessors even a decade ago did. The profiles in the next chapters will underscore that point. But this is not to suggest one should forget the continuing struggle of the majority of women horn players. As Norma Teagarden, a popular Dixieland pianist, still working regularly at age eighty-two in San Francisco, has observed about women saxophone and trumpet players during her long career, "They'll do anything to keep them hiring a woman. If they're going to use just one woman, they'll hire a pianist. The best thing to do is get your own group." It's as if she had a direct line to such players as saxophonists Laura Dreyer and Paula Atherton.

Laura has had three NEA grants for performance and composition. She worked with several well-known musicians—Walter Bishop, Jr., was one. She played as a substitute with Mel Lewis in the Village Vanguard's Monday night band. She co-led a group with Carol Chaikin, hiring Mel Lewis, pianist Larry Willis, bassist Ron McClure, and drummer Victor Lewis on different occasions. Now she plays and arranges for Diva—itself an indication that she is one of the best women horn players in jazz. She leads her own groups to showcase her own compositions at Visiones, Birdland, and Le Bar Bat. In Birdland, she, like every other group leader on weekdays, must attract a quota of patrons to the tables near the bandstand, to assure herself of earning full payment for the band.

Summing up her position, she said in 1993: "There haven't been any momentous highlights. My career has been a real struggle. As a jazz musician, I've been working, and I've learned to adapt to so many different styles that I've gotten a really good practical training. You get pigeon-holed and called for all the women's groups. We're out of the mainstream and have to fight extra hard to be in the mainstream. That's why a lot of women haven't had the experience that the men have. It's an old-boy network. The [women] rhythm section players get called, but I can't think of any of the horn players except for Rebecca Franks [who do.] And there are some very excellent woman horn players who haven't gotten the exposure. Women married to male musicians get more chances. It's political. I'm thirty-two years old, and I've been here [in New York] for eleven years, and the only way I'm able to survive creatively is by doing my own thing."

Paula Atherton concurs. A member of Kit McClure's band, Paula was planning to release a recording, primarily of her own compositions, with her group, a five-piece fusion band, Interplay, on the Rave Records label. She was offered that chance to record as a result of being a finalist in the Hennessy Cognac Jazz Search in 1993. "It has been an absolute struggle," she reflected. "This recording coming out is a highlight of my career. I'm very happy about it."

Chapter Twelve / / /   Laurie Frink and Stacy Rowles

By age forty-three, Laurie Frink could look back at having played lead trumpet in the big jazz bands of Buck Clayton, Benny Carter, George Russell, Mel Lewis, Benny Goodman, Bob Mintzer, Eddie Palmieri, Machito, Ed Palermo, Gene Harris, and Gerry Mulligan. In her position, she makes a band swing, sets its tempos, asserts its style.

One of the greatest influences on her career was Carmine Caruso, a trumpeter and teacher, mentor and healer of other trumpeters' chops. It was he who devised exercises for many horn players so they could repair any damage their playing—or anything else—might have caused to their mouths.

Caruso gave Laurie trumpet lessons; from the time she was twenty-three until he died, in his eighties, in the 1980s, he also transmitted to her an unshakeable self-confidence. She learned how to pass on his lessons to younger musicians—Rebecca Coupe Franks, for example—who found Laurie invaluable as a role model.

Her odyssey began in Pender, Nebraska, where she was born on August 8, 1951. Her family had no records and didn't listen to music. Her father was a candy salesman, her mother a housewife in the tiny farm community of about 1000 people. Her mother forced her to take piano lessons. Laurie hated the lessons but loved music and wanted to play in the school band. Her mother agreed to let her quit the piano, if she would take up another instrument. "I picked the trumpet," Laurie recalls, "because it was shiny. And I knew it was like a bugle."

She became quite good at it, because she had nothing else to do but practice. After hometown high school, she went to major in music education at the University of Nebraska at Lincoln. She would have majored in performance, but the school didn't permit women to do that. No woman played in the school's marching or jazz bands either. Eventually the director of the jazz band, who was her trumpet teacher, became fed up with the strictures against women. Because of Laurie's abilities, he simply said to himself, "I'm going to do this. I'll bring her in." So she played trumpet and mellophone in the jazz band when it needed another trumpet player. In her years at the university, she was the only woman out of forty trumpet majors.

"I was mostly into practicing," she recalls, "And I usually had a job, too, to stay in school." She worked as a nurse's aide at a home for the aged on the night shift, from 11 P.M. to 7 A.M. during the summers, and from 4 A.M. to 8 A.M. in winters.

One summer, she attended the Aspen Music Festival in Colorado, arriving there as a classical player and ending up in the jazz band. "I said to myself, 'This is fun'." At the end of the summer, trumpeter Jimmy Maxwell arrived and played the trumpet. "And I had never heard a trumpet like that before. I knew that was what I wanted to do," she recalls.

She decided to go to New York and study trumpet with Maxwell and Gerard Schwarz, another musician whom she met at Aspen. Her parents opposed the move. So in 1971, a rift occurred in Laurie's relations with her family.

Arriving in New York without any money—"zippo," she says—she immediately found several menial jobs. More important, she studied with Gerard Schwarz, who was the first trumpeter in the New York Philharmonic Orchestra and then the conductor of the 92nd Street YMHA/ YWHA Chamber Orchestra. She also studied jazz with Jimmy Maxwell. "He charged me $5 a lesson, when the going rate was $30, because he liked me," she says, "and he thought I wanted to play."

She also began to take trumpet lessons from Carmine Caruso. "He had a system teaching you to approach trumpet playing from a muscular standpoint. He taught you physically to play so that the physical didn't get in the way. Trumpet players always have problems with their chops," she reminisced.

"He was also a great psychologist. I used to watch him in the studio. Inside of one hour, he could give somebody self-confidence. And you thought you were fine." Laurie was devastated by her loss when he died. "Carmine taught me that, for people who are really into music, all that matters is that you play. He was always assuring me, when I was crying, that I could play. I was crying sometimes because it's not easy to be on the road with fourteen men in a bus. They weren't used to having a woman on the bus. Now they're used to it. 'Frink's here,' they say offhandedly. But they had to get used to changing their clothes in front of me. I can't change my clothes in front of them. I'm shy. I'll always find a ladies room or a closet, or I'll change in the bathroom of a bus, no matter how tight a squeeze it is. And they had to get used to my screaming about neatness in the bathroom."

She played a variety of styles—big-band jazz, contemporary, classical, chamber, and orchestra music. On Broadway, she played in orchestras for *Anything Goes,* and before that, in no particular order, she played in the orchestras for *Barnum, Dream Girls, 42nd Street, La Cage aux Folles, Nine, Les Miserables, Starlight Express, Doonesbury,* and *Jerry's Girls.*

"I much prefer jazz," she says. "I like the feeling and the expressiveness and the individual personality. My favorite musicians are Miles Davis, Lee Morgan, Duke Ellington, and Johnny Hodges. Those are my all-time favorites, although I do love Ornette Coleman," she says.

In the late 1970s, Gerry Mulligan, who had broken up his concert jazz band in the mid-1960s, when Birdland closed, decided to start a big band again. Laurie was still studying with Jimmy Maxwell to learn to play by ear, singing what he sang and then playing it. He recommended that Gerry Mulligan hire her. Mulligan ordinarily wouldn't have even listened to her audition, but he happened to hear a woman trumpeter, Marie Speziale, who held the trumpet seat with the Cincinnati Symphony Orchestra, when Gerry played there for a night. He knew that she could play, so he counseled himself: "If one can play, maybe two can." Laurie auditioned and got the job. The first engagement with Mulligan happened to take her to Cincinnati, so she met Marie Speziale and thanked her for paving the way.

With Mulligan, Laurie toured the world, playing lead trumpet, and recorded the Grammy-winning album, "Walk on the Water." In 1986, Laurie worked in Benny Goodman's band, which she considered a highlight of her life, even though other musicians in previous decades had not always found the experience pleasant. "Working with 'The King of Swing', we had standing ovations before we played a note. He knew that we were his last band, and we were young and loved his music. So he was real nice to us. He took us out to lunch after rehearsals, gave us bonuses and Christmas presents, and, if we sounded good, he gave us raises. All of us cried when he died. It was quite an experience."

Increasingly she has been sought out as a teacher, in the 1980s at the Harbor Junior High School for the Performing Arts at 109th Street and Second Avenue and as a private studio teacher at the Manhattan School of Music, at New York University, the New School for Social Research, and at the State University of New York at Purchase. At the First International Women's Brass Conference in St. Louis, she gave a master class and took part in several panel discussions. In the 1993–1994 academic season, she gave a clinic at the International Trumpet Guild in Illinois and appeared as a soloist and clinician at the University of Kentucky.

Kit McClure felt that it was a great coup for her first record with her band that Laurie Frink played lead trumpet. Maria Schneider, a young composer, bandleader, arranger, who was leading a big band in a Manhattan club, Visiones, on Monday nights, regarded Laurie as a star of the group.

Laurie thought that the women who came before her paved the way. "And I've been lucky. I'm making a living. Women twenty years older than I had it harder. Younger women have it easier because of women like me."

In complete contrast to Laurie Frink, Stacy Rowles was born into a musical family where she was encouraged to play and develop as a musician and an artist from her earliest days. Her father is pianist Jimmy Rowles, one of the few stylists for whom other pianists show up in droves to take lessons by ear during his gigs. His wife, a dancer, also had a good musical ear for melody and time. And so many of the Rowles' friends have been instrumentalists and singers that the Rowles children bathed in music all their lives.

Gary, born in 1944, plays bass guitar, piano, and organ. He has his own recording studio, and he writes jingles. Stephanie, born August 4, 1958, has musical inclinations and plays the flute. And in the 1980s, Stacy Rowles, the middle child, born on September 11, 1955, began to become internationally known as a jazz trumpeter.

Some musicians hunger for the opportunities to play that Stacy's family presented her with. But from the start, the gifted child had a reserved aura. When her family started her playing the piano, she found the instrument put too much pressure on her. For three years, she toyed with an over-the-shoulder marching drum. Then she found a trumpet, which belonged to her father, in his drawer. She became tantalized.

"He taught me the chromatic scale. Then I taught myself. I took lessons and taught myself more. I took more lessons," she says. She liked the way the instrument made her lips tingle. In her early lessons with Graham Young, she learned proper embouchure and found out where the sound came from, with support from the diaphragm. When her father invited friends to the house, he called Stacy downstairs with her horn. "He put me out there to play in front of everybody. I've always had a lot of support since I started playing," she says.

She was first charmed by an old Chuck Mangione record, "The Land of Make Believe." Then her father put her in touch with a Freddie Hubbard record, "Here's That Rainy Day." Lee Morgan, Clifford Brown, Ray Nance in Duke Ellington's band, Dizzy and Clark Terry—all the right people—became her teachers from their records. She loved the way Clark "got around on his horn," she says, Chet Baker and Jack Sheldon instructed her too.

"I listen to everyone I can and put something new into my brain from them. I'm spongy, and I take apart what I hear, and I change it, and that process keeps everything fresh and moving," she says.

Perhaps the immediate immersion in the music world gave her the luxury of early insight into its vagaries. Certainly at moments, she has been dismayed by events in musicians' lives, in the world where she was to the manner born. In junior high school, where she played third trumpet in a twelve-trumpet band, she challenged another trumpeter to a contest. "And he quit playing afterward." That bothered her, she recalls. "I didn't mean to stop the guy from playing because I played better than he did on that particular day."

At Los Angeles Valley College, which you attend for four years, says Stacy, but which you usually go to for a "continuing education" program until you decide what you want to do, her teachers supported her playing. Actually she didn't need any guidance for her instincts about music by then. Furthermore she had already begun making jewelry in high school. She worked at becoming an artisan too until she produced pieces— necklaces, bracelets, rings, and belt buckles made of genuine turquoise and sterling silver—good enough to satisfy custom orders and sell through a friend's shop. She made one belt buckle in the shape of a horn tilted up for Dizzy Gillespie. "Jewelry-making is on the side," she says. Yet her pieces are distinguished. It's clear that she takes the artisan in herself seriously.

A nearly magical acceptance by her colleagues began, on a professional level, when she was eighteen, in an all-star band in high school. It played at the Monterey Jazz Festival, where her father was accompanying singer Carmen McRae. Then Stacy was asked to play Freddie Hubbard's "Moment to Moment" apart from her band. "I got a standing ovation," she recalls. "Dizzy Gillespie escorted me offstage. And I sort of went on from there."

Two years later, she played in the Wichita (Kansas) Jazz Festival, in a big band led by Clark Terry. Terri Lyne Carrington, the drummer, who was ten years old, played with Clark there too. Afterward, Stacy joined an all-women's big band, Maiden Voyage, with musicians from the Los Angeles area.

By 1984, she made her entry into the recording world, playing on Concord's "Tell It Like It Is" with her father. The next year, with Red

Mitchell, the bassist, and Colin Bailey, the drummer, and her father, she recorded the album, "I'm Glad There Is You." With Bailey on a record called "The Jimmy Rowles-Red Mitchell Trio" the next year, Stacy played as a guest. Her records circulated in the United States and abroad, so her name became known. "She's good," people told each other in cities where she had never played.

She was married at the end of 1987 and for a while she practiced the fine art of dividing her time productively between her domestic life, her music, and her jewelry. She didn't feel an urgent need to play in public all the time. That's not to say that her laid-back attitude extended to the quality of her performance. "I try to practice every day to keep my chops up," she said. "I play an hour to ninety minutes a day, or I'm in trouble. Playing the trumpet is not something you can pick up every once in a while and expect to play well. I have to play music. That's a big part of my life, but it's not taking over my life. I saw so many people consumed by music, as I was growing up. But I take a step back. . . . Music can make you crazy, because it's so demanding and personal. When you play music, it's your essence. And when people don't respond, or if they look at you funny because of gender, they can make you angry. I know a lot of angry musicians, so I'm willing to go with the flow and travel to great places, wherever people want me to play. But I won't kill myself over music. I'm so sensitive that my sensitivity makes me not want to go headfirst into a bowl."

Leonard Feather, the influential *Los Angeles Times* critic, "has helped out with gigs and reviews," she says. He was helpful in finding her a job on a cruise from Vancouver, British Columbia, to Los Angeles in 1988 with the Jazz Birds, her own group. In 1989, Feather pressed George Wein, the producer of the Grande Parade du Jazz in Nice, France, to hire West Coast artists. As a result, Stacy was hired, and she played a set with George Wein on piano and Oliver Jackson, the drummer, and with many different rhythm sections. Al Grey and Bill Watrous, the trombonists, Red Mitchell, saxophonist Ernie Wilkins, and trumpeter Joe Newman played with her there too. "There were no other women instrumentalists that I saw there or know of," she says.

Just before the festival, she played in New York City in a jazz quartet behind the Jazz Tap Ensemble, a West Coast group, and went with it to France in December 1989. She also played at Le Petit Opportun, a well-known jazz club in Paris. And she has been back to Europe, mostly playing in France, occasionally in Belgium, Switzerland, and Holland. At least twice she performed in Europe again with the Jazz Tap Ensemble. At home she used to play regular Thursday night gigs, for about two years, from 1989 until 1991, with her father and a bass player at Linda's, for a while a trendy Melrose Avenue restaurant, with artfully mismatched furniture, fanciful recipes, fashionable young audiences—and an owner who liked to sing with the groups she hired.

Stacy was very happy about her CD, "Looking Back" on Delos, released at the end of November 1989, with Donald Bailey on drums and Erik Von Essen, bass, and Jimmy Rowles, and another record, "Sometimes I'm Happy, Sometimes I'm Blue" on the French Black and Blue label, with Bailey and her father, trumpeter Harry "Sweets" Edison, and bassist Ray Brown, and then a trio album with Nels Cline, a Los Angeles guitarist, Tim Brine, the alto saxophonist, and herself playing contemporary originals on "Angelica"—"a more avant-garde album," she calls it, released by Enja in Europe in 1989.

Jimmy Rowles is distinguished by, among other attributes, a seemingly laid-back piano style with a sometimes melancholy sound and by his fanciful line drawings, one of which hangs in Bradley's internationally famous piano "joint," as the late Bradley Cunningham called it. The drawing is the club's logo. Stacy's jewelry-making and laid-back trumpet style with a sometimes melancholy sound come as no surprise.

By 1993, things had changed for Stacy, in part due to marital troubles. "Because of some hard times, I'm trying to work as much as I can in Maiden Voyage and in the Jazz Birds, which I co-lead with Betty O'Hara, a valve trombonist. Our bassist is Mary Ann McSweeney, the drummer is Jeanette Wrate, and Liz Kinnon is the pianist. And I'm struggling to survive."

In New York, she played at the Joyce Theatre with the Jazz Tap Ensemble in spring 1993. She also did a record, "Till Next Time," on the September label in Belgium, with Belgian musicians, led by Ben Fluijs, an alto saxophonist.

In April 1993, with some funding, she finished an album with her father. He had been urging her to sing, and so she did six vocals on the new album. Her father sang some songs too. The rest were instrumentals. The Rowleses then began to look for the right deal with a recording company.

She was working with the quintet, Velvet Glove—trumpet, tenor, and soprano saxes and a rhythm section—which had done "Round One," a CD on the Fishhorn label live at the Top of the Senator club in Toronto. For the summer of 1993, the group had a Canadian government grant to tour, for two and a half weeks, playing in the Canadian jazz festivals, in Toronto, Montreal, Ottawa, Quebec City, Edmonton, and Vancouver.

A freelancer totally reliant on herself (which means she must always have at least a mild case of freelancer's apprehensiveness), Stacy was hoping the fall would be as busy as the summer of 1993. One of her plans was to work more with her father, who turned seventy-five on August 19, 1993.

"I really can't say if I'm having a hard time from gender," she mused about her quest for more work. "I don't get calls for studios or jingles. That's so clique-y. But Carl Reiner and Estelle, his wife, a singer, called me to record with them. That's the first time in a while that I was called to work with string and horn players on a session. The Reiners have been hiring me for club work in town for a long time. I can't say if it's because I'm a woman, but I don't get many calls to work in Los Angeles. There are so damn many musicians in Los Angeles and so few gigs. So you have to go where the work is. It's working out that I'm doing more traveling than playing at home. But I don't mind it at all, because I love to travel."

In early 1994, she heard rumors that Maiden Voyage would be traveling to Japan in the fall. And she was working in clubs all around California.

Chapter Thirteen / / / Flautists
Elise Wood and Ali Ryerson

In 1992, flautist Elise Wood finally got the recognition she had been working and hungering for. In the 1970s, she left Philadelphia, where she had studied classical flute, for New York. She met a group of jazz players, including bassist Vishna Wood, whom she married. He drew her into the jazz world, and they worked together in groups for years. But by the early 1980s, they were beginning to lead their separate personal and professional lives. Elise performed in a concert at St. Peter's Lutheran Church with pianist John Hicks, and they began working together and soon formed a business partnership—John Hicks-Elise Wood, Inc.

During the 1980s she performed with Hicks in New York and on tours of the United States, Japan, and Europe. For years, they worked on recording songs that matured into "Luminous," her first album as leader, for which she uses both her C and her full-bodied alto flute. The recording, released on Evidence, presented her as a ripened, assertive, imaginative flautist and composer, who fit in eloquently with the rhythm section. Critics responded so enthusiastically to her voice filled with light and song that she felt vindicated for all her years of devotion to her instrument.

She plays only the flute, historically an instrument that most jazz wind players use for doubling. Frank Wess and James Moody, legendary saxophonists, are renowned jazz flautists. John Hick's support for Elise's flute playing, of course, helped her advance. Like so many jazz musicians, he is always looking for something new to inspire him, and he has enjoyed the lift of Elise's fey flutes and the music they have allowed him to play with her. Not surprisingly, he has preferred the alto flute. Also intrigued by the sound of the flute, pianist Sir Roland Hanna invited her to work with him in clubs in the 1980s.

The C flute's very register has impressed people as feminine. Parents of little girls with musical talent have often thought it was acceptable for their daughters to play the flute instead of any other wind instrument. So it has been a popular instrument for women eager to explore their musicality. Some women have gone on to make other wind instruments their priority. Many women jazz saxophone players began with flutes and continued to use them as part of their professional careers, just as Wess and Moody have done. A few contemporary women saxophone players who double on flute are Canadian soprano saxophonist Jane Bunnett, and multi-instrumentalist Kit McClure, and multi-reeds player Carol Sudhalter. Rarely does the flute alone, whether played by a woman or even a male virtuouso such as Jeremy Steig, usually portend a bright, economically prosperous career in jazz. Sherry Winston made some very popular jazz fusion recordings that received a lot of airplay in the 1980s. But flute players who don't double usually cross from classical to jazz to pop and back. Ali Ryerson does that, and she has even taught classical flute playing.

In the 1980s, Ali Ryerson went to live in Europe. She was invited to play in concerts with Stephane Grappelli in Spain and Scotland, then in Carnegie Hall. Record producer Bob Thiele was so enchanted by Ali's ease, warm sound, and musicality when he heard her at Carnegie Hall that he invited her to lead an album, "Blue Flute," for his Red Baron label. He included one of her tracks in a Red Baron sampler in 1993. Ali has always had that sort of effect—the ability to engage listeners completely and immediately.

"I've played with a lot of big names," she says—among them Chico Hamilton, the drummer, Lou Donaldson, the saxophonist, and flugelhornist and trumpeter Art Farmer, trombonist Bill Watrous, and guitarist Laurindo Almeida. In Bradley's in the early 1980s, she was featured with various pianists on Sunday nights. Bradley Cunningham teased Ali by asking if she could bring back Art Tatum to accompany her. But Ali herself attracted fans repeatedly to the club, and Bradley kept booking her because she was so good; on Sunday nights, he was willing to deviate from his usual format—piano-bass duos—and give her a platform.

Before that she had toured for two and a half years with a show's band, gotten her bachelor's in classical performance at the Hartt School, and even moved to Montreal to play in clubs in 1980. Beginning in 1981, she used New York as her base and played in Bradley's and Sweet Basil and other places.

Fame was elusive. She started tacking back and forth from Europe to the United States for more playing opportunities. She regards her encounter with Thiele, which led to a three-year recording contract, as "that fateful day." Thirty-nine years old at the time "Blue Flute" was released, Ali reflected, "You always feel it could have happened ten years earlier, but the later it happens in life, the more you know about music. So I don't wish I had the recording contract when I was twenty-two. It's a thrill now." Her ideal "is to realize myself artistically by touring with guys like Roy Haynes, Kenny Barron, Santi Debriano, and Red Rodney" whom she played with on her first CD as leader.

She moved back to the East Coast in 1992 from a temporary hideaway in Carmel Valley, California, where she had taught master classes and played with her former teacher, well-known classical flautist Julius Baker. After touring in Europe in June 1992, Ali played in her brother's jazz restaurant in Gaylordsville, Connecticut—(their father is retired guitarist Art Ryerson)—and set about putting herself back into New York's action. She led groups in such places as Birdland. Other group leaders—pianist Kirk Lightsey for one—were happy to invite her to sit in with them when they saw her in their audiences. Her second album on Red Baron, "I'll Be Back", came out in 1993. In 1994, she was touring in the United States and Belgium.

Her playing is filled with momentum. She has a seductive vibrato that interprets "I Fall in Love Too Easily" as a poignant cry on "Blue Flute"; enhanced by Haynes's tasteful drumming, she can swing hard. If a flautist can have anything like a fat tone with expressive breathiness, Ali, one of the best flautists in jazz, has it.

Chapter Fourteen /// Carol Sudhalter, A Role Model

Carol Sudhalter, who plays baritone saxophone with enough lyrical feeling to make it a fine instrument for her solos, began by playing the flute at Smith College in the early 1960s. Her parents hoped she would live a conventional life, but she didn't want to do anything except play music. She eventually wended her way to a conservatory in Israel, then returned to her native Boston via Milan, where she studied, under conditions of extreme hardship, with a flautist whom she idolized.

Throughout the 1960s, when she tried to sit in for jazz gigs, the men had stock responses: (1) "What's a chick doing here?" (2) "You play okay for a chick." (3) They would make sexual overtures, but never talk shop about music or instruments. In Israel, the men wouldn't even let her sit in. Since those days, jazz has become more familiar in Israel, and the few women jazz players get chances to jam, according to Hana Dolgin, a woman saxophonist who grew up in Israel and was playing in New York as a leader in the 1990s. By the 1980s and 1990s, the stock, prejudiced reactions that had bothered Carol stopped.

She had begun to play saxophones and clarinet by the 1980s. At the Lynn Oliver Studios in New York, the men were still a little reluctant to get into shop talk with her. But sometimes she walked into situations where no barriers existed. She was called to play at a resort in the Catskills, and she drove to the job, taking along two saxophonists in their mid-twenties to early thirties as she estimated their ages: Jeff Hittman and Larry Vejmola. Beforehand, she worried not about the music or the paycheck or the route to the job, but about whether the young men would talk to her during the ride. She had the heartwarming experience of finding herself included in a trio of friends, who discussed their lives and experiences, sharing their confidences intensely and candidly. They talked about horns and reeds, as saxophone players do, and discussed relationships as

117

well. That happened in 1982, the first time Carol had found herself so naturally accepted.

"I noticed a progressive change in the 1980s," she said. "I walk into a band, and the men introduce themselves to me with a handshake. I think it's a rare case where sexism prevails over acceptance—at least acceptance on the surface and usually more than that. I feel comfortable." In 1993, bass player Jimmy Butts, known as "The Face," called her to round out his group playing New Orleans-based jazz for brunch on Sundays in New York's Cajun restaurant. If anything, her gender worked in her favor there. Men in the audience were particularly charmed by the slender, attractive multi-instrumentalist who could also sing. "It has been ages since anyone said to me, 'Why would a girl choose a saxophone?' I think it's easier for me now [to be a jazz musician]" Carol mused between sets at the Cajun. "There are some guys that I just know to avoid. They're still in that rut. But it's easy to avoid them; you go with the supportive ones. You know there are negative people out there, and you don't hang with them. That's how I keep my energy up."

Carol Sudhalter was born on January 5, 1943, in Newton, Massachusetts. Her brother Dick, two years older, would become a professional jazz trumpeter and author of a book on Bix Beiderbecke. Another brother, two years younger than Dick, would play saxophone strictly for his own enjoyment. Their father was an alto saxophonist, who had a sweet tone, Carol thinks, because he had classical training on the violin. As a jazz player, he had a penchant for florid improvisation in the style of Frankie Trumbauer. "I heard my father practice etudes and concerti on his sax every night, and on rare occasions I heard him play violin," Carol remembers.

Growing up without a woman musician in the family, she had no role model to suggest that she could become a musician. "I had crushes on musicians and was a groupie as a child," she recalls. She heard records by Beiderbecke and Bud Freeman; she listened to recordings of her father's radio show, "The Voice of the Saxophone," which he had broadcast as a side venture from his business. As a bachelor, he had dropped out of Harvard University to play music, then married and gone into business to support his family, giving up opportunities to travel and play as a career. "He was a homebody, and I'm glad that he didn't go on the road," Carol reflects. "I loved having him home every night. And I can't fault my father in any way as a musician. He was a beautiful player and a perfectionist. Sometimes he took me along to the gigs when I was quite small, and he put me in the front row in clubs."

He always regretted dropping out of college and insisted that Carol go to Smith College. She began to study biology and discovered her talent for languages. But the lifestyle at Smith depressed her. "There were so many rules. You had to wear a skirt to dinner. You had to wait for the housemother to pick up her fork before you began eating," Carol recalled. She sought out a therapist because she felt so depressed, out of place, lost. In therapy, it gradually came to her that she wanted to play music. And not just music, but jazz. Twenty years old then, she felt she was a late beginner. "So I stayed in my room instead of going to meals and taught myself to play," she recalled.

The school had an African-American cook, Mattie, who owned a collection of Billie Holiday records. Carol used to visit the middle-aged woman and listen to the records. She was delighted to have found her first friend at college. The housemother called Carol on the carpet and forbade her friendship with a cook. Carol defied the order, but it left her with a bitter feeling. "Smith was awful in those days," Carol summed up.

The local radio station in town, WHMP, started a "Sounds of Smith" radio program that played Louis Armstrong, Billie Holiday, and others. But when baseball games came on, they took precedence over music. However, between her father, the radio, and records, Carol acquired "good roots," she reflects.

She wanted to switch her major from biology to music ("from butterflies to music", she reminisces). But it was too late. She obviously switched her passion, however, to music, and prompted relatives and friends to offer their negative opinions. "You're starting too late. And what will you do with it? You'll never succeed," they told her. She answered them, "It's too early to say what I'm going to do with it." She didn't appreciate the interference. And she found playing experience by sitting in with bands in Northampton, Massachusetts, the country town where Smith is located.

When she graduated, she wanted to attend a conservatory, but couldn't afford it, and so she worked at part-time jobs. All the while, she took lessons and practiced. Her father advised her to study with someone whose sound she particularly liked. She went through every flute record in the Boston Public Library and decided on Bruno Martinotti, a flautist in Italy. That was a long way to go for lessons. Instead, her parents offered to pay for her trip to Israel, where she could study free of charge at the Jerusalem Conservatory. However, she didn't enjoy her stay in Israel and decided to head home, with a detour to Venice.

She searched the city for Martinotti. A man whom she met by chance gave her a clue. A conductor named Martinotti lived in Milan, but he didn't play flute, the man said. Carol went to a phone book and looked through the Milan section for his name. It had "Prof." after it. She took a train to Milan, telephoned him, and said one of the few Italian words she knew at the time: "Flautista?"

He answered, "Si."

"English?" she said.

"No," he answered.

"French?" she said. She had been practicing her French on dates with North Africans in Israel.

"Si," he said and put his French-speaking wife on the phone.

The wife made an appointment for Carol to have an audition for lessons. Mrs. Martinotti also translated at the audition. The professor told Carol that she had a good sound, but her interpretations were bad.

"That was the first thing that I ever did for myself out on a limb," Carol recalls about her Milan adventure.

He gave her two lessons a week. She lived in a basement and had no money to eat. After about a month, she developed ulcers and had to go home for treatment. Recuperating in Boston, she worked as a Spanish translator, saved money, and went back to study with Professor Martinotti for a year. "I had a great time and learned a lot about the flute, and about life, and about how to eat." Then she went to live in New York, where her life was so unsettled that she became ill with a variety of maladies—colitis and allergies among them. Dissatisfied with her playing, she again headed for Italy. This time she learned about opera and Baroque music. But Italy put up barriers for a woman who wanted to play jazz.

"You couldn't step out and play jazz, if you were a woman. You couldn't even take a big stride in good, solid shoes, or they thought you weren't feminine. You had to wear high heels. Italy was not liberated. So I had to go home. And my life got better."

She went to the New England Conservatory, where she studied Third Stream music under pianist Ran Blake; she took a course with trombonist Phil Wilson, became very close to the flute, and played some "way out, experimental things." She formed a duo with another flute; they called it The Duodenum and played impressionist improvisations for art openings, exhibits, and parties. "One time we played for a sunrise ceremony in the woods, beginning at 5 A.M., for the Thoreauvian Society. We hid from each other and played responses," she recalls with a laugh.

She was still fairly ignorant about bebop. "I came out of Billie, Louis, Bix, Chicago jazz, Django Reinhardt. I owe my brother and my father exposure to that."

Carol's father died at that time. In one of those mysterious twists of the mind, which bare and free its hidden desires, on the day that he died,

Carol suddenly realized she wanted to play the saxophone. "It had occurred to me only in one dream years before that day. In the dream, I saw myself in a bathroom, where the acoustics are intensified. I was playing a saxophone made out of a carrot, with a bobby pin for a mouthpiece. It sounded wonderful. I loved it. But I still never knew that I wanted to play saxophone until he died." Then Carol was on her own.

"He had thought that jazz would be terrible for me," she reflected. "He had saved all his life to put me in Smith. He thought that I should be a translator at the United Nations or a mathematician. And he worried that I would be a pauper. He loved to worry. My mother at least approved when I began teaching music lessons in the early 1970s. She thought there was some hope in that. At the end of each day, I practiced until 2, 3 A.M."

"I got a hold of a tenor, not an alto, fixed it and started taking lessons in 1976, a year after my father died. I was in my thirties, no kid. And I knew I could do it by then. I also had a terrible experience, which gave my playing a push."

Her mother was managing her life as a widow. So Carol moved out of the family house and into her own apartment in Somerville, Massachusetts. Her neighbor was a ragtime pianist who taught engineering at the Massachusetts Institute of Technology. Between April, when they met, and September, they became close, affectionate friends. He didn't tell her, but he had lupus. In the fall, he had a heart attack, probably related to the lupus, Carol thinks. At age thirty-seven, he died.

"It was his privilege not to tell me," she says. Nevertheless, she found it hard to overcome her feeling of great loss. She went out one night to hear a girlfriend, Lisa Brown, play with a Latin band. Inspired by the sight of a woman playing a horn in a Latin band, Carol soon found a job playing tenor saxophone and flute as the only woman in a Dominican meringue band. "I had always liked that music and had a feel for it. I played my guts out. That got me through. That's how I survived."

After a year, an offer came for her to play in a woman's band, Latin Fever, in New York City. Larry Harlow recommended Carol to his wife, Rita, who led, booked, and managed Latin Fever. So Carol rushed to New York, auditioned, and found herself replacing Jean Fineberg, Deuce's tenor player then going on the road with Chic, another women's band, and leaving Latin Fever.

Carol's debut with the group took place in Madison Square Garden. "I saw 23,000 people in front of me. That was exciting and great," she recalls. The gig was part of a Latin festival. Rosa Soy, a singer, lyricist, and arranger, who later left music to become a lawyer, wrote one of the group's tunes, which Carol particularly liked: "La Mujer Latina," about a woman getting up out of her bed and doing something with her life. Carol worked with Latin Fever until it broke up a year later.

Thrust on her own resources, she formed a quartet and also "discovered" the baritone saxophone for herself. "I was really getting into it. Cobi Narita perceived that it was a special thing. She booked me to play for the Universal Jazz Coalition. And I got interested in playing in big bands and started taking my baritone to the Lynn Oliver Studio. By 1981 and 1982, I was playing baritone quite a bit—even in the Damrosch Park Bandshell at Lincoln Center for the annual women's jazz festivals. By that time, I had a lot of private flute students and had branched out into teaching piano."

So she managed not to become impoverished. To augment her income, she sometimes worked as a medical transcriber, having learned to type in the seventh grade. She never spelled anything wrong and could go at top speed. She had learned transcription, typing as fast as she could listen to material through headphones during her first year in college. Also, for income, she set up an office for Jorge Calandrelli, an arranger, who has written for such people as clarinetist Eddie Daniels, and who has had awards and Grammy nominations. Carol became friends with him on the night she first played with Latin Fever. She was highly paid as his bilingual secretary for about ten hours a week until he moved to Hollywood. The friendship lingered. When she formed her Astoria Big Band in Queens in 1987, he donated his arrangement of "Summertime" for the band's repertoire.

Keeping her quartet afloat as often as she could find gigs, she went to work in Sonny's Place, a jazz club in Seaford, Long Island, where she was so excited by the quality of her rhythm section with Jack Wilson as the pianist that she decided to record the group. A sound engineer went to the club to tape it. From the tape, she extracted an album, "Hey There," on her own label, Carolina Records.

She also played in duos for flute and guitar for private parties. And with growing entrepreneurial spirit and self-confidence, she decided to found her own firm, Mix and Match Music, to supply groups with varied instrumentation or any type of music for private parties.

"Gradually I learned about booking, business, files, keeping good biographies on hand, tapes, hunting out the talent," she said. "I've built a small business. I pay my musicians well. I'm putting my Smith education to a practical use. I can deal with people who throw posh parties. I have patience with their demands and their questions. I understand the musicians' points of view and the clients' needs."

"I don't force a jazz musician to play rock. Sometimes I have to book a bagpiper, a singer of sea chanties, a bassoonist. I find it. We play Cole

Porter and George Gershwin and Harold Arlen or show tunes, or Haydn or Mozart. I get great doublers [people who play two instruments or more professionally]. There are a lot of great doublers in New York. One fellow, Lewis Kahn, who went to Juilliard, doubles as a trombonist and a violinist."

Her last enterprise was to found Carol Sudhalter's Astoria Big Band in 1987. "I got tired of schlepping long distances to play in different rehearsal bands from Long Island to Fort Lee, New Jersey, and there was nothing good in Queens. 'Why don't I start a big band right here in Queens?' I asked myself. 'Queens is filled with great musicians'."

"So that was another big step, like studying in Italy. I had to face serious questions: where do I get the music? where do I rehearse? Men and women showed up to play in my band. I think I bought the first few charts. Then we got keys to a church and to a community organization and carte blanche to rehearse. Charts have been donated and bought. People say to me: 'I've written a chart. Want to hear it?' They're most generous. Robin Connell, a pianist and a good arranger, started bringing her charts. And a man, a friend of a friend in Beverly Hills, sends us beautiful charts that he buys; he asks for nothing in return."

The band received grants from the Queens Council on the Arts to present concerts for three years in a row, and in 1993, the council awarded the band a second grant for promotion. Carol decided to record the band during a performance at St. Peter's Lutheran Church at Citicorp in Manhattan, and she sells the album, "Who Will Buy?" on her Carolina label by mail order.

She was always busy working in music, playing, leading, and teaching too. She was especially charmed by one of her students, a multi-talented girl, who went to the Manna House School in Harlem, and played flute, saxophone, bass, and piano, and wrote arrangements and composed her own rags. She was very religious and answered her family's telephone by saying "Praise the Lord," just as her mother did.

"I had no role model as a kid. I could be a role model now myself for kids. I wish I could be on television. I should be on kids' shows, like 'Sesame Street,' playing baritone sax. That would give young girls some inspiration."

Chapter Fifteen / / / Jane Ira Bloom, Soprano Saxophonist and Experimentalist

In the late 1980s, petite, sandy-haired Jane Ira Bloom, with the classically pretty features and clear eyes of an ingenue, gave her Upper West Side apartment in Manhattan a distinctively feminine touch of pink-colored flowers. They abounded and dominated the setting for her private life with her husband, comedic actor Joe Grifasi, as intensely as her soprano saxophone had always ruled the foreground.

Noticing her attraction to instruments, her parents started Jane Ira with piano lessons when she was four years old. As a third grader in Boston, she was offered the chance to play soprano saxophone. Afterward, she dabbled briefly with an alto sax; she learned to play piano and drums but continued with the piano only to compose.

Her concentration helps explain her virtuosity with the soprano sax, which is more difficult to control and keep in tune than any other saxophone, sax players agree. Exactly why she gravitated to the soprano remains a mystery to her. However, once she fell in love with it, her teacher, Joseph Viola, reinforced her affection for its sound. A soprano sax player himself and head of the woodwind department at Berklee School of Music, he tutored her privately through her high school years at the private Cambridge School in Weston, Massachusetts.

Nobody in her family was a musician. "My mother had Duke Ellington and Ella Fitzgerald records in the house, and when she went to New York, she went clubbing. But my early career in music was totally self-motivated, an enigma."

When she was studying for her bachelor's and master's degrees in music at Yale University, she kept traveling back to Mr. Viola for lessons. In New Haven, she blossomed as a professional, playing club and concert dates and brimming with enough drive to make her first record on her own Outline label with bassist Kent McLagan on the campus in 1978.

By then she had left the American songbooks behind and played jazz classics such as the haunting "Chelsea Bridge" with an eerie sound and stealthy control on her first record. She was also gravitating all the way toward "new music," her own compositions, drawing inspiration from Sonny Rollins and Ornette Coleman among the sax players and from trumpeter Booker Little on recordings. (He died in 1961 in his twenties.). Abbey Lincoln also intrigued Jane, who calls all the people she liked "mavericks." Perhaps most important about her playing was her clear, full sound. Critic Nat Hentoff, hearing her first record, was struck by her finesse. By 1979, she ranked in *Down Beat* magazine's poll for Talent Deserving Wider Recognition. She stayed in the *Down Beat* polls after that for soprano saxophone as well as for TDWR.

In her early thirties, she made her debut album for Columbia records, "Modern Drama," her fifth album as leader. She played with such extraordinary ease to her sound that she could devote herself to technological experiments and interpret her affinity for charismatic artists in other fields and for athletes too. Jane's attention had been riveted by Shirley Muldowney, a woman race car driver and champion, who accelerated to a speed of 250 miles per hour in six seconds. "She excelled where no woman was supposed to, in a man's world, by excellence alone. The experiences she had to go through [as a woman] and her determination—I can relate to that," said Jane.

As part of Columbia's promotion of her recording, she appeared with other Columbia jazz artists in a JVC Jazz Festival concert in New York City in the summer of 1988. As usual, she went through continuous idiosyncratic gyrations on stage—"doppler-like arcing motions," Jane Ira calls them. They had become so integral a part of her playing at that time that she commissioned bassist Kent McLagan, now a mechanical engineer, to design a velocity sensor—a machine in three parts with a strain gauge and a wire that attached to the bell of her sax. The gizmo translated the velocity of her horn's movements into the quality of her sound. So she became conscious of how fast she moved, because the speed changed her music. "I'm interested in how sound changes when it moves," she says. "But I'm a saxophonist, and the acoustic sound is always at the center" of her attention, she adds.

On her fifth album, which showcased her virtuosity and languid ease, no matter how intense her music became, you could hear the velocity sensor making a sweeping, gossamer sound—Jane called it "silvery"—in the tune "Overstars." On other tunes, the mechanism added shrillness—

"punctuation," she describes it—or mystery, or simplicity for the sake of entertainment. So Jane blended her natural gifts with technology for a record more exciting than she had ever led before. On her tune "Cagney," which strutted with toughness, the gizmo allowed Jane to sound as shrill and brassy as Cagney's spirit.

"NFL" started with a whistling sound (possibly the velocity sensor), calling the ensemble together. The instruments huddle; then the soprano heralds the game's excitement, which builds to a pitch resolved by soft vibes. The team pulls together again and ends with a victory song, which leaves everyone in good humor. (For anyone baffled by football, Jane's composition makes the pristine spirit of the game clear.) And the intense, fast-paced little tune, "Modern Drama," showcased Jane's sax and gizmo, which led into excellent drumming that melded into the versatile Fred Hersch's exquisite piano playing, from which the sax emerged as a forceful, complex protagonist. You have the illusion of characters talking in a scene on stage.

Naturally Jane enjoyed the prestige of being the centerpiece. The pressure was part of her continuing personal drama. "I keep pushing myself to 120 percent," she said. "I think there's something called the 120 percent syndrome," she added with a smile, referring to the tendency for career women to work harder to excel than men. Analyzing the way her sex put special strains on her public progress, she summed up, "There was covert discrimination, phone calls that didn't come, opportunities that didn't arrive and should have. And in the 1970s, anyway, the young artists weren't being recorded, and it was hard for any of us to get hired in clubs. So I had to develop my own direction. There's no other choice, if you're passionately interested in music. I chose a lonesome trail, doing original new music. I constantly thought about ways to get the music before the public." Her efforts made her a high-profile woman instrumentalist who gave frequent performances in New York in the early 1980s. "I improvised a career. Now I finally have an opportunity to create and play."

Even though her Columbia contract ended after her second release, "Slalom," in 1988, the recordings gave her greater exposure. In 1988, the NASA ART Program invited her to become its first participating musician and interpret the experience of space flight with her compositions. She wrote a suite, "Rediscovery," which had its premiere at the Kennedy Space Center and eventually was performed at Carnegie Hall. And she crossed back and forth from playing new music and jazz in clubs, festivals, and concert halls. She performed Augusta Read Thomas's "Sinfonia Concertante for Soprano Saxophone and Orchestra" as part of the Absolut Concerto Series at Lincoln Center in February 1993. Jane Ira was pleased that her sound had inspired the composer to write the piece specifically for her. She then led a group at Manhattan's Blue Note, never noted as a forum for experimentalists. And she received a commission to compose a piece, "Einstein's Red/Blue Universe," for the American Composers Orchestra, performed at Carnegie Hall for the Meet the Composer (AT&T/Rockefeller) Jazz Program in May 1994. In 1993, she was also awarded a Ford Foundation grant to compose a thirty-minute score for the Pilobus Dance Company. And she congratulated the Arabesque Jazz label for its commitment to her first recording for them, "Art and Aviation."

"For a small American jazz label, I think they've really got their heads in the right place about their commitment to recording musicians' unique sounds . . . they want to get that music out there," she told *Cash Box* writer Felicia Scarangello for a February 1993 column.

She had prestige, respect, and a high profile. But the route had never become easy for a woman soprano saxophonist who plays and writes unusual and experimental music. "When I was coming up," she says, "women's jazz festivals were very much in the air. But it's not about that anymore. It's about people in power in the music industry catching up with the rest of the country in recognizing women coming into positions of equality in all fields of experience."

Other albums by Jane Ira Bloom as leader are: "We Are," with Kent McLagan, Outline, 1978. "Second Wind," with Larry Karush, piano, Kent McLagan, Frank Bennett, drums, David Friedman, vibes, Outline, 1980. "Mighty Lights" with Fred Hersch, piano, Charlie Haden, bass, Ed Blackwell, drums, Enja, 1982. "As One," with Fred Hersch, piano, JMT, 1984. "Modern Drama," with Fred Hersch, piano, Ratzo Harris, acoustic and electric basses, Tom Rainey, drums, Isidro Bobadillo, percussion, David Friedman, vibes, marimba, percussion, Columbia, 1987. "Slalom," with Fred Hersch, piano, Kent McLagan, bass, Tom Rainey, drums, Columbia, 1988. "Art and Aviation," with Kenny Wheeler, flugelhorn, trumpet, Ron Hort, trumpet, Kenny Werner, piano, Rufus Reid, bass, Michael Formanek, bass, Jerry Granelli, drums and Elektro-Acoustic percussion, Arabesque, 1992.

Introduction to the Drummers

New Yorkers, having a parochial view of themselves as the quintessential sophisticates because their city is the world capital of so many activities, with a palpable dynamism, had never experienced anything like drummer Terri Lyne Carrington before. She showed up regularly on the bandstands of the most illustrious jazz clubs beginning in 1984. And she never faltered in any gig or in the continuity of her career. Terri Lyne, of course, took herself for granted. At age ten, she had played in her first jazz festival.

In the mid-1980s, she was getting a lot of invitations to play with male musicians, as if there were nothing revolutionary about her playing with them, and as if she were the only woman drummer good enough to play with them. Actually several other women percussionists and drummers were acquiring good reputations for playing jazz and popular music by the time Terri Lyne arrived. Already mentioned are Sheila E., Carolyn Brandy, and Marilyn Mazur, who plays both percussion and the drumset and works primarily in Europe. Jeanette Wrate is based on the West Coast, where she is well known.

And Carol Steele, who does so much of her work in studios, has been a roaring success. A beautiful blonde, she elicited cheers when she sat in with Dave Valentin's group at the Blue Note in the late 1980s. The Latin players know her well.

Marimba player Valerie Naranjo, of Indian background, leads groups around town and on tours, playing jazz, folk, and new music; she has recorded with Philip Glass. Nydia Mata, of Cuban background, has worked as a conguero in Latin jazz and American pop groups. Jazz drummers who work fairly often in New York are Sylvia Cuenca and Cindy Blackman. Kit McClure's drummer Bernice Brooks also works in many other groups— singer Nancy Donnelly's is one.

Sue Evans, a very successful drummer and percussionist, has an awesome resume. Even before Sheila E. played with Prince, Sue won a Talent Deserving Wider Recognition Award in Down Beat in 1975. In 1984, she *won the Most Valuable Player Award from the National Association of Recording Arts and Sciences for mallet percussion, then for hand percussion in 1987 and again in 1989. "I usually send out my resume and let it speak for me," she says. "If I had to choose one thing that has helped to make me successful, it would be the variety of things I do." Her credits range from playing as a substitute with the New York Philharmonic Orchestra under Michael Tilson Thomas in 1985 and Leonard Slatkin in 1989, to performing at Town Hall for Scott Joplin's* Treemonisha, *to working as a percussionist and drummer for Judy Collins over a twenty-five year period, to playing percussion with the New York Pops, to recording with the Gil Evans jazz band and playing with him in clubs. Few people may have noticed Sue playing percussion for Aretha Franklin on the crowded stage at Radio City Music Hall in 1993. So not all jazz musicians know of her.*

But in the jazz world, she maintains a fine reputation; Jon Faddis and Dick Hyman hired her for a Carnegie Hall tribute to Erroll Gardner, for example. She has also played for numerous film soundtracks, including the Spike Lee films Jungle Fever *and* Malcolm X. *She has made over twenty jazz recordings with well-known leaders. These credits are just a small sampling of her work. Technically, she is thought of in the category of a studio and commercial world drummer and percussionist.*

All these drummers keep time with authority and taste. Older drummers who have heard Cuenca and Blackman, both with high profiles in jazz by the 1990s, acknowledged that these women have arrived. Reviews praise Bernice Brooks. Bernadine Warren has played in Cobi Narita's jazz festivals. Sherrie Maricle from upstate New York caught the attention of bassist Slam Stewart, and she recorded with him long before she made her way in New York City as a performer and teacher. Barbara Merjan was working in the Broadway show orchestra for Cats *and playing in club dates with Carol Chaikin in June and leading her own group on Long Island in July 1993. Terri Lyne is probably the best known, though the others have gained on her. Percussionist Vicki Randle has become prominent in Branford Marsalis's band on the "Jay Leno Show."*

(In Caribbean and Latin-American jazz groups, women percussionists are viewed differently. These groups use women horn players; Sue Terry did a lot of work with Haitian groups when she was new in New York. But women percussionists were just beginning to play more in Latin dance bands by the 1990s. The subject of women percussionists in Afro-Cuban music is touched on in Chapters Eighteen and Nineteen.)

Chapter Sixteen / / / Terri Lyne Carrington

Solomon Matthew Carrington II, a drummer, had decided to stay in Boston and play with the artists who passed through town. That way, he could help raise his family on a day-to-day basis.

He finished a gig with Gene Ammons, the saxophonist, one night in 1965. As soon as Matt Carrington walked offstage, he collapsed and died of a heart attack. His son, Solomon Matthew Carrington III, who was nicknamed Sonny, played saxophone as an amateur in Boston. His daughter Terri Lyne, born on August 4 the same year her grandfather died, began picking up that saxophone and playing some tunes.

Illinois Jacquet and Rahsaan Roland Kirk, who played many of the reeds, stopped at the Carrington house, since the family was a part of the music scene. Kirk gave Terri some advice about playing a few simple songs. She could play "Tangerine" by the time she was five years old. Then one of the worst things that can happen to a horn player befell her. She lost her teeth; she couldn't play anymore. So her father slipped her a remedy—her grandfather's drumsticks.

"I had natural talent. I could keep time immediately," she recalled, "So my father thought I had talent. He showed me a few things. I progressed, and he sent me to a teacher."

Sonny played rhythm and blues, organ, and other music on records for Terri's edification. "It was stuff I could easily understand, not Coltrane or James Brown. And I started to get on a schedule to practice before my mother came home from work. But it was normally pretty musical around the house."

Her mother, Judith, who had studied classical piano for nine years and loved playing duets with her best friend, could listen to Terri and tell her what was happening in her early playing. And Terri's understanding of music broadened. Soon she was recognized as a child prodigy. She studied with Keith Copeland at Boston's Berklee College of music long before she went to college. At age ten, she went to a Wichita, Kansas, jazz festival and sat in with Clark Terry's group; she was in fancy company that day, playing with Terry, George Duvivier, the bassist, Garnett Brown, the trombonist, Al Cohn, tenor saxophonist, and Jimmy Rowles, the pianist and a few others. At age twelve, Terri led her own group in an all-night jazz concert in a Boston church.

With his connections in the jazz world and the prodigious talent of his daughter on his hands, Sonny Carrington assumed the role of stage father, managing her career moves. She went to Berklee on a scholarship for about a year and a half. But then she got "tired" of Boston, "tired" of the academic approach. She decided to go to New York. Clark Terry, who had known for a while that she was arriving in town, hired her. She played with him for a year and made her presence known in a variety of other groups. She also hung out in clubs and made many friends among her own generation of jazz musicians. At the time, she was the best known of their group, and she was very generous about lending a hand to help them find jobs whenever she could.

Everybody knew about the hot new woman drummer in town in 1984. She led her own group at Cobi Narita's jazz center; she had the drumset with famous groups in the most prestigious clubs. Terri Lyne could barely imagine the old sex discrimination that had dogged her predecessors on drums. "For one thing, she can play," was how several male clubowners and musicians explained her acceptance into the top male-run groups.

Terri reveled in her career. She wore jump suits in bold patterns and fashionable clothes on the bandstands; her eyes burned; there was a glow about the electrifying young drummer with perfect time and an ability to radiate the message: "Listen and look at me!" She had a glow off the bandstand too when she mingled with her male colleagues in audiences at clubs. She exuded self-confidence. To a great extent, she attributed it to her father, who had nurtured and directed her, setting a high standard for her. "He didn't care if I was nine or ninety, he said, or male or female, because all that anyone would ever care about was if I could play," she said soon after she came to New York.

Her connections led to an increasingly steady stream of jobs. Jack DeJohnette, *Down Beat*'s perennial poll winner as the world's best drummer, took her under his wing and became her adviser and confidante. She visited his family in their home in the woods near Woodstock, New York. She constantly learned from him, while she answered the calls for tours, festivals, record and club dates with Pharaoh Sanders, the New York Jazz Quartet, trumpeter Woody Shaw, Dizzy Gillespie's protégé Jon Faddis, and reeds player James Moody. One of her biggest problems was pacing herself, lest she become run down from overwork and excitement. There were times when she was overcome by the joy of working and depleted by the spent energy of her days.

Another problem, despite the constant calls, was money. She shared an apartment with her old schoolmate, Greg Osby, in Brooklyn, and bought a car to carry her drums to and from work in Manhattan. But the financial picture kept getting better. In 1987, she toured only with David Sanborn, Wayne Shorter, and Stan Getz. In the late summer, she ended several months of nonstop touring around the world to go into the Greenwich Village Jazz Festival in guitarist John Abercrombie's group at Sweet Basil.

In Brooklyn, a loosely knit but intensely proud group of young, rising jazz stars—Geri Allen, Steve Coleman, and Greg Osby among them—included her in M-Base, essentially an organization that played together at the Brooklyn Academy of Music and in their private apartments, encouraging and advising each other about their original compositions. They were trying to offset the wearying competition they found on the jazz scene, sometimes from their young colleagues overly protective of their gigs. Terri was one of the stars of M-Base, even though she had little time to sit home in Brooklyn and mingle with other members. But her stardom enhanced M-Base's credibility, with bassist Dave Holland and drummer Marvin "Smitty" Smith and singer Cassandra Wilson adding to the luster of the group's image and function.

Soon, Terri's association with M-Base would become history. Toward the end of 1988, she was recording her own album as leader for Polygram; she did part of it in Los Angeles, where her friend, keyboardist Patrice Rushen, lived. Patrice would play on the record. Terri toyed with the idea of moving from New York to Los Angeles because of the warm weather, the easy lifestyle, as she perceived it, in a pretty place with bright green palm trees. She headed for a European tour with Niels Lan Doky, an exciting young Danish-Vietnamese jazz pianist, whom she had known in Berklee and whom she had "hung out" with all night many nights in New York clubs when they were new in town and mesmerized by the music. When she returned from the tour, a Los Angeles friend called her and said, "Arsenio Hall has been asking about you. He's interested in you."

So Terri went to the studio to audition for the job as his television show's first staff drummer. Then she moved so quickly to Glendale that she left most of her old things behind and bought Scandinavian furniture to fill the first, one-bedroom apartment she had ever occupied totally by herself. In short order, as her photograph appeared in magazines, even on their covers, she became a recognizable celebrity when she walked down the street. "Oh, that's Terri Lyne!" shouted one young man, spotting a photograph of her in full action at the drumset; the shot was done in blazing colors.

At age twenty-three, she could reminisce about the changed attitudes of audiences and musicians. "People in audiences looked at me. They were very attentive or in shock to see a woman playing the drums," she noticed in the early days of her career in New York. "Some musicians were fine, and some were full of it," she summed up. If there were any negative vibrations in operation, she thought, "I can feel them from people who are insecure," she said.

As time went on, she observed that people seemed less startled by the sight of her at the drums. "They might say, 'Wow, there's a girl. She can play, she can swing'." And that was it. If they came backstage looking for an autograph, they might mention their surprise. "And that's normal for them to be surprised, I guess," she said.

For the most part, Terri sloughed off prejudice to the point where "I don't see it," she said before going to work for Arsenio Hall. "If those feelings are underneath, I don't pick up on it. It's a waste of time. I get along with all the men musicians, and I always have. It's becoming passé, that mentality. I'm getting more involved with other scenes," she said, referring to her switch in early 1989 from the mainstream bebop groups to her rock, fusion, and pop music orientation on the West Coast. "And prejudice against women players is not happening in that scene. The pop music musicians have respect for women, or at least for me," she said. "It's becoming more fashionable in the crossover environment to hire a woman. Every time you look up, they're using a woman instrumentalist for videos. They even audition a woman just because she's a woman," she echoed Tracy Wormworth.

Working for union scale on the Hall show, she commanded a salary that young lawyers would like for themselves. Union minimum, when she started with Hall, was $57,200 a year plus benefits and $53.54 for every hour of rehearsal over four hours. And she could pick and choose, when it came to playing with acoustic jazz groups. When her album, "Real Life Story," was released in February 1989, Arsenio Hall featured it briefly on a show. Terri Lyne got the feeling, before the year was out, that she would like to travel to promote the record. Perhaps she had the itch to be on the road again, not confined to a daily routine in a studio. She left the show's staff and thereafter showed up in very well-known, traveling groups, emphasizing pop music in her life. She played with Stan Getz's group for the rest of his life, and she began working with singer Al Jarreau.

If it seemed she had taken a giant step far away from her life in acoustic, bebop-rooted music, Terri Lyne didn't care how surprised people might be. "I'm more interested in high tech than in acoustic music," she said, settling right away into Los Angeles in the late 1980s. Far from the chill winds of Boston and New York, and at a distance from her family, she had friends her own age in the music world. Nurturing her career all her life, she had begun going to clubs in the early evenings with her father when she had been really too young to stay up very late. When she played music, it had always been with people much older. Pianist Lee Ann Ledgerwood, meeting Terri in Berkeley, California, when Terri had been an adolescent, had worried about Terri's social life. The girl had been such an outstanding player and always in the foreground. Perhaps she didn't have time to mix with people her own age. That had been true, Terri would think later. She had socialized with her numerous cousins, as she had been growing up. Otherwise she had been maturing in music first and foremost.

At the end of the 1980s, however, she was asserting her independence. And she had plenty of company. Patrice Rushen and Geri Allen had played, along with Terri, on various tracks of a Wayne Shorter album, "Joy Rider," an album virtually unique at that time for the number of women instrumentalists in a mixed group. Terri had to pause to remember a less savory time when, at age eighteen, she went through a bitter period. She thought she had a double liability as a woman and an African-American. For a year, she was in distress. "But then I said, 'The hell with it. That's my kharma.' And I haven't looked at it since."

She never considered moving back to the East Coast. "I can't imagine being anyplace else," she said in Glendale, where she had bought a condominium by 1993, taking the Scandinavian furniture with her and adding much more. She still loved the weather, the people, the trees. In comparison to Boston and New York, "Los Angeles is a new city," she said, "and it's health oriented. I work out in a gym, I eat healthy foods. And I like the social and political activism here."

"Real Life Story" was nominated for a Grammy for Best Fusion Jazz Album. She was also nominated for the National Association for the Advancement of Colored People Image Award for a new artist. She played on pianist David's Benoit's last recording out by 1993, and on saxophonist Gary Thomas's last two records by 1993. She had also recorded with Joe Sample and with Donny Hathaway's daughter, singer Lalah Hathaway.

Though she was looking for a good deal for a second recording as leader, she was, even without it, eminently successful. It was a routine part of life for her to play with Al Jarreau at the Hollywood Bowl for the Playboy Jazz Festival. And from her vantage point, she had the breadth of vision to see what was happening for women instrumentalists in jazz and pop. "There are a lot more women playing and coming into their own. It's no longer a matter of women being fashionable or a fad. It's really serious. When a woman says she plays, you have to listen and find out now."

Chapter Seventeen / / / Cindy Blackman and Sylvia Cuenca

Cindy Blackman and Sylvia Cuenca seem to have traveled parallel paths—primarily because both emerged in the 1980s in New York, and both have found acceptance in top-notch men's groups. Saxophonist Joe Henderson was one of the first to hire them. Cuenca came from a musical family in San Jose, California. In the late 1980s, ambitious to try her luck in New York, and reassured by the prospect of seeing a close friend who played bass in New York, she crossed the country. Pretty and extremely quiet in manner, but very talented and forward enough to hang out and sit in with groups in clubs, she steadily gained confidence. Everyone was impressed by her work. By the 1990s, she had enough self-assurance to ask Clark Terry if she could sit in with his group. After he heard her play, he started calling her for his gigs in New York. Due in large part to Terri Lyne Carrington, then Sylvia and Cindy soon afterward, the novelty wore off for jazz audiences to see a woman playing the drums in swift-moving, contemporary jazz rhythm sections.

In June 1993, Sylvia was recorded in Clark's quintet live at Birdland for a Candid label release. That was her third recording. Her first was in bassist Ron McClure's group on the Steeplechase label and the second was with the Vienna Art Orchestra on the Amadeo label. Within about five years, she had chalked up an impressive list of credits: N.E.A. performance grants in 1988 and 1991, appearances in festivals, clubs, and concert halls all around the world—the New Orleans Jazz and Heritage Festival in the United States, the Taxi International Jazz Festival in Milan, and several others in all the countries in western Europe, and an NEA concert played with saxophonist Gary Bartz in February 1993.

"I feel like the quality and level of what I'm doing is better than it used to be. Things are opening up for me," she summed up the direction of her career. "And Clark is a wonderful guy and a great guy to learn from, too."

Born on May 19, 1964, she was actually having the time of her life. "I love the road life—the environments and the situations and learning experiences you're put into with different musicians. You may not be feeling very well, but you go on stage and make it happen. I love seeing the world and reaching those audiences. That's what it's all about," she says.

In spring 1989, trumpeter Wallace Roney took his group into Fat Tuesday's. When he and his sax player, Gary Thomas, stepped aside to feature the rhythm section, you could really hear how tightly and sensitively the musicians played with each other. Mulgrew Miller, the pianist, began at a breakneck tempo, playing unusual, dissonant harmonies, all of which supplied a perfectly straightforward interpretation of the tune, "What Is This Thing Called Love?" Love had become a discordant relationship lived at a pace too fast to keep up with. The bassist Charnett Moffett emulated Mulgew with virtuosity. And Cindy Blackman's drums, starting third, played the same melancholy philosophy adroitly. The music washed like a powerful wave through the rhythm section.

Nobody stared at Cindy, who was dressed conservatively in an Armani-style jacket over a dancer's leotard and dark slacks—her favorite attire at that time for playing drums. Her hair was neatly coifed. The only touch that might have attracted special attention was the bright red lipstick she favored to accent her slender, pretty face. But the dim lighting in Fat Tuesday's muted her lipstick. And her performance shone more brightly. She had achieved the ultimate goal of a woman drummer: she was taken for granted on the bandstand and applauded for her confident, creative playing with fine time.

She has been living in New York since about 1981. Only in the last several years of the 1980s did people begin to know her name in the jazz world. For a while she was with Al B. Shure, a pop group, but she left to work with Joe Henderson. She wanted to challenge herself by working on his level at creative imagination. And that was her consistent choice, though she knew she could follow the more lucrative and open route for women instrumentalists—to fusion and funk.

"I like music that challenges me mentally. I like to come off the bandstand exhausted mentally and physically. You can put out a great deal of energy for a soft roll for a ballad and for what you're playing over a song. It can be exhausting. I like to know that I've given everything I can at all times," she said.

Cindy Blackman's mother was still fussing over her wispy child in the 1980s. Cindy is five feet nine and weighs between 110 and 115 pounds. But Cindy, who let her record company, Muse, change her first name officially from Cynthia to the nickname Cindy for her first record as leader,

is not a child. Her record, "Arcane," includes some of her own compositions, which record producers from several companies have admired. Her
record came out even before Terri Lyne Carrington's early 1989 release.
Cindy had a second recording, "Code Red," released by Muse in 1993,
with a mixture of her own and other people's compositions. Her third
album was "Telepathy," issued in 1994. Muse had another album in the
can. The trick for any drummer, man or woman, Cindy learned, in a city
brimming with fine drummers was to be so good that a leader would hire
her above all others.

Cindy's odyssey began in Yellow Springs, Ohio, where she was born
on November 18, 1959. At age eleven, she moved with her family to
Connecticut and lived in several cities in the Hartford area, where she
eventually graduated from West Hartford High School.

She grew up in a house where her maternal grandmother played
classical piano; her mother played the violin; her maternal uncle played
vibraphone and acoustic guitar, sang, and gave Cindy her first guitar
lessons. Cindy's paternal grandmother also played a little church music on
the piano. "Everybody played piano a little in those days," Cindy recalls.
She thinks there may have been fewer distractions in the "old days," the
1950s and before. Cindy's father, a salesman, didn't play any instrument.
And her mother stopped playing the violin when Cindy, the third child,
was born.

Inexplicably, Cindy was always attracted to drums. She first tried to
play during a rehearsal of a group in which her sister sang. During a break
in the action, Cindy ran to the drumset and started banging. The drummer made a motion as if he was cutting his throat. Cindy's feelings were
hurt. "I thought I had been really saying something," she laughs now with
a wry smile.

She begged her parents for drums. They bought her a paper drum
set, which her cousins quickly beat to shreds. She played a snare drum in a
marching band in parades around her city for a couple of years. But the
parades seemed to get longer, the weather hotter, she noticed, every year.
She gladly gave up the marches, valuing the bit of technique she had
learned, and turned her attention to school bands.

When she was about nine years old, she happened to look at the back
of one of her father's Modern Jazz Quartet albums. There she read:
Drummer—Connie Kay. "Oh, well, if she can do it, I can do it!" Cindy
told herself, mistaking him for a woman because of his name.

By age thirteen, she was begging again for her own drumset. Her
father finally started to listen to her. "Are you going to put it to good use?"
he wanted to know. "Or are you going to throw it away like you did with
the skis?"

"No, I'll use it," she said.

He paid $123 for the set, she recalls exactly. She played the drums all day every day. In summer she went down into the basement and listened to records, trying to learn from them while she practiced. She coaxed some friends to play instruments with her, but they weren't interested. Her passion for the drumset isolated her slightly, except for her rapport with a boy who had his own set. He had let her play it before she had her own.

When she was still in high school, drummer Tony Williams arrived in Connecticut to teach a clinic in a music school near her house. He asked the students if they had any questions. Cindy was so overwhelmed by his presence that she couldn't talk. (Later she met him; he even used her drumset when he played on a recording. Afterward Cindy asked him what tips he could give her about tuning her drums. "They sounded fine," he said. He had no criticisms.)

She went to study for three semesters at Berklee College, beginning a year before trumpeter Wallace Roney, drummer Marvin "Smitty" Smith, saxophonist Branford Marsalis, and many other talented youngsters showed up. She spent a great deal of time practicing the drums and playing in all kinds of gigs—weddings, parties. She led a group, played in a rock group, and got a taste of all the possible musical directions. She liked the effects that could be achieved with synthesizers, but acoustic jazz allowed her more freedom to play rhythmically, explore her abilities, and hear harmonically. She liked the wider range of textures in acoustic jazz.

At Berklee she weathered some gossip that a male student was disparaging her drumming, though he was an even more inexperienced player than she in those days, she knew, and he would be inept for quite a few more years. Wallace Roney never disdained her drumming. They became confidantes at school. Then she dropped out to accept a job with The Drifters, and went to play with them on the island of St. Thomas. The repertoire was doo-wop—"On Broadway," "Sweets for My Sweet." Cindy stayed with the group for three months, "until I couldn't stand it anymore," she recalled. She headed back to Boston, where she packed her things for a move to New York City. To keep expenses down, she used her family's house in Connecticut as headquarters for three months and constantly traveled back and forth to hear the music in New York. Wallace Roney often joined her; they hung out and even played together in New York, wherever they could find a place to sit in or jam.

"There weren't a lot of people I felt comfortable talking to about my feelings about music," Cindy has recalled. "I never had a close association with other musicians in school. I sensed some male chauvinism, so I slipped in and out of classes quietly. But Wallace was easy to speak to. We had the same direction in music.

"People hire you to play but sometimes with a stipulation that's sexual. I'll head off trouble if I see something looming down the road, or, if a leader's wife doesn't want you to go on the road with him. As a woman, you get some of those things," she says about some of the roadblocks she first encountered.

Cindy had never been prepared for discrimination and chauvinism, because her parents had never told her that the drums were not for women. Her father had said only that they were noisy. But even when people hurt her feelings, casting aspersions on her playing because she was a woman, they never detered her from playing drums. Slender though she was, she had always been an athlete. And she had always played with toys and drums. "To me, my upbringing meant I was well-rounded," she reflected. "Children shouldn't be stifled from doing what they want because of gender."

Soon after she settled in New York City, Wallace Roney came to work in Art Blakey's group to replace Wynton Marsalis. Later Wallace did a recording called "Verses" for Joe Fields, the owner of Muse Records. On the album are two songs that Cindy wrote, "Float" and "Topaz." Cindy went to a rehearsal and had the thrill of hearing Tony Williams play her songs with the group. Michael Cuscuna, record executive with Blue Note, was there too and, along with Fields, was curious about Cindy's work.

Joe asked her, "Do you have any more songs?"

"Yes," she said.

"Would you be interested in doing a project?"

"Of course," she said, thinking that it was sociable chatter. But Joe Fields followed through. Familiar only with her songs and the praise he had heard about her drumming from a few people, he offered her the chance to do her first recording, "Arcane," named for one of her songs in 1987. Two more originals, "Mirrored Glances" and "The Awakening," were on the recording. The other songs were by Buster Williams, Larry Willis, and Joe Henderson. The recording came out on LP and CD. In the 1980s, she and Wallace Roney helped each other through the crises, challenges, and decisions of building careers. He sometimes heard her playing an original song on the piano. (She can play piano well enough to compose or accompany, she says.) And if Wallace liked the song she was writing, he would say, "What's that? That's great."And he learned it and played it with his group. His encouragement was important for Cindy at that time; she thought she might have had difficulty presenting her songs to other people without his enthusiasm. "So I feel more comfortable with my writing now," she said soon after the release of her first recording.

Some of the best, older bebop drummers in town gave Cindy a heartwarming amount of encouragement too. Art Blakey, who exerted a strong influence on her, spent time tutoring her informally. They met on the scene and talked about drumming. He was looking for someone he could trust to babysit for his young children. So Cindy took the job. "A lot of times he was at home while I was babysitting," she says. "He just didn't have the patience to be changing diapers. We would wind up talking. He would tell me stories about everything. He helped me out with his personal attention.

"Philly Joe Jones was influential. Arthur Taylor helped me out. He told me stories about how the scene used to be compared with the way it is now. He told me about the people who came and went, and who he played with—Miles, Bud Powell, Bird, Sonny Rollins. By sharing his memories, he gave me a feeling of what was happening, and that inspires me and gives me a lot of insight.

"I've gotten to know every drummer whom I used to admire, with the exception of Max Roach. Jimmy Cobb gave me a cymbal that Tony Williams gave him. Jimmy didn't like all the overtones of the cymbal. But I like those overtones that Williams gets. Tony finally heard me play in 1988. Elvin Jones and Art Blakey gave me cymbals too. Billy Higgins has been very sweet and given me insights about things that happen on the scene and how to handle them."

Higgins advised her what to do when a famous musician guaranteed her a week's salary for a job in a club, then went to play with another group and left her to cover for him in the club. The club paid the replacement group less money, so Cindy's fee was smaller than she had expected. Taking Higgins's advice, she decided to grin and bear it—and survive to play another day in a group. "I like to focus on music. I don't focus on negative vibes. I just try to play with the best musicians available," she says.

Among them have been Larry Coryell, Joe Henderson, Sam Rivers, Jackie McLean, Don Pullen—demanding musicians ranging from bebop traditionalists to avant-garde experimenters. She played in Don Pullen's group, which appeared many times at the Village Vanguard. In the 1990s, she was the regular drummer in the group of masterful trombonist Al Grey and also with rock and roll star Lenny Kravitz, a guitarist, singer, and songwriter. She traveled the world with famous groups and with her own group too.

She had learned everything that thousands of male musicians had learned before her. Cindy had her baptism in raw fish and learned not to eat it at every meal in Japan because of the monumental stomach ache it gave her that she then had to play with on bandstands. Such lessons were now far in the past for her.

The only thing she faced differently from male drummers was how to

dress and play drums and look feminine. Offstage she favored the elas-
ticized little dresses in which only a woman with the slender grace of a
birch tree can look pretty. She decided to wear leotards—dance clothes—
on stage, so that she could move easily, under a nice jacket with pants. One
summer, she also bought a dress with skirt-length pants for a bloomer
effect under the dress for gigs in hot weather. Otherwise all the flash had
resided in the drums and the crimson-colored lipstick.

It had been a long haul for her, with hurdles and disappointments,
but she had emerged, ahead of the pack, as one of the best musicians of her
generation. Nobody refers to her as a woman drummer; people call her
Cindy Blackman.

Chapter Eighteen / / / Percussionist Carol Steele

Carol Steele, who was born in San Francisco on September 22, 1952, into a Scotch-Greek family, has bright, straight, platinum-blonde hair and a kinetic, forthright manner. For a long time she had been thinking about buying a house with the money she has made as a *conguero* and Afro-Cuban percussionist in the studios. She has been living in her Upper West Side apartment in Manhattan since 1976.

"It's really simple," Carol says about her decision to play Afro-Cuban music. "I went to an all-girls, Catholic high school in the Mission district. Next door at the YMCA, the brothers [African-Americans, Mexicans, and Filipinos] used to hang out, drink wine, and play conga drums. I heard them playing—bu bup, bee bup, and I couldn't concentrate." She played the *clave* on her knees to emphasize the seductive sound. (The *clave* is the distinctive Cuban rhythm combining short and long beats in three-two or two-three patterns. They underlie all but one of sixty-one varieties of Cuban rhythms, most of which are unknown outside Cuba. The *conga* is actually one of those rhythms, and that's how the word *conguero* came into being. The correct name of the instrument is *tumba;* the player is a *tumbadora*.) "So I'd get a pass from Sister Mary Joseph to go to the bathroom and hang out. 'Hey, guys, can you show me something?'"

"Get out of here, white girl, you're not supposed to do this."

"I'll bet I could. I'll bet. Show me!"

She learned in a minute what it took one of the young men a week of practice to play. "And that's how I started," she recalled. She has no idea why the sound touched her so profoundly. Soon she was jamming in Dolores Park, playing rhumba. After she had been practicing there and in her bedroom for a year, a Nicaraguan with a gig in a motel in the redlight district called the Tenderloin hired her. He billed the group as Carol y Los Quatros Latinos. At age eighteen, she was earning $125 for four nights a week.

"That was slammin' money," she says. "I was paying $65 rent to my roommates and hanging out at a record store. Santana and Sly Stone went there. I invited them to my gig in the Tenderloin. Ha ha. I was so proud to have a gig. Carlos Santana treated me like a mascot. He asked me to sit in when I went to his gigs. I was always bold. That's how I got the gig with Mongo Santamaria. I went up to him on one of his gigs and said, 'I want to play with you.' He said, 'Are you crazy?' 'No, I want to play a song with you and take a solo.' He hired me that night.

"I played in East Oakland funk bands, black bands. I love them drums, honey. My family was waiting for me to get it out of my system. But getting mentioned on the Grammys and playing on a triple platinum record with Steve Winwood made a difference to them. I bought them video equipment with my earnings. But my dad used to introduce me to his friends as 'the bongo beater'. I sat in with his Moose lodge's combo and played and sang 'La Bamba' just to make him feel good.

"In 1974, I first came to New York City, featured in Mongo Santamaria's band in a club on 52nd Street and in the Village Gate when I was twenty-one. And I'd thought that I'd made it. That was it! Later I was to find out that it was a good start. Some negative things happened, so I didn't stay with the band. I'm not going to compromise my personal life for any job. So after a year, I left and was taken in by [Brazilian-born singer] Flora Purim and [her husband, percussionist] Airto just before she went to prison [on drug charges]. She said to me, 'We know you're going to get your shit together.'"

Flora and Airto had a tiny studio apartment sandwiched between their larger apartment on one side and bassist Stanley Clarke's apartment next door. Clarke and his wife, Carol, and Flora and Airto had a connecting backyard. Carol Steele took a secretarial job to pay the rent and went to the Corso on East 86th Street, a huge, popular Latin dance hall, and other clubs to play Latin music. She also played in rhythm and blues bands. Her attitude was, "If someone asked me, 'Can you play Mozambique?', I'd say, 'No, but if you want to tell me what it is, I'll learn it'."

"But the city kicked my ass. I went home to San Francisco to study and came back to New York in 1976 to play Latin music. In the 1970s, the scene was really happening here. I sat in with Willie Colon, Tito Puente, Nelson Gonzales—he was a *tres* player [a player of a Cuban instrument with three double strings]. I joined his band, did a record. And there were no other women, especially white women, doing what I did on the Latin scene. It was unheard of. But I was in heaven, playing in after-hours clubs. If I see the guys today, I love them. They taught me Spanish. I had to learn Spanish to hang out with them, because that's the language they talked. And they pointed out to me that there were ten of them and one of me, so I had better learn Spanish. They weren't going to speak English.

"I was working to support myself in a drum shop from 9 A.M. to 5 P.M., the Professional Percussion Center, owned by Frank Ippolito. He told me that I would starve on the Latin scene. He was right, but I was happy. I worked for him six days a week."

"I took a job with Latin Fever, an all-female band, and went to Venezuela." Many other women instrumentalists, also not of Latin background, worked with that group. It made one recording. "It was the only all-women's band I ever played in. I wanted to be good enough to be with the cats. And 'all-women' is a novelty. So I came back to New York and went to work for Frank again. He told me to leave the Latin scene so that I could support myself. He kept telling me that. And then he died.

"I got a call out of the blue to go and work for Diana Ross in 1978. I was down and out at the time, and suddenly I had this chance. 'This is the next phase,' I told myself. 'Let me tour to make some money'."

Also with Diana Ross on the tour of Europe, Japan, and the United States was Alex Acuna, a Peruvian drummer, with whom Carol became friends. The whole adventure gave her commercial viability. She played conga, timbales, and Brazilian percussion in the group, though her main music has always been Afro-Cuban. "I'm a Cuban head to the max," she says.

From Diana Ross's group, Carol went to singer Angela Bofill, Tom Brown, the Manhattan Transfer, and saxophonist Sadao Watanabe, with whom she made a record in the United States and then toured Japan. She went on to the Jeffrey Osborne rhythm and blues band. Between all these good gigs, which paid "nice money" and lasted three to four months, she would return to her West 91st Street apartment and not work in music for six-month periods, except for the odd recording date. Since the work wasn't enough to sustain her, she took secretarial jobs at the Afro-American Institute.

"That was my little secret to keep me from becoming the poor, starving musician," she says. Her colleagues, all men, lived with women who had nine-to-five jobs, so the men were able to stay home, practice, and wait for calls to play. "But I had no one. So I just did the secretarial work," Carol sums up.

Worried that she was "losing her chops" by playing with rhythm and blues groups, she also worked on occasional jazz gigs in town with singer-composer-arranger Carmen Lundy, a newcomer to New York in the early 1980s, and with pianist Onaje Allen Gumbs, and singer Sybil Thomas, and pianist Kenny Kirkland with Alex Blake, the bassist from the Manhattan Transfer, in trio gigs. She also played in Grand Street, a SoHo club that had a vogue in the early 1980s showcasing young musicians and singers such as Roseanna Vitro.

Then Carol capped all these good musical experiences with a tour with Jaco Pastorius. She thought the affiliation would give her enormous prestige. But he behaved abusively and threatened her behind the scenes. "I thought it was possible that he might actually hurt me," she said. "I have never put myself in a sexual situation in a gig, even if I've been so attracted to the bandleader. So I wasn't sending out any sexual vibes to Jaco. But there was a love-hate thing going on. He was weird. One night he went onstage, before thousands of Italian kids, and he walked across the stage, giving them the finger. The kids threw garbage at us," she recalls.

She quit the tour and went back to New York City so depressed that she barely worked in music for six months. "I'm level-headed," she says. "And he was adored, and yet he was a complete lunatic." (By the time she met Jaco, he was already in deep trouble, and he would die young, remembered as a tormented genius.)

She did only one tour, with Jeffrey Osborne, whom she had already worked with. And then, still down over her memory of the Pastorius fiasco, she got a call to work with Steve Winwood. He phoned from England and talked for an hour. Someone in his band, whom Carol didn't know, had referred her to him.

She quit her secretarial job again, because, she recalls, recovering her *esprit,* "Suddenly I had money! I was on my way to his fabulous estate in Gloucestershire, England. And he was very good to me. I did his hit single, 'Higher Love', from his album, 'Back in the High Life'. And that gig put me on the map. I started doing studio work like crazy and a lot of jingles, records in Los Angeles, England."

She shook shakers, played a triangle, "and the money rolled in." After a while, the commercial music began to make her worry that she was losing her ability to play well, and she began to plan to visit Cuba. "Losing your chops? Go to the motherland of the music," she told herself. "I had collected records of master drummers from Cuba. And if they let me play with them, okay, and if they said: 'What are you doing,' I would go home and find something else to do. But the trip to Cuba in the spring of 1987 changed my life. I've been there five times since."

To arrange her travel visa with the government, she wrote to say that she was going for professional work and study. "In Cuba, there is a rhumba group called Los Papines from Havana, which comes to the United States, and another called Los Munequitos de Matanzas, an obscure group. But conga players who study Afro-Cuban music know the group."

In Cuban music, the difference between Havana and Matanzas styles of rhumba could be compared to the difference between New York City's

From left to right: At a Women's Jazz Festival, Bertha Hope on piano, Willene Barton on saxophone, Jean Davis on trumpet, Barbara London on flute, Carline Ray on Fender bass, Paula Hampton on drums, and singer Evelyn Blakey. Credit: Raymond Ross, Photography, New York City.

Melba Liston led her own group in performance at Sweet Basil in 1981. Credit: Raymond Ross, Photography, New York City.

Trumpeter Jean Davis is a veteran on New York's jazz scene. Credit: Raymond Ross, Photography, New York City.

Amina Claudine Myers sings, plays piano and organ, and composes; shown here at Environ, New York City, 1977. Credit: Raymond Ross, Photography, New York City.

Patrice Rushen, first a star as a singer and pianist, has become a highly respected film scorer, arranger, and musical director.

Renee Rosnes, much in demand as a sideperson in groups and on recordings led by men since the late 1980s, has become a well-known leader. Photograph by William Claxton, used with permission.

Sumi Tonooka, pianist and composer, was especially inspired by studying with Mary Lou Williams. Photograph by Rick Dunoff, used with permission.

Akua Dixon, cellist and composer, crosses the line easily from classical music to jazz. Photograph by Rennie George, used with the knowledge of his family.

Kim Clarke plays acoustic and electric basses in New York City and on international tours with jazz and pop groups.

Composer and guitarist Jane Getter can swing a whole room as leader of her fusion groups. Photograph by Barbara Mensch, used with permission.

Cynthia Sayer, one of the best-known and most respected banjoists, plays New Orleans-based jazz.

Rebecca Coupe Franks, trumpeter, was called by Bill Cosby for a record date after he heard her play in a concert with bassist Milt Hinton at the New School. Photograph by David Hughes, used with permission.

Saxophonist Carol Chaikin works as a sideperson, leads her own groups, and plays in Diva, an all-women big band. Photograph by Henry Diltz, used with permission.

Stephanie Fauber, French horn player, worked in the Monday night band at the Village Vanguard. Photograph by Mollie Hoover, used with permission.

Fostina Dixon, who plays all the reeds, composes, and sings, leads her own group. Credit: Teri Bloom, New York City. All rights reserved.

Stacey Rowles, daughter of jazz pianist Jimmy Rowles, plays trumpet in Maiden Voyage, the Velvet Glove, and her own group, performing primarily on the West Coast. She also plays at jazz festivals and in concerts in Canada and Europe. Photograph by Linda Sparks, used with permission.

One of multi-reeds player Carol Sudhalter's enterprises is the Astoria Big Band, which she founded. To her right is Bertha Hope, who plays piano in the band. Photograph by Glenn Reinhart, used with permission.

Recognized for her talent when she was still a student at Yale University in the 1970s, Jane Ira Bloom went her own way, composing and performing new music on recordings and in concerts, with prestigious commissions. Photograph by Thomas Lau, used with permission.

Drummer Terri Lyne Carrington, who became a star in the 1980s, has worked with many of the most popular jazz groups. Photograph by Carolyn Greyshock, courtesy of Terri Lyne Carrington and Verve.

Cindy Blackman, drummer and composer, leads her own group on recordings and on tours, and she has played in jazz groups led by pianist Don Pullen and trombonist Al Gray. Photograph by Rick Laird, used with permission.

Sylvia Cuenca established herself as a fine mainstream, bebop-rooted drummer in New York in the 1980s. One of the groups she plays with is led by Clark Terry, who has always included women in his groups. Photograph by Israel Fishman, used with permission.

Vicki Randle, percussionist and vocalist, plays in Branford Marsalis's band for The Tonight Show. *She has toured and recorded with some of the best-known and most adventurous jazz musicians, including saxophonist Pharoah Sanders and pianist Herbie Hancock. Photograph by Paul Drinkwater, used with permission, courtesy of NBC.*

Maria Schneider, who was a protégée of Gil Evans, composes and arranges for her own band. She tours to work with European bands, too. Photograph by Dennis J. O'Brien, used with permission.

Shirley Horn and her old friend, Miles Davis, played together on one of her hit recordings. Photograph by Susan Regan, used with permission.

In the 1990s, Joanne Brackeen has won praise from The New Yorker *magazine as a "jazz authority." Photograph by Teri Bloom, used with permission.*

Pianist and composer Marian McPartland, hostess of the prize-winning show "Marian McPartland's Piano Jazz" on National Public Radio, is one of the best-known jazz musicians.

Pianist and singer Emme Kemp performs in the United States and Europe, often presenting her original musical show in concerts. Photograph by Leslie Gourse.

Versatile pianist, composer, and singer Patti Bown, who earned recognition in the jazz world in the 1960s when she toured in Europe with Quincy Jones, has had a wide-ranging career in concerts, on recordings, and in clubs. Photograph used with permission of South Carolina Educational Television.

Toshiko Akiyoshi, composer, arranger, and pianist, leads her own band. Photograph by Teri Bloom. All rights reserved.

Maiden Voyage has built a reputation over the years on the West Coast, winning praise from influential jazz critic Leonard Feather. Left to right, back row: Martha Catlin, trombone; Betty O'Hara, valve trombone, trumpet, and double bell euphonium; Stacey Rowles, trumpet and fluegelhorn; Anne King, trumpet; Katherine Moses, saxophone and flute; Jill De Weese, trombone; Maria Benedict, trumpet; Jennifer Hall, saxophone. Right to left, second row: Sydney Lehman, piano; Barbara Watts, baritone saxophone; Valerie Clemente, (substitute) bass; Kathy Cochran, tenor saxophone; Christy Belicki, trombone. First row, left to right: Judy Chiknick, percussion; Jeanette Wrate, drums; Jodi Gladstone, trumpet; Ann Patterson, reeds, leader, in front. Personnel changes have taken place. Linda Small now plays bass trombone in place of De Weese; Maria Shaap has replaced Moses; Jennifer York has replaced Mary Ann McSweeney, who was the regular bassist. Photograph by Nels Israelson, used with permission from Ann Patterson.

contemporary urban jazz and the roots of the music in New Orleans. All the rhumba styles—and there are many—are played with percussion, drums, and voices. Carol knew that she wasn't going to visit only Havana; she was heading for Matanzas, a two-hour bus ride outside Havana. The ride became part of the adventure.

"It took me two-and-one-half hours in line to get a ticket," she says. Bus-ticket vending was a world unto itself in Cuba. The ticket seller called everyone to the window, asked each person where he or she was going and at what hour, and assigned everyone a bus departure time. He required the travelers to sit down and wait for the moment of the ticket sale. He wrote down everyone's name, so that he could call it out and sell with the personal touch. For some reason, he thought that Carol, who called herself "Carolina," had said "Eugenia." So he kept screaming "Eugenia" while she was chatting with other people waiting for their tickets. Finally she realized he was calling her.

"But, man, I went to Matanzas. Just to be there, I was completely overcome. I found an anthropologist who spoke English. She introduced me to the people I was going to see. I had letters of introduction to them. One was my idol, Estaban Vega, better known as Chacha.

"Two master congueros work in New York; one played with Eddie Palmieri and many others; he is my godfather, Julito Collazo; the other one is Francisco Aguabella; both came to the United States in the 1950s, playing with Katharine Dunham for dance. Both studied with Chacha in Matanzas. He was the first quinto player in Los Munequitos de Matanzas. Quinto is the drum that does the solo. Chacha is retired now. I first went to his house. And he interrogated me. Who was I? What did I know? We drank a few beers. And he walked me to a Los Munequitos rehearsal."

"So here we are in a black *barrio*. Even white Cubans don't go there. Matanzas is a pretty, black city. And everyone is checking me out. I could feel my heart beating in my throat!"

"'What are you going to play?', Chacha asked me."

"I said I wouldn't play anything."

"He said, 'No, no, no, you don't come to this province and say that you play conga drums and not play. So what drum did you play?'"

"I said, 'Well, I'll play quinto.'"

"I got the idea that you have to go for it. Chacha was a little, bald, black guy, with his arms buffed to the max. 'Oho, quinto!' he said."

"I hadn't played rhumba in years, since Nelson Gonzales's band. Chacha played with me. Everyone completely went wild. And more than money in the bank, that was the real thing. They either touch your forehead or put a hat on your head, and that means you're crowned."

"Chacha told me, 'Well, now you can say that you came here and played with us, and you have graduated.' And he made me sing a song for this deity, that deity."

Carol, a student of Afro-Cuban folklore, has for years believed in the Yoruba religion, from West Africa, and generally accepted as the religion of the ancestors of many of the most talented African-American jazz and Cuban music players. In Cuba, the religion, called Santeria, blends Catholicism with the Yoruba religion.

Her pilgrimages to Matanzas kept her inspired. 'I'm among the top congueros that work in the studios," she says. "But that's not what I came to New York for. The Munequitos are like my family. And I sit in with all the guys. I write my own music now." She blends Afro-Cuban with Latin, fusion, jazz and funk. "It sounds like funk with traditional African rhythms. And if you know the rhythms, you know what you're hearing. And if you don't know, you don't."

In common with many women jazz musicians, Carol stayed single. (The last chapter in this book deals with the complex domestic situations and personal lives of women musicians in general.) In mid-life, Carol Steele fell in love with an Afro-Cuban folkloric dancer, a Communist in Cuba. "I can't see my way clear to going there, and he can't come to live here," she said in the late 1980s. She saw him over a period of four years. But the demands of their established lives and careers kept them apart, and eventually they separated.

In 1992, she toured the United States and Europe with a British singer and acoustic pianist named Howard Jones, with whom she played percussion and sang duets—a novel experience. The Italian singer and guitarist, Pino Danieli, heard her with Jones and wanted her to do the same thing with him. "For the last two years, I've been doing gigs with just me!" she says. She played on Pino's recording, "Che Dio Te Benedica," which went into the international popularity charts in 1993. She also played on an album by another Italian singer, Renato Zero, and that album went into the charts too. She played for "Love Is," a single song taken from the television show 90210, done as a duet by Vanessa Williams and another singer. Those were some highlights of her professional life.

In 1993, she recorded with Angelique Kidjo, a singer from Benin, at Prince's studio in Paisley Park, in Minneapolis, Minnesota. Carol loved the singer, and she herself was playing a type of music closest to her heart. She was given the latitude to play extensive solos. The recording appeared in 1993 on the Mango label, a subsidiary of Island Records. "This is very good for me," she said with her customary enthusiasm, as she went out the hotel door in Minneapolis, on her way to see *Jurassic Park* with Angelique during a break in the action.

Recently, Peter Gabriel asked Carol to go to the studio and play rhythms for him for four days, to inspire him to write the music for his new album, and he gave her credit in the liner notes for laying down the original grooves. She has played for the following leaders, in addition to those already mentioned: Curt Smith, "Soul on Board," September 1993; Tears for Fears, "Sowing the Seeds," 1990; and Terry Haggerty, guitarist; Richie Zambora, Eric Clapton, Steve Winwood, Chaka Khan, Bruce Willis, Brian Wilson, Oleta Adams, Boy George, Cindi Lauper, jazz saxophonist Gato Barbieri, Angela Bofill, Tom Brown, and Nelson Gonzalez for his self-titled salsa album. For Orquestra Batachanga, she sang background vocals. This is just a sampling of her many credits.

Chapter Nineteen / / / Individualists

Although all the women in this chapter play piano, they exemplify the great diversity in the backgrounds and experiences of all jazz women. Their commitment to jazz is their only common ground. Jon Hendricks's explanation of the artistic urge applied most especially to these jazz women, perhaps to all women musicians, for they had little of the world's possible material bounty and physical ease to gain by dedicating themselves to an art in which they were usually regarded as interlopers primarily because of their gender. "Artists . . . operate by a sort of instinct," Hendricks has said. "It's nature's instinct, not just an accidental thing. It's not involuntary but a gift given to those blessed. Some people have the faith to go with it. If you don't believe, you will certainly be subject to it, because those are the ones it attacks." Perhaps one reason the following women fell in love with jazz is because jazz insists on and celebrates the individualist's spirit. All jazz musicians must improvise, once the theories are under their fingers. Most jazz musicians feel compelled to compose.

Judy Carmichael: "Basie Called Me Stride"

One of the most individualistic pianists is Judy Carmichael, who can faithfully reincarnate the stride style. She plays melody, harmony, and rhythm all at once, recreating the technique that made the great Harlem stride pianists, in effect, one-man bands in the 1920s and 1930s. Later, pianists relied on bassists and drummers to supply rhythmic support, and contemporary pianists were freed to stress melody and harmony. Stride has all the healthy spirit of a person striding proudly down the street, showing off technical finery.

Judy Carmichael, playing the piano since the 1970s in a well-defined stride style, definitely chose a road almost never taken anymore, and that has made all the difference. Earl "Fatha" Hines modified the stride style for his purposes as a bandleader in the 1930s in Chicago, paving the way for contemporary pianists. Mary Lou Williams gave Thelonious Monk lessons in playing stride piano, which served a foundation for his quirky style and contributions to bebop in the 1940s and afterward.

By the time Count Basie's rhythm guitarist Freddie Green heard Judy Carmichael in the late 1970s, she had been playing stride style piano professionally for years, working seven hours a day, five days a week, at Disneyland in California. Somebody had passed the word to Freddie Green that the young woman was playing authentic stride, and he should listen to her when he traveled to the West Coast.

Freddie was so impressed that he advised Judy to go to New York City and make a career out of playing stride. "Everyone there will know what you're talking about," he said. In Disneyland, nobody understood that she was playing the music of Fats Waller, James P. Johnson, and many more including Count Basie.

"And although they paid me well in Disneyland," Judy recalls, "nobody even listened to me."

Freddie introduced Judy, a slender woman with cascades of blonde ringlets and a peaches-and-cream complexion, to Basie and Sarah Vaughan. Inspired and encouraged, Judy, an anachronism in a generation of pianists usually eager to dilute the roots of danceable jazz with a variety of international musical influences and experiment with odd meters and harmonies, decided to produce her own first album. She would take it to New York City and try to sell it. It was called "Two Handed Stride" and featured Judy with none other than Count Basie's band men Freddie Green and saxophonist Marshall Royal, with Red Callender on bass and Harold Jones on drums. They recorded it in 1980, but Judy had difficulty finding a distributor. Audiophile released it in 1982 when all the eras, or styles, of jazz became more popular.

The early 1980s were the beginning of the sophistication of Judy Carmichael in the business and politics of the music industry. She had been born in Pico Rivera, California, south of Los Angeles, and had worked as a ragtime pianist, evolving into a stride pianist before she had ever heard of Fats Waller. A Basie record, "Prince of Wales," "stretched-out stride," as she calls it, convinced her that stride was her metier. She kept working on the harmonies and rhythms to evolve into an individualistic stride pianist. "I consider myself a jazz pianist," she says, "and I think of jazz as what came out of the danceable music and early roots of jazz. I'm along the evolutionary path. I use stride to launch my improvisations. I'm not a re-creationist or a revivalist or a traditionalist; I'm a jazz pianist who can stride rather than a stride pianist, because I continue to evolve. Stride is timeless."

During ten years of professional playing in California, she learned all about the tradition and literature. Then in New York she began to learn more about her unique place on the contemporary jazz scene.

Several companies offered to distribute her first record—until their executives met her. They were aghast. "You don't look like Fats Waller. What are we going to do with you?" they told her.

"I finally signed a contract for distribution for my first album with one man before I sent him my photograph. Then he said in wonderment: 'Is this what you look like?' He hadn't expected a young, pretty blonde."

"No, I hired someone," she said.

Hanratty's, an Upper East Side room, which liked to feature stride-based pianists such as Dick Wellstood, asked her to perform. She began working there in 1982, just about the time her record came out.

"And then I knew that was what I wanted to do," she says.

She was born on Thanksgiving Day, November 27, 1952. "Mom had a feeling about that day," Judy says she has been told. Both her parents were amateur musicians; her father sang, her mother played ballads and standards on the piano. Because she liked the sound of her mother's playing, Judy decided to study piano. In college she found a summer job playing ragtime, while she majored in German at Cal State Fullerton. She had also sung in the Civic Light Opera group as a child, but she never mentioned that after she began to play piano professionally, because she always wanted to focus on the piano—"and get better and better. The piano is enough of a challenge," she says. And her gift for the instrument far exceeds her singing talent, she thinks.

Her first job was on the Balboa Pavilion Queen Riverboat, which cruised Newport Harbor. The boat was owned by the Balboa Pavilion, a charming saloon, not a dive, she says, on the water. Soon she was hired to be the off-night pianist.

"I knew only five tunes when I went in. I played 'Maple Leaf Rag' for the audition. So I learned other songs real fast. On my nights, I drew a bigger crowd than the full-time pianist, so I became the full-time pianist. And I decided to make playing a career. As I worked there over a period of four or five years, I focused more on stride instead of ragtime. People brought me tapes of early Benny Moten, Fats Waller, Basie. The records convinced me to make a career of it."

"I dropped out of school after two years, because I was booked solid right away. I was always booked solid. I played in the Balboa for about five years. Then I sat around practicing for about six months, when I was between the jobs at the Balboa Pavilion and Disneyland," she recalls.

Once she decided to try her luck in New York and market her first album, she traveled back and forth between Hanratty's, the Nice, France, jazz festival, Disneyland, and the Kool Jazz Festival in New York City. She owned a house in Newport Beach, California, purchased when she was only twenty-four years old. She also maintained an apartment in New York City. In California, none of her friends were jazz musicians, and all her girlfriends were married in the late 1970s.

So she found herself in an isolated position socially, with no well-worn path to follow professionally. "The typical way to approach a jazz career," she knew, "was to become a sideman and work with bands to develop a style and go forward." But from the start, she became a soloist. her second album, "Jazz Piano," also distributed by Audiophile, was a solo. "I didn't want to wait twenty years for a break," she says. "I usually hired other people. So I took a lot into my own hands, producing my own records and booking my own concerts. I decided, 'I'm not going to have a jazz career. I'm going to have a Judy Carmichael career'." Retaining all the rights to her records and leasing them for a limited number of years, she made sure that rights reverted to her. Then she could do what she wanted with them. "It's a lot better that way," she says, savvy about the business end of her career.

It was not only choice that made Judy take matters into her own hands. A woman stride pianist is so unusual that Judy didn't get the same kinds of calls as contemporary jazz musicians receive. Much of her support came from outside the jazz world. She was called to play for museums and by people in the art world. "Sometimes I was the only jazz musician called to play in a classical performance—five string quartets and me," she noticed. Her friends were also outside the music world. One good friend for a long time was an architect. Other friends worked as graphic designers and other types of artists.

In almost every festival I've played in, I've been the only woman instrumentalist in piano jams. I've worked in only one festival where there was another woman: Emily Remler. I did a lot of things with Dick Hyman, Ralph Sutton, Jay McShann, Dick Wellstood (who died in 1988), and Derek Smith. When I did concerts in Nice, I played duo pianos with Joe Bushkin one night, John Lewis another. They supported me once they heard me play.

"Preconceived notions still endure. Everyone in jazz is supposed to be down and out. The good players are supposed to be black. The good ones are men. I definitely think that's what goes on," she says. "But I really like being a professional musician because you can't fake the music. You have to sit down and play. You put everything else aside and play. I never have problems with good musicians. The good ones think I'm honest and serious. They don't care if I'm pink with polka dots. Basie called me 'Stride', not Judy. 'Hey, Stride,' he'd say.

"I've felt prejudice based on my being a woman more than on race. I used to have people walk into Hanratty's, see a woman at the piano, and walk out. They would come back years later and tell me, 'Oh, you're great.' My records introduced me. Then the people asked me 'Were you amplified?' That's because I'm female. And stride style on piano is considered the most demanding physically. So stride is thought of as macho by people who conjure up the images of Fats, Basie, Albert Ammons. People think I'm too small to play stride. I think that, as I get older, all that controversy will be moot and die down. Some people already don't know about the era when stride started. I have a lot of young audiences who have no idea of Fats Waller's style and simply like the way Judy Carmichael plays."

Relegated to the past are her memories of the nights when she walked into clubs with a male musician, and all the other men assumed she was a male musician's girlfriend, not a musician herself. If she said she was a musician, the men didn't take her seriously. They didn't believe she had gone to the club to listen to music. Men wanted to listen, they thought, while women simply wanted to meet men.

"But it's the same for men and women. You listen to mature as a player," she says.

Ordinarily she goes to clubs only to play, not to drink or hang out, and she talks to people when she introduces tunes and between the sets. At the end of the night, she leaves quickly. She prefers to play in concerts. "When people come to concerts, they come to listen," she says. "I always knew that I wanted to get out of clubs and into concert halls."

Isolated though she is from the mainstream, contemporary jazz piano milieu, she has established a reputation for her style and has met and played as leader with excellent, older, contemporary musicians. For her third album, "Pearls," she played with Warren Vaché, the trumpeter, and Howard Alden, the guitarist, and bassist Red Callender on Audiophile. By the time she made her fourth record, "Trio," a CD released on her own C&D label in 1989, she was working with her own group: Mike Hashim on saxophone and Chris Flory on guitar. Though she produced the recording herself, for the first time she also had an executive producer.

In 1987 and 1988, she was selected to serve on the National Endowment for the Arts fellowship panel. The U.S. Information Agency sponsored her on a tour of India in December 1987. She played concerts in New York City at the 92nd Street YMHA/YWHA, at Weill Recital Hall next to Carnegie Hall on May 22, 1989, with Skitch Henderson and the New York Pops Orchestra, and at the Great Hall at Cooper Union, and at Merkin Hall near Lincoln Center. During JVC Jazz Festivals, she played at the outposts of Waterloo Village and Saratoga Springs. Though she traveled primarily in the United States, she also played in Switzerland, Germany, France, Brazil, and Holland as well as India.

By 1990, she was able to buy a small summer house in Sag Harbor, in the fashionable, expensive Hamptons on Long Island, New York. Her fifth album, "Old Friends," was on the drawing boards. It came out on her own C&D label, and was distributed by City Hall in San Francisco.

It has given her particular pleasure to become "pals," she says, with Marian McPartland. "I've been on her radio show. She's savvy. I admire her. That radio show has made her even more famous. She created her own career. To do well in jazz, you have to live forever or else create your own opportunities."

"You look for concerts in unlikely spots. You can't make a good living by just playing in the local clubs. Or else you go into the studios. The classical music world has many umbrella organizations that fund, hire, and network. Jazz doesn't have that. And the couple that we have are very narrow in scope and often pro-black. And they know who they are. They don't promote jazz in a big way, either. And many in government funding think that jazz is black. How can you say that when whites have been making real contributions?

"All the older musicians were very supportive of me, when I arrived in New York City," she recalls. "Why? I asked. Freddie Green told me that black musicians had few other choices than jazz careers. They thought I could have been a lawyer, or done toothpaste ads. I could have done anything, because I was white, and yet I chose this rotten life. Therefore he wanted to see me get ahead. Is it rotten? No, but jazz is a hard art to pursue because there's not even the hope of making a good living. Big breaks don't come often in jazz. I'm thrilled, though. I wouldn't do anything else." The legendary trumpeter Roy Eldridge, who was working in Jimmy Ryan's club, was very impressed. Tommy Flanagan, one of the most influential contemporary pianists in the 1970s and 1980s, asked her to sit in and play during one of his gigs in Bradley's. Hank Jones, another of the most important jazz pianists, complimented her. So did pianist, teacher, and jazz entrepreneur and spokesman Billy Taylor. "I know you, you're really serious," he told her when he met her, giving her a thrill. "I think that's the bottom line," she says. "Are you serious? Or are you fooling around?"

So it was important for her to add: "Any of the racism I've dealt with has been in the hiring of musicians, and not done by musicians. Promoters have stereotypes. A major producer was going to produce my first album. He met me, and he was nonplussed and dropped me. Freddie Green told me I was dropped because I was white." The producer had the preconception that she was unmarketable.

Her career keeps gaining momentum. She feels she has become a less dense, pianistic player and has developed a lighter approach. "I'm into ballads, space, rhythm . . . a wider range. I'm not just a repertory player. I feel that I'm doing my most original work." That seems to be an accurate self-analysis. And her schedule is busy.

In 1991, she was the subject of a program on National Public Radio because of her position in the tradition. She has been a guest on Garrison Keillor's Show, "The American Radio Company." She became a Steinway artist. In 1992, the U.S. Information Agency sponsored her tour to China. She took her trio with Mike Hashim and Chris Flory on the first U.S.-sponsored tour to China after Tianamen Square. "We didn't even know for sure if we would be allowed to play. But they let us play in 12 different cities. It was a huge success," she says. Because her music is stride, Leonard Miller took a special interest in her and invited her to be a guest on ABC's "Entertainment Tonight." She appeared on CBS's "Sunday Morning." Between the fall of 1992 and spring 1993, she performed 90 concerts, "in big cities, small cities, everywhere"—cities and countries where she usually played in the past. She still often found herself part of a classical series. It's the stride style that gives her entree.

While she was aware that more women jazz musicians were emerging in the late 1980s and early 1990s, she didn't think the general public had the slightest idea of their existence. Many times people came up to her after performances and remarked, "You and Marian McPartland are the only women jazz musicians, aren't you?"

Judy has her own distribution company for her albums: C&D Productions, 64 W. 21st St., New York, N.Y. 10010.

Michele Rosewoman, Composer and Pianist

Ever since Michele Rosewoman won her first *Down Beat* magazine poll as Talent Deserving Wider Recognition in 1983, critics have been talking about the way this gifted pianist has blended Afro-Cuban musical traditions and European harmonies in her very modern jazz compositions. She sometimes keeps a low profile, but when she surfaces, she does it in a big way, as she did in 1993 with two new CDs demonstrating her longstanding interests. In the spring, Evidence issued her trio album, "Occasion to Rise," originally released a couple of years earlier by Toshiba/EMI-Somethin' Else in Japan. In the fall, Enja issued "Harvest," an aptly named quintet album with her group Quintessence. That last recording showcases every aspect of Michele's interests. Enja was her label for two previous CDs as leader with her group, Quintessence. Before that, Soul

Note released her debut album as leader. With "Harvest," Michele seems to have mellowed, if one can say that without being misleading about her highly charged, eminently rhythmic music. "The percussion—my rhythmic orientation—is what makes me different from other piano players," she says.

Michele has played congas since she was seventeen. "I play seriously too," she adds. "I've played with the best. I play Afro-Cuban rhumba and a lot of the Haitian drumming." She worked with Reggie Workman's group as part of a play, and in California she worked in clubs as a conguera, playing piano and congas at the Keystone Korner in 1977 and 1978. She stopped playing congas in public after that, when she moved to New York, because the drums were too hard on her hands. "It messes with the articulation for a piano player," she explains. "And it's a hassle being out here in New York with all the men. In Cuba, they're teaching the women to play *bata,* and in Africa they have drums that only the women play—the *yessa* drum is one. But here, there's a real tension about women playing congas. It's not acceptable for women to play *bata,* not in the folklore tradition. Women play in bands, for dancing."

Drummers—Billy Hart and the late Freddie Waits, and California-based Donald Bailey, and Orlando "Puntilla" Rios, a master Cuban drummer, singer, and folklore expert, and Puerto Rican percussionist Eddie Bobè, "my compadre", she calls him—have told her how much they appreciate her work.

She does know how to write a shocking, alerting piece, such as "Occasion to Rise," which appears on both on her trio and quintet albums. But she also clearly delights in creating airy, eerie melodies in the Billy Strayhorn tradition, and that influence dominates much of her most recent quintet album. Above all, both her albums recorded in the early 1990s show that she was blazing her individualistic trail with increasing confidence and polish, as she continued to blend the experimental harmonies and atonality of the jazz avant-garde and European modernists with the vocal and drumming rituals of Afro-Cuban religious rites derived directly from Africa. That stone-African drumming tradition was first introduced to bebop by Chano Pozo in Dizzy Gillespie's band in 1947. The ideas were there for her to collect and elevate to a new plane in a fresh way. She did, and now she serves as a bridge between all the strains in mainstream, post-bebop jazz. Sometimes with delicate beauty and intensity, Michele's music bends the borders of cultures, not just jazz. Her affinity for Afro-Cuban music undoubtedly attracted the attention of Dizzy Gillespie, and he was instrumental in her receiving a prestigious commission.

At least part of her success in integrating the mystical power of the Latin heritage with the abstractions of the avant-garde and the melodic grandeur of the Ellington influence stems from her growing, attention-getting technique. You never know where her very fast fingers are going to go next.

Petite, and pretty, with an exotic, Mediterranean cast to her features, auburn-haired Michele can look like a starlet in her leather jacket and delicate jewelry, but she is nevertheless proving herself, through her artistry and stamina, to be a major messenger. She was born in 1953 in California. Though recording companies are making it fashionable, or even necessary, for young musicians to hide their age, Michele says, "How can I go through that? You have to age with grace and excitement." Her father, who was born and brought up in New York, loved to go to jazz clubs and record shops. After marrying Michele's mother, a visual artist, he opened a record store in a small town near Oakland. Michele grew up listening to classical, international folk, pop, and jazz—everything. The family was also committed to a left-leaning social order. Her father went on to teach political science and economics in a California college. The message of espousing an all-encompassing world view—including the music of a once-enslaved people—wasn't lost on Michele.

"When I was seventeen, I discovered in particular this Afro-Cuban music," she recalls about falling under the spell of fine conga and bata players. "In every city I lived in, from Oakland to Seattle to San Francisco to New York, I was always with that music," she says. "And it will run parallel to my pursuit of jazz for ever and ever." She found African, Latin, and American friends and musicians who taught her more about it. She began playing *kalimba,* "a thumb piano, called *mbiri* in Zimbabwe," she explains. "In Seattle, I was with the Shona from Zimbabwe." Though she never played *bata,* a two-headed drum originally from Nigeria and now an integral part of Cuban music, she was invited to attend Puntilla's classes. She declined, but she knew it was a real honor he had extended. She kept learning about African and Cuban religious traditions as well as the music.

Experimental new music always engrossed her too. Her route was not going to be easy. When she arrived in bebop-happy New York in 1975, she found an eighth-floor loft. It had no elevator service on weekends or after 5 P.M. Less hardy souls might have hesitated, but she has lived there—and stayed trim—ever since. Without a piano of her own at first, she practiced in piano stores, where she made friends. "That was important, because my first gig was with Oliver Lake at Carnegie Hall Recital Hall (later Weill Recital Hall). And I had to make arrangements to practice." Through her skill as a piano tuner, she met another tuner who sold her a piano for $85. Slowly, she found her way in town, or around the edges of the town's mainstream players and composers—an historically male-dominated world, of course.

In 1983, she was chosen Talent Deserving Wider Recognition for the first time by *Down Beat* magazine; she had that award again in 1988. She attracted fascinated fans, such as Enja's owner Matthias Winckelman, who says: "Michele has a special role to play." She formed her own group, New Yor-Uba, to play her innovative compositions. Right before she left for Europe to tour with New Yor-Uba in 1984, she was informed that she had been nominated by three people—Dizzy, Marian McPartland, and Lester Bowie—for an ASCAP/Meet the Composer commission. When she returned, she got a letter. "I was so shocked. I had been chosen by the three of them on the basis of the music I sent them. I had total access to the Brooklyn Philharmonic Orchestra to write a piece it would perform, to be conducted by Lukas Foss.

"So I spent five months writing. I didn't get to hear it until the day before the performance. It was an incredible experience—positive in how much I grew musically, and negative because of the atmosphere I was thrust into. I had to deal with the orchestra and the classical mentality." She wanted to dedicate the piece to Gil Evans, Marvin Gaye, and Duke Ellington, "because I was listening to them during the time I was writing, and they had a lot of influence on the piece, 'The Heart of Answers'." Forces above her had slated the piece for dedication to Aaron Copeland that year. She had to learn to live with the decision—not an easy compromise for a musician passionate about details of her work. To end the new Enja quintet album, for example, with the song "Warriors," she pointed out, with the instincts of a teacher, that she signalled the presence of a Yoruba deity, Eleggua, by opening a barely audible, creaking door, while the drummer was still playing. She wrote "Warriors" for New Yor-Uba, her big band, and played the song on the album, "Harvest," with overdubbings, singing with conguero Eddie Bobè in the Yoruba language. "The tune acknowledges three Yoruba deities, *orishas,* who are warriors that help us fight our battles," she explained—first Ogun, then Ochosi defined by rhythm, and then Eleggua acknowledged by the door. "All ceremonies (in the Santeria religion derived from the Yoruba tribe) are opened and closed for Eleggua," she said as she disclosed her fascination with minute details.

It's important for her to play in public. She performed in a Toronto club with her trio, with bassist Santi Debriano and drummer Gene Jackson, in 1993, and with Don Moye, Jimmy Heath, Julian Priester, and others at a tribute to the late saxophonist Clifford Jordan at the memorial festival for the drummer Eddie Moore in Oakland, and in a concert with bassist Ray Drummond and drummer Donald Bailey in 1992. In past years, she has played solo and in groups in clubs such as the chic restaurant Garvin's, which had a jazz program in Greenwich Village in the 1980s, and more significantly for jazz world prestige, at Sweet Basil, the

Jazz Forum, and the Tin Palace. She has led youth choirs under the aegis of the New York City Parks Department—a type of project she wants to repeat, in part because she herself loves singing so much. In the summer of 1993, she flew to Germany to play with violinist Billy Bang's group and came back to set up her own group's tour of the west and Canada. She led a group in New York's Yardbird Suite.

All the while, composing opportunities have kept coming her way. In 1993, she was commissioned at New York University to do an independent study recommended by pianist Muhal Richard Abrams. "I'm dealing with computers and electronics. I have access to a studio. They've asked me to present a piece for the School of Musical Technology. That's exciting," she said.

Synthesizers have fascinated her for a long time. "There are warm ways to use synthesizers. I like them for certain colors, warm kinds of colors. And I'm pursuing them for a lot of reasons. It's like having a multitrack recording studio. You can use that as a writing tool, putting things against things and hearing how they sound. You can emulate instruments and get an idea of what the music will sound like in performance. That's a very useful tool. And I did come up listening to Jimi Hendrix, Earth, Wind and Fire, and guitars and electric guitars. So my interest is the creative mix of electronic and acoustic instruments. I don't know where I'm going with it, but I'm just going with it, because it has come my way, and I'm sure it's for a reason," she says.

Yet to be realized is her plan to record with New Yor-Uba, with which she has played at festivals in Amsterdam, in Atlanta, and at the New York Public Theatre. That project is her primary goal.

In addition to "Harvest" and "Occasion to Rise," Michele's recordings as leader are: The Michele Rosewoman Quartet on "The Source," Soul Note, 1984; "Quintessence," Enja, 1987; "Michele Rosewoman and Quintessence: Contrast High," Enja, 1988.

Lee Ann Ledgerwood—A Member of the Bradley's Set in the 1980s

Professional jazz musicians, finding each other in areas from Baja, California, to Pori, Finland, have gotten together beneath the moon and talked about the fine times they've had listening to the great jazz piano-bass duos at Bradley's in New York. Beginning in 1969, it grew in reputation from a saloon with jazz played on a little upright piano to a great jazz club. Saxophonist Paul Desmond left his Steinway to Bradley's. Bradley died in 1989. The club changed its focus from piano-bass duos to larger groups including horns, drums, guitars, and vibes. The piano in Bradley's was still tuned every day. Almost every jazz pianist of note has played there—to name a few, George Shearing, Bill Evans, Hank Jones, Tommy Flanagan, Kenny Barron, John Hicks, Kirk Lightsey, Jimmy Rowles, and in the 1990s many newer stars. Bradley Cunningham once said that nearly every pianist he admired had played in his "joint," as he called it. Few women have played there, however; among them have been Joanne Brackeen, Bertha Hope, Renee Rosnes, Eliane Elias, and Lee Ann Ledgerwood. Fledgling jazz pianists used to dream of the day when they could go to New York and hear jazz at Bradley's—or even play there. Lee Ann Ledgerwood, who arrived in New York when she was twenty, in 1980, was no exception.

"The first time I was there, I was thrown out, because I didn't have enough money for my beer," she recalled.

She went back soon afterward and gave Bradley Cunningham a tape of her piano playing. She kept going by to see if he had listened to the tape.

Finally he told her, "Dear, if I listened to your tape, I'd fall in love with you."

A Bronx cheer fizzed out of Lee Ann Ledgerwood, as she reminisced. However, it must be said for Bradley that he was probably telling it, in part, like it is. Lee Ann is one of the best-looking jazz pianists, man or woman, in the world. Bradley did listen to her play and hired her for one weekend brunch gig she was supposed to play solo, but she brought along a bass player. Bradley must have admired her "chutzpah," she says; the blonde Midwesterner learned Yiddish words during her odyssey in New York. He hired her to play the brunch gig regularly, but he never came back to hear her.

Eventually she decided to confront him about his oversight, and she called him.

He said, "Is this call about work in my club?"

She said, "Well, you can provide some answers for me. I really need a nighttime gig for a week to make an impression, to get any focus on my talent."

So he listened. She had been playing the brunches for eleven months by then, she reminded him. He said, "Well, I'll come in and listen to you, and if I can do something, I will, and if not, I'll tell you why."

He came in for two brunches, disappeared for a couple of weeks, then telephoned her to say, "How would you like to work for a week this May?" She would like it very much, she said.

Born on May 10, 1959, in Warren, Ohio, a town of 40,000 people involved in football, beer, and steel, she had left home early, determined to find her way in music. In her first days in New York, she played at One Fifth Avenue, then a fashionable place. Her gig ended at 1 A.M. She went around the corner to Bradley's, the "in" place for jazz until 4 A.M. There she felt herself in communion with her fellow jazz musicians.

"Fellow" is the word. Lee Ann heard that Bradley's friends thought he had gone off the deep end by hiring a young, unknown woman. At about the same time, he also hired a young unknown man, Fred Hersch, to play in the club. Bradley was a good judge of piano players—and all the instrumentalists, even those who hadn't been subjected to media critiques yet.

After one week of a nighttime gig in Bradley's Lee Ann felt that she had been initiated as a member into a special society. She was among the pianists who had the status, an unofficial award, of having played there. "And when you love jazz piano, it's really nice to be part of it and to contribute to it," she said. "The arts keep the world in balance. You really have to love this to do this, because it's so hard."

Bradley called her at the end of a week and told her, "You did real good, kid." He hired her again for several weeks in the next few years. She adored establishing her name there. People who mattered in New York jazz circles heard her.

"Bradley treated me with equality," she recalled. "One night we were in the kitchen in the club. And I was leaning on Bradley. A famous jazz musician said to Bradley, 'Who is that? Your niece? Your girlfriend?'"

"No," Bradley said. "She's my piano player and my friend."

Lee Ann met Red Mitchell, the bassist, whom Bradley commandeered to play in the club with many pianists. Mitchell played for several weeks in the club with Lee Ann, and also with George Mraz, and Reggie Johnson, among others. Red Mitchell tried to encourage Lee Ann, sharing with her his views about the lifestyle in jazz. "The hardest part of any gig is having a nice day before you get there," he told her. That helped open her eyes. He also arranged for her to play in Sweden. She stayed with him and his companion, Diane, in their large Stockholm apartment. "He (had) a great piano; he was real good to me," Lee Ann recalled, and she was impressed with the lavish trappings of his success in Europe.

Pianist Richie Beirach, who had matured in the loft jazz scene in the 1960s and 1970s, heard Lee Ann and also saw her at Bradley's. He really did fall in love and married her while she was still in her early twenties.

During the marriage, Richie taught her many things about jazz. He had a fantastic collection of all kinds of classical and contemporary records and played them for her. He also dazzled her with his excellent books about music. Though they would remain friends, the marriage ended after four years. She continued working as usual with the musicians who had become her admirers. Bassist Ron McClure hired her. And when she was playing in Bradley's again, another musician, flautist Jeremy Steig, heard her and hired her for his group. In 1987, Lee Ann and Jeremy were married. And Lee Ann decided that she wanted to get away from relating to music as a series of gigs. Instead she wanted to write music, play, and develop in private. The music she began to write had a very different sound from what she had played in gigs.

"I don't want to say it's atonal, but it's a more open thing," she said. "I use a lot from classical contemporary harmony. I like to play bebop, but if I'm going to write, it's going to encompass a broader harmonic base. And I also feel inspired by funk and fusion electric things, by things that would appeal to a commercial jazz market, not that I want to do this kind of music simply to make money. I spend a lot of time with this."

She made a recording as the keyboards player on the fusion record, "Power Play" led by bassist Eddie Gomez. She did some arranging and a good deal more to polish the final product. And instead of getting the credit on the album cover, she was listed with the singers. "I don't have anything against singers," she said, "but I did more and different things. It'll change. Too many women are playing too well now. But it's still funny how they separate you, the men from the boys.

"I think anyone has a hard time being young in New York. the politics of being young are hard. You take a lot of hard knocks. You see some people whom you've heard that were so great on records, and they're down and upset. And then you get the gig and understand what's bothering them. It's hard to keep a smiling, happy front when people are belittling you. Some people, men or women, do okay with it, and some don't. Joanne Brackeen said to me, 'This is New York. What did you expect? They would welcome you with open arms?'"

But Lee Ann believed that somehow, even if you're young, and especially when you're young, you really have to find your way. Versatility is one means for a musician to take the pressure off. She began working for television. She became acquainted with Gary Anderson, a vice president at Score, who had played on the road with Woody Herman and also had admired Lee Ann's playing in Manhattan. So he hired her for a soundtrack for a PBS movie, and also bought a few songs she wrote for a "Dr. Seuss" special. "I love it," she said about composing. "It gives me a sense of craft. And the money is comfortable enough to support my craft. I feel very well-rounded now."

Her odyssey began in a place far from the jazz scene, with her attraction at age three, to Ray Charles records—"What Did I Say?" for one. She also liked a Nancy Wilson/Cannonball Adderley record—"for the sound. And I also liked it that Nancy had yellow shoes that matched her yellow dress on the album cover." Lee Ann was so young that her family hesitated to give her piano lessons. But she finally began at age four; though she studied classical music, she preferred improvising. Her father played tenor sax in jazz groups on weekends. Weekdays he taught in an elementary school. And he had a record collection that really swung, Lee Ann recalled.

The record that changed her life, she thinks, was "From Left to Right" by pianist Bill Evans. She was about thirteen years old. "The harmonic support that he gave his lines just killed me. I wanted to know what that left hand was doing. One piano teacher helped me with what Bill was doing—his voicing. I was already disenchanted with interpretation. I was a ham. I liked to play Mozart with the pedal down for two pages. And my teacher, Pat Pace, said if I could be stopped from improvising, I should be stopped. And he helped me with jazz."

After high school, she went to North Texas State (now the University of North Texas), which had a big band laboratory. She was required to "comp"—accompany—for twenty horn players. She decided that it was a good school for horn players, not for her. After one year, unhappy with the lack of emphasis on piano and the location of the school, she went to Youngstown, Ohio, to study for a little while, then headed to Berkeley, California. Not only did she study, but she played with Branford Marsalis, Terence Blanchard, Donald Harrison, and even Terri Lyne Carrington, who at age fourteen was already, quite plainly for Lee Ann to hear, "such a good player—and nice."

In Berkeley, Lee Ann took every type of job she could find—gospel, comping for vocalists, bebop, rhythm, and blues. Whatever a musician wanted to play, he or she could find it. And Lee Ann heard more jazz than ever before, Bill Evans, bassist Scott LaFaro, and pianist Hampton Hawes included. Finally she decided that she wanted to go to New York and find out where she was in the scheme of things. "I may have the feeling," she told herself, "but can I do it?"

In New York, she knew people were telling each other that she could play. They helped her persist when she found herself in bad situations. More than once she had gigs where she was the leader of a group, yet the club owner put the paycheck into the bassist's hands. (That never happened in Bradley's or the Knickerbocker, where she often played in the mid and late 1980s.) She grew musically and underwent a metamorphosis. She became a vegetarian for a while; she started to walk a great deal. The healthful effects of New York stunned her.

Her musical development in that period made her recall the blossoming of Arthur Rubinstein's joyous outlook on life: "Rubinstein was depressed as a kid, because he wasn't really serious about the piano. He played cards, smoked, and lived a wild life. Finally he tried to hang himself one day, but the cord he was trying to kill himself with broke. And he instantaneously got this passion for life. No matter how many terrible things happen in life, there was still great beauty—painting, music, art. That attitude is what it takes. You go through a thing to come out the other end. You have to feel bad in order to feel good. That has been my experience too. And I'm very excited about the future. I've been working for it."

In 1991, she recorded her first album as leader, "You Wish," on the Triloka label, with bassists Eddie Gomez and Steve LaSpina, drummer Danny Gottlieb, and Bill Evans on tenor and soprano saxophones and Jeremy Steig, the flautist. "It has 'Nardis' and 'I Want to Talk About You', plus a lot of my own compositions, and it was nice to feature my own writing."

Her second marriage ended. She went on the road for a long time with Eddie Gomez in 1991. "When you're away, you're not writing, and so I decided to give myself a more stationary kind of life and go into teaching," she says. She was teaching piano, theory, composition, and ensemble playing at the Mannes School of music on Manhattan's Upper West Side. She really liked teaching. "It's a good thing for me to be doing right now," she said. "You get a lot back from teaching, from the process of verbalizing your ideas. I think it has helped my playing to become stronger."

During her years in New York, she had seen a change in the status of women jazz musicians. "The field of jazz was one of the last bastions of male chauvinism. Now there's just more of us, and it's not such an oddity anymore. It's nice—there's a feeling of community there. It has become natural, and it's something that was bound to happen. Nobody is handing my bassist the check anymore."

Bertha Hope: Salvaging Elmo and Writing and Playing in Her Own Right

In 1992 and 1993, Bertha Hope led groups for her nights in Bradley's and several other notable clubs and restaurants in New York City. She also spent months working in Japan and Europe. Her first three CDs as leader came out in the early 1990s, with the extraordinary support of the powerful, rhythmic talent of bassist Walter Booker, Bertha's longtime companion, on all of them, along with two great drummers of the middle generation—Billy Higgins on "In Search of . . . ," Steeplechase, (1991), and Jimmy Cobb on "Between Two Kings," Minor, (1992). On her third

CD, "Elmo's Fire," Steeplechase, 1991, she worked with trumpeter Eddie Henderson, tenor saxophonist Junior Cook, drummer Leroy Williams, and Booker, and guest tenor player Dave Riekenberg. These were her first recordings since she played duets with Elmo Hope for his album, "Hope-Full," on the Riverside label in 1961.

But through the years, and throughout her fifties, she kept developing her own playing and composing. And she consistently worked at preserving the compositions of her late husband, pianist Elmo Hope, who had helped develop bebop.

The couple married in 1960; though both worked in music throughout the 1960s, life was a struggle. Not only was jazz in commercial eclipse in those days, but Elmo was an addict. Bertha worked regularly in a club called the Blue Morocco in the Bronx in early 1960s. She also worked for the New York Telephone Company. "But the nature of the job and the corporate situation was making me sick," she reminisced, and she quit the phone company. Then Elmo died in 1967. At age thirty-one, Bertha was left alone with the job of raising three young children. First she worked in a Head Start program. She played piano professionally only on the weekends, so that she wouldn't have to travel and leave home for more than a few hours.

Born on November 8, 1936, in Los Angeles, California, she had been a very young woman and budding musician in a family that stressed education when she had fallen in love with Elmo and thrown her lot in with his. There is no doubt that her affection and loyalty for Elmo were inseparable from her respect for his music. Because he had died so young, he had never gotten proper credit for his work. Bertha decided to try to perpetuate his musical legacy. It was as if Bertha—a serene-looking, highly educated, and graceful woman with chiselled features—at some point decided to live for two.

After Elmo's death, she went to Antioch and earned a degree in elementary education with a minor in teaching bilingual children so she could support her family by teaching. After graduation, she took courses at City College toward a master's degree in education. But she didn't want to be tied down to a regular job in a public school that would prevent her from traveling to play music. She kept working in the Head Start program, and taught music workshops in the public schools.

With Don Sickler of Second Floor Music, a music publishing company, she has, in recent years, been working on books of Elmo's compositions. When she rented Walter Booker's recording studio, which he built himself on Manhattan's Upper West Side, she first met the bassist. She was making a tape to apply for a grant to document Elmo Hope's work.

In her playing and in her manner, there's always a touch of class and never a hint of complaint. She doesn't regard her past as having been fraught with difficulty. Music has always helped her—a warm and vulnerable woman involved with community projects and quick to assume responsibilities for her friends in those projects—rise above it all. "Writing and exploring are part of my personal course in how to stay sane. I try to find a way to let the music just flow, and that helps me stay centered. I never made money the goal, and I think if I did, I would lose it"—lose her sense of purpose.

In 1992, she spent three months playing in one club in Hokkaido in the north of Japan. It was located way off the beaten path, part of a golf course. She was able to spend a lot of time, after waking up surrounded by trees and songbirds, writing her own music. "It was lonely and peaceful. Sometimes you need that to write music," she says. Surfacing in New York again, she played in clubs and bands, Carol Sudhalter's in Queens, and Kit McClure's, among others. "So things are happening," she said.

Maria Schneider: Jazz Composer for Big Bands

Not only petite and fair, but very fragile-looking, Maria Schneider dispelled that image when she led her own contemporary jazz orchestra in May and June 1993 at Visiones. Most people had never heard of her, yet she had some of the best musicians in her orchestra, and they were playing her exciting compositions and arrangements. Laurie Frink ordinarily played lead trumpet in the orchestra, and Marvin Stamm has played when Laurie was away. Walt Weiskopf on tenor saxophone, Scott Robinson on baritone sax, and others of that ilk constituted the personnel. It was a serious band.

Schneider's music made Visiones sound at times like Monday nights at the Village Vanguard, with the Thad Jones-Mel Lewis Orchestra after Thad left and Bob Brookmeyer was writing for it, with its legacy of a powerful, brass sound from Thad, an alumnus of the brassy, blues-based Basie band. The rest of the time Schneider's band sounded like an offshoot of Gil Evans's orchestra, with mutes and woodwind coloring. Schneider herself thought the Evans influence was paramount, though both Gil and Brookmeyer had been her main teachers. She didn't know exactly what to call the style she was composing and arranging for her band, except that it was contemporary music without being avant garde.

It accomplished the feat of swinging on the far side. There was no doubt that it was jazz, with classical European overtones. Her piece called "Worldly" sounded worldly—replete with the anxiety of contemplating the unknown. The band played her exciting, intense song called "Goofer

Blue," and another song actually entitled "Gosh," with a soprano sax solo. If she had come from California, she might have written a piece called "Awesome"—a California-style word. But Maria is from the sticks, Windom, Minnesota, and has no discernible affectations.

She was born on November 27, 1960, in a family that encouraged her in her desire to write music. Her mother wrote prose, one sister did too, and another was artistically inclined. Maria's father invented machinery. Maria played the piano, taking lessons from a woman who had played stride as well as classical music in Chicago. Maria learned a little about stride and grew up under the impression that stride had been the last style of jazz to evolve.

She attended the University of Minnesota, where she majored in theory and composition. Performing had never interested her very much, and no one tried to discourage her from becoming a composer. At college she finally discovered contemporary jazz. "People turned me on to Herbie Hancock, McCoy Tyner's chordal voicings. I realized that jazz had a huge tradition of writing. Gil Evans really became special to me when I was in college," she says. She took her bachelor's degree and went to study jazz composition at the University of Miami but soon transferred to Eastman School of Music in Rochester, New York, to get her master's. She studied with a Brazilian named Manfredo Fest, then moved to New York City with a National Endowment for the Arts grant to study with trombonist, arranger, and composer Bob Brookmeyer.

In New York, a few musicians were incredulous that she was dreaming of writing music for big bands. It was a dead art, they told her, trying to discourage her. Their advice had nothing to do with sexual discrimination. She simply didn't want to write commercial music, and so she got a job working for a music copying company and wrote her music on her own time. "I was just set on writing the music I wanted to write. You can always earn money some way," she reminisces about her attitude.

One day, standing at a Xerox machine, she was looking at a picture of Gil Evans on the album cover of "Priestess," and she had an image of herself as an apprentice to Evans. But she didn't try to look him up. "He looked too old in the picture. And people said he didn't teach, or he didn't like to teach," she recalls. Tom Pierson, who has led his own big band, was working in the music copying house with her. He invited her to go for coffee, and they talked about Gil Evans at length. Not long afterward, Tom telephoned her to say that Gil wanted her to work for him as a copyist and assistant with his books. Maria hadn't even known that Tom knew Gil.

"After a while, Gil asked to hear one of my tapes," she recalls. "Then we started to do writing projects together. He turned over projects to me to write, when he was too busy, or tired, and he guided me. That was an apprenticeship, from 1985 to 1988, the year he died. So this wonderful thing fell into my lap. If I'd had my dream, it would have been that."

"Bob Brookmeyer opened up my writing apropos form. He introduced me to Mel Lewis, and I wrote for Mel, who advised me to start my own band." She collaborated with John Fedchock, a trombonist who had played with Woody Herman. Maria and John started their own band, and they married too. But then they grew apart musically, separated their bands, and eventually got divorced. The encouragement of her teachers remained constant. They also provided her with connections. By the early 1990s, she found herself in the lovely position of supporting herself by her composing and arranging for big bands. "I don't know if it's a dead art, but I'm surviving this year," she said in the spring of 1993.

At that time, Anita Evans, Gil's widow, invited Maria to lead Gil's band at the Spoleto Music Festival in South Carolina, where they played "Porgy and Bess" and excerpts from "Sketches of Spain," "Miles Ahead," and other selections. "We hope we'll do more of that kind of thing, reviving the music," Maria says.

In the autumn, as she had done the previous year, she was going to work with bands in Europe. She would do a concert with the Umo Band in Helsinki, Finland, then work with the Stockholm Jazz Orchestra, and do some concerts with the Danish Radio Orchestra in its club—the orchestra Thad Jones worked with after he left his Vanguard band—and then in December she would go to the Cologne Radio Orchestra. Bob Brookmeyer had passed the word about her book to the Europeans. He knew them well and was living in Europe himself. Pianist Kenny Werner, who has worked with the Mel Lewis band and played with Maria's band and on "Evanescence," the Maria Schneider Jazz Orchestra recording released by Enja in 1994, has also recommended her to Europeans.

She writes for schools; Endor Music, Inc., a publisher that has also published Brookmeyer, Thad Jones, and Toshiko Akiyoshi, distributes her work. Maria's sales through Kendor are not a big part of her income, but everything helps her "to work on my own voice and my own thing. And it has paid off (for me to pursue that). I make a living by going to Europe three months of the year and by teaching jazz theory at the New School.

"It was fine with me to do music copying, and I thought the music I was writing was my own pleasure. The big band has been expensive, and I have invested a lot in it and the recording too. It's difficult to get a recording company to listen to a big band. But now people who never heard of the band are coming down to Visiones to hear it," she said.

Views from Women at the Top

Not one of the veteran women players who became a star in the jazz world attributed her success to any special ingredient in her life or personality. But as the women talked about themselves, it became clear that they were dedicated to music, willing to make personal sacrifices without even seeing them as such, and able to overcome sexual prejudice by sloughing it off or ignoring it—usually. None became sidetracked by prejudice, and each confronted the myriad challenges, including male chauvinism, by continuing to work. All these women have had the advantage of playing piano.

Chapter Twenty /// Shirley Horn: "I Got Older and Bolder"

Shirley Horn, the ballad singer and jazz pianist, was on the brink of a major breakthrough when I talked with her about her life and career. Neither of us knew it then, but her reputation was about to spread far beyond her loyal fans who had kept going for years to hear her in jazz clubs.

She had signed with Verve and was beginning to record. "I Thought About You: Live at Vine Street," issued on LP in 1987 and on a CD in 1992, and "Close Enough for Love," issued in 1989 on LP and CD, began her contact with a wider audience. Next came "You Won't Forget About Me" in 1991, done with guests Miles Davis, Branford and Wynton Marsalis, Toots Thielemans, the Belgian-born harmonica player—all stars, along with Buck Hill, a saxophonist. Her fresh exposure with Miles Davis, an old friend and colleague, brought her more attention.

By 1992, she had the most popular recording, "Here's to Life," at the top of the Billboard jazz chart for fifteen weeks. She had also led her trio and sung behind Toots in 1991 for his recording, "For My Lady," on the Gitanes Jazz label, and played piano without singing a note for Carmen McRae's Novus album, "Sarah—Dedicated to You," both released in 1991. Her work as a pianist for Carmen informed the public that Shirley could have built a career on her piano playing alone. She also appeared in a film, *Tune in Tomorrow* with a score by Wynton Marsalis. A new album, a tribute to Ray Charles, "Light Out of Darkness," on which she sings Charles's repertoire, was released in September 1993.

The tables are turned now. In the old days, saxophonist Buck Hill was able to get jobs in jazz in their hometown, Washington, D.C., and Shirley was never called, because of prejudice against women musicians. Now Buck's work with her for some of her appearances and recordings brings him the national exposure he might otherwise not have. The *San Francisco Chronicle* jazz critic has written that he knows that "Superlatives are always dangerous." But he's willing to go so far as to say: "Shirley Horn is the best singer in jazz today." Everyone agrees she is a unique stylist.

Shirley became a star and overcame the legendary prejudice in the music world when she was deep into middle age. She has also won out against ageism, which some younger women musicians found so threatening to them in the 1990s. The younger they were, the better, was the point of view of the record companies.

In 1989, Steve Margolin, then the manager of Fat Tuesday's jazz club in New York, replied to a question about why the club didn't usually book women as leaders of their own groups. "They don't draw the crowds," he explained. Not even guitarist Emily Remler did, unless she performed in collaboration with Larry Coryell. Women leaders probably didn't have the drawing power because jazz is considered a man's music, and, even more to the point, a black man's music; historically that's what jazz was, and nobody wanted to change its image. Perhaps nobody could change it, Margolin thought.

But a week later, Fat Tuesday's was jam-packed during Shirley Horn's engagement, even though the weather was so bad that a flood warning was issued one day. By mid-week, reviews in the local newspapers appeared; all were excellent. Lee Jeske in the *New York Post* was the most effusive:

> Shirley Horn is an enchantress, a weaver of romantic musical spells. The Washington, D.C.-based singer/pianist, who is at Fat Tuesday's this week with her trio, draws you into a song with the simplest means; a cool, dry haze of a voice, elegantly precise phrasing, an uncluttered piano style that complements her singing and, in everything she does, the very best of taste.
>
> Her too-short first set Wednesday night—55 minutes that went by in a blink—began with a pair of understated instrumentals, "Isn't It Romantic?" and "Emily," before she pulled the mike over for a warm, intimate vocal on "Our Love Is Here To Stay." She embraces a song—trusting her talents, trusting the song. It's mood music in a sense, supper club music from a more dignified, gentler time, and it's delightful.
>
> "I Thought About You," slow and tender; "Beautiful Friendship," joyous and swinging; Irving Berlin's . . . "I Got Lost in His Arms," soft and dreamy; Jack Segal and Marvin Fischer's more obscure "Something Happens to Me," playful and ebullient; a blues instrumental, end of set. Her bassist, Charles Ables, and drummer Steve Williams, provide fine support, as they do on her "Close Enough for Love" (Verve label), one of the year's best jazz albums.
>
> The key word here is "romance"—hopeful, generous, mature romance. Horn avoids the two poses that characterize most female jazz singers—girlish naivete and brokenhearted bitterness. She has been a musician's musician for 30 years; go discover her for yourself.

When it was suggested to Steve Margolin that a woman who sings and gets good reviews can pack a room, he replied, "You can do it with anyone who is good. Well, I guess you really have to get it out there. You really have to publicize it. Some people have fanatical followings, who show up. But usually you have to publicize it."

By 1989, Shirley, who had spent twenty of her thirty-five professional years traveling, didn't have to publicize to fill a club. Critics did it for her, and all that clubowners had to do was give her the bandstand and a notice in the paper.

Since then, she has become more entrenched at the top, drawing crowds to an expensive new Five Spot club revived in New York in 1993. She arrived there because of her soft-voiced interpretations of standard songs, primarily at slow tempos. She and Chet Baker created a vocal genre of their own. And when she talks, no matter what she says, it's with that some soft voice that cushions all of life's shocks and experiences—for others anyway.

That hushed voice sometimes faded away to inaudibility during our interview in the spring of 1989. She had been working in Fat Tuesday's for a week and going out on the town with musician friends after each performance. She talked so quietly that the humming air conditioner in her hotel room almost drowned her out. She and her girlfriend and traveling companion, Dorothy, from Washington, had infused the room with their sensuous perfumes—one by Paloma Picasso for Dorothy, and Calvin Klein's "Infinity" for Shirley.

At age fifty-two, she had been playing the piano for forty-eight years. She wanted to make sure her birthdate, May 1, 1937, went on record correctly, if it was going to be mentioned, because the *Washington Post* had recently credited her with two extra years. That bothered her. She had begun her studies with lessons in classical music. But when she was thirteen, she heard a recording by Erroll Garner, "Penthouse Serenade," she recalled. "I fell in love with it and copied it note for note. He was a great musician, more like Debussy in his pastels. . . . And then I got hip to Ahmad Jamal . . . and Debussy and Rachmaninoff are my favorite classical composers. And Oscar Peterson is my Rachmaninoff."

Her parents held civil servants' jobs; her father also drove a taxi at night part-time to support the family, which had no money to spare. Shirley's uncle was a doctor, who paid for her piano lessons in the afternoons and evenings, when she was supposed to be attending Howard University's School for gifted musical children. She was under the legal age to be working; nevertheless she was sneaking in to play the piano for two hours a night, for $125 a week, at Olivia Davis's Maryland Club.

Every night, an old man used to arrive, order dinner, tip his hat to her, and leave. One night, he came carrying a turquoise-colored teddy bear; it was so big that, if she stood it on her feet, it reached her chin. The old man sent word to her that if she sang "Melancholy Baby," he would give her the teddy bear.

"So I sang 'Melancholy Baby', I sang that song," she remembered with a laugh.

An item about her playing at the club appeared in the newspaper.

"I told my mother the truth," she said.

Dorothy reminded her, "You didn't have a choice!"

"I had a strict mother. She didn't let me work anymore," Shirley recalled. "I cried and screamed and protested and banged my head against the wall. But I was underage."

Nevertheless, the sojourn in the club taught her that she could earn about double the money if she sang and played piano. "I never studied singing. It came naturally to me. And I started to like singing. It's all second-nature to me," she summed up.

She also started to compose a little when she was in Howard University's music school. Among the musicians who went to school with her was Frank Wess, the arranger and reeds player, who later joined Count Basie's band in the 1950s and became a star in studios, clubs, and concert halls. Shirley, the only girl in school, felt very lonesome. She knew two things for sure—that she was shy, and all she wanted out of life was to play music. Frank Wess befriended her more than any of the other boys and young men in the school.

"He was nice to me; I was like an oddity. We had a crisp old teacher. I wrote a composition for her class. She didn't like my composition. 'What kind of music is that?' she said. She was very critical of it and hurt me. Frank Wess told me it was lovely music. But I haven't studied composition since then. I've written some things, but they're at home, put away."

After high school, she was accepted at both Juilliard and Xavier University, but her parents couldn't afford either, and her rich uncle had died. At age eighteen, instead of continuing with classical training, she made the difficult shift from classical to jazz and popular music and became a professional performer on the Washington scene.

"The guys didn't help me in Washington. And it didn't make a darn bit of different to me. Not one gig for me came from the men. I adored Buck Hill, a tenor saxophonist, but even he wouldn't let me sit in. Well, maybe he let me sit in, but no jobs came from him. The other guys never let me sit in."

"But I got older and bolder. And I decided to get into this crap. And I took their jobs. I didn't know much then. I knew how to play 'How High

The Moon'. A vibraphonist taught me that. He was stiff and clinical, but I thought he was raising hell."

"Now Buck Hill is working for me. He played on my last album, and he'll play with me at Lincoln Center," she noted. (He would continue playing with her as her fame became greater and she earned more money and played at Lincoln Center many times; she was asked to sit in for an ailing Carmen McRae there in 1992.)

At age nineteen, Shirley married "a stable man who is a bit older than I," she said. "My husband understood that I was all about music. The only thing that ever interfered with my music and career was my daughter, Grady, who was born on October 25, 1959, the year Billie Holiday died. I didn't want to travel until Grady was about ten years old. So I worked in Washington."

She was accepted in the music world as a singer. People simply didn't realize how good a pianist she was for many years. (It was also years before people realized how well Nat Cole played piano; "He played a mean piano," Shirley says. His playing received short shrift from a public that focused on his singing.)

She did a record as a singer-pianist, then made several recordings including movie themes that Quincy Jones produced. She didn't make any records as a piano player until the late 1980s, when she did one instrumental track on her album, "I Thought About You: Live at Vine Street." "Somehow people got to know that I could play piano," she said. She decided she would one day make an album with one side consisting of all instrumentals. The singing and playing sides would both be of Johnny Mandel's music, she decided, because she had fallen madly in love with it. Then her album, "Here's to Life," produced by Johnny Mandel, included some of his songs.

She never worried about people not paying more attention to her piano playing. In the 1980s, when women were playing all the instruments, and more women than ever were playing piano, it was a good time for Shirley to push her piano playing—or simply to have the public realize its quality. But she never let the business side of music or politics of any kind get in her way. "I love the music and have to perform; the hell with the rest," she said.

In addition to recordings mentioned in this chapter, "Loads of Love/Shirley Horn with Horns" was released on CD in 1990 (they were separate LPs released by Verve in the 1960s).

Chapter Twenty-One / / / Joanne Brackeen Lives and Plays Without Any Dos and Don'ts

Joanne Brackeen's playing contains multitudes. She can sound lush and jubilant, or airy, ethereal, and tremulous, or ominous, rolling, and low-voiced; she has a firm, occasionally adamant touch. Playing anyone's music, she runs the gamut of the whole piano, infusing even the far reaches of the treble and bass registers with her vitality. Her approach to the standards "Thinking of You" and "The Most Beautiful Girl in The World" makes them happy, romantic, and spontaneous. She gives her original songs the same infusion of energy, even when they sound cacaphonous. And she can reinterpret her own avant-garde music to make it funky and crowd-pleasing, as she did with "Picasso" one night in 1993 at the Village Gate. The crowd shouted for her resilient and resonant, dramatic and romantic composition played with her usual strength and attention to melody and rhythm. To hear her play this is to understand why she can inspire adulation in some discerning jazz fans. She is even capable of playing Brazilian music with authenticity. No one has ever been lulled by Joanne's assertive performances, which can charm, or make merry, or puzzle and shock an audience.

Helen Keane, who produced Joanne's 1992 album of originals, "Where Legends Dwell," with bassist Eddie Gomez and drummer Jack DeJohnette, on Ken Records, stands in awe of Joanne's gifts. The women first worked together on an album, "Special Identity," ten years earlier, with Gomez and DeJohnette, after Bill Evans advised Helen to work with Joanne. "It was excitement for me," Helen recalls. "I loved her work, because she was so different, something new. Technically, melodically, and harmonically she had it all together." Now Helen admires Joanne's maturity. "She's in another place, and she's a stronger person emotionally and musically. There's a serenity about her, an aura that comes from gifted people."

Joanne has traveled a long way from her musically sheltered childhood. Born in 1938 in Ventura, California, she taught herself to play by copying Frankie Carle records note for note. Her family didn't travel; she didn't hear adventurous jazz until she joined the scene in Los Angeles in her late teens and felt a kinship with the avant-garde players. Her admiration has remained steadfast for three decades, through her gigs with Art Blakey and Stan Getz.

She called herself to the attention of Art Blakey with a touch of magic in her approach. She was sitting in the audience at Slug's, a Lower East Side jazz club, listening to Blakey's group. The pianist was so lost, because the music was too difficult for him, that he stopped playing. Joanne got on the bandstand. When Blakey looked up, he saw her playing the piano. "After that, we went to Japan," Joanne recalled.

She was married to saxophonist Charles Brackeen, and they had four children. All of them were young, but they were in school when Joanne started traveling, first with Blakey, then Joe Henderson, and after that Stan Getz. She loved working with Getz, because he was such a good musician, in love with melodies, and he gave her opportunities to stretch and play her more experimental music. She waited for him to tell her when to do her own thing.

When she began freelancing as a leader, she often compromised and muzzled her urge to play her own compositions, so that clubowners didn't alienate their mainstream jazz-loving customers. Usually they became absorbed in Joanne's brilliant interpretations of the standards—songs she always found fresh ways to play because of the amount of time she had spent in private, composing, playing, and experimenting at the fringes of atonality.

In the 1980s, her marriage ended in divorce. Her children were grown, and a few were professional musicians. Joanne began to develop more as a musician and a personality. Always friendly with musicians, but rather shy with fans, she grew forthright, gregarious, and sociable. And she became more aware of the way the world worked—especially the machinations and politics of the music world.

"I had never paid any attention to the world at large," she recalled about the early period of her career. "I couldn't name any other women pianists, but it never occurred to me that there weren't any. Was that simple-minded of me? But I think it was probably a great asset. I was playing with all guys. My friends were all guys. So I'm with the guys. I never thought I was doing anything different. I had no business management, and I didn't pay attention to it. I never said that I wanted to be a millionaire. I was in love with music. That really helped me develop and progress at the beginning.

"And I heard a lot of really good music. Ornette Coleman, Billy Higgins, Charlie Haden," people who persuaded her to fall in love with experimental music when she was still a teenager living in California. "There was no one person who encouraged me. If someone called me for a job, I did it. Charles Lloyd, Dexter Gordon, and others called me in the late 1950s in California."

With her husband and four young children, she moved to New York in the mid-1960s. She didn't go out very much because of the children. Her husband helped; occasionally there were babysitters; the children themselves started to babysit for each other. She usually went to the Village Vanguard and Slug's—places where she heard the musicians she was most interested in. "Then I ended up with these great bands, Blakey, Henderson, Getz. That was encouragement."

She is, and has been, her own primary manager, booker, and accountant. She plans concerts and club dates for herself in such places as Europe, Canada, Australia, Israel, Turkey, Toronto, and Hong Kong—and in cities across the United States. Even though other women musicians—and men too—regard her as successful, she notices that she works less than some of her eminent male colleagues. She forces herself not to focus on the fewer opportunities for women to lead groups in New York clubs. Naming many of the best women pianists who have established fine reputations, and whom everyone admires, she remarks that they aren't working very much. "They're touring," she is told. "They are? Where?" she asks rhetorically. She knows that they're not. And then she goes to work, for when she is in New York, she makes sure she is performing.

A relentless pioneer for music that could alert and even sometimes alarm, Joanne in the 1990s sounded more mellow in general as a composer. "Where Legends Dwell" has a touch of pensiveness—a laid-back quality balancing the intimations of maelstrom that often made her music sound fierce. In one week in 1992, she entertained an audience with her trademark, forceful ruminations in the bass register as endings to distinctive, pretty standards at Knickerbocker restaurant, then moved to the jazz club Visiones where she led a quartet in relentlessly exciting music that avoided her earlier fascination with shocking harmonies. She has earned a great deal of success with her Brazilian albums in the 1990s, "Breath of Brazil" and "Take a Chance," happy, romantic, brilliantly executed music.

What remains unchanged is her exuberance, adventuresomeness, fearlessness, and confidence. Asked to explain why she sounds the way she does, she doesn't differentiate much between her playing and composing.

"For me, it's the way I hear life. Music is a study of the life energies and forces, the way they move through the universe, more than music is a subject [the way I was] taught in school, [where I was asked only] to learn notes and chords."

She was motivated by her musicality and passion to transcend lessons and become an original. "I am well aware that it is impossible for a human being to create anything that doesn't already exist. We become a center for (energy) to flow through," she says. "Once you get a view of the magic taking place all the time everywhere, then all you have to do is become an opening for that to come through. . . . As soon as I put my hands on the piano, I'm in what people call an altered state—I go to another dimension instantly. And I'm often in that dimension anyway. The music that I hear is, first of all, a kind of silent energy. As that translates into sound, it sounds more like a voice." And that voice isn't restricted to the piano notes but falls between the cracks. Joanne can play nearly anything on the piano and, in part, because of her impatience at being unable to play quarter tones, she has become attracted to writing for orchestral instruments. "I really want to write a symphony," she says.

She studied her predecessors—"lines, phrasing, and chords," she says, to learn to play. "But in composition it's really exciting, because you can take these same elements and move them in different ways,' phrasing differently, changing rhythms, beginning phrases at different spots. "When you study jazz, there are places where most people phrase in a certain way. . . . When I compose, it's easy for things to come to me that aren't in that . . . form. And when I improvise . . . things that I'm doing just fall in a different place from where everyone would expect." She has even been surprised by tapes of her performances. "Oh, what did she do?" she says to herself. Playing the tape again, she realizes, "Oh, that was all right."

She's trying to find more time to analyze her own playing and composing, so she can extend her work—and "pass it on to my students," she adds. She feels increasingly responsible to them.

As for her touch, which is generally thought of as percussive, but can be very light and even gossamer, especially in the upper registers, or in her Brazilian compositions and interpretations, again she says, "That's the way I feel music. And that may be everyone's reason for playing the way they do, or they may have an influence. My style is my own. I don't have any dos or don'ts. I have a lot of different feelings when I play. I know some people may move things around slightly, but they're still not up there to play anything that comes into their minds. But . . . the way children think and the way I play are very close . . . I have a sense of wonder about the universe's sound and rhythm. I think my touch reflects that. And I

enjoy being that way. I prefer to listen to people who are unpredictable . . . I like the newness of things."

Far from disdaining pianists who differ radically from her forceful-
ness, she says, "I think everyone has a place." Listening to a low-key player
may be an ideal way for an audience "to get into something more evolved,"
she theorizes. She approaches her students with the same open-
mindedness, taking the time to listen to their weaknesses, strengths, and
goals. Then she tries to give them exactly what they need. The idea is to
get them to use their gifts, supported by technique, so they can assert their
individualism, as she does. For Joanne, her music is her real fingerprint.

Chapter Twenty-Two / / / The Wily Miss Dorothy Donegan, Mistress of Fiery Medleys

From *The New York Times* story, by Peter Watrous, on the White House Jazz Festival, June 21, 1993: "The pianist Dorothy Donegan came out, and as usual she tore the place apart with a gloriously strange improvisation that mixed 'I Can't Get Started' with classical flourishes, ominous movie-music chords and boogie woogie. She had the crowd on its feet." Whitney Balliett was similarly taken, and he wrote in *The New Yorker,* July 26, 1993, of the "three or four dazzling minutes" when she played, "finishing with a blinding two-handed run."

Dorothy Donegan, who was playing professionally in Chicago, her hometown, in the 1940s, has always been regarded as a masterful pianist, with a strong, clear, inventive style and an independent spirit. One might even call her eccentric but, after all, it is Dorothy Donegan who has borne the responsibility for being Dorothy Donegan, a great pianist with a sharp wit and refreshing candor, and who started her career under the double onus of de facto racial segregation and male dominance in jazz. She knows that well-established male pianists can suffer by comparison when they play before audiences right after she has dazzled them.

Sally Placksin in *American Women in Jazz* included the glowing reviews that jazz critics have always given Dorothy's pianism. John S. Wilson in *The New York Times* mentioned her "almost subliminal sense of swing" for a "dazzling" performance in 1980, and Wilson, the most balanced and tasteful of critics, wasn't normally given to effusiveness. He might have said "sublime" too, instead of subliminal, and he wouldn't have been wrong either. In 1992, the National Endowment for the Arts rewarded her with a $20,000 award.

Dorothy has always practiced a great deal on the best pianos she could find and has kept herself in fine physical shape to support her natural stamina and power. She has alluded to the solitary life of the committed artist, when she has spoken, in interviews and in a recorded monologue, of eschewing parties, drinks, and drugs. It was no sacrifice for her to avoid life in the fast lane; her wild, exciting times took place at the keyboard. Then she went home to muster strength for her next performance.

As a child, she studied the classics and could play them as well as she played jazz. She loved classical pianists, but also adored Art Tatum, whom she knew and studied. Early in her life, she saw that her way to becoming a classical concert pianist was blocked by racial prejudice. She then recorded many jazz piano records for Decca, Continental, and Jubilee. Not only are those records out of print, their masters have been lost or misplaced. So posterity may have been deprived of some of the truly fine jazz records of the 1940s and 1950s.

Nevertheless, Dorothy Donegan was able to hold onto a mind of her own, deciding what she has wanted to do with her career in jazz and how much she wanted to earn. And with her own methods, Miss Donegan has been able to make a roaring success of her career and its bottom line.

There have been times when Dorothy Donegan seemed out of the public eye. That's because she chose to work mostly in Europe after the era faded in which she had become a reigning pianist at the Embers, a very fashionable supper club in the 1950s on Manhattan's Upper East Side. Some colleagues have mentioned she might have shown a bit too much temperament to clubowners in New York. But from time to time, she still showed up to play in New York City clubs and concert halls. Not only were the reviews consistently wonderful, but the clubowners, by the 1980s, who offered her the conditions and fees that she liked, loved her, despite her temperament—or self-protectiveness. Either she or the clubowners had mellowed. It depended on whom you chose to believe. Her loyal fans came to hear her; as easily as a leaf blows in the breeze, she entertained them thoroughly.

People constantly asked her why she didn't record more.

"I have recorded in the U.S. and in Europe," she said about her recording activity up to 1990. She named some records made in Europe: "Makin' Whoopee!" released in 1988 as a CD and an LP on the Black and Blue label in Paris, done originally in 1979; "Four Leaf Clover," she thought, done in Sweden, though Four Leaf Clover is the name of a label and may not be the title of her album. She made one or two more albums in Switzerland, probably on the Jaylin label, she said, vague about the details. Anyway, the records have been done, she said, and several more were made in the United States.

The records in print lineup in 1989 listed only "The Explosive Doro-thy Donegan" for Progressive Records in Decatur, Georgia. By 1994, that one was not listed. Instead there was "The Dorothy Donegan Trio, Live at the 1990 Floating Jazz Festival," recorded on a cruise ship, and released by Chiaroscuro Records in New York in 1991. It's a wonderful album, enriched by Dorothy's monologue about memories of her early life and entire career, and her philosophy about her devotion to her work. She mentioned a friend's assessment of her ranking as a pianist—as good as Oscar Peterson—at least sometimes. (Other pianists have said similar things about themselves, but they have said them only in private.)

It was the late bebop singer Babs Gonzalez, Dorothy recalled for her audience, who had told Oscar Peterson that Dorothy had outplayed him one day. "She's got more hands . . . and more fire than you," Dorothy relates that Gonzalez told Peterson. Dorothy gave her own opinion about her work: "Some people can play but can't entertain an audience." Her monologue echoed her hands, which had begun the album with some heavy-handed boogie woogie, from which she pulled out "The Battle Hymn of the Republic," and moved to the calypso song, "Matilda," and then on to a delicate, tinkling "Bye Bye Blackbird," from which she darted back to the heavy-handed boogie woogie riffs. The exciting medley, in which she revealed herself a bonafide heir of Art Tatum, showed the magical sleight of hand that has made her a star for decades. In *The New York Times* in 1980, John S. Wilson had noted her "ability to go from subtle brilliance to a pre-gut appeal that rocks the house and moves nor-mally sedate audiences to cheers and whistles." Her medleys are nimble-ness incarnate.

In her monologue, she also spoke of the great influence Art Tatum had on her elaborate and virtuoisic work. "I watched how he fingered all the runs," she said. She liked to listen to Horowitz, Ashkenazy, and Alicia de la Rocha. With her irrepressible wit, she said, "There's no better item to steal from than Tchaikovsky." Borrowing from the classics gave her work "snob appeal," she had decided. "It proves you didn't learn to play in reform school."

Other current recordings are "The Incredible Dorothy Donegan Trio," with Dizzy Gillespie as a guest artist, 1991, and her second cruise ship album, with her trio and guest Clark Terry, 1992, both on Chiaroscu-ro. "Dorothy Romps," (1953–1976), was issued by Rosetta Records, 1991.

"I'm in competition with the men," she added to her explanation about the paucity of her recordings. "But I am going to record," she said about a year prior to the first recording done on a cruise ship.

In mid-summer, 1989, she was having a very successful engagement at Fortune Garden Pavilion, an elegant restaurant on Manhattan's Upper

East Side. It had invited her back, of course, after its owners found out how smart they had been to book her in the first place. Well-heeled jazz aficionados had showed up *en masse*.

Jazz fans liked to speculate that Donegan, surely one of the strongest jazz pianists, with one of the most elegant yet forceful touches, had suffered gross maltreatment or mismanagement in the music world. It might also be said that she was not the most avid publicity-seeker in the world. It is difficult to convince her to make time for an interview. She can be busy paying bills, which seem to follow her around the country. Or else she might be trying to track down lost luggage, or attending shows in which old friends star. In 1989, she had a wonderful time going to see Ruth Brown and Carrie Smith in *Black and Blue* on Broadway. Then they came to see her. Miss Donegan loved keeping in touch with her old buddies. Her life in music has provided a continuity.

She has been married three times. Her first husband, John T. McClane from Des Moines, Iowa, recalled meeting her when she was twenty-five years old. She had gone to the West coast from Chicago and was in the movie, *Sensations of 1945*. (Other film highlights of her career would include a 1950 CBS-TV show with Harry Belafonte and Pigmeat Markham and a BBC-TV show made in London in the 1960s.) She was playing in a club near Sunset and Vine. McClane had owned several clubs in Los Angeles—The Trip, the Livingroom next to Ciro's, the It Club, and the Morocco Supper club. From the first time he heard her, he thought she was a great pianist. He always believed she should have received more recognition for being "one of the best from Bach and Beethoven to dirty blues and boogie woogie." She can move easily from the classics to pop music, perhaps too easily, he surmised. She doesn't think about it and doesn't discipline herself, he said.

"You don't know what she is going to do, and she doesn't like to be told what to do," he summed up. Furthermore, "you must make it simple. She plays too many keys." She has suggested the same thing herself. "When you record," Mr. McClane went on, "you've got to make it simple." Actually he doesn't like to criticize her because, "I love all her playing, I really do. She's a first-rate artist," he said. He thought that she knew her instrument far better than nearly anyone else did, and she should make her own judgments about how to play.

Mr. McClane, retired from his enterprises and living in Beverly Hills, gave Dorothy the house she has lived in for a very long time in Los Angeles. At times, he had undertaken the job of helping her manage her career during their marriage. She played in his clubs, of course, most notably the It Club, where, he recalled proudly, many wonderful jazz musicians played. Dorothy was formally managed by Music Corporation of America, where one of the executives wanted to book her into the

Embers. The club's owner, a lawyer, as Mr. McClane remembered, was worried he would lose money if he booked Dorothy. So Mr. McClane, who accompanied the MCA executive to a meeting with the lawyer, said, "If you lose money, we'll make the loss good." She was very successful and played there twice a year for six weeks during its heyday.

Eventually she left MCA to go to Joe Glaser's management company. He managed so many black artists—Louis Armstrong among them—that Dorothy told him he had a plantation, Mr. McClane recalled. "She said the damnedest things."

Mr. McClane confirmed that she had recorded a number of records for Decca, and for Birdland's owner Morris Levy's label, Continental, and for Capitol, which probably bought the rights to records she had done for Jubilee. "But the records may have been used as a tax write-off," Mr. McClane believed. Like Dorothy, he didn't know exactly what happened to them. She told Sally Placksin that her recordings for Decca were put on the shelf for a long time, then sold to another company, which put them together with other records by women pianists. The experience taught her that she had to make and own her own records.

To get away from all her frustrations in the United States, she went to play in Europe, where audiences always appreciated her work, and paid her substantial fees. "Some of these artists get robbed by everybody and have nothing left," says McClane. "She's doing pretty good, because she has nothing but a booking agent. She has no publicity nor road manager. She knows how to do it all for herself," said Mr. McClane.

She married twice more after she and McClane divorced in 1959. They had one son John McClane, who plays the guitar beautifully, his father says. The son became an executive with a record company. With her second husband, she had another son. Her third marriage to a man considerably older, who owned some real estate in Chicago, didn't last either. He is now dead. Her friendship with McClane endured.

On August 6, 1989, on what was probably the hottest day in one of the most afflicting summers in memory for New Yorkers, Dorothy Donegan left her air-conditioned suite in a midtown hotel and went to Queens to visit Rose Murphy, the chi-chi girl. Dorothy would have to get back to New York City and revive herself from the heat so that she could play the last night of a week's engagement. But she set out to visit her old friend anyway, because Rose Murphy had suffered a stroke, Dorothy thought, and was on a dialysis machine. "And she's almost not with us anymore, you know," Dorothy explained when she returned to her room to prepare herself for the night's performance. She didn't feel like talking or playing or doing anything at all, because she was so depressed from the visit. (Rose Murphy survived another three months.)

But Dorothy pulled her frazzled ends together at the end of that sweltering August day. In Fortune Garden Pavilion, she could see the sky through a skylight. Plants hung above her head, over the piano. Dorothy must have taken a modicum of pleasure from that elegant setting. Her practiced joyousness lit her face with a smile that night, though her old friend lay gravely ill.

Her medleys, as usual, seemed to have a life of their own, with their own logic because of her harmonic sense. "The Sunny Side of the Street" led into "There Will Never Be Another You," which started out slowly and metamorphosed into so much improvisation that any contemporary pianist would envy her imagination and technique. Her striding left hand, however, marked her as a product of an earlier, perhaps more livable, happy, and comprehensible era. Her boogie-woogie playing was infused with her authentic feeling for the style. There are not many people who can make a whole room fall in love with the emotional power of boogie woogie fifty years after its heyday in Chicago.

When she went on to sing "Time After Time" with a lot of vibrato in all the right places, she said, "Ruth Brown taught me to sing that." She heard a glass break, and she quipped, "That's all right, honey, you'll pay." At some point, she got up and, in her long, dark, sequined dress and turban—a conservative stage outfit by modern standards but one that prompted critics to call her ostentatious—she shimmied and shook a bit. Jazz critics have always affected a pose of annoyance with her entertainer's instinct, wishing she would stick to playing the piano with high seriousness. But Dorothy told the audience, after a few gyrations, that she had played for actresses Tallulah Bankhead and Ava Gardner and the Duke and Duchess of Windsor and perked them up.

So she must know what she is doing, she said offstage. She gets paid for being an entertainer and a pianist, she has always maintained. Dorothy is perfectly capable of playing with high seriousness. She has played with the New Orleans Philharmonic, and was thinking about practicing one concerto. "You can live off one concerto for an entire year. Andre Watts," whose playing she loves, "does that," she says. And the level at which she performs in clubs is its own standard of high seriousness.

Late in the last set of her evening, she mentioned causally, "Do any of you know Rose Murphy?" A few people seemed to stir. Dorothy sang, "Chi chi," got a murmur here, a laugh there, and she sang it again. "Chi chi." Everyone seemed to recall. Dorothy imitated Rose Murphy for a while, then launched into a parody of Lena Horne's singing style—the voice, the phrasing, the enunciation. More people were familiar with the great beauty's stylistic hallmarks. Dorothy has the rare knack of being able to imitate all the great jazz pianists. She has exceptionally long, strong fingers that can do anything with a keyboard. But for her last set, she stuck to parodying the singers.

So she worked her old friend, Rose Murphy, into the evening, spinning a bit of her personal angst into a bright strand in the tapestry of her art. In her own way, she was keeping Rose Murphy alive and well and before the public. And nobody knew the trouble Dorothy had seen that day. She talked about how her friends from the cast of *Black and Blue* had come to see her at the club. For her audience, she made her life metamorphose into the story of a wonderful time. She is a witty, wily, and warm performer. Executing dazzling, bravura runs up and down the piano, she fascinated all with her ornate embellishments.

It had been passing through her mind for a decade that she was losing all her friends, and she sometimes longed for them. "Oh, Mary Lou, Hazel, come and get me," she quipped a few years ago to some friends who visited her backstage and asked her how she was. Actually, despite a problem with cataracts, she was very well, with a bright smile and eyes that could make her chiselled face look ravishing. She still had the ability, confirmed in Peter Watrous's report from the White House, to save an entire festival from slipping into the doldrums. A month later, she made a whole room swing and an audience alternate between listening raptly and cheering roundly, as she carried on her career as usual, with a summer engagement at the Village Vanguard, where she often performed when in New York.

Chapter Twenty-Three /// Marian McPartland: ". . . Something You Really Need in Life, Someone to Encourage You"

In 1985, as the occasional woman emerged in groups in jazz festivals and clubs, and there was that intimation of good things to come from the younger generation, Marian McPartland played a concert in the Kool Jazz Festival's solo piano series. Her concert launched the series, which became a gem of the festival for a while. Every pianist wanted an invitation to play in it, even though it took place at the awkward hour of 5 P.M.

Miss McPartland, who was born on March 20, 1920, in Slough, England, close to Windsor, and who never gave up her British citizenship, was first noted for her engaging, Swing-era interpretations. Her light touch and soulful ballad playing were her lauded hallmarks. But there was something about the opportunity to play in Carnegie Hall Recital Hall, later renamed Weill Recital Hall, that especially inspired the stout-hearted musician. And so the delightfully genteel but witty and earthy Miss McPartland created an exceptional mixture of musical moods with fastidious technique and a feeling for all the styles of jazz from the era of her birth to the cusp of the next century. Her playing made the air seem buoyant. For that, she received a standing ovation and was invited back the next year. Word of her triumph made her concert a sell-out.

With dissonance and intensity, she began Duke Ellington's obscure "Clothed Woman" dramatically, then lightened her touch to swing deftly. She actually sounded somewhat like Ellington. "It's The Little Things That Mean So Much" came next by and for her old friend, pianist Teddy Wilson. The song was a love ballad eventually supported by a surprising walking baseline in her left hand. Then Miss McPartland explored blues, standards, and originals—"Easy Blues," by Mary Lou Williams, in which her left hand rumbled around in the bass, compensating for the lack of a string bass. "Emily," for which she is particularly known, soared forcefully. You can always count on her to be bright, forceful, and enlivening—and to do the unexpected. Her enduring appeal has nothing to do with nostalgia.

"I wanted to have a mixture of things that people recognized," she said of her repertoire for the 1985 concert, "and also something new and different, even new to me." She had the aplomb to explain her preparation for the concert right after she finished playing. One could see that she was exhilarated and happy to offer more to the public. "The Teddy Wilson song: it just happened that Carmen McRae sang it for me when she did 'Piano Jazz'. And I wanted to show some different moods. I did improvise in new ways. I have done 'From This Moment On' with a tempo change before, but not the way I did it tonight. In the past few years, I only played it as part of the trio arrangement. So things came out differently. And I thought: 'Oh, what's this? What am I doing? Well, it's happening, so deal with it.

"It was exciting. I did prepare and spend time choosing the tunes. And you can be comfortable, because you're not on trial. I thought about how I would feel out there in the audience, and I wanted to be entertaining as well as musically valid."

Miss McPartland could have rested on her laurels and repeated her repertoire from the 1950s, when she became a jazz star with popular appeal in a long engagement in the Hickory House, a famous midtown Manhattan jazz club and restaurant. She could have played the same songs in the same way for the rest of her career and maintained her reputation. But since her girlhood in England, when she defied her conservative parents and played jazz in the 1930s, she has always challenged herself.

As a teenager in England, Miss McPartland, whose maiden name was Margaret Marian Turner, began piano lessons at the Guildhall School of Music with the understanding that she would pursue classical music studies. Her parents hadn't wanted her to go even that far with an unconventional career. She had second cousins, she would reminisce, who had musical talent. One sang in St. George's Chapel in Windsor, when the royal family was in residence in Windsor Castle. Another played cello. A third became mayor of Windsor and was knighted by Queen Elizabeth. Several people in her family were knighted earlier, she knows. The musical talent was on her mother's side.

Marian had always heard music on the BBC, even jazz, which was popular in Britain in the 1920s and 1930s. Her younger sister, Joyce, brought home a boyfriend who owned a fine collection of jazz records, a precious commodity to Marian. Her sister wasn't interested in jazz. So Marian welcomed the boyfriend and his records into her life.

Her parents disapproved of her contemplating a career in jazz to the degree that Marian could only look at the Palladium's bills starring Duke Ellington and Fats Waller. "With such parental disapproval," she has recalled, "it never occurred to me to ask to go to the shows. I knew my parents would only tell me I couldn't go." They were shocked when she dropped out of the Guildhall to take her first professional job. She went on the road, playing jazzy-sounding pop music in a four-piano vaudeville act. The leader was Billy Mayerl, a novelty piano player, whose music is still popular to this day. Marian's parents were so upset by her decision that she used a stage name, Marian Page.

In the 1940s, when English and American musicians traveled to entertain the troops in Europe, it was inevitable that Marian would meet American jazzmen. One was Jimmy McPartland, well-known cornetist in the Chicago tradition. "I was with the first group of U.S.O. performers that went from England to Normandy Beach and into France. I met Jimmy in Belgium. He was a G.I. who got transferred from combat to Special Service. We performed for the troops in the front lines with a G.I. bass player and drummer for several weeks," she reminisced. The couple fell in love, married in Aachen, Germany, and went to the United States in 1946.

"I was Jimmy's war bride. He was always so proud of me. He praised me all the time. The day we arrived in New York on a Victory Ship, he took me to Eddie Condon's [a legendary jazz club]. There was no jealousy and no male chauvinism in Jimmy. It seems like no matter what I did, he was always in my corner forever. If my self-confidence was low, he would say, 'Don't be ridiculous. You're great!' He'd *always* say I was the greatest. This is something you really need in life, someone to encourage you. That was how he was, he never tried to bring anyone down, he always spoke well of people."

With entrée into the jazz world through him, Marian McPartland, as she became known, distinguished herself quickly. She won rave reviews for her lyrical, touching interpretations of ballads. She established her pattern of constant growth, bolstered by an underlying determination, an instinct for self-motivation, and the stamina as well as the talent of the superior artist. It amazed her husband how her playing always seemed to keep up with the times.

In the 1960s, she did more touring than she had been able to make time for during her Hickory House days. She also began writing songs that were recorded by Tony Bennett, Sarah Vaughan, Gary Burton, Cleo Laine, and Peggy Lee. She started her own record company, Halcyon. By the 1970s, her social consciousness led her to become involved in jazz education in the public schools and colleges—Harvard and Howard Universities among them.

Critic Leonard Feather wrote about "the rhythmic agility of her left hand and the skillful way with which she used it, sometimes to accompany, more often to complement and correlate what was going on in the right." In a chapter about her in his book *Jazz Live,* Michael Ullman revealed that she took some good advice from Lennie Tristano and became a more rhythmically accomplished player, paring down her romantic embellishments, gaining in emotional impact in her ballads. "I went once for a lesson to Lennie," she has recalled. "He was intimidating, in a way, but he gave me good advice about improving my rhythmic concept to keep better time."

Her drive to be contemporary added earthiness and resonant feeling to her style. At the same time she was poised in a natural way. She never affected the pose of a snob, or a patrician, or a fussy artist—though she was always very particular in the sense of being critical and analytical about her own work and enormously interested in other musicians, performances and ideas. She was simply so devoted and equal to whatever she undertook that she achieved a firmness and classiness without sacrificing any of her delicacy.

Her career took an upward turn in the 1970s, when Bobby Short requested her as his vacation replacement in the very fashionable Cafe Carlyle on Madison Avenue on the Upper East Side. President Kennedy and his family had made the Hotel Carlyle the epitome of chic in the 1960s. During what turned out to be Marian's annual engagement, William Hay from South Carolina Educational Radio approached her to see if she would do a thirteen-week radio series, to be distributed by National Public Radio.

"They left the format up to me," she says. "I thought that two pianos seemed the easiest way to do it." Primarily funded by Exxon and also by the National Endowment for the Arts, "Marian McPartland's Piano Jazz" was first recorded in the Baldwin studios in 1979. "We started on a shoestring," she recalled, "so Jack Roman of the Baldwin Company offered us the use of the showroom. It had about ten pianos in it. Mary Lou Williams was the first guest. We picked two pianos that we liked. Someone pulled them side by side. And off we went."

Other early guests were Hazel Scott, Eubie Blake, Bill Evans, Teddy Wilson, Billy Taylor, Tommy Flanagan, Ellis Larkins, John Lewis, Dick Hyman, Barbara Carroll, Bobby Short, and Cedar Walton. "I was like a kid in a candy store," she remembers. "I was phoning everyone and got all the people I wanted."

After a year, the show won a Peabody Award, one of several broadcast awards in the show's history. "We had a big party to celebrate that," she recalls. "We gave everyone a miniature Peabody medal. I'm very proud of it."

Among the show's awards have been:

1. The George Foster Peabody Broadcasting Award (University of Georgia).
2. The Edwin H. Armstrong Award (Columbia University).
3. The International Radio Festival of New York Gold Medal Gabriel Award.
4. The Corporation for Public Broadcasting Program Award.
5. The Southern Educational Communication Association (Cultural Documentary Award/Best Performance Award/Best Public Radio Program of the Year).
6. The *Jazz Times* 1992 Readers Poll (Best Syndicated Jazz Radio Program).
7. An ASCAP/Deems Taylor Award.

Over the years, Marian would also receive honorary doctorates from Union College in Schenectady, New York, Bates College in Lewiston, Maine, and Ithaca College in Ithaca, New York.

Her show had replaced "American Popular Song," a program with guest singers hosted by her friend, composer Alec Wilder. She eventually found out that he had recommended her as his replacement; so great was his admiration that he wrote several pieces for her. Not only did Marian's show continue beyond a thirteen-week season, it grew into a twenty-six week show, then a thirty-nine week show every year in the 1990s.

At first she spent afternoons taping shows, then packed up and went to play in the Carlyle at night. For a while she set aside a period of every year to plan and record the shows; the rest of the time she traveled, performing in clubs or more often in concert halls, sometimes with symphony orchestras. By the 1990s, "Piano Jazz" was nearly taking over her life, she felt at times. She reserved one week a month to tape. She often found herself organizing or coming up with ideas for the show. She had to delay the autobiography she was trying to write so she could continue to play her concerts and host "Piano Jazz."

On "Piano Jazz" her guests take turns soloing, chatting, and playing duets with Marian. For each show, she takes into account the guest's strengths. "I want to do the right thing with 'Piano Jazz'. I have a responsibility to make it good. It's kind of an historical record. Whoever listens to it in the future will learn something about the people I'm talking to."

As the country went through a renaissance in the public's appreciation of jazz in the 1980s and 1990s, Marian McPartland was the ideal renaissance musician—accomplished, articulate, and curious about everything musicians were playing. She began inviting people who were not jazz pianists to be guests. One show featured Tony Bennett. For another, she had the classical pianist Ruth Laredo as a guest. Miss Laredo played some Chopin; Marian improvised on it. "And she talked so interestingly," Marian recalls. Dizzy Gillespie was a guest, playing trumpet, piano, and demonstrating rhythms with his hands.

Marian's naturalness has had a great deal to do with the show's success. She has a trace of a British accent. At times she hesitates slightly, dispelling any hint of hauteur, clearly thinking carefully about what she wants to say. A subtle vibrato in her voice adds warmth and poignancy to her presentation. Nothing about her is slick. Yet her thoughts flow supportively and enthusiastically for her legions of guests. Her thorough understanding of their musical talents leads her to strike up intimate, profession-centered conversations with them right away.

With Mulgrew Miller, she focused on composing. She explored Wynton Marsalis's all-encompassing musicality and introduced the public to his piano playing. She enticed the charming, ebullient Hazel Scott to talk candidly and humorously about her career, from her childhood as the talented daughter of pianist Alma Scott to her friendship with singer Mildred Bailey and her marriage to Reverend Adam Clayton Powell, a powerful U.S. Representative. Perhaps most intriguing, in each show, Marian also proves that, with her fastidious technique, vitality, and command of the history of jazz styles, she can blend with other pianists with exceptional ease. Her duet on an Ellington song with Hazel Scott was a masterpiece.

Throughout the 1980s, her bright blonde hair was teased into a gossamer style. In the 1990s, she wore it longer, straighter, for a more casual image. Because of her trim figure, she wears a pants suit gracefully. In the Penny Lane Studio in the MGM building, where she tapes her shows in midtown Manhattan, she moves with the reflexes of a woman half her age. Her aplomb, undoubtedly born of experience, covers up a trace of nerves, which she says she has never really lost. Every show is a new adventure.

Marian and Jimmy McPartland co-owned a house in Merrick, Long Island. At some point in the 1960s, they decided to get a divorce. Even so, they remained very good friends. He lived in half of the house, she lived in the other half until, in the 1980s, she bought another house and moved to Port Washington. Quite often he went to stay with her. "I feel as if I always want to look out for him. I really care for him," she said of their relationship. "And I know Jimmy cares about me."

Although their careers had brought them together, their different musical directions had something to do with their divorce. They traveled separately and met and played with different people. Jimmy never wanted to move away from the traditional jazz style. "I wanted to go forward, and I still want to improve, experiment, and keep up with what's happening," she said. "He always had very good insights, and he heard all the harmonies I played. But musically he had his own style, which is more traditional. I occasionally played a gig with him. I loved it. But I didn't want to play in that style all the time. When I think of people getting up and doing the same job every day, and complaining about it, hating it—no, that's not for me. I'm so grateful to be working at something I really love. Life goes by so fast. You should take advantage of everything that's around you—and enjoy what you do."

From listening to Marian McPartland play the piano and interview guests of diverse musical interests and accomplishments, one gets the impression that her word means everything; she thrives on change. She feels impelled to stretch and leap over those odd measures of time, the decades. She likes new challenges. "I try not to be too busy, but then I can't resist," she summed up her urge to work. In the summer of 1990, she was thinking of inviting Miles Davis on her show. She had once reached him by accident on a hotel telephone in France. They had a long conversation. Miles always asked her, "How's your old man?" Marian would later muse, "Miles was always fond of Jimmy." She wasn't sure, however, if Miles would like to do the show. She encouraged herself: "All he can say is no." But Miles died. She regretted having let the time pass without calling him. "I think he would have liked to have done the show," she said.

During the 1960s, when she had been playing for Benny Goodman, she had become emotionally unsettled and decided to spend two weeks at the Menninger Clinic. "I'm quite open about it," she says. "I like to joke about it and say that Benny Goodman *drove* me to the Clinic!" After two weeks, she headed home to Long Island and went into therapy. Her doctor encouraged her to try anything she wanted to do. "Don't be afraid of rejection. What have you got to lose?" he counseled her. She took that lesson to heart and made it an instinctive reaction. "In fact, I've turned out to be downright persistent."

Her acquired wisdom has helped her to maintain the energy she needs to face the demands of her career. "You have to take care of yourself and keep trouble at bay. I'm always exercising. I put my feet under a chest of drawers and anchor my feet there. Then I do ten half sit-ups. I walk and swim. When you get right down to it, my priority of all time is to take care of my health, to stay in good shape, and not get sick, so I can withstand the rigors of the road and late planes. After that, the rest is easy."

Because of her radio show, she has found herself more popular as years have gone on. When she played in Yoshi's in Oakland in 1989, the club was packed. People told her they had heard her show and wanted to meet her. She was playing her original music with symphony orchestras— for example, the North Carolina Symphony Orchestra in October 1990 and the Milwaukee Symphony in May 1991. And she had discovered: "I can do anything I want to as long as I have the time and energy. Isn't that great!" she said in response to a remark about all the options she could consider.

By the 1990s, she wanted to get "Piano Jazz" on television. "Radio is great, but TV is even better," she said. She and Bobby Short made a pilot, but only one educational station aired the show. Prospective producers told her that they didn't find anything interesting in watching two pianists play and talk to each other. But she doesn't agree. Her show, is, of course, for musicians, the intellectually curious, and the musically inclined. Good jazz pianists are invariably "interesting," she says. And their music ranges from the pleasant or intriguing to the electrifying.

She decided to start teaching again, and she began by taking her trio to play with the Schreiber High School Jazz band in Port Washington in March 1991, a month designated for highlighting music in the public schools on Long Island. At first she was unsure about how to entertain "those television obsessed kids who have a very limited attention span. How can you play Duke Ellington's music and hold their interest?" But she wanted to try to reach the students.

She remembered a time when Duke himself helped her teach a class in the 1970s. She was playing his "C Jam Blues" for school kids in Washington, D.C., when he arrived to play for the program. He was already quite ill at the time, but he kept the date. "That was the biggest thing I ever did, working for three months in different schools. The program was very well funded. Billy Taylor was in it. He has always helped me. And Duke helped a great deal. That's the kind of thing I'll never forget," she said.

All along, she has tried to keep track of young musicians building careers, because she wants them to find opportunities and grow musically. Countless tapes and phone calls keep coming to her for "Piano Jazz"; it's impossible for her to follow up all of them. But some she does.

In 1990, a young pianist, Lynne Arriale, was a guest on "Piano Jazz." Marian had been impressed with Lynne's playing and devotion to development—and perhaps saw a trace of herself in Lynne. She was developing self-confidence and superb technique. When Marian found out she couldn't go to Japan that year for "100 Golden Fingers," a concert tour with nine other master jazz pianists, she recommended that Lynne go instead. (Later, on April 3, 1993, Marian joined Lynne to play in a concert at the Pabst Theater in Milwaukee, Lynne's hometown. Lynne played for 45 minutes with Marian's rhythm section, then Marian played, and afterward Lynne and Marian played three duets—to a standing ovation.)

Jimmy McPartland became ill with lung cancer in 1990. He was staying with Marian so often that she simply kept him with her all the time during his illness. One day, he didn't look well. "I can't leave him today," she told herself. She cancelled a trip to the West Coast to record a solo concert live at Maybeck Hall for Concord Records, her label since the late 1970s. When Jimmy seemed better, she flew to California and headed to the concert in high spirits. She knew she would have a good audience in a wonderful, small hall with a nice piano. Though she still hadn't decided what to play she told herself, "Well, play this thing. It's all going to work out. I'm going to enjoy myself."

Some of her choices were standards—"My Funny Valentine," "Willow Weep for Me" and "A Fine Romance." She also played her own composition, "Twilight World" and an exciting newer piece, "Kaleidoscope," the theme from "Piano Jazz." She had never played more than the opening phrase, and she decided to take advantage of the opportunity at Maybeck Hall to stretch out and extend the piece. She also included Ellington's "Clothed Woman" with its dark, discordant, repetitive introduction filled with strange chords. When Duke had heard her play that song in the Hickory House in Manhattan in the 1950s, he had been startled—and delighted. "*I* don't even play that tune," he said, and was very complimentary about her work—no doubt cognizant of the keen wit it takes to interpret that tricky song.

Jimmy and Marian remarried in 1991. "The divorce was a failure," she has explained. Soon afterward, two days before his eighty-fourth birthday, he died. Marian has missed him very much. They were together for about forty-five years. She had been scheduled to go to Europe with Benny Carter, who led a sextet, with trumpeter Harry "Sweets" Edison, trombonist Al Grey, bassist Milt Hinton, and the drummer Louis Bellson. She decided to go on with the tour. "That was the best thing I could have done," Marian recalled two years later. Her eyes became luminous and moist at the memory of the tour so soon after Jimmy's death. "So many countries. The last was somewhere in Spain. Such a pretty place. Then I went to England to see my family, and I came home."

"I guess I've been doing the same thing over and over for the past few years, booking 'Piano Jazz' and doing symphony and trio concerts, but I want to keep doing things a little different. Concord has just put out a CD with my trio and a twenty-two-year-old alto and tenor saxophonist, Chris Potter, who works with Red Rodney," she mused in the spring of 1993. This CD *was* different. Called "In My Life," it was dedicated to Jimmy, and she played songs that had special meaning for her. A sense of profound nostalgia for her relationship with her husband came through in her pensive interpretations.

When Chip Deffaa, who wrote the linear notes, told her how moved he was by her performance of "Singin' the Blues," she explained, "I played it for Jimmy. It was a tune he really loved, and I first learned it from hearing him play it." Saddened, and grieving too by then for Dizzy Gillespie, who died in January 1993, Marian included "For Dizzy," a song she built around some chords he had played on the piano when he had been a guest on "Piano Jazz." An expressive, autobiographical album, it featured young Chris Potter, who could play with brilliance and rhythmic excitement, maintaining the spirit of the jazz tradition.

Her next album was part of the 2-CD Concord Silver Anniversary set. She started out in a dramatic, adventurous, and swinging mood and ended up rich and romantic—altogether a joyful musical experience, with a fresh approach to standards. It was a very pleasurable experience for Marian. First she commented off-the-cuff, "It's the best thing I've done." Then, surprised she had said that, she corrected herself. "I think it's pretty good." But her first remark reflected her enthusiasm for her work. The conditions under which she led her group helped make the music so ripe. "There's something about playing in the open air, to a live audience. It's so romantic, and you can do no wrong," she recalled about her feelings that day in Concord, California.

The label has been reissuing CDs of Marian's earlier releases from her own label, Halcyon, and some have Jimmy and Marian playing together. "He played some wonderful ballads. He almost sounded like Miles, he really did." Marian never has understood how Jimmy could be dismissed as just a Dixieland player. "That wasn't fair to him. He could play so beautifully, using the Harmon mute on ballads, and he could really swing elegantly. He was like a totally different player with that Harmon mute," she reflected. "Even to the end, Jimmy himself was so encouraging to me. He always accused me of being too critical of myself—and others. He'd try to get me to relax. One of his favorite expressions was, 'Okay, but let's do it gracefully.' If I wanted to leave a party, he'd say that. We'd shake hands all around and say goodbye. He died that way too; gracefully."

She has noticed, with gratification, how many more women players of all instruments were emerging in the 1990s. "They seem to be playing with more confidence, realizing, 'I have a perfect right to be here.' They're not apologetic." Marian never really thought much about being a woman in the male-dominated world of jazz. People used to ask her how it felt. "Nobody asks me anymore. That's such an archaic view. But if they do ask, I just laugh and say, 'It feels damn good!'" Recalling again how shocked her family was when she set out in the world as a touring pianist, she said, "Now I'm really happy that I did it."

Marian McPartland has written a collection of articles, *All in Good Time*, published by Oxford University Press. On "The Benny Carter Songbook" CD, she plays Carter's easeful, romantic music with stunning clarity and ebullience. Her duo piano record, "Alone Together," with George Shearing has taste, elegance, and fascinating high style. Both recordings are on the Concord label, which has also reissued "From This Moment On" including "Emily." Her latest album by 1994 was "Marian McPartland Plays The Music of Mary Lou Williams," Concord.

Chapter Twenty-Four / / / A Few Words About Love, Marriage, and Motherhood

Alluded to throughout this book has been motherhood. In society in general women have been postponing marriage and motherhood until their thirties and even their forties. For women musicians, who must be free to travel at a moment's notice, the logistics of raising children present nearly insuperable problems, especially when the women are very young and must establish themselves. No matter how much the married woman players with children love their families, these women would cease to function as rational contemporary human beings if they had to give up their music. Their ardor for playing their instruments, which frequently begins in childhood, usually rules all their instincts.

Eliane Elias, the critically praised Brazilian pianist, a club, concert, and recording artist and producer, was a child prodigy. When she began teaching at age fifteen, she sensed that her happy childhood had ended and she had become an adult. "I was lucky, a beautiful young girl. . . . But the music had to come first. I had to do it. Nothing made me as happy as what I did, and I did it with love." When you make that sort of choice, it affects your personal life profoundly, she found out. "You give up many things." She noticed that men, and women too, could feel intimated by women "out there and doing something and working with men," she has said.

Society now permits women to be consumed with passion for their art first and foremost. And if the music hadn't fired them, most of them would never have met their husbands and started the families that so complicate their lives.

Tania Maria, the Brazilian singer and keyboardist, met her husband when he fell in love with her as she performing. He made sure that he met, wooed, and won her. A French businessman, Eric Kressman gave up his formal job with a corporation and started to manage her. Her career went very well. Eventually they became parents. And Tania Maria, who had her last baby, Tatiana, on February 11, 1977, presented her family life to an audience in the Blue Note in the late 1980s by saying, during her last set one night, that she was going home to see her little baby. She said that she knew the audience didn't care, but she cared very much, and so she had to stop the show. Everyone laughed. Actually her little baby had been out of diapers for a while, but she was still far from college age at that time. Tania Maria had worked throughout Tatiana's life and, from the beginning, hired people to help her with child care. Tania Maria had no alternative, because her career was in a crucial stage in the early 1980s. She had just come from Paris to live in the United States. If she had stayed home with a child, she would have sacrificed her career—and livelihood.

Artist manager Linda Goldstein's first child was born when she was thirty-six and in the throes of enjoying the financial success of "Don't Worry, Be Happy." Her infant daughter started logging miles in international travel. To take care of her young daughter, bassist Kim Clarke, separated from her baby son Mikey's father, relied heavily on her mother and babysitters; otherwise she would not have been free to tour or even able to play in gigs in New York City at night.

Pianist Eliane Elias, who played with Steps Ahead, then as leader of her own group, had a baby daughter, Amanda, with her husband, Randy Brecker, the trumpeter, in 1984, when Eliane was twenty-three. Since the Breckers sometimes traveled together, or simultaneously in different groups, child care became a major challenge. Through the happy accident of her birth into a financially secure family, Eliane could put Amanda on an airplane and send her to her doting grandparents in Sao Paulo, Brazil. That's what Eliane did every time she made an extended tour. For shorter tours, she could afford to leave the child with a trusted babysitter in New York. But Eliane spent too much time either worrying about Amanda or telephoning to talk with the babysitter. As often as she could, Eliane simply took Amanda along on tours, because "mamae" didn't like to leave the child with a sitter, Eliane said.

"I believe that when you want to do something, you do it," she said. "It's very hard, but you prove it's not impossible."

Occasionally she had to curtail her traveling to stay home and take care of the baby. And the baby interrupted Eliane while she was practicing or composing. "The first two years were very hard," said the slender woman with honey-colored hair and an expressive face with mobile features and a generous mouth. "Now I'm doing more," she said when Amanda was four in 1989. "But I have to plan life around her. In the first two years, when I couldn't leave home, I was practicing ooooooooooo. I'm playing classical music. I'm growing. It's very hard, it's very hard, it's much harder than for any man to even imagine it. You have to plan well."

"For me to be a sideman is impossible. If Wayne Shorter would say, 'Can you go on tour for three weeks?' what can you do? So I work my bookings around her too." Every day she learned again "how to keep it all together," as new situations confronted her. In 1989, she surmised, "I don't think I have as much time these days to do all the things I want to do in music. But I also don't think I would be able to say the things in music that I do, if I hadn't had all these demands . . . on my time. A maturing comes from having a life. So the music is getting more complex."

Sumi Tonooka had a similar attitude about her maturation and enrichment as a woman and a musician because of her children. She had a great deal of help with child care from her husband and babysitters. But the problems were enormous. "Life is full," she explained. "I feel very fortunate, with a good marriage, which gives me good support. My husband" (an artist) "works at home. Our time is flexible. That's definitely to our benefit. We give and take. He pulls the load, then I do. We have babysitters as well. It helps to have some base of support, babysitters, family and friends. That base of support definitely comes into play." Bertha Hope recalled that she too relied heavily on family and friends to help her with her children, after her husband Elmo died.

Sumi felt strongly about leaving Nami, who was only eight months old, in anyone else's care for a long period of time. "I left her once for a week," Sumi said. "Sometimes I want to be playing a lot more than I am, but life is more balanced this way. When she's walking and on her feet, it may be easier for me to leave her. I hope both kids will be more independent when they're in school. My friends tell me that I will have more time then." Eliane Elias found that was true. Her schedule became easier when Amanda started school in New York and became more occupied with her own friends and various lessons.

"Sometimes," Sumi said, "you feel half crazed, when it's at its worst. I feel like I'm not doing either thing well, but [motherhood] has enriched my life and my feelings about being alive. I really wanted to have kids, and I feel good about that. Music needs to be integrated. But it's true that I'm doing a lot at one time. I don't even realize how much energy I'm putting out sometimes. The boy is just three, and she's eight and a half months. It's very intense."

"Yet both my kids are mellow. It's almost as if they're custom-made. Kai loves the drums and Bobby McFerrin, and he likes to get up and play the drums anytime he sees them. At my gigs, I have to talk to the drummer and see if he minds if Kai plays for a minute. At home, Kai has set up pots and pans. He did it himself. It's interesting how their personalities come out at such early points. Nami likes to listen to someone sing. She likes music, period; she seems to tune in. And they do listen to me practice. The more they see you doing something, the more they get into it themselves."

"But it's not easy for me. They want my attention. Maybe I can practice an hour at a time without being disturbed or worried, unless there's a babysitter here. [The organization for child-rearing] isn't a fixed thing. It's flexible," she summed up her situation.

Joanne Brackeen, who depended primarily on herself and her husband, a freelance musician, and occasional babysitters to help raise their four children, often stayed home with them. It wasn't until they grew up a little, and the elder children could look after the younger ones, that Joanne became free to travel and take jobs on the road. While the children were babies, she remained home for the most part.

Cellist Akua Dixon Turre, wife of trombonist Steve Turre, has been able to take her daughter, age eleven, and son, only two, on the road, because the girl is so smart and reliable. Akua went on tour with Steve's group to Martinique and California when she was still nursing her son. "I would not have made it without my daughter. The band would start playing, and I would take the boy off my breast, fix my blouse, and run out on stage. I could leave my son in my daughter's care while I played."

Bassist Melissa Slocum has custody and responsibility for raising her daughter, Sonora, who was four in 1993. Her parents, who might be able to offer her some help, live in the Midwest. So Melissa's options for pursuing a career have narrowed. She cannot travel, unless she earns high fees and can afford to take the child with her, and she cannot even go out often at night to hear music, "hang out," and continue to make valuable connections because of the high cost of babysitters on a regular basis. In 1993, she was concentrating on finishing her master's degree on a scholarship at the Manhattan School of Music and playing freelance for singers in New York City and with Diva and Unpredictable Nature. "Aren't you satisfied just being a mother?" some people have asked her, to which she has replied, "Yeah, but I have to support my child." Although she was already giving music lessons, she decided, after her daughter was born, to get a master's degree so that she could have the best qualifications for a staff teaching position. "I'm not going to give up my music. I really want to earn a living in this field. I don't really want to do anything else," she says.

Before she became a mother, Melissa was able to make some progress. "I felt my career was really taking off," she recollects. While working in a regular gig every week for eight years at Arthur's Tavern, she auditioned for Lionel Hampton's band and played for several months as his bassist. One of his Town Hall concerts was on her schedule. She also played with Art Blakey's group, and Charli Persip's Superband, and groups with pianists Walter Davis and Bobby Enriques, and a Brazilian group, and with drummer Ralph Peterson's groups on his Blue Note recordings: "Ralph Peterson Presents the Fo'tet," a quartet, and "Ornettology." She played on some tracks for singer Dakota Staton and also in a group with pianist Kirk Lightsey and drummer Doug Hammond for a Turkish singer named Ozay. In 1993, Unpredictable Nature made the album "Dedication."

She yearned to play in a high-profile quartet or quintet and also lead her own band. While she was confined more to the apartment, taking care of her daughter, she was studying and practicing to improve her technique. "I like my ideas and the shape of the music, but I hear technical stuff that I want to work on," she explained. "I'm trying to prepare myself for the time when I'll be free [to go any place at any time to play]. I know enough musicians." They would be able to offer her work. In the meantime, she added bluntly, valiantly grappling with the stress, "I hope I survive."

Women musicians are always curious about how other women manage to have careers and children at the same time. "It's a subject for a book in itself, the way women in music handle their child-rearing," says Linda Goldstein.

Some women musicians are lesbians. The majority are not. Sometimes they postpone marriage for so long that they find themselves living as single women forever. Carol Steele has stayed single. Other women have married and divorced and remarried—and divorced and remarried. For most women, the difficulties entailed in simultaneously maintaining a close love relationship with a man and a consuming career in music have proven too arduous. They suffer from conflicts about which love—the husband or the music—takes priority. And they have difficulty in finding men who can tolerate the demands of a creative career on a woman's mind, energy, and time—especially a career for which a woman must travel and may become famous. (Shirley Horn solved the problem by staying home and playing primarily in Washington, D.C., when her daughter was young.) And if a man is paying the bills, he may take the liberty of interrupting his wife's work. If he isn't paying the bills, he may feel excluded. No matter who pays the bills, or if the couple is sharing them, the man may simply become jealous of the woman's devotion to music and her position in the limelight, and he may demand that she leave her instrument alone and pay more attention to him—just at a moment when she needs to practice or rehearse or go to work. He might break a dish to interfere with her concentration.

If the man is a musician, jealousy of another kind can arise. Melba Liston, who was married and divorced three times and had no children, recalled how competition might arise if she played better than a man. That competition would preclude the relationship from ever becoming a marriage—or even getting off the ground to become a friendship. She expressed it diplomatically, saying that troubles could arise "if I happened to play a little better than a man did once in while." On the other hand, Melba recalled her happiest love relationship had taken place with a musician who was married and could not marry her. He was a particularly encouraging mentor—not a competitor—for her.

Women thoroughly understand the tension that their passion for music can provoke. Some instinctively protect themselves and their creativity and stay free, no matter what the personal sacrifices may be. Some delay making a commitment until they feel secure in their careers and know a man cannot presume to take precedence. But there are no rules. Some women thrive on the challenge of a dual role as musician and wife, or a triple role as musician, wife, and mother. Some marry early and divorce when their careers are established, eventually no longer interested in diversifying their energies, whether they have children or not—especially if their mate is difficult. Some women marry and divorce early when the strains of marriage prevent them from pursuing careers effectively. And some drop out of the music world and devote themselves to marriage because they defer to tradition, or because a career in music can be so tortuous that marriage seems the more attractive and reasonable way of life. Or their nurturing instinct for their children may take precedence.

Some women musicians choose to live with their lovers rather than marry, and their relationships do not appear to be any more or less stable or longer-lived than those of married women musicians. Some women musicians, who have married happily or had long, happy, if complicated, relationships with men, have derived enough satisfaction from their careers that their marital status never assumes overriding importance. Or some may even find it easy, or at least possible, to take refuge in their creativity when their relationships, though on the whole satisfactory and worth continuing, are exceptionally complicated. If they've never had children, they don't deeply regret or resent that they haven't. As Marian McPartland, who never had children, has joked, "I didn't have any children, but I had bassists and drummers." A life in music can be so rewarding that it can actually compensate a woman for not having had children—or a husband—or an enduring love relationship.

No formal study has been done about the family lives of women musicians. The decisions they make for their domestic arrangements are as individualistic as their professional paths. Women musicians are as apt to stay single, or live with, or marry several men over the long haul as they are to remain married to one man all their lives. Some couples who share music as a focus find it enhances their love and compatibility; others find that nothing helps them get along, although both are dedicated musicians.

The biggest stress on love, marriage, and motherhood is a life on the road. Rebecca Coupe Franks, the trumpeter, learned about sacrifice after she moved from California to New York. She had been seeing a man for a while, and when she left California, one of her best friends began to see him. Rebecca wrote a strikingly effective song called "You Bitch!" Trumpet notes sounded exactly like the title.

■ ■ ■ ■ ■ ■ ■ ■ ■ ■

A View from the West Coast,
by Frankie Nemko

■ ■ ■ ■ ■ ■ ■ ■ ■ ■

A number of the jazzwomen who live on the West Coast have been heard in Los Angeles, where I lived for years, or I have visited them on their home turf—for example, flautist Holly Hofmann in San Diego, where she also books gigs for other musicians, and the respected saxophonist Mary Fettig, from San Francisco, who has opportunities to tour the country with her own groups and other bands.

A major phenomenon on the West Coast is Maiden Voyage, a seventeen-piece, usually all-female band, that was founded in 1980 and plays at important festivals, clubs, and concert halls. Its leader, alto saxophonist Ann Patterson, is a regular player with other big bands in southern California and with the group called the Four Winds. Trumpeter Stacy Rowles, percussionist Jeanette Wrate, and trombonist Betty O'Hara, members of Maiden Voyage, also lead their own groups, and their reputations have spread beyond the West Coast and even to Europe.

Women have been playing on the West Coast almost since the birth of jazz. Pianist and singer Nellie Lutcher, born in 1915, was already a professional by age fifteen, working in Los Angeles nightclubs during the 1930s and 1940s. Similarly, Mary Osborne, one of the most accomplished guitarists of the 1950s and 1960s, moved to Bakersfield, continued for many years to accompany some of the jazz greats, and led her own successful small combo. Saxophonist, clarinet, and vibes player Peggy Gilbert, while not best known as a jazz artist, was instrumental in forming in 1928 an all-women orchestra for tours in the United States and Canada.

In the bebop period, many women earned respect in jazz, among them saxophonist Vi Redd and trumpeter Clora Bryant—and both were still blowing strong in the early 1990s. One of the most famous women in jazz, trombonist-composer-arranger Melba Liston, who was born in Kansas City, was raised in Los Angeles; she toured with Count Basie, Dizzy Gillespie, Gerald Wilson, and Billie Holiday.

For this caliber of artist, it's hard to apply a label such as "West Coast jazz," because all these musicians—a mere fraction of the talented women—are simply consummate jazz artists playing that most diverse of musical idioms. Possibly the most expedient way to put the East-West controversy into perspective is to describe the environment and circumstances pertaining to both these geographical regions.

As Ted Gioia explains in his *West Coast Jazz,* published by Oxford University Press in 1992: "One can look to the sprawling suburban landscape of southern California. . . . There was no uniform gathering place for West Coast players after the decline of Central Avenue." His book covers the years 1945 to 1960; fortunately, since then, quite a number of gathering places have sprung up, most notably the famed Shelly's Manne Hole, a hub of West and East Coast and international jazz for twelve years. There was the even more storied Lighthouse in Hermosa Beach, from whence much of the notorious "cool sound" emanated during the 1950s, 1960s, and 1970s.

The San Fernando Valley also had its musicians' hangout, Donte's, which was a spawning ground for emerging talent in the 1970s and 1980s. There have always been such places along the western seaboard, where many women, for example, pianist Cecilia Coleman, could try out new material and new permutations of groups and hang out with contemporaries. A recent addition to the Los Angeles jazz club scene is Catalina's, named for its woman owner; many top jazz players of both sexes appear here.

So it's not a lack of venues that influences West Coast jazz. Gioia, however, has a point when he talks about the movie industry settling in southern California. The studios have attracted accomplished players, composers, and arrangers to try writing for films and television. One prolific film scorer is the diminutive, multi-talented pianist and singer Patrice Rushen, with credits also as musical director for a late-night talk show. Without doubt, one of the busiest studio bassists, male or female, was Carol Kaye, who appeared on more than 10,000 pop and jazz recordings and dozens of film and television scores. From the 1950s to the 1970s, she played with many jazz greats when she was between studio gigs. Eventually she moved to the peace and tranquility of Colorado, leaving an enormous legacy on records, videos, and in publications.

The stringent requirements for the style of writing and playing on these sessions has had a marked influence on the way musicians played outside the studios. So has the fabled "laid-back" atmosphere of the idyllic West Coast scenery in such places as Malibu. Los Angeles itself doesn't have the frenetic pace of life of New York or Chicago. Like proverbial chameleons, transplanted musicians have adapted to the West Coast, forging what most avid fans regard as a viable form of their favorite music. One such transplant, Toshiko Akiyoshi, flourished in Los Angeles during the 1970s, with a sixteen-piece band featuring the cream of the studio crop that adeptly handled her daringly different charts. Though she and Lew Tabackin, her reeds-playing husband and co-leader, moved back to New York, Toshiko left her mark on the West Coast jazz community.

Another notable fact puts the East-West debate into perspective; the East Coast generally connotes New York and the tri-state area, and Boston, Philadelphia, even Washington, D.C., and big mid-Atlantic cities east of Chicago. East Coast musicians travel a great deal in this area, getting exposure with varied audiences. The West Coast's paucity of major metropolitan-like cities limits such touring. Maiden Voyage from time to time makes pilgrimages to Sedona, Arizona, and to Seattle, Washington; Hoffman will get a gig in Los Angeles, as does Colorado-based Ellyn Rucker. Pianist Joyce Collins plays pretty regularly in Aspen, Colorado; she also makes an annual trek to Brazil. However, all West Coast musicians generally travel far less than easterners.

Even so, more women than ever before are studying jazz at the college level, planning for careers in the studios for the financial reward, while they moonlight in jazz clubs. One native Californian, Joanne Grauer, has chosen to stay home and help train a new generation of jazz pianists and singers who believe they can live up to their own expectations, jazz's standards, and assert a strong voice in jazz.

■ ■ ■ ■ ■ ■ ■ ■ ■ ■

Appendix / / / Women
Instrumentalists Active in
the 1980s and Early 1990s

■ ■ ■ ■ ■ ■ ■ ■ ■ ■

This list, ranging from women with long, illustrious careers to emergent musicians, was compiled primarily through the author's personal knowledge and recommendations by musicians.

Their burgeoning numbers make an exact listing impossible. Many are college and conservatory graduates, some have advanced degrees, and more to come currently study in schools. The emphasis is on women who have played in New York at least once from the late 1970s into the 1990s, or have recorded or had an album reissued and distributed nationally or internationally. Where known, albums are listed, unless they're in the body of the book.

The author apologizes to any women left off this list. Some represent a larger group of women—for example, several based in Canada, and on the West Coast, and singers who accompany themselves as pianists. The author also apologizes to singers who may play instruments primarily in private, to please themselves, to practice, or compose. More apologies go to lyricists, arrangers, and composers not known for playing instruments professionally, and to the growing number of women on the business side of the music industry—such as publicist Diane Patrick and artists' manger and lawyer Gail Boyd.

Many women not profiled in this book and included primarily apropos of their recent activities were written about previously in Sally Placksin's *American Women in Jazz,* Linda Dahl's *Stormy Weather,* Mary Unterbrink's *Jazz Women at the Keyboard,* Antoinette D. Handy's *Black Women in American Bands and Orchestras,* and *The Grove Dictionary of Jazz.*

An Asterisk (*) connotes a musician who has been mentioned in some detail in the body of the book. Two asterisks (**) indicate a musician for whom the most current or complete information was not available at the time this book was published.

TOSHIKO AKIYOSHI, pianist, composer, arranger, bandleader, leads an award- and poll-winning band with her husband, saxophonist Lew Tabackin. She performs with the band and smaller groups in clubs and concert halls. Her most recent recordings are "The Toshiko Akiyoshi Jazz Orchestra at Carnegie Hall," featuring Lew Tabackin, on Columbia, 1992; "Remembering Bud: Cleopatra's Dream," on Evidence, 1992. In 1986, Mayor Koch presented her with the New York Liberty Award in recognition of her achievements as a foreign-born New Yorker. She was written about in Placksin's book.

JUDY ALBANO, electric and acoustic pianist, has played for jingles and recorded music used as educational material by Jim Henson in schools. She tours the United States, England, Canada, and Japan with r&b musician Benny King and plays with jazz trios in New York clubs. Three tunes she recorded for group leader, drummer Bernard Purdie, were scheduled for release on Lexington Records in Europe.

ALIVE!, a cooperative women's band, recorded "Alive!" on Uranus, 1978; "Call It Jazz" on Redwood, and "City Life" on the Alive! label, in the early 1980s. Founded in 1976 in the San Francisco-Oakland area, the group broke up in the 1980s. It had two reunion concerts in 1993, produced by Redwood Cultural Works, San Francisco and Oakland, and scheduled an appearance at the Michigan Women's Festival in Hart. Members are Carolyn Brandy, percussionist, spokesperson for the group; Rhiannon, vocalist; Susanne Vincenza, cellist and acoustic and electric bassist; Barbara Borden, drummer; Janet Small, acoustic and electric pianist. Alive's recordings can be obtained through a distribution firm for recordings by women, Lady Slipper, Inc., in Durham, North Carolina.

*GERI ALLEN, pianist, teacher, composer, recording, club, and concert artist, ranked among the critics choices in *Down Beat* and won first place as Talent Deserving Wider Recognition in 1993.

GIA ARNETT, guitarist, played blues in trios with a tenor sax and an organ, studied with trumpeter Bobby Bradford, who played with Ornette Coleman, and performed in U.S. Army big bands for six years. She leads her own bebop-rooted band in Cincinnati.

*LYNNE ARRIALE, pianist, group leader, is based in New York. Her debut album, "The Eyes Have It," was released by DMP, 1993. She won first place in the great American Piano competition, Jacksonville, Florida, 1993, and tours in the United States, Canada, and Europe with her trio.

*PAULA ATHERTON, alto saxophonist, flautist, and singer, plays and records with Kit McClure's band and other groups. As a finalist in the Hennessey Cognac Jazz Search in 1993, she was offered a chance to record her own compositions with her jazz fusion quartet, called Interplay. She is also on some rock recordings.

KAREN ATKINSON, classically trained flautist and jazz and classical bassist, plays with her husband, jazz bassist Lisle Atkinson, in the Neo-Bass Ensemble. She also plays with the Bergen Philharmonic in New Jersey and in classical concerts in the New York area. The Neo-Bass Ensemble, which has performed at Merkin Hall, the Harlem School for the Arts, the Henry Street Settlement House Playhouse, and the Lake George Jazz Festival, recorded an album, "Bird Lives Through the Neo-Bass Ensemble," 1988, available from Karlisle Productions, 51 W. Englewood Ave., Teaneck, New Jersey 07660. Karen plays flute on the jazz album, "Bass Contrabass," on Jazz Craft, 1979.

AZIZA (Mustafa Zadeh), pianist, singer, from Baku, Azerbaijan, composes new music with the exotic influence of her country's folk music. Her debut album, "Aziza," is on Columbia, 1993.

SARINA BACHLEITNER, pianist, composer, plays standards in New York restaurants and clubs. She also accompanies dance classes at the Rudolf Steiner School for grades one through 12. She studies with Manny Albam and Jim McNeely at Broadcast Music Inc.'s excellent Composer's Workshop.

SHERYL BAILEY, Baltimore-based guitarist, has won the Jim Hall Jazz Master and Harris Stanton Awards, played with Leni Stern, and toured Japan with saxophonist Gary Thomas. She is known for her strong, lyrical, versatile style.

**LESLIE BAKER, California bassist, who studied with the late Red Callender, has received excellent reviews for her competence and promise from Leonard Feather and others.

NANCIE BANKS, New York-based singer, leads a big band, including Lynne Arriale, on "Waves of Peace," on Consolidated Artists, 1993. The band, with well-known journeymen musicians such as bassist Michael Fleming, saxophonist Patience Higgins, and baritone saxophonist Charles Davis, performs in clubs and halls.

LOUISE BARANGER, trumpeter, plays with Diva. Previously she played with Maiden Voyage, the Harry James band for the last year of that trumpeter's life, then had the lead trumpet seat in "Sugar" in Las Vegas for a year. Returning to Los Angeles, she freelanced for Nelson Riddle, Ray Anthony, Frank Sinatra Jr., Bobby Vinton, with whom she did two TV specials, George Burns, Rich Little, and many others. Among her studio jobs, she worked for "Dallas" on TV and on the soundtrack of the film *For the Boys* with Bette Midler, and for jingles. She is on the albums: "Alumni Tribute to Stan Kenton," with the Paul Cachio Big Band, Happy Hour Records, 1980s; Holly Near's "The Speed of Light," Redwood Records, 1980s; and Bobby Womack's "The Last Soul Man," MCA, 1987. She has toured the United States, Japan, and Europe. Married to Fred Mills of the

Canadian Brass group, which plays for the Mostly Mozart festival annually, she had her own brass quintet for several years in Los Angeles. She lives in Tampa, Florida.

**PATRICIA BARBER, Chicago-based singer, composer, and pianist, had her first major-label CD, "A Distortion of Love," on Antilles, 1991. (Singer Carla White among others provides finger snaps.)

*WILLENE BARTON, tenor saxophonist, played with a quintet under Anna Mae Winburn's direction in the 1950s after the International Sweethearts of Rhythm disbanded, and with the Jazz Sisters in the 1970s. For a Kool Jazz Festival concert at Carnegie Hall, at 1981, she led a group including Bertha Hope, pianist, Bernadine Warren, drummer, Nydia Mata, percussionist, and Lucille Dixon, bassist. In the 1980s, Willene toured Europe with singer Sandra Reeves Phillips and, in 1993, played in the Big Apple Jazzwomen's band with pianist-leader Sarah McLawler for concerts in the New York area.

JAMIE BAUM, flautist, has played experimental music in the Knitting Factory's 1993 festival. Previously she worked with George Russell and Donald Brown in Boston and with Vic Juris in New York. Her album, "Undercurrents," is on a German label, Konnex, 1992.

ANN BELMONT, guitarist, plays commercial music on dinner-dance cruises and works in jazz groups in clubs, for which she is usually called by other women musicians. "There's the old boy network, and the old girl network. I call my friends, and they call me," she describes the system as it works for her, in New York. She has worked with Kit McClure's band.

*LOLLY BIENENFELD, New York-based trombonist, who played in the Thad Jones-Mel Lewis Orchestra at the Village Vanguard, in Broadway orchestras, and the circus, plays lead trombone in Diva.

*CINDY BLACKMAN, drummer, composer, and group leader, lives in New York.

CARLA BLEY, well-known pianist, keyboardist, composer, arranger, and found of New Music, a record distribution company, toured Europe leading a twenty-piece band with her husband, bassist Steve Swallow, in 1993. Carla works in piano-bass duos with Swallow, and in larger groups, one of which she led in Fat Tuesday's in New York in the 1980s, and writes on commission for orchestras. Her recordings on her label Wattworks, distributed by Polygram. She has appeared on TV—for example, a show hosted by saxophonist David Sanborn. Among her recent recordings are "Duets" with Steve Swallow, ECM/WATT, 1988; "Fleur Carnivore," ECM/WATT, 1989; "The Very Big Carla Bley Band," ECM/WATT, 1991; "Memoirs," Soul Note, 1992; "Go Together" with Steve Swallow, ECM Records, 1993.

*JANE IRA BLOOM, soprano saxophonist and composer, lives in New York.

ESTHER BLUE, pianist, played at the Blue Note's late night sets, at the Knickerbocker, Horn of Plenty in New York, and Singapore hotels in the 1980s. In the 1990s, she played keyboards with Richie Havens and Sara Dash and led her own groups in New York. She also accompanies singers and works in contemporary gospel and Latin jazz groups.

**JULIE BLUESTONE, New York-based flautist and saxophonist, plays classical music and jazz.

BESS BONNIER, well-known, much admired veteran pianist, composer, and teacher, says about a career as a woman jazz pianist, "For one reason or another, it's hard, but either you survive or not. It's a choice that you make." Despite vision problems, she was artist-in-residence at Grosse Pointe North High School, Detroit, for the fourth year in 1993–94, in a program funded by the NEA and the Michigan Council for the Arts and Cultural Affairs. She plays for concerts such as the annual Montreux/Detroit Jazz Festival and helped establish Detroit piano summits, which have starred Barry Harris, Earl Van Riper, Hank Jones, Tommy Flanagan, Oliver Jones, and Bess. She has written "The Bess Bonnier Song Book" and a show, *Sweet William,* with tunes inspired by Shakespeare's plays and sonnets for production first in her high school. She is on the album "Xmazz," with the Jack Brokensha Quartet, on AEM Records, 1993, which includes her tune, "Christmas Rag."

**KIM BONSANTI, trumpet, has played with Diva and other groups.

BERYL BOOKER, pianist, led a much praised, popular all-women trio in the 1950s, with Bonnie Wetzel on bass and Elaine Leighton on drums. Booker died in 1980. In a compilation of recordings available in 1993, called "Jazz Round Midnight: Piano," she plays the song "Let's Fall in Love."

*KYSIA BOSTIC, pianist and singer, who lives in New York, has traveled with Charles Aznavour, Liza Minelli, Julio Iglesias, and pop singer Will Downing, and recorded with Regina Belle, The Manhattans, Melba Moore, Marlena Shaw, and Alex Burgnon. She received an ASCAP Special Award for Musical Theater and a Hollywood Dramalogue Award for composing music for "The Colored Museum."

*PATTI BOWN, Seattle-born, New York-based pianist, composer and singer, has played in the Newport and JVC Jazz Festivals in the 1980s and 1990s, in concerts with Joanne Brackeen and Marion McPartland, and has worked in Upper East Side and Greenwich Village clubs (e.g., the Village Gate). She has traveled to play in Europe and London.

She has had an NEA grant for composing and performing, and

served on NEA panels in 1988 and 1989. In 1988, she was on the State Department's panel to choose musicians for tours to represent the U.S. government.

The governor of the State of Washington presented her with a plaque for humanitarian service for the business community of Seattle on June 3, 1989. She was artist-in-residence at Howard University in 1989. And she received the Centrum Grant in Washington State for composing in 1990. With the University of Mexico Symphony Orchestra, she performed a piece by composer Rolf Lieberman.

She recorded jazz for Columbia, Prestige, Altantic, and r&b and pop for Motown and Scepter, and gospel for Savoy and Jubilee, working with Aretha Franklin, James Brown, Duke Ellington, Charles Mingus, Rahsaan Roland Kirk, Billy Eckstine, Benny Golson, Gene Ammons, Sonny Stitt, Marvin Gaye, Patti Labelle, Jimmy Rushing, Big Joe Turner, and others.

ANDREA BRACHFELD, New Jersey-based flautist, composer, and singer, leads a group, Phoenix Rising, with Rick Hozza, guitarist, and Jeff Presslaff, a pianist. She also plays in their groups. Most of her recording has been with Latin groups—for example, "Charanga 76." As leader, she recorded "Andrea," Casa Latina Records, 1978.

*JOANNE BRACKEEN, pianist, composer, and group leader, lives in New York.

KAREN BRIGGS, California-based violinist, works with Yanni, a New Age player, and for special events plays in a group with reeds player Ann Patterson, plus a cellist, an acoustic guitarist, and a percussionist. She plays mainstream jazz, Latin, and contemporary music. As part of a fiddle festival, she appeared in a duo with pianist Dave Grusin in Carnegie Hall. She has played in famous halls and theaters around the world, including Radio City Music Hall, and has appeared on "Soul Train" and "The Joan Rivers Show." With Soul to Soul, a British pop group, she toured Japan, Australia, and Bulgaria. She was nominated for a Grammy for her music for the soundtrack album of the TV show, "Thirtysomething," and led a group including Nedra Wheeler, bassist, for her album, "Just Karen," Vital Records, 1992.

CAROL BRITTO, pianist, works in New York clubs such as the Knickerbocker, the Village Corner, and Zinno's, tours in the United States, Canada, and Switzerland, and plays concerts at American colleges. Her albums as leader, on the Town Crier label, are "Alone Together," and "Inner Voices," both in the 1980s, available from Town Crier Recordings, 59 W. 19th St., New York, New York 10011. In the 1980s, she often performed with the late bassist, Major Holley.

Before moving to New York in 1984, she worked in Toronto for twenty-seven years. A Baldwin artist, she was organist for the Toronto Blue Jays and played with the Tommy Dorsey band in the 1970s.

BERNICE BROOKS, drummer, plays in New York clubs such as La Cave on First with singer Jeree Wade and pianist Frank Owen. She also plays with a Latin-rock-pop group, the T-Dolls, and with Toshi Reagon, daughter of Bernice Reagon Johnson of Sweet Honey in the Rock, and with singer-pianist Terri Thornton. For four years she played for the gospel show, "Mama, I Want to Sing," with which she toured Japan. She has played with shows in workshops: "A Thrill a Moment" at the Henry Street Settlement House Playhouse, and "God's Trombone" at the Riverside Church. Praised for her work in Kit McClure's band, she played at the Inaugural Ball for President Clinton.

CLEO PATRA BROWN, pianist, born in 1907, the daughter of a strict Baptist minister, first played in church, then became a jazz and boogie woogie musician. For a while she was caught up in life in the fast lane. Tiring of that, she became a Seventh Day Adventist in the 1950s, changed her focus to church music, and settled in Denver. In 1989, she traveled to Atlanta to be a guest on Marian McPartland's "Piano Jazz." Patra Brown, as she preferred to be called by then, played for the Park Hill Seventh Day Adventist Church in Denver, Colorado.

CLORA BRYANT, trumpeter and composer, a Los Angeles resident from 1945 to 1993, moved to New York to finish work on her biographical "Suite for Dizzy," for which she had her third NEA grant. She incorporated songs by Dizzy Gillespie, at his request, into the suite. In 1993, Clora was honored at the University of Massachusetts at Amherst for her contributions to American music. In April 1993, she served as music director for a tribute to Dizzy in California, with trumpeters Jon Faddis, Clark Terry, Freddie Hubbard, Marcus Belgrave, Oscar Brashear, Al Aarons, and Chuck Findley. In May 1993, she attended and wrote articles about the International Women's Brass Conference at Washington University in St. Louis.

In the late 1980s, she toured Europe with the Johnny Otis band, then with Jeannie and Jimmy Cheatham, and played at the Hotel Meridien in Paris, with her son, Kevin Milton, a drummer, and visited the Soviet Union to perform in five concerts accompanied by her son Darrin, a singer. Her only available recording, "Gal With a Horn," done in 1957, was reissued on VSOP, a Japanese label.

JANE BUNNETT, Toronto-based flautist and soprano saxophonist, leads her own group with trumpeter Larry Cramer, her husband, and also co-leads Music in Monk Time with Jane Fair. At the Hennessey Greenwich Village Jazz Festival, Jane recorded "Live at Sweet Basil," Denon-Canada, 1990. She also did "New York Duets," with pianist Don Pullen, on Music & Arts Programs of America, 1989.

She has visited Cuba many times, where she has played in Havana's International Jazz Festival, winning critical acclaim. In Paris, using her Canada Arts Council grant in 1993, she was praised by Mike Zwerin in the *International Herald-Tribune* as a improvising experimentalist who has risen above sexual bias and explored Afro-Cuban music. Her album, "Spirits of Havana," Denon, 1991, is unavailable in the United States.

She led the Critics Poll for soprano saxophonists in the Talent Deserving Wider Recognition category, *Down Beat* magazine, 1992. She has ranked as TDWR previously. In winter, 1992–93, she led a group at Sweet Basil.

ELAINE BURT, experienced trumpeter, moved from Tyler, Texas, to New York in 1993.

**ANN HAMPTON CALLOWAY, singer and pianist, is a major attraction in New York nightclubs, cabarets, and supper clubs.

VALERIE CAPERS, critically lauded pianist and composer, has received two NEA grants for composition. With one she wrote an "operatoria," as she calls it, about the life of Sojourner Truth, staged by Opera Ebony in New York. In 1987, she had a commission from the Smithsonian Institution to write a classical work for voice, piano, and cello, "Song of the Seasons," praised in the *Washington Post*. Commissions for jazz compositions have come from the Research Foundation of City University of New York and the New York All City Chorus. Her Christmas cantata, "Song About Love," was presented in 1974 at St. Peter's Lutheran Church, then produced by George Wein at Carnegie Hall. Mongo Santamaria had a big hit with her song, "El Toro."

She has performed in concert halls in the United States and played in European festivals—la Grande Parade du Jazz in Nice, France, and the Hague, Holland's North Sea Festival. In 1982, she appeared on a video *Jazz in America,* Sony Corp., with Dizzy Gillespie in Redondo Beach, California.

She believes she's the only sightless person with bachelor's and master's degrees in music from Juilliard. She's chairman of the music department at Bronx Community College, within CUNY, and conducts jazz workshops around the country for students from elementary grades to college. Her last recording as leader was "Affirmation," KMA Arts, 1982.

She has never been aware of discrimination against her in the jazz world because of her visual handicap, but when calls for work did not come—probably because she is a woman, she has mused—she turned to teaching for security as well as satisfaction.

*JUDY CARMICHAEL, stride pianist, lives in New York.

*TERRI LYNE CARRINGTON, drummer, composer, leader, lives in Los Angeles.

BARBARA CARROLL, pianist who originally became prominent as a swinging musician in the early days of bebop's development, has worked at Bemelmans Bar at the Hotel Carlyle for six months a year—October through December and April through June—since 1978. In the 1990s, she played for several months at the Westwood Marquis Hotel in Los Angeles. Among her concerts—some solo, others with rhythm sections—was one in a series at the 92nd St. YMHA/YWHA in New York in July 1993. New albums available are "Live at the Carlyle," on the DRG label, 1991, and "Old Friends," Audiophile Records, 1989. She also recorded "Let It Snow! Let It Snow! Let It Snow!" for a Christmas collection for DRG, 1993.

ELISE CATERA, New York-based flautist and composer, who plays classical music as well as jazz, and doubles on alto sax, performed at the Blue Willow, West End Gate, La Cave on First, and Hudson Bar and Books, in duos and quartets in the 1990s. Supporting herself with a day job, she hires musicians for jazz groups. "Sometimes I pay the musicians myself. I take responsibility for that. Some places pay us the door [admission fee], and then if there isn't a huge crowd, I have to pay musicians," she says.

*CAROL CHAIKIN, alto and soprano saxophonist, who also plays the EWI (electric wind instrument,) lives in New York.

JEANNIE CHEATHAM, singer, pianist, in her bluesy band with her husband, Jimmy, appears at the Blue Note, on the "Today" and "Tonight" TV shows, and travels to Europe to play at Nice and The Hague jazz festivals, and other places. Among the Cheathams' albums are "Blues and Boogie Masters," 1993; "Back to the Neighborhood," "Basket Full of Blues," in 1992; "Homeward Bound," "Luv' in the Afternoon," in 1990; and "Midnight Mama," all on the Concord label. She has appeared on McPartland's "Piano Jazz."

The Cheathams won the Grand Prix du Disques in France for their first album, "Sweet Baby Blues," Concord, and have been nominated for W. C. Handy awards. In 1993 and previous years they ranked in *Down Beat's* Talent Deserving Wider Recognition category. They played in a TV special—their concept—"Three Generations of the Blues," with Sippie Wallace and Big Mama Thornton. The show won a critics award at the International Film and Television Festival of New York.

SARAH CION, pianist and composer, has played in Kit McClure's band, with which she toured Portugal and Japan. She leads her own trio in New York clubs and also in Boston Globe Jazz Festivals in 1989 and 1990. She has performed at the Banff School for the Arts in Canada and played with tenor saxophonist Shlomo Goldenberg for his CD, "To You," released on an Israeli label. She has received three NEA grants for study in the 1990s and the Boston Jazz Society Award in 1988. She teaches at Mt. Vernon Music Academy, Westchester County, New York. In 1994, she played with Diva.

*KIM CLARKE, acoustic and electric bassist, is based in New York.

CECELIA COLEMAN, highly praised pianist, has her own CD out,

"Words of Wisdom," on L.A.P. Records, 1993, and has played on a CD led by Benn Clatworthy, jazz tenor player, "Thanks Horace," on Discovery, 1989. Also recorded were "Long Ago and Far Away," with Dan St. Marseille, on Resurgence, 1993, and a ten-piece ensemble album led by Jimmy Cleveland, trombonist, for VTL Records. She leads her own trio in Los Angeles and has played with Lee Konitz, Jack Sheldon, Eddie Harris, and others in concerts and clubs.

GLORIA COLEMAN, New Jersey-based organist and pianist, worked with alto saxophonist Sonny Stitt until his death in the 1980s. She plays in Rose's Restaurant in Atlantic City, with saxophonist Pete Chevez, a bassist, and drummer Duck Scott, Shirley Scott's son. Gloria's son, drummer George Coleman Jr., played with her in an outdoor concert for WBGO in Newark, New Jersey, in June 1993. She is on a Hank Crawford album, done in the 1990s, including her composition "There's a Way." On Etta Jones's recent Christmas album are Gloria's tunes "Christmas Time" and "Ring the Bells." On Boston-based saxophonist Nat Simpkin's album, Gloria plays piano.

FELICIA COLLINS, guitarist, from Albany, New York, crosses from pop to jazz.

JOYCE COLLINS, pianist, teaches privately and taught at the Dick Grove School, a music college, for the duration of its existence. In 1990, she was named Jazz Educator of the Year by the Los Angeles Jazz Society. On her album, "Sweet Madness," Audiophile, 1990, she led Andy Simpkins and Octavio Bailly, bassists, and Ralph Penland and Claudio Slon, drummers. She has been on Marian McPartland's "Piano Jazz."

In 1993, she was preparing a solo album and planning a return trip to Rio de Janeiro, Brazil, to do seminars, concerts, and recordings. She plays in the Jazz Bakery and other Los Angeles clubs.

Her album "Street of Dreams," 1980, was nominated for a Grammy. She performed at Michael's Pub in a program called "A Fusion of Ellington and Gershwin," 1982, and at Bradley's in New York with bassists Red Mitchell and Michael Moore in the 1980s. In Los Angeles studios, she has played for the Mary Tyler Moore and Bob Newhart shows, and others.

**ALICE COLTRANE, pianist, composer, organist, widow of John Coltrane, based on the West Coast, played at a concert for an enormous audience at the Cathedral Church of St. John the Divine in New York in the 1980s. Her recording, "Journey to Satchidanada," is on the Impulse label.

ROBIN CONNELL, pianist and composer, worked in New York in the 1980s, then received a graduate degree at the University of Northern Colorado, and from 1989 through 1993 taught jazz at Interlochen Center for the Arts in northern Michigan. With an NEA grant for teaching and performance, she moved, as artist-in-residence, to Garden City Community College in Kansas. A member of Robin's current quartet is flautist and artist-in-residence Jill Allen.

INDIA COOK, violinist, is based in San Francisco.

GLORIA COOPER, pianist and vocalist, plays in trendy New York rooms and teaches at Long Island University in Brooklyn. From 1972 to 1988, she lived in San Francisco, where she played in hotels and jazz clubs and taught in Chabot Junior College in Hayward.

SHEILA COOPER, plays alto and tenor saxophones with Kit McClure, subs in Diva, and leads her own quartet in Birdland, the Squire, Caliban, and the Brooklyn Arts Council. She has played for *Cabaret* and other Broadway shows and toured Japan, the Middle East, and Europe, playing jazz and r&b. Born in Canada, she moved to New York in 1983 with a Canada Arts Council grant. She recorded an original composition for an industrial film for a Sony Corp. product.

**MARILYN CRISPELL, a classically trained avant-garde pianist, praised by the critics for her intensity and imagination, sometimes leads her own groups at the Knitting Factory and frequently performs with Anthony Braxton's quartet. Among her albums are "Live in Berlin," 1982, reissued by Black Saint, 1993; "Live in San Francisco," 1989, "Highlights from the Summer of 1992 American Tour," with bassist Reggie Workman and drummer Gerry Hemingway; "The Marilyn Crispell Trio," 1993, all on Music & Arts Programs of America. She was in *Down Beat*'s Critics Poll for Talent Deserving Wider Recognition in 1993.

CONNIE CROTHERS, pianist, experimentalist, who improvises her performances, has played at the Blue Note, Sweet Basil, the West End Cafe in New York, and in European countries. Her quartet's drummer is Carol Tristano, daughter of the late pianist and teacher Lennie Tristano; bassist is Cameron Brown, and tenor saxophonist is Lenny Popkin. Among Crothers's albums are "Swish," done with Max Roach in 1982 and reissued in 1993 on New Artists, Crothers's label. Also on new Artists are "Concert at Cooper Union," "New York Night" recorded at the Blue Note, "Love Energy," and "In Motion." Crothers recorded "Solo" on the Jazz Records label and "Perception" issued in 1974 on Steeplechase and reissued by Inner City in the 1980s; that album received special critical attention in the mid-1980s.

*SYLVIA CUENCA, drummer, lives in New York.

BEVERLY DAHLKE, Los Angeles-based baritone saxophonist and doubler on other instruments, has played with the orchestra for *The Will Rogers Follies* at the Pantages theater, the Dallas Jazz Orchestra, the Hollywood bowl Orchestra, and toured with Doc Severinsen's band and in the past Harry James's orchestra. She and her husband, baritone saxophonist

Greg Smith, made on album, "Mr. and Mrs. Smith and No Baggage," Intima Records, 1980s. She plays in studios in Los Angeles.

CLAIRE DALY, baritone saxophonist in Diva, doubles on alto, tenor, and flute. She has played with Joel Forrester, pianist and composer, in Greenwich Village and SoHo clubs. As a composer she works with Dan Froot, who has had grants for composition. She recorded in the horn section with Taj Mahal on "Like Never Before," Private Music label, 1991.

**MEREDITH D'AMBROSIO, singer and recording artist, also plays piano. Her recordings, all on Sunnyside, are: "Another Time," 1981; "It's Your Dance," 1985; "The Cove," 1988; "South to a Warmer Place," 1989; "Little Jazz Bird," 1990; "Love Is Not a Game," 1991; "Shadowland," 1992. She has starred at the Tavern on the Green in Central Park.

DARDANELLE (HADLEY), singer, vibraphonist and pianist, came to New York as a player, started singing, and modeled her popular trio after Nat King Cole's in the 1940s. She moved to Chicago in the mid-1950s and worked for WGN radio and television until 1961. Based in Winona, Mississippi, she works in the United States and London, where she recorded at Pizza on the Park for two CDs for Audiophile.

Her other Audiophile albums are "A Woman's Intuition," "Dardanelle Down Home," and "That's My Style" with Dag Walton's big band for which she played vibes and sang. Stash released "Sounds of the Apple," with Dardanelle and Slam Stewart and Company, and has reissued two of her albums on CDs named "Colors of My Life." In the history books, she was praised by Mary Lou Williams and others.

**RUTH DAVIES, bassist, based in San Francisco, where she has played in a group with pianist Jane Hastay, worked with singer and pianist Charles' Brown's group in 1993. Brown became prominent with his Nat "King" Cole style trio in the 1940s.

JEAN DAVIS, trumpeter, recently played with the Big Apple Jazzwomen in various concerts. She also works in clubs in New York and at the Peppermint Lounge, Orange, New Jersey. She lived through the era when people told her to stay in the kitchen and stop taking jobs away from men, she says. She played with the Jazz Sisters. "Everyone was good in that band," she says.

SUE DAVIS, percussionist, plays on singer/composer Tom Brigg's album, "Moonlight," available directly from Briggs, P.O. Box 34328, Los Angeles, California 90034-0328.

**BLOSSOM DEARIE, prominent pianist and singer in jazz history, has starred at the Ballroom. Her albums are "Blossom Dearie" on Verve, and "Christmas Spice So Very Nice," "Et Tu, Bruce," and "May I Come In?" on the Daffodil label.

CLAIRE DeBRUNNER, bassoonist, plays in jazz and improvisatory groups at the Knitting Factory, Cornelia Street Cafe, and other places.

BEATRIZ DeMELLO, pianist from Brazil, was playing professionally in New York clubs and restaurants by 1993.

**BARBARA DENNERLEIN, highly praised organist from Germany, made her recording debut as leader with "Straight Ahead," for Enja in 1990. The came "Hot Stuff," Enja, 1991, and "That's Me," 1992, on Mesa Blue Moon. She was ranked as one of the top organists in *Down Beat*'s Critics Poll, 1993.

DIANNE DeROSA-PARKE, baritone saxophonist, who doubles on clarinet, bass clarinet, and flute, played in a jazz concert led by Clark Terry at Town Hall in the 1980s. She worked with Kit McClure and with the Ringling Brothers Circus, 1982 to 1990. She also traveled with Broadway orchestras for such shows as *Evita,* and played in summer stock orchestras.

DENA DeROSE, pianist and singer, came from Binghamton to New York in 1992, to study, work consistently in restaurants and clubs, and plan for a far-ranging career.

**JOYCE DiCAMILLO, pianist, was living in New York in the 1980s.

BOEL DIRKE, Swedish pianist, plays in the Cornelia Street Cafe and other rooms and with a group of friends in jams. Her album "Sweet Fulfillment," with her husband, Andy Fite, guitarist and singer, and tenor saxophonist Charley Krachy, came out on New Artists in 1994.

*DIVA, an all-women big band, made its New York debut at New York University, Leob's Student Center, on March 29, 1993.

FOSTINA DIXON, highly praised flautist, clarinetist, soprano-alto-baritone saxophonist, composer, and singer, leads her group Winds of Change. She had an NEA grant in 1980 for study and served on the NEA panel in 1989. Dr. Billy Taylor presented her with the Eubie Blake Award for artistic excellence and gratitude for her contribution to jazz, given in 1986.

On the album "Our Music Is Your Music," Esoteric, 1980, she was a featured soloist, with baritone and clarinet, with the Leslie Drayton Big Band from California. She also recorded with James Blood Ulmer in the late 1980s. She has worked with Roy Ayers, Tom Browne, the trumpeter, Gil Evans, Cab Calloway, Charli Persip, Bobby Vinton, Melba Liston, Slide Hampton, Frank Foster, Gerald Wilson, with whom she recorded in 1981, and Jimmy Cleveland. Her first professional gig was with Marvin Gaye. She has also played in orchestras for Joe Williams, Nancy Wilson, and Sammy Davis, Jr.

She teaches a woodwind choir of flutes and clarinets in P.S. 183 in

Brownsville, Brooklyn. She taught music in the summer of 1992 at the Jackie Robinson Center for Physical Culture. In 1991 and 1992, she toured for five months in twelve countries in Europe, playing concerts and conducting workshops. She has also taught workshops at New York University, the New School, and other schools.

She has played in the New York Summer Arts Festival, Third Annual Black Women's History Conference in New Jersey, the Kool and Greenwich Village Jazz Festivals, Third Heritage Arts and Humanities Festival, Jackie Robinson Festivals, and the 14th annual Afrikan Festival in Brooklyn in 1993, and others.

GAYLE DIXON, classical violinist, also plays jazz and records for albums and film soundtracks. From 1987 into the 1990s, she played in the Broadway orchestra for *Phantom of the Opera,* among her many Broadway credits. She also works in classical orchestras and chamber groups for diverse cultural events. A member of the Quartette Indigo founded in 1972, she also played for a while in the Uptown String Quartet. Those quartets had some overlapping of personnel in the 1980s. Quartette Indigo's personnel now includes her sister, cellist Akua Dixon Turre, violist Melvin Roundtree and violinist John Blake. In the 1990s, they played in the Berlin Jazz Festival, at Lincoln Center Out Of Doors, and at colleges and concert halls in the northeastern United States. See AKUA TURRE for the quartet's recording activity.

Gayle played for the video of *Black and Blue* telecast on Great Performances on Channel 13, WNET-TV, in New York and over the Public Broadcasting System. She was a very prominent soloist for the title tune of the album "Louella," led by flutist James Newton, on the Gramavision label, 1994.

She served on the executive board of the American Federation of Musicians, Local 802, from 1986 to 1993, for which she acted as a trustee of various funds and the musicians assistance program and as a spokesperson on minority issues.

LUCILLE DIXON, bassist, left Brooklyn College for two years to play with the International Sweethearts of Rhythm, then worked with Earl Hines's band, 1943–44—probably the first female bass player with a name band. After a long career written about in history books, including her work at Radio City Music Hall, she played for shows at the Westchester Broadway Theatre, in Elmsford, New York, 1974 to 1991. She also played in community orchestras.

She recorded with Tiny Grimes for Atlantic, with Ella Fitzgerald on Norman Granz's label, and with Dinah Washington on her first record after she left Lionel Hampton, and in the 1980s played in a Kool Jazz Festival concert at Carnegie Hall. Though technically retired by 1993, she divided her time between New Rochelle, New York, and Puerto Rico. A member of the unions in both places, she sits in with bands on the island.

*DOTTIE DODGION, drummer, settled in California after her work for a Washington, D.C., area club came to an end and then Melba Liston's group broke up in th 1980s. All her professional life, she was helped and encouraged by pros, she reminisced—first her father, a drummer, and then her husbands, bassist Monty Budwig and alto saxophonist Jerry Dodgion. By 1990, she moved to work in Monterey, California, with leader Jackie Coon, flugelhornist, guitarist Eddie Erickson, and bassist Eugene Wright. Her career, which is well delineated in Sally Placksin's book, has included complicated experiences because of sexual bias.

With Coon's group, she sings and plays on a CD, "Live One Take," the Breakers label, 1993. She recorded her first vocal album with Arbor Records in August, 1993.

HANA DOLGIN, saxophonist, born in the United States, raised in Israel, played in a duo with a pianist in Man Ray and with her quartet, Hana and Her Brothers, at Birdland and Yardbird Suite, New York, 1993. She has worked with singer Evelyn Blakey.

**BARBARA DONALD, saxophonist, pianist, singer, is reported to be living in the State of Washington.

*DOROTHY DONEGAN, pianist, singer, concert artist, lives in Los Angeles, California. In early 1993, she was honored at the University of Massachusetts at Amherst for her contributions to American music. She received a $20,000 grant from the NEA in the 1990s, among her other honors.

**DIANE DRAKE, former trumpeter with Kit McClure and the Harp Band, Las Chicas de Nueva York, La Contessa, and other Latin bands, leads a quartet and quintet on Long Island. She was organizing a big band with men and some women players in this book, among them Bienenfeld, Mayhew, and Lilly White.

LAUREN DRAPER, trumpeter, formerly played with Kit McClure.

*LAURA DREYER, saxophonist and composer, plays with Diva and leads her own groups to showcase her compositions in New York clubs. She has had three NEA grants for performance and for composition—the most recent in 1992 to study with Lyle Mays, the keyboardist with guitarist Pat Metheny. She has also worked with Brazilian pianist Dom Salvador, pianist Walter Bishop, Jr., and once subbed with Mel Lewis's band at the Vanguard. She used to co-lead a group with Carol Chaikin, in which Mel Lewis, Larry Willis, Ron McClure, and Victor Lewis, the drummer, played at various times. She arranged a chart of one of her compositions for Diva's engagement at Tavern on the Green in New York in August 1993.

**CANDY DULFER, pop jazz saxophonist, has played at the North Sea Jazz Festival at The Hague, Holland, on Arsenio Hall's TV show, and in many concerts—at Town Hall, New York, for example. Recordings are

"Saxuality," Arista, 1991, which was nominated for a Grammy and certified gold, and "Sax-A-Go-Go," RCA Records, 1993. Her song, "Lily Was Here," is in an Arista compilation; another song, "Sunday Afternoon," is on *Jazziz* magazine's CD, Jazziz on Disc, 1993. Daughter of a Dutch saxophonist, she leads her own band, Funky Stuff, and has worked with Prince, Madonna, Aretha Franklin, Van Morrison, and Pink Floyd.

**AMY DUNCAN, pianist, composer, bandleader, writer for the *Christian Science Monitor,* who led her own band at the Blue Note in the 1980s, moved to Brazil in 1993.

MADELINE DURAN, saxophonist, is in the San Francisco area.

KAT DYSON, Virginia-born guitarist, lives in Montreal, where she primarily plays and sings the blues. She also performs in pop, jazz, and gospel groups, aware of an increasing number of women who play keyboards, bass, guitar, drums, and saxophones in Montreal.

**SHEILA E, percussionist, formerly with Prince, and daughter of musician Pete Escovedo, California, sings on jazz pianist Michael Wolff's self-titled album for Columbia in 1993. She has made her own video, *Live-Romance,* Warner Reprise Video, and albums, "Romance," "Sex Cymbal," 1991, "Sheila E," and "The Glamorous Life," all on Warner Brothers Records.

ELIANE ELIAS, Brazilian-born keyboardist, occasional singer, group leader, recording artist, and award winner, played with Steps Ahead in the 1980s before leading her own group. Leonard Feather gave her the Golden Feather Award in the *Los Angeles Times,* and her albums go to the top of the radio popularity charts for jazz. A jazz recording, "Paulistana" on the Blue Note label, and "On The Classical Side," her first classical album, done for EMI Classics, were released in 1993, and both were critically praised and won her such notice as a cover photo on *Jazziz* magazine. She lives in New York.

CECILIA ENGELHART, singer, has played shakers, temple blocks, cowbells, and more percussion in groups lead by Cuban-born reeds player Paquito D'Rivera, and Brazilian percussionist Airto, and Willie Colon, and Martinique-born percussionist Mino Cinelu, and bassist Santi Debriano. She has written lyrics for Paquito, Claudio Roditi, and New York Voices. With her own Brazilian/Latin jazz band, Tanaora, she has played original compositions at Yard Bird Suite and other clubs and festivals in the New York area, and in Mexico and Turkey.

SUE EVANS, percussionist and drummer, works and lives in New York. She studied with Warren Smith. When he was asked to sub for a percussionist in Judy Collins's group, he couldn't make it and recommended Sue, then a high school student. She worked for Collins for years. That exposure led to studio work—eventually as many as ten to twelve sessions a week for jingles and recordings. When synthesizers started to displace musicians, Evans turned to orchestral and chamber work and other live performances.

In addition to playing with the New York Philharmonic Orchestra occasionally and as the regular percussionist with the New York Pops Orchestra, she often works with the Brooklyn Philharmonic and the New Jersey Symphony Orchestras. She worked with arranger-composer-bandleader Gil Evans, recording with him on "Ampex 1969," and touring in South East Asia and Europe. She has a master's degree from Juilliard, where she is a doctoral candidate. She had teaching fellowships there in ear training and theory. She has played with scores of famous pop and jazz musicians in live performances and on recordings—among them Jon Faddis and Wynton Marsalis at Carnegie Hall, and Aretha Franklin at Radio City, and on recordings with George Benson, Lee Ritenour, Eddie Daniels, Derek Smith and Venus, Michael Franks, Art Farmer, Urbie Green, Jeremy Steig, Hubert Laws, and Marvin Stamm. She played for the video, *Peter Paul and Mommy, Too!*, a concert, on Warner Brothers, and for soundtracks for Spike Lee's *Jungle Fever* and *Malcolm X*.

She won the National Academy of Recording Arts and Sciences Most Valuable Player Award in 1984 for mallets and timpani, and the same award for Latin percussion and congos in 1987 and 1989.

ROBERTA FABIANO, guitarist and singer, was in New York in the 1980s.

JANE FAIR, Toronto-based tenor and soprano saxophonist and flute player, where she plays in concerts and clubs, also performs with the group the Velvet Glove in the Canadian jazz festivals, in Quebec City, Montreal, Toronto, Edmonton, Saskatoon, Calgary, Vancouver, Victoria, and Ottawa, along with trumpeter Stacy Rowles, pianist Jill McCarron, drummer Sherrie Maricle, and bassist Rosemary Galloway. Jane teaches in private sessions and as a freelance instructor in Toronto schools. Velvet Glove's first album was "Round One," Fishhorn Records, 1992; a second CD was recorded. She has also recorded on a CBC Transcription Series on the CTL label (Canadian Talent Library) in the 1970s.

KATHI FARMER, New York-based singer, organist, and pianist, graduate of the New England Conservatory of Music, fell in love with playing the organ when she subbed in a group for her schoolmate, saxophonist Ricky Ford, at Wally's in Boston. Later working in Harlem's Red Rooster, Showman's, La Famille, Baby Grand and Blue Book, she attracted great jazz organists to her gigs; they taught her fine points of organ playing— Jimmy McGriff, Jimmy Smith, and Lonnie Smith. Jack McDuff gave her private lessons. In saxophonist Lou Donaldson's group at DeFemio's, Yonkers, she played in the funky style, similar to Eddie Lockjaw Davis's work with Shirley Scott, that she had liked in her father's extensive organ records collection. In 1992, she toured as organist with Lester Bowie's Organ Ensemble in Spain.

In virtually a separate career, Kathi sings, occasionally accompanying herself on piano but preferring to stand up to sing, with pianist Walter Bishop, Jr., and others. Pianist Kirk Lightsey played when she sang with Brook Benton in the 1980s.

ZUSAAN KALI FASTEAU, emphasizing improvisation, composes, plays many instruments, and produces recordings for her own label, Flying Note. She sings and plays soprano saxophone, ney (an Arabic flute), shakuhachi (a Japanese flute), piano, cello, sanza (a thumb piano), mizmar (a reed instrument), jew's harp, trap drums, and percussion instruments such as Brazil's berimbau, for jazz, world, and experimental music.

Her CD, "Prophecy: The Whale and the Elephant Trade Notes on the State of the World," Flying Note, 1993, was in the top ten for airplay on college radio stations, as reported by the *College Music Journal*. She released "World Beyond Words," a Flying Note CD, 1989, and made five more albums as leader and three with co-leader Donald Rafael Garrett. She also recorded two albums with Archie Shepp.

She played in concerts in India, Europe, Turkey, Africa, and the United States from 1970 to 1993. With a master's degree from Wesleyan University in world music, she traveled for about thirteen years in Asia, Africa, Haiti, and Europe, including Denmark, where she recorded with Marilyn Mazur as part of the International Women's Music Festival, for Olivia Records, Copenhagen, 1978. With Mazur, she played in the Montmartre club in Copenhagen and toured Europe. In New York, she has played at the Alternative Museum, Greenwich House, and Roulette for experimental music in TriBeca, the Blue Note, Knitting Factory, Donnell Library, and St. Peter's Lutheran Church, 1985–93, and avant-garde music festivals. Albums are available through Flying Note Records, P.O. Box. 1027, Canal Street Station, New York, New York, 10013–1027.

*STEPHANIE FAUBER, French horn player, lives in Santa Fe, New Mexico.

MARY FETTIG, saxophonist in San Francisco, performs in concerts, in orchestras for Broadway shows, and on records for Concord Jazz. She has appeared in Monterey, Concord, and Playboy at the Hollywood Bowl jazz festivals in California and at Montreux and the North Sea Festival in Europe. On the East Coast, she has worked with Flora Purim and Airto Moreiro and Marian McPartland. In 1973, she was the first female instrumentalist to travel with Stan Kenton's band. She toured with Tito Puente on the West Coast in late 1980s. Her album as leader is "In Good Company," Concord, mid-1980s, with Marian McPartland, Ray Brown, bass, Peter Sprague, guitar, and Jeff Hamilton, drums. She also played in Tito Puente's band on Concord and for small labels and movie soundtracks, for example, a *Star Wars* CD with the music re-recorded, and Garfield the Cat specials, and *Soap Dish*.

* and ** JEAN FINEBERG, tenor saxophonist, co-leader of Deuce, a fusion band, with trumpeter Ellen Seeling, was last known to be living in

San Francisco. "Deuce" is the name of their album. In 1991, Deuce received a Reader's Choice Award for Wind Players from *Hot Wire, The Journal of Women's Music and Culture.*

**ROBERTA FLACK, starring pianist and singer, has made many albums on the Atlantic label, including "Set the Night to Music," 1991, "Oasis," 1988, "I'm the One," 1982, "Best of Roberta Flack," 1981, "Roberta Flack Featuring Donny Hathaway," 1980, and several others in the 1970s—"Chapter Two," "Feel Like Making Love," "Quiet Fire," "Killing Me Softly," and "Roberta Flack and Donny Hathaway," and her first album, "First Take," 1969.

PAM FLEMING, trumpeter, singer, based in Brooklyn, subs with Kit McClure's band. She's a member of a horn section that began as Steppin' Razor, with Jenny Hill, saxophonist, and Nilda Richards, trombonist. When it opened a festival concert for the reggae band Burning Spear, that group hired the women. In 1985, they formed their own reggae-based horn section, Burning Brass, adding funk and rap to the repertoire.

Burning Brass won the Brooklyn Lager World Beat Competition and was featured at the Burlington, Vermont, Reggae Festival in 1990. The women have played with Maxi Priest, a reggae group (which had a top ten hit, "I Just Want To Be Close to You.") Pam has made a demo tape with her own group, Fearless Dreamer. The group's style is "celestial rock," she says. "It's soft rock and love songs."

In 1993, Burning Brass played at the Plattsburgh, New York, festival, the Lakeside Reggae Jam, and with a rhythm section in a castle converted to a concert hall in Stuttgart, Germany.

*EILEEN FOLSON, cellist in the Uptown String Quartet, was a member of the Black Swan Quartet, a jazz group in the 1980s, with one violin, two cellos and a bass. She has many prestigious credits as a cellist in classical music. In 1993, she worked in Rainbow and Stars with the Lerner and Loewe review.

**KIM FORMAN, pianist, based in New York, plays in the United States and tours Europe.

MIMI FOX, San Francisco-based guitarist, has recorded two albums as leader, "Against the Grain," Catero Records, 1987, nominated for a Bay Area Music Award for Outstanding Jazz Album, and "Mimi Fox Live," TuSco, 1993, recorded live at Yoshi's in Oakland, 1991. Inspired as a teenager to play jazz when she heard John Coltrane's "Naima," she has played in scores of clubs, including Blues Alley in Washington, D.C., Foxy's in Minneapolis, the New York Hilton, Kimball's in San Francisco and Oakland, and at the Kansas City and Michigan Women's Jazz Festivals, and colleges ranging from Yale to San Francisco State University. Among the people she has worked with are singers Holly Near, Linda Tillery, Rhiannon, and pianist Julie Homi.

ARETHA FRANKLIN, soul singer, organist and pianist, based in Detroit, is busy with concerts and recording dates. Mentioned on the cover of *Newsweek* magazine as one of the older r&b stars who could still thrill audiences, she has many albums available—on Rhino Records, Atlantic, Arista, Mobile Fidelity Ultradisc, and Chess, and a video, *The Queen of Soul,* A*Vision Entertainment.

*REBECCA COUPE FRANKS, trumpeter, composer, lives in New York.

(AHNEE) SHARON FREEMAN (her adopted first name means "The Tribe" in several American Indian languages), pianist and French horn player, primarily played horn with George Gruntz's band in studios and radio stations in Europe and in festivals and concerts in the United States and Europe in the 1980s. She composed and conducted for a concert, recorded by the BBC, with Gale Force at the Camden Jazz Festival and other British sites.

She has toured in Europe with Charlie Haden, David Murray, and others. With NEA grants, she arranged the music of Mary Lou Williams, for production by the Nanette Bearden Dance Company, and composed "Time Piece" for a big band. She has had Meet the Composer grants and a New York States Council of the Arts grant for composition.

In 1993, she was working as musical director for Jazzmobile Workshop and the Bearden Company. She was composing an opera; one aria, "Free Space," sung by Jeanne Lee, was released on a CD, "Natural Affinities," Owl label, 1992. Sharon was also working as musical director and pianist on "Queenie Pie," Duke Ellington's opera for production in New York halls. She's a partner in a concert production company, Freeman-Rowan, New York.

She has arranged, conducted, and played for Warner Brothers, A&M Records, a new label called Shemp, and Geffen Records. She is also writing a book about French horn player Julius Watkins.

JANICE FRIEDMAN, a pianist, toured with Woody Herman's orchestra in the late 1980s. From 1990 to 1992, she worked with her trio at the Sign of the Dove in New York. At the JVC Jazz Festival in 1991, her work was reviewed as "explosive piano playing that carried the aura and variety of a big band with only bass and drum accompaniment." She works with Warren Vache's trio; with Sue Terry and the Holy Terrors, along with bassist Sue Williams. In Nancy's trio, John Goldsby plays bass, Tim Horner, drums. Playing at Arthur's Tavern, she met Cedar Walton, the pianist, who asked her to sub for him at a Newark club. She has led a quintet album, "Finger Paintings," Jazz Mania, 1993, with bassist Goldsby, Tom Rainey, drums, Claudio Roditi and Rick Savage, trumpets.

As a child she won awards for classical piano from the Musical Education Council in 1971 and 1972, and second place in an international competition. She began teaching at age ten.

NANCY FRIEDMAN, Latin percussionist in New York, plays with Nydia Mata in the Harp Band. She is also musical director of Retumba con Pie, which plays Afro Cuba, Latin, Puerto Rican, and Brazilian music as part of a dance group.

*LAURIE FRINK, trumpeter and teacher, lives in New York.

**ROSEMARY GALLOWAY, bassist, is a member of the Velvet Glove. See JANE FAIR for personnel, activities and album details. She leads a "trad" jazz band, the Swing Sisters; Jane Fair works in that too.

LORRAINE GELLER, pianist, who was married to saxophonist Herb Geller, died at age 30 in 1958. Her recordings have been reissued on "Memorial," a Fresh Sound CD.

JANE GETTER, guitarist, collaborates as a composer with drummer Lenny White, who worked with the group Return to Forever. Their tune, "Pablo," is on the album "Acoustic Masters," on Atlantic featuring Ron Carter, bassist, Bobby Hutcherson, vibes player, Lenny White, Mulgrew Miller, pianist, and others. Her song, "Road Town," is on the album, "In a Loud Way," Blue Note/Manhattan, led by her husband Adam Holzman, former keyboardist with Miles Davis.

She won an ASCAP/Gershwin Award for composing a dance piece. In her own group, she has played with pianist Richie Beirach and emergent jazz and jazz funk players in clubs. She has worked with drummer Jimmy Cobb in trumpeter Joe Shepley's group; with Lenny White; with Kit McClure; with pianist Michel Petrucciani at the Montpelier, France jazz festival. With her husband, she leads a jazz funk band, No Soap Radio, in clubs, with drummer Rocky Bryant from Cindi Lauper's band and the Family Stand, and bassist Freddie Cash from Jean-Paul Bourelly's group and also from Arrested Development. On tour with Jack McDuff, she played in festivals with David Fathead Newman and Hank Crawford. In 1994, she took a sabbatical from performing to have her first child.

PEGGY GILBERT, saxophone, clarinet, and vibes player, was a pioneer in all-girl bands and films in the 1940s. She currently has a Dixieland band, the Dixie Belles, which plays for special events, in clubs, and on TV in Los Angeles. She leads an album on cassette, "Peggy Gilbert and the Dixie Belles," Cambria Records, 1982. Another Cambria cassette has a sampling of her work from 1938 to the present. Born on January 17, 1905, she's this list's senior member.

MABLE GODWIN, singer who accompanied herself at the piano, retired after thirty-three years at Arthur's Tavern in Greenwich Village, 1993. Bassist Milt Hinton was host at her retirement party.

LIZ GORRILL, jazz pianist, plays improvisatory music at the Knitting Factory and other places.

JOANNE GRAUER, Los Angeles-based pianist and synthesizer player, plays in Monte Leone's in the San Fernando Valley, in Tarzana, and other clubs. She was credited for playing solo pianist for the film, *Nine and a Half Weeks*. She has done jingles, works in the studios, was discussing a possible film project for her to score, and working on an album of Charlie Chaplin's compositions—"Smile," for one—from his movies. She has coached Michael Feinstein for a performance at the Hollywood Bowl, Clint Eastwood for his piano playing in a film in which he played a secret service agent, Ellen Burstyn for the film, *Alice Doesn't Live Here Anymore,* and the late Audrey Hepburn for her role as a concert pianist in a TV film. Cassettes of "The Lonely Giraffe," her album of original music that she intended for use in healing animals, are available from Joanne Grauer, 6812 Woodrow Wilson Drive, Los Angeles, California 90068-1846.

CAROLA GREY, German-born drummer, group leader, composer, arranger, led her first recording, "Noisy Mama," on the Lipstick label. Based in New York, she tours in Europe with her own group, including saxophonist Ravi Coltrane, and she works with other groups there. She sits in at jam sessions at the Squire.

**JANET GRICE, bassoonist, has two albums, "The Muse," and "Song for Andy," on the Optimism label.

**JOYCE GRIMES, a bassist, played with Kit McClure's band.

CORKY HALE, pianist, harpist, and occasional flautist, lives in Los Angeles. Currently musical director for Hal David, who appeared at a concert in the U.S. Congress, she has also recently played at the Montreux Jazz Festival, Switzerland, recorded a "Piano Jazz" show with Marian McPartland, and performed at exclusive restaurants in Los Angeles and New York. She has a television, film, and theatre production company, Hale/Arnold Productions, Inc.

She is on several current recordings—as a harpist on "Bjork," by an Icelander rock singer, and on retrospective reissues of Tony Bennett and Barbra Streisand. Her career is in the history books. She accompanied Billie Holiday in 1957.

*KATHY HALVORSON, oboist, baritone saxophonist, flautist, based in Boston, toured Europe with Mingus's "Epitaph" in 1991, and played with George Russell's orchestra at Wolf Trap in 1992.

*PAULA HAMPTON, drummer, plays in clubs, for special events and on cruises in the New York area. She worked with singer Dakota Staton in the late 1980s and early 1990s.

FLORA HARRIMAN, trumpeter, has played with Kit McClure's band and the New Jersey National Guard band. She plays the cornetto as part of her fascination with early Renaissance music, though her focus is jazz.

JILL HARRIMAN, New York-based pianist, has led her own band and played with other leaders—for example, drummer Barbara Merjan.

LEE ANN HARRIS, Los Angeles-based percussionist, plays congas, bongos, timbales, and Indian, African, and electronic instruments, in new wave and popular jazz groups. She has recorded an album on Brainchild Records with the group Kilauea; she is also on Toni Childs's "The Women's Boat" on Gefen Records, and on guitarist Charles Broughtman's Brainchild album. She has played with guitarist Peter White and with trumpeter Rick Braun who has toured with the singer Sade.

JANE HASTAY, Minnesota-born pianist and composer, recipient of the Flora Boyd Award for piano at Mills College in Oakland, California, worked as an accompanist in groups for singer Denise Perrier in San Francisco until moving to New York in 1992. Married to bassist Peter Martin Weiss, she sometimes works with him in groups. Weiss has played for singer Etta Jones at the Blue Note for Saturday brunches. Jane is setting up an electronics studio and wants to compose for films and TV.

ANDREA HAVERBACK, pianist, lives in San Francisco and plays with Mimi Fox.

DAPHNE HELLMAN, harpist, had the sterling experience of being profiled by Whitney Balliett in *The New Yorker* magazine, December 1990, when she was seventy-five years old. In 1993, the spirited musician celebrated her 30th year of playing on the Village Gate's terrace. When it closed, she freelanced in other clubs. She also played in situations ranging from the subway, where she met a spoon player whom she performs with, to the Metropolis restaurant, at a convention at the Sheraton Hotel, at CBGB's, in schools and colleges, and at special events such as a benefit for the Martin Luther King Jr. Scholarship Fund at the Manhattan County School in May 1993. She worked years ago, under the direction of Julius Monk, at the Ruban Bleu and Upstairs at the Downstairs on New York's Upper East Side. Her albums are available from the Enterprising Shih label, 228 E. 61st St., New York, New York 10025.

DEBORAH HENSON-CONANT, harpist, based in Cambridge, Massachusetts, has recorded "Naked Music" released in 1994. Earlier recordings are "Budapest," White Cat Records label, and "Caught in the Act," "On the Rise," and "Talking Hands," a compilation in 1991, all on GRP Records. She has performed at such places as Blues Alley in Washington, outdoors at the World Trade Center in New York, and other clubs and concert halls. She tours Europe, usually in Germany, Britain, and France, for concerts and club dates; she has performed at the Montreal and Pori Jazz Festivals. She won the Boston Music Award for best instrumentalist in 1990 and had grants for composition from Meet the Composer and the NEA.

HILDEGARDE, known as The Incomparable, singer and pianist, turned eighty eight in 1994. In 1993 and 1994, she performed at the Algonquin Hotel, the Russian Tearoom, and other New York clubs.

JENNY HILL, tenor saxophonist, formerly with Kit McClure, co-leads Burning Brass, with Nilda Richards, trombonist, and trumpeter Pam Fleming. (See FLEMING for more details.) The group has backed up reggae artists Maxi Priest, Dennis Brown, Andrew Tosh, and others.

ELLEN HOFFMAN, pianist, is in the San Francisco area.

HOLLY HOFMANN, flautist, has made three albums, "Further Adventures" and "Take Note," both on Capri, and "Duo Personality," with guitarist Mundell Lowe, bassist Bob Magnusson, pianist Mike, Wofford, and Ronn Satterfield, guitarist, pianist, and vocalist, on Jazz Alliance, 1992. In 1993, she was working on a new album with bassist Ray Brown. She books entertainment and runs a jazz program at the Horton Grand Hotel in San Diego. She tours festivals and clubs in the United States, Japan, and Australia, and teaches college clinics.

Leonard Feather wrote in the *Los Angeles Times* in 1991: "she is on her way to becoming one of the major forces in jazz flute."

JULIE HOMI, pianist, synthesizer player, and composer, based in Los Angeles, tours for about three months of the year with Yanni. She has toured with Angela Bofill and Robert Palmer. She has led her own group, including Vicki Randle, percussionist and vocalist, at the Festival at the Lake in Oakland and in Los Angeles clubs.

**HELEN HOOK, violinist, plays in jazz and funk groups in New York.

*BERTHA HOPE, pianist, composer, lives in New York.

*SHIRLEY HORN, pianist and singer, lives in Washington, D.C. She has made a video, *Here's To Life,* Polygram Video, 1992, in addition to her very popular albums.

**BOBBI HUMPHREY, flautist, in California, has an album, "The Best of Bobbi Humphrey," Blue Note, and has appeared on late-night TV.

EFFIE JANSEN, singer and blues and jazz-influenced pianist, often works solo in New York clubs.

NADINE JANSEN, pianist, flugelhornist, singer, in Scottsdale, Arizona, plays solo in a little club, J. Chew's. She has also played at a women's jazz festival in Tucson. In 1988, at the women-in-jazz concert, Marian McPartland, Judy Roberts, and Nadine led their individual trios, then sat down at three grand pianos without side people and played together.

Nadine's albums are "A Little Taste," with John Daley, bass, Forrest Nye, drums, Bob Culbertson, guitar, 1990, and the release of "A la Mood," done originally in 1964. For cassettes, write to Jantone Records, 8485 East McDonald Drive, Suite 343, Scottsdale, Arizona, 85250.

JANE JARVIS, New York-based pianist, whose once was a vice-president of the Muzak Corporation, 1963 to 1979, plays in clubs, sometimes with bassist Milt Hinton. She has two albums on Audiophile Records—"Cut Glass" with bassist Jay Leonhart and drummer Grady Tate, and "L.A. Quartet," with tenor saxophonist Tommy Newsome, arranger for the Doc Severinsen band.

In 1993, she was involved in a project that she called "The biggest thing in my life." She wrote thirty-one songs and some lyrics for a musical, *Take Two,* that opened in a Honolulu theater in 1993. Comprised of all styles of music, even an Argentine tango, the play ended with a jazz waltz. "So it's good for young women to know you can put jazz to work anywhere," she said.

In January 1993, Lionel Hampton, Clark Terry, and Milt Hinton celebrated her career with a party at the Chelsea Center, Long Island. "It was just like Ralph Edwards and 'This is Your Life,' with people who started with me in radio stations, former bosses from television, fans from Switzerland. It was amazing, two hundred people, including musicians who played—Grady Tate, Bucky Pizzarelli, Warren Vache, Al Grey, Oliver Jackson, and bassist Mark Elf and others. It was a fun party, I'll tell you that. It was non-stop music." She's in the history books.

SONYA JASON, Nebraska-born, Phoenix-raised alto saxophonist who doubles on flute and soperanino saxophone (an octave above the alto, in the key of E flat), plays jazz in the David Sanborn style. Sanborn and Phil Woods were her main influences. Her CD is "Tigress," Discovery label, 1993. Her band plays her music and compositions by Sanborn, Grover Washington Jr., Spyro Gyro, and Kenny G. in such clubs as the Baked Potato in North Hollywood, Jax's Bar and Grill in Glendale, and Le Cafe in Sherman Oaks. Women have played in her band—keyboardists Kathy Shoemaker in Los Angeles and Beth Lederman in Phoenix, and guitarist Linda Taylor in Los Angeles.

INGRID JENSEN, Canadian-born trumpeter and flugelhornist, who plays with Diva, taught jazz at the Bruckner Conservatory in Linz, Austria, and played in many groups in Europe from 1990 to 1993. She recorded with the Vienna Art Orchestra, on "Fe + Males," Polygram, 1992, with Sylvia Cuenca, drummer, and plays on six more albums, one led by Carl Ratzer, an Austrian guitarist, Warner Chapel label. Among her favorite accomplishments, she played in the Austria Center, Vienna, with Lionel Hampton and the Golden Men of Jazz group. "I moved to Europe, because people are more open-minded there," she reflected about the way she dealt with bias against women horn players in the 1980s. She came to the United States to live in 1993 because of increased opportunities.

ANITA JOHNSON, primarily a bass trombonist, plays with Kit McClure. She has also played for Carol Channing, Rita Morena, and Illinois

Jacquet's band at the Village Vanguard in 1990. She has done national tours with the shows *Cabaret* and *Sweeney Todd* as the only woman in the orchestra. "But I roomed with a woman dancer—so it was no problem," she says. She once missed an opportunity to travel with a jazz band because the leader didn't want her to share rooms on the road with male musicians.

Primarily a classical player, she works with small opera companies in New York and co-leads a trombone quartet, playing mostly classical and some jazz, with Anna Mondragon.

JOY JULKES, bassist, primarily in funk and pop groups, has accompanied Angela Bofill.

KAROLYN KAFER, alto saxophonist, plays on several albums—the University of North Texas, One O'Clock Lab Band's "The Best of the One O'Clock," Amazing Records, 1992; on the unreleased "Turnin' Twenty," made in 1993, with the Dallas Jazz Orchestra; and on "Thank You, Leon," Seabreeze, 1990s. She lives in Denton, Texas, and teaches at the University of North Texas. She began playing lead and second alto and tenor in the Doc Severinsen band in September 1992, appearing in Atlantic City, Malibu, and on the Arsenio Hall show.

**KOMIKI KAMOTO, percussionist and singer in experimentalist circles, has performed at the Knitting Factory and, in 1990, at a JVC Festival concert.

REBECCA KANE, pianist, leads groups at the Knitting Factory, Birdland, Cornelia Street Cafe, and other clubs in New York.

**DEBBY KATZ, drummer, is from Chicago.

**CAROL KAYE, electric bassist, who played guitar first, broke the barrier in the studios in California, where she was on countless albums. She has moved from California and may not be performing.

**DEBBY KEEFE, tenor saxophonist, married to drummer Steve Johns, lives in New York.

EMME KEMP, singer, pianist, composer, wrote for *Bubbling Brown Sugar,* for *Captain Kangaraoo,* and plays for concerts and gigs in established New York rooms, including Peacock Alley in the Waldorf-Astoria. She also tours in Europe and performs her original show, *Someone To Sing To* there and in the United States. On college campuses, she gives concerts and lectures; one talk is "Realities of the Artist's Life." She had an NEA grant for composing in 1977. She sang and played on Eubie Blake's recording, "Eubie Blake Song Hits," EBM, in 1976.

LIZ KINNON, versatile pianist, composer and arranger praised by *Los Angeles Times* critic Leonard Feather, sometimes plays with Maiden Voyage and with Latin jazz groups, in Los Angeles. She is currently marketing her own project, Latin and Brazilian-flavored acoustic and electric jazz, and has toured lately with Andy Williams. Other jobs have been with Raul de Souza, Brazilian trombonist, Poncho Sanchez, conguero, Kenia, Brazilian pop singer, Bill Holman, big band composer and arranger, and Anita O'Day, singer. She has played in the United States, Mexico, Japan, and Brazil with jazz, Latin, and pop groups, and on a jazz cruise with Dizzy Gillespie.

She had an NEA grant in 1979 to study composing and arranging at the Dick Grove School of Music, where she then taught for ten years. She wrote arrangements for the Duke Ellington Memorial Concert broadcast in Europe featuring Sonny Fortune, Bobby Shew, Pepper Adams, and a full orchestra. Her songwriting credits include "Say Goodbye," music and lyrics, recorded by Kenia, on her album "Love lives On," A&M Records, 1991. Among her many other songs, she wrote "J.J." especially for Stacy Rowles on flugelhorn.

**HIROKO KOKUBU, pianist, played in New York with Carol Sudhalter's group in the early 1980s, then returned to Japan. Her album, "More Than You Know," is on JVC Compact Discs, 1988.

KAREN KORSMEYER, primarily an acoustic bassist, plays with Kit McClure, including the first album, and for Off-Off Broadway shows, club dates, parties, and special events. She has had an NEA grant to study with Rufus Reid. She also works with computers by day.

DIANA KRALL, singer and pianist, who has studied with Jimmy Rowles and Jim McNeeley, was featured at the Ottawa Jazz Festival in 1990. As a leader, she has an album, "Stepping Out," on the Just in Time label in Canada, distributed by Enja in Europe and JVC in Japan, 1993. Bassist Ray Brown wrote the liner notes. Sidemen were Jeff Hamilton, drummer, and John Clayton, bassist.

She arrived in the United States with a Canada Arts Council grant and has taken her trio to Canadian jazz festivals, to Boston's Harbor Hotel with her close friend, Finnish drummer Klaus Suonsari, and the Canadian Embassy in Washington. She began a promotional tour for her album at the Just Jazz club in St. Louis.

KATHLEEN M. LANDIS, pianist and singer at Cafe Pierre in 1993 in New York, has also played in the jazz world with bassist Don Pate.

BRITTA LANGSJOEN, trombonist, plays with Diva, Kit McClure, and leads her own group at such places as The Squire in New York and Champs in Brooklyn. She also plays 6/8 music in a Persian band, and in a contemporary blues group, and in the Blue Birds group, which performs music from the 1920s through the 1940s, at the Red Blazer, and with Stan Rubin at the Red Blazer, and in salsa bands.

"The most challenging things for me now are the jam sessions, at St. Mark's Bar on 132 First Avenue, and the Local 802 jam run by pianist

Harold Mabern," she says. As an undergraduate, she played in a local jazz band in Champagne-Urbana and toured Russia with it for a month. Occasionally she plays on a Tuesday night set aside as women's night at the Peppermint Lounge in Orange, New Jersey.

MARIA LAZZARO, tenor saxophonist, plays with Kit McClure and freelances in a quintet with her husband, trumpet player Bill Mobley, and with her own group. Maria received an NEA grant to study with George Coleman. She was on Kit McClure's first CD.

**ANNE LE BARON, harpist, improviser, experimenter, lives in New York.

ANNIE LEBEAUX, vocal coach, musical director, singer, and pianist, performs in restaurants and clubs.

*LEE ANN LEDGERWOOD, pianist in clubs, composer and arranger for albums and TV, released her first album as leader, "You Wish," on Triloka, 1991.

**PHEBE LEGERE, pianist, singer, and novelty entertainer, has worked in the Knickerbocker, the Ballroom, and other New York clubs.

REBECCA LEVENSON, pianist and keyboardist, worked in Boston for five years, then moved to New York in 1985. She has played on Kit McClure's album, and at the Blue Note with Manny Duran for the jam session, and in restaurants and clubs, including Chita Rivera's restaurant, with bassist Santi DiBreano, Boots Maleson, Ed Schuller, and others, and with studio musicians at Visiones and other clubs in New York. She has worked with drummer Frank Bambara in an organ trio, for which she played synthesizer. She also works often with women musicians.

ERICA LINDSAY, tenor saxophonist, who doubles on soprano and flute, leads her group on "Dreamer" on the Candid label, 1990—her first recorded appearance. She has composed music for two off-Broadway productions, *Song of Sad Young Men* and *Feed the Beast*.

She moved from New York to the Woodstock area in the 1980s. Lately she has been writing for singers, in collaboration with lyricist Kathleen Sannwald, an electric bassist. With her own group, Erica plays in Albany at Justin's, a club and restaurant, and has done an NPR show. She has traveled with leader Bakida Carroll, an American avant-garde trumpeter, to Holland in 1993. She has also performed with McCoy Tyner's big band and with performance artists, combining poetry, solo saxophone, and painting.

*MELBA LISTON, legendary trombonist and arranger, led a New York-based group, in the early 1980s, until she became ill. Moving to the West Coast, she continued to write arrangements. In May 1993, she was inducted into the Pioneers Hall of Fame at the Intentional Women's Brass Conference, Washington University, St. Louis, Missouri. Available in compilations are instrumentals by Melba—"Christmas Eve" and "Blue

Melba." She also plays on the recording "Jazz Club: Trombone." Most of the arrangements on the album, "Volcano Blues," which bills Melba and pianist Randy Weston as co-leaders, were written by Melba on Antilles, 1993.

ROBYN LOBE played conga at Rainbow and Stars atop the RCA Building with flautist Mauricio Smith for six months in 1992 and again in 1993, and performed as a mambo dancer with the Eddie Torres Orchestra and the Orchard Beach All-Stars. She has worked with pop musicians Robert Palmer, Deee Lite, James J. T. Taylor from Kool and the Gang, Debbie Gibson, and Lisette Wilson. She also dances with groups led by Tito Puente, Iris Chacon, and Jose Alberto and plays congas with Eddie Torres and Angela Carasco.

She recorded as a percussionist with Palmer, on "Heavy Nova," EMI, 1980s, and with Deee Lite on Elektra. She has played percussion for her dance company, Robin Lobe and Company, at Rainbow and Stars and for Retumba Con Pie, which performs often in Riverside Park, in public schools under Arts Connection, a lecture demonstration-program, and in colleges, Caribbean festivals, and clubs such as S.O.B., Club Broadway, and the Village Gate. She plays with a new group called La Noreste. "It's very difficult to break in," she says about women playing percussion in Latin groups. "In Retumba Con Pie, we're using the bata, which women are not usually allowed to play, and it's controversial."

BARBARA LONDON, flautist, pianist, singer, and teacher, who played flute with the group Ariel at the Kansas City Women's Jazz Festival in 1979, has played at Lincoln Center's Avery Fisher Hall and at the United Nations as a solo flautist. She teaches harmony as an associate professor at Berklee and played in concerts at St. Peter's Church, New York, 1991, at the Berklee Performance Center, and in the Willow Jazz Club and Zachary's in the Colonnade Hotel in Boston. She had three NEA grants, in 1986, 1988, and 1990, for jazz performance. The Berklee Bookstore sells her workbook on harmony. She has led and produced four albums, among them "Flat Out-Dreaming," on Wild Aster Productions, late 1980s, available from Miss London, P.O. Box 972, Dover, New Hampshire 03820.

VIVIAN LORD, singer and pianist, recorded "Love Dance," on Stash, reissued as a CD; "Two for the Road," 1993, with singer Anne Marie Moss on half the tracks, Vivian Lord on the other half. Another album is CBS/Sony's "Route 66," with pianist Kenny Kirkland, trio leader, with Vivian, vocalist, in the 1990s. She teaches vocal jazz at William Patterson College, Wayne, New Jersey, and subs as a piano teacher. "My four years in Japan were a highlight of my life, 1982–1987. I played round the clock, in clubs and concerts, five months a year," she recalls.

NELLIE LUTCHER, singer and pianist, bought property years ago in Los Angeles where she lives. Though she rarely performs in public, she played at Barney Josephson's Cookery in New York in the 1980s.

MAIDEN VOYAGE is an all-women's big band on the West Coast, led by Ann Patterson. Leonard Feather has written: "Patterson has never relied on the novelty of leading a female orchestra. Foremost on the agenda are the quality of music, the spirit and accuracy of the interpretation and the talent of the soloists." It has never recorded, but it has played at the Playboy, Monterey, and Concord Jazz Festivals among others, and for many high profile events, such as NBC's "Tonight" show, and was the opening act for Billy Crystal at the Hollywood Bowl by invitation of the Los Angeles Philharmonic for a tribute to American music.

In addition to women mentioned elsewhere in this book, Maiden Voyage's personnel has included Kathy Rubbicco, piano, Anne King, trumpet, Sharon Hirata, tenor sax, and Mary Ann McSweeney, bass. (Mary Ann has recently moved to New York, where she plays with Diva, in Broadway orchestras, and with trombonist Al Grey.)

NANCY MARANO, pianist and teacher, has become best known as a singer with accordianist and synthesizer player Eddie Monteiro in New York. Whitney Balliett wrote a profile about the unusual duo in *The New Yorker* in 1993. They have played at Michael's Pub, in a JVC Jazz Festival concert, and on two CDs: "A Perfect Match" and "Double Standards," both on Denon.

**RITA MARCOTULLI, pianist based in Gottesburg, Sweden, has played with Dewey Redman, Joe Henderson, and Billy Cobham.

**MARIE MARCUS, pianist, plays in Dennisport, Massachusetts, on Cape Cod. She celebrated her fiftieth anniversary in the music business, according to the Unterbrink book, by playing in the Kool Jazz Festival, New York, 1982. One of her teachers was Fats Waller; among her friends and acquaintances have been Hazel Scott, Mary Lou Williams, Marian McPartland, and Norma Teagarden.

TANIA MARIA, pianist and singer, from Brazil, lived in Paris before becoming a starring performer in the United States in the 1980s. She was profiled in *Louis's Children,* a history of jazz singers. Her 1993 album, "Outrageous!," has an apt title for her bombastic, creative, Latin-jazz fusion style, Concord Picante, 1993. Other albums for the same label are "Piquant," "Come With Me," "Taurus," "Love Explosion," and "The Real Tania Maria: Wild!" "The Best of Tania Maria" was released by Capitol/EMI, 1993. Other albums are "Forbidden Colors," Capitol/EMI, "Made in New York" and "Lady From Brazil," Manhattan/EMI, and "Bela Vista," World Pacific/EMI.

*SHERRIE MARICLE, drummer and percussion teacher at New York University, has also taught jazz history and conducting. She leads on "The Time Being," Jazz Alliance, 1993, an album of original music, and on "Cooking on All Burners," Stash Records, 1990. She has played with Slam Stewart, Clark Terry, and other jazz stars. She's the drummer for the

New York Pops Orchestra, Diva, Unpredictable Nature, and the Velvet Glove. In October 1993, she had her first original symphonic work presented by the New York Pops at Carnegie Hall. She won the Eubie Blake Jazz Scholarship, the Foundation Award from SUNY, Binghamton, and the Kennedy Center Alliance Award for outstanding contributions and achievements in the arts. She has ranked in *Down Beat*'s Talent Deserving Wider Recognition category.

SUE MASKALERIS, composer and lyricist, pianist and singer, works as a soloist and small-group leader in established rooms and for special events in New York. She was a quarter-finalist in an American Song Festival competition and has won composing awards. In August 1993, she led her Trio Rio, plus guests, in performances of her own material at a Greenwich Village club, Yardbird Suite.

NYDIA "LIBERTY" MATA, percussionist and drummer, who came from Cuba at age four, lives in Long Beach, New York. She was nineteen, an amateur drummer, when she was introduced to Laura Nyro by Nyro's staff light man at the Fillmore East in the 1970s. Nydia had played conga drums at Cuban parties and played them informally for Nyro, who hired her for a record date; Nydia recorded more and toured with Nyro and other pop stars, and with Isis and Latin Fever, women's groups. She became the first woman to teach at the East Harlem School of Music run by Johnny Colon.

She works in the studios, plays Latin jazz, country-western music, and concentrates on gigs with Harpbeat, a duo with harpist Ellen Uryevick. They also play in the Harp Band, including such instruments as harp, vibes, Latin percussion, acoustic bass, flute, and saxophone. She has played in a Kool Jazz Festival band at Carnegie Hall and with the Big Apple Jazzwomen. Among her recording credits is "Carol Chaikin."

JEAN MATISSE, classically trained pianist, began playing jazz in New York clubs in 1973. She studied with Sir Roland Hanna, met jazz bassist Major Holley, worked with him in Zinno's, and has played with bassists Jimmy Rowser and Marty Rivera. She has had long engagements at Robert's and Ying's, New York restaurants featuring jazz, and played at the Village Gate with the Jazzmobile band and at other clubs and restaurants.

*VIRGINIA MAYHEW, California-born alto saxophonist, plays tenor in Diva, arranges, and leads a group; she is based in New York, where she works in clubs and concerts with Norman Simmons and Al Grey.

* and ** MARILYN MAZUR, American-born percussionist and drummer, lives in Denmark and plays primarily in Europe.

*JILL McCARRON, quintet leader, pianist, composer, leader of a finalist group in the 1990 Hennessey Cognac Festival, played in Diva and recorded for LRC with Unpredictable Nature. She's also in the Velvet Glove (see JANE FAIR), has played in Virginia Mayhew's quartets, and leads her own group in New York clubs. She played solo in an "I Love A Piano" series at the Village Gate.

*KIT McCLURE, lead alto saxophonist with her big band, also plays tenor, flute, bass clarinet. She recorded her first album, "Some Like It Hot," on Red Hot Records, 1990, New York. She took her band, with the fine singer, Giselle Jackson, and show-stopping trumpeter Rebecca Coupe Franks, into Tavern on the Green, in spring 1993.

ARLETTE McCOY BUDWIG, pianist and singer, widow of bassist Monte Budwig (Budwig, a well-known jazz musician, played with Maiden Voyage as a substitute), recorded "I Still Love You," Jazzabel, 1993, solo and with trumpeter Conte Candoli and saxophonist Bob Cooper, who worked with Budwig, and Colin Bailey, drummer. She also plays in clubs and festivals such as the Otter Crest in Oregon and the Los Angeles trad jazz festival. Her tune, "Devastating Cherub," was recorded by Jimmy Rowles—"a high point in my life," she says. She has taught piano to Shelle Manne and recorded on "Dig Monte Budwig," Concord, in the 1980s.

PATTI McCOY, pianist, known as Pat Moran when she played at the Hickory House in New York in the 1950s, now plays gospel in churches in the Jacksonville, Oregon, area. She recorded a children's album, "Shakin' Loose with Mother Goose," jazz with rap by Steve Allen and Jayne Meadows, on the Kids Matter label, 1990.

*SARAH McLAWLER, pianist, organist, and keyboardist, had played in Cafe Nicole in the Hotel Novotel, New York, on Tuesdays through Saturdays, for nine years by 1993. An experienced, respected jazz pianist and singer, she led several all-women's groups in Chicago. Record producer Teddy Reig persuaded her to bring a group to New York. Sally Placksin's book says the Moe Gale Agency brought the women east. McLawler married violinist Richard Otto, with whom she worked in a duo until his death in 1979. She has played organ in Cobi Narita's Big Apple Jazzwomen band and has traveled abroad extensively to work.

*JILL McMANUS, pianist, composer, and teacher, lives in New York.

*MARIAN McPARTLAND, pianist, concert artist, Peabody Award winner for "Piano Jazz" on NPR, is also a composer, role model, and mentor. Among her latest Concord recordings are "In My Life," 1993, and a Concord Silver Anniversary celebration CD, 1994. Alto and tenor saxophonist Chris Potter plays on both albums.

CARMEN McRAE, one of the great jazz singers, Grammy nominee, concert artist, based in Los Angeles, began as a pianist in the 1940s and continued to play occasionally in performances throughout her career. She was profiled in *Louis's Children*.

MARY ANN McSWEENEY, bassist, played for years with Maiden Voyage and moved to New York where she joined Diva in 1994. See MAIDEN VOYAGE.

**MOLLIE MacMILLAN, pianist, was heard playing by Marian McPartland in Ithaca in 1993 and encouraged to move to New York.

MYRA MELFORD, pianist, composer of new music, in the avant garde, has played at the Knitting Factory. She has two CDs on the Enemy label—"Jump" and "Now and Now," both with her trio. The Swiss label, hat Art, released her latest album, "The Myra Melford Trio Alive in the House of Saints." She's on avant-garde trumpeter Butch Morris's recording, "Dust to Dust," New World, done in the 1990s. She was awarded a New York Foundation for the Arts fellowship for composition, 1992, and has received numerous Meet the Composer grants.

BARBARA MERJAN, drummer, has worked with McClure, McPartland, Chaikin, and others, including funk and r&b groups, and has played with the road show of *Cabaret* starring Joel Grey. She's on an album led by Nana Simopoulos, guitarist and sitar player—"Gaia's Dream," B&W, 1993. She has substituted in *Cats* on Broadway and worked as a sideperson and leader in New York area clubs. John S. Wilson wrote about her in *The New York Times:* "(She) propels the Kit McClure Big Band through a strutting St. Louis Blues with rolling drumming that would do credit to Art Blakey."

*LYNN MILANO, who played bass with the Jazz Sisters, works at Harrington's, a jazz club in Port Jefferson, Long Island, with various groups—pianist-singer Mose Allison's, pianist Wayne Sabella's, and others. She also played for a show at Hofstra University in 1993.

She teaches in the Commack public schools and at C. W. Post College. She also plays in classical groups, is working on an album of her compositions at Sabella's recording studio, and finishing a book on rhythm section playing with Charlie Perry, drummer, author, and clinician. She has invented a string tuner.

**ANNA MONDRAGON, trombonist, has played with Kit McClure. See ANITA JOHNSON.

*DIANE MONROE, violinist, plays in the Uptown String Quartet.

AUDREY MORRISON, New York born-trombonist, based in Chicago, plays in Diva and combines classical, jazz, and ethnic (klezmer and Latin) music as a playing career. She has taught jazz ensemble, trombone and tuba, and coached brass ensembles and jazz combos at Wheaton College since 1981. In September 1993, she began teaching at the University of Wisconsin at Parkside in Kenosha. She's principal trombonist with the Barrett Deems Big Band in Chicago, with two professional classical brass quintets, and with the Elgin Symphony Orchestra and works as an extra with the Chicago Lyric Opera Orchestra and the Milwaukee Symphony Orchestra. She also plays with various chamber orchestras. She has also taught at Clark Terry's jazz camp in LaCrosse, Wisconsin, and at the classical music program at Monterey, California, in summers.

KATHRYN MOSES, a multi-reeds player noted especially for flute, played with Maiden Voyage in California and returned to her native Toronto, Canada, where she plays in a variety of pop, jazz, and classical groups in studios, clubs, and concert halls. She composes for Canadian radio, TV, and films.

Her album, "Kathryn Moses," Jazz Canada, won a Canada Music Council award for the best Canadian jazz album in 1976. On her album "Music in My Heart," PM Records, 1979, she played flute, soprano sax, and she sang. She recorded as a flautist on Chuck Mangione albums, and has played as a sideperson on thirty-four albums, ten of them jazz, in the 1980s and 1990s. With her own group she played at the Toronto Jazz Festival, 1993.

She composed for the films, *Sadness of the Moon,* DaRuma Productions, and *Dreams of the Night Cleaners, Forbidden Love,* and *Children of Jerusalem.*

ROSE MURPHY, pianist, singer—the "chi-chi" girl—died in 1989. Available on a recording is "Rose Murphy Sings Again," MCA Records.

DIEDRE MURRAY, cellist and composer, who has played mainstream jazz, is more often associated with the avant garde and new music. She also works as a curator for the Fire Wall Total Arts Festival in New York and Philadelphia, and for P.S. 122, and the YWCA at 52nd Street in New York. In 1993, she was playing in a group with Pauline Oliveros, accordianist and composer, singer Jeanne Lee, and dancer Blondell Cummings. Her albums are "Song for the Lost People," About Time label, late 1980s; "Fire Storm," Victo Records, 1992, and one to be released on the Black Saint label, co-led with Fred Hopkins. Though she has played r&b, she is primarily a jazz-based musician, performing at the Knitting Factory, Village Vanguard, Village Gate, and Avery Fisher Hall in the 1990s. She played in the Victoriaville Music Festival in Canada and at the Willasau Jazz festival in Switzerland, 1992; and at District Curators, in Washington, D.C.

SUSAN MUSCARELLA, pianist, is in San Francisco.

AMINA CLAUDINE MYERS began playing in churches and gospel groups in Texas, Arkansas, and Kentucky, studied piano in college, and later became an organist and keyboardist. In New York since 1976, she composes, leads groups and vocal choirs, and has taught at Jazzmobile and SUNY at Westbury. Recent albums as leader are: "In Touch," on Novus, and "Jumping in the Sugar Bowl," Minor Music. Her song, "Happiness," is included on a Novus sampler.

A live trio recording, "Amina Claudine Myers Trio," recorded at the Women in (E)Motion festival, was released in Germany, 1993, where she often plays. She plans to write a piece for dance and orchestra in honor of Harriet Tubman and to work in music therapy. With the Art Ensemble of Chicago Representing the Chicago Blues Tradition, Amina played in a trio touring Europe in 1993.

HARUKO NARA, pianist, teacher, composer, leader on "My Favorite Things," Jazz City, 1990, and has recently recorded with Lonnie Plaxico, bassist, Chris Hunter, alto saxophonist, Robin Eubanks, trombonist, and others, for a CD yet to be released.

She gave a solo concert in Rome for the Japan Foundation in 1993 and was studying for her doctorate in music and music education at Columbia University, where she taught piano. In 1992, she recorded a track, "Maiysha," by Miles Davis, on a tribute album to him, on Crown. She was playing in Birdland and other clubs.

In 1990, she played in a concert at Weill Recital Hall. At that time, she was teaching, playing in restaurants, and composing at home, expressing her belief, through her compositions that combined Japanese, European, and American jazz influences, in the oneness of mankind.

VALERIE NARANJO, who plays marimba, also plays African percussion and records on African xylophones. She co-leads the group, Mandara, emphasizing percussion, trombones, vocals, and keyboards. She also plays under the auspices of Cobi Narita's Universal Jazz Coalition, and in contemporary classical and experimental groups.

Twice a year she tours with Philip Glass; she sings, plays percussion and keyboards on his album, "Powaquatsi," Elektra Nonesuch, 1988. She has also recorded "Cool Blue Halo," 1988, and "Primal Dream," 1989, with pop musician Richard Barone, on MCA. Other albums are "Carabali," 1990, and "Carabali 2," 1992, a Latin jazz sextet, and "One Shield We Walk" with singer Purafe's Native American group, 1993.

With a master's in ethnomusicology from Ithaca College, Naranjo, of Native American and Latin descent, has studied and played in Africa. The highlight of her life, she says, has been her work in Ghana, from which she received the official Kobine Award for contributions to the arts in Ghana's upper west region. She has had two NEA grants and several Meet the Composer awards. She lectures at the Schomburg Center for Research and Black Culture in New York and the Charlin Jazz Society, which presents jazz history in forums and performances, in Washington, D.C. She has also composed for dance and theater companies and has toured with the Zimbabwean jazz group called Mudzimu. In August 1993, she and co-leader Barry Olsen, a multi-instrumentalist, took Mandara, which has performed at S.O.B., Lincoln Center, P.S. 122, and Central Park, to the Asia Pacific Music Wave festival in Osaka—Naranjo's third trip to Japan. She has toured in Europe, Latin America, and the Caribbean and has performed at the Knitting Factory and other clubs, and has collaborated with Zusaan Kali Fasteau.

**LINDA NEEL, trombonist, plays with Kit McClure, in New York.

YOLANDA NICHOLS, saxophonist, is in the San Francisco area.

BETTY O'HARA, valve trombonist, flugelhornist, double bell eupho-nium player—"with two bells, you can trade fours with yourself," she says—and trumpeter, singer, arranger, and composer and a star of Maiden Voyage, has been praised by that band's leader Ann Patterson, *Los Angeles Times* critic Leonard Feather, and others. She co-leads Jazz Birds with Stacy Rowles, writes for that group, and works in Dixieland groups. In September, 1993, she appeared for the tenth year in the Los Angeles Classic Jazz Festival as an all-star and also with maiden Voyage and with another band. She has played in national festivals too. Until 1991, she worked for five years for TV shows including "Magnum P.I." and "Hill Street Blues," until synthesizers came in. She played second trumpet under the name Betty Peterson in the Hartford, Connecticut Symphony Orchestra and then moved to Los Angeles in 1960 when she married bass trombonist Barrett O'Hara. They have two children. Her album as co-leader is "Horns Aplenty," Magnagraphic label, 1985.

JUNKO ONISHI, Japanese-born pianist who attended Berklee, made her United States debut album, "Crusin'," on Blue Note and played for a week at the Village Vanguard, with Wynton Marsalis's sidemen, bassist Reginald Veal and drummer Herlin Riley, in May 1994.

MARY OSBORNE, guitarist, died in the 1990s. Available on a recording is "A Memorial," Stash Records, 1959.

ELIZABETH PANZER, harpist, an improviser in the avant garde, free-lances with such artists as critically praised singer Judi Silvano, trumpeter Butch Morris, and Kitty Brazelton, a rock singer. Panzer has a classical duo called Giverny, with a flautist, Carol Shansky. She has put out a private cassette of her own music, recorded with the North South Consonance, a classical group, and has had a fellowship to Waterloo, a music festival in New Jersey, and fellowships to France to study composition. She has played in CBGB's, the Knitting Factory, New Music Cafe, Ear Inn, Cooper Union, Carnegie Hall, Weill Recital hall, and Merkin Hall in New York.

**ZINA PARKINS, keyboardist, who also plays a homemade electric harp, has performed in a JVC Jazz Festival concert in the series called The Knitting Factory Goes Uptown.

STARR PARODI, primarily known as a pop musician in the Los Angeles area, has been playing keyboards for the Arsenio Hall show since 1989. Before that she toured with pop jazz saxophonist George Howard. She also played and composed for "Fame."

Her album "Change" was released by Gift Horse Recordings in 1991. For composition, she has won an Omni Gold Award for a *Better Homes &*

Gardens magazine commercial, 1992, and a B.D.A. Bronze Award for the main title of *Angel City,* a TV film. She has composed for many TV shows, commercials such as Chanel, and film trailers for *El Mariachi, Last Action Hero, Prelude to a Kiss,* and *Straight Out of Brooklyn.*

LISA PARROTT, alto and baritone saxophonist, received a grant from the Australian Council for the Arts to study with Steve Coleman in New York. Arriving in 1993, she began playing on Tuesday nights at the St. Mark's Bar and First on First. In Sydney, which has four million people and only four women saxophonists, she led groups playing her compositions influenced by Ornette Coleman. At a summer camp, she fell in love with recordings by Bird, Ornette, and Eric Dolphy. Her sister, an acoustic bassist, accompanies groups visiting Australia. Longwinded, strong, and gifted, Lisa can play funk, mainstream contemporary, classic jazz and experimental music.

SALLY PATELLA, trumpeter, plays in a nine-piece band specializing in the music of Ellington, Basie, Goodman, and Fletcher Henderson in Denver, Colorado.

ANN PATTERSON, alto saxophonist, multi-reeds player and teacher, leads Maiden Voyage. (See MAIDEN VOYAGE.) Her father, a Dixieland drummer, encouraged her to play music. A graduate of North Texas State (now called University of North Texas), where she studied classical oboe and dated a jazz saxophonist, she switched to alto in her late twenties. Acutely aware of the music scene for women in Los Angeles, she says, "About fifty women currently play here. There are some good young players coming along. I think there will be more. Women in their twenties didn't get the discouragement, and some women even get encouragement. It's not great but it's better."

Ann played on two Don Ellis albums before 1980, one John Mayall blues album, and one saxophone quartet album called the "Four Winds" on the Discovery label. She has played for many well-known jazz and pop artists and taught in midwestern and California colleges.

JEAN ARLAND PETERSON, pianist, based in Minneapolis, played with Doc Severinsen at Orchestra Hall, with the Minnesota Orchestra in 1993. She plays for parties, in clubs and theatres, and for industrial conventions for such stars as Bob Hope and Diahann Carroll. She has toured the United States, England, and Europe. In Russia she performed with a group, Women Who Cook, in 1988.

She has played with Dottie Dodgion, Mary Fettig, Mary Osborne, Marian McPartland, and others. She sometimes works with her children, all professional musicians—Patty, a singer; Ricky, a keyboardist for David Sanborn and a producer at Prince's Paisley Park, who has recorded on several albums; Billy, a bassist, who also plays piano and tours with the Steve Miller band; Linda, a pianist and singer; and Paul, called St. Paul, pianist, guitarist, and bassist, on the Atlantic and Capitol, who has also made videos.

Her albums are "Jeannie Arland Peterson," renamed "Wee Small Hours," and "Triplicity," and "Wish," on the Celebration label. She was organist for the film, *Grumpy Old Men,* with Jack Lemmon, Ann Margaret, and Walter Matthau.

ROBERTA PIKET, pianist, admired by musical contemporaries, ran the jam session at The Squire when Virginia Mayhew was touring. Piket won third prize in the American Pianists Association 1992 Biennial Jazz Piano Competition in Indianapolis. In 1989, she performed in a group that opened for Dr. Billy Taylor for the Bright Moments Festival in Amherst, Massachusetts. Freelancing in jam sessions and little clubs in New York, she has led groups. Her quartet was a finalist in the jazz division, Brooklyn Lager Band Search, in 1991.

LEIGH PILZER, tenor and baritone saxophone player, based in Washington, D.C., and nearby Silver Springs, Maryland, co-leads She-Bop, a quartet playing in D.C. clubs, with Sheryl Bailey on guitar, Cyndy Elliott, acoustic bass, Stephanie Oshry, piano, and Alison Miller, drummer. Sheryl has played with saxophonist Gary Thomas. Leigh and Sheryl used to play with a group that performed at Baltimore's Left Bank Jazz Society, with Kendra Holt, Hammond B3 organ, Roberta Washington, drums, Ann Hairston, alternate drummer, May Pat Hughes, saxophones and vocals. Hughes now leads an r&b and funk band, in which Leigh and six other women play.

LESLIE PINTCHIK, pianist, wife of guitarist and bassist Scott Hardy, has played at J's, the Knickerbocker, other clubs, and private parties in New York. She and her husband worked with bassist Red Mitchell at Bradley's in 1980s. Pintchik and Hardy usually play in a rhythm section with drummer Richard De Rosa.

**TRUDY PITTS, pianist and organist, is a Philadelphian.

TERRY POLLARD, much admired pianist, "a natural bebop player," known especially for her work with vibrist Terry Gibbs, is inactive due to illness, in Detroit.

MARGIE POS, jazz bassist and composer, teaches at Berklee in Boston and plays in performance spaces and clubs in the northeast, occasionally touring the United States, Central America, and Europe.

GLENNA POWRIE, keyboardist, from Vancouver, has worked with Kit McClure, accompanied Phyllis Hyman on the road, played at a benefit with Dizzy Gillespie, and toured with her own band including Tracy Wormworth, bass, Gene Jackson, drums, and Greg Osby, alto saxophone. Glenna's album, "Asba," is on Muse, with Tracy, Kevin Eubanks, guitar, Darryl Jones, drums, Osby, and Mino Cinelu from Martinique on percussion. She has had Canada Arts Council grants, recorded for Vancouver companies and written music for a PBS film, *Psyche Pursued,* about the experiences of a woman in New York City streets.

With Sophie B. Hawkins, a Grammy nominee for 1992, Glenna along with Tracy toured and made an MTV video, *Damn, I Wish I Was Your Lover.* Glenna has led a group at Canadian jazz festivals.

*VICKI RANDLE, percussionist and vocalist, plays in Branford Marsalis's band for the Jay Leno show and has recorded a CD with Branford for Columbia. She also works with Julie Homi's band and has recorded with George Benson ("In Your Eyes," Warner Brothers), Lyle Mays ("Street Dreams," E.M.I.), toured with Wayne Shorter, Dr. John, Lionel Ritchie and Kenny Loggins, and recorded with Herbie Hancock ("Mr. Hand") and Pharaoah Sanders ("Journey to the One").

LENORE RAPHAEL is a singer, pianist, arranger, and composer based in New Jersey, where she has taught piano in a summer workshop at Montclair State College. Her album, primarily of originals, "The Whole Truth," Swingin' Fox Music, 1991, is available from that company at P.O. Box 792, Livingston, New Jersey 07039. Her sidemen were Vic Juris, guitarist, Mark Vinci, saxophonist, Mike Richmond, bassist, and John Paul Biagi, drums. She has played in New York and New Jersey clubs, libraries and cultural centers, and on an *S.S. Norway* jazz cruise.

*CARLINE RAY, veteran electric and acoustic bassist, singer, guitarist, and accompanist for Ruth Brown, who starred in Broadway's *Black and Blue,* has many credits. With Brown, Carline, toured the United States, Europe, and South America in the early 1990s. She has been teaching at the New School and at Jazzmobile. She worked with the Alvin Ailey Dance Company for fourteen years, into the 1980s, and recorded Ailey's ballets, "Revelation" and "Blues Suite." Profiled in Placksin's book, Carline lives in New York.

ANDREA RE, percussionist, keyboardist, and singer, has only tangential relationship to jazz, playing in soulful Delmar Brown's band, Bush Rock (Delmar worked with Gil Evans). She has written some lyrics and sung backup vocals for saxophonist Chico Freeman.

**VI REDD, alto saxophonist and singer, daughter of a saxophonist, has been a woman pioneer in jazz. Last heard of as a teacher and performer on special occasions in California, she has been written about in the jazz histories by Placksin and Dahl.

*EMILY REMLER, guitarist and composer, died in 1990.

NILDA RICHARDS, trombonist, plays in the horn section, Burning Brass. (See PAM FLEMING and JENNY HILL.) She has appeared on reggae recordings by Burning Spear—"Live in Paris," 1989, and "Mistress Music," 1988, and "People of the World," 1987, all on Warner

Brothers—and on a small label with The Toasters, a ska group. Her sextet, Sister Love, plays "rap-funk," her original music, as she raps about social and political issues and romance, at Nell's and S.O.B.

She meets with traditional bias: "People are always shocked and ask silly questions like: 'Do you have very big lungs?'" Security men at clubs think she carries an instrument for a man.

LIBBY RICHMAN, alto saxophonist and composer, leads bands and has played at Birdland, the Squire, the 55 Club, the Plaza Hotel, the Carlyle Hotel, the Guggenheim Museum, the Empire State Building, McGraw-Hill Park, the Daily News Building, One Penn Plaza, in city parks, and at colleges in the tri-State area. She employs Latin percussion instead of the drum set and combines classical European and Latin influences in her songs. As a sideperson, she has worked with Lesley Gore, Martha Reeves, the Shirelles, McClure and others.

*MAXINE ROACH, classical viola player, daughter of drummer Max roach, plays in his double quartet and the Uptown String Quartet.

JUDY ROBERTS, a pianist based in Chicago, has toured extensively to play in clubs and concerts. She has played with Marian McPartland and Nadine Jansen in a jazz concert in Scottsdale, Arizona, in 1988. Judy has been interviewed on "Piano Jazz" by McPartland. As a leader, she has recorded ten albums—one with Ray Brown and Jeff Hamilton, "Trio," Pausa, 1985. Between 1982 and 1984, on the Inner City label, her albums became very popular—"The Judy Roberts Band," "The Other World," "Nights in Brazil," and "You Are There," which included the theme from "Star Trek" and a version of Ahmad Jamal's rendering of "Poinciana" that was nominated for two Grammys. Her album, "My Heart Belongs to Daddy," with saxophonist Richie Cole and her father, a big band era guitarist and arranger, was released on Judy Roberts Productions, 1992. She has played at all the European jazz festivals and has toured in Singapore and Japan.

JANICE ROBINSON, an experienced, respected trombonist, lives in New York. Married, with two children, she did not play professionally in the early 1990s.

DIANA ROGERS, pianist and singer, sings jazz-influenced pop songs in hotels and supper clubs.

**NOMI ROSEN, flautist, has played at The Squire jam session, New York.

MARLENE ROSENBERG, Chicago-based bassist, who has had NEA grants for composition, has played in rhythms sections for saxophonist Joe Henderson. "I wish I didn't have to say that we still have our problems, but things are better," she says. She accompanied singers Joe Williams and Nancy Wilson, when she worked with the Jazz Members, a big band in Chicago, in Orchestra Hall. She has played with Stan Getz, Marian

McPartland, Frank Morgan, and Ed Thigpen with whom she recorded a CD, "Easy Flight," early 1990s, Reckless Records. There's also a recording of Joe Henderson, "Punjab," taped in Paris, with Renee Rosnes, Sylvia Cuenca, and Marlene, released on Arco, 1990, probably taken from a radio broadcast. She was also on a video "Fe + Males," with the Vienna Art Orchestra, in the 1990s. Her critically praised album "Waimea" was released by Lake Shore Jazz, 1994.

DASSI ROSENCRANTZ, electric and acoustic bassist, from Israel, plays on the Latin scene in New York. In Israel she played in pop and ethnic groups.

*MICHELE ROSEWOMAN, California-born composer, pianist, and group leader, has led her own groups and lives in New York.

*RENEE ROSNES, Canadian-born pianist and composer, lives in New Jersey.

MERCEDES ROSSY, pianist, from Barcelona, Spain, where she won prizes in jazz piano and chamber music, was based in Munich from 1985 to 1989 and primarily played in Germany, Austria, and Switzerland. With a grant from the Generalitat de Catalonia, she studied at Berklee and played in Boston until she moved to New York in June 1992. She has played at the Village Gate, Visiones, Cameo's, other New York clubs and restaurants, and the Peppermint Lounge in Orange, New Jersey. She was invited to play in the Festival at Sand Point, Idaho, by Gunther Schuller.

**ELLEN ROWE, pianist, composer, band director, is a highly respected teacher on the faculty of the University of Connecticut.

*STACY ROWLES, trumpeter and flugelhornist, lives in the Los Angeles area.

ELLYN RUCKER, pianist and singer in the Nat Cole style, preferring to stay based in Denver, Colorado, played at Bradley's for one night in 1989. She was a guest on "Piano Jazz" in 1993. She has recorded "Live in New Orleans," a trio album; a video, Leisure Videos, 1992; "Ellyn," with tenor saxophonist Pete Cristlieb, bassist John Clayton and drummer Jeff Hamilton, 1987, and "This Heart of Mine," with bassist Red Mitchell and drummer Marvin "Smitty" Smith, 1989, both albums on the Capri label. In 1992, she played in the Guinness Jazz Festival, Cork, Ireland, with bassist Michael Moore and European musicians. She tours Britain and Europe, playing at festivals and for jazz societies—for example, Holland's North Sea Festival in 1986, 1987, and 1988.

*PATRICE RUSHEN, keyboardist, singer, composer, scorer for films including *Hollywood Shuffle* and *Without You I'm Nothing,* Grammy nominee, musical director for Robert Townsend and for TV personalities, has eleven albums out, including "Anthology of Patric Rushen" and "Straight from the Heart" on Elektra Entertainment, and "Watch Out" on Arista. She has written scores for the TV series "Jack's Place," "Brewster Place," "The Midnight Hour," "Robert Townsend and His Partners In Crime" for HBO, and the critically acclaimed special, "Comic Relief V." She produced Sheena Easton's "The Nearness of You" for the film *Indecent Proposal,* and later produced an album of standards for Easton. Patrice was the first woman musical director for the Emmy Awards show in 1991 and 1992, the first woman to serve as musical director for the NAACP Image Awards, and the only woman musical director for the People's Choice Awards. In summer, 1993, she arranged the music for Janet Jackson's band for a world tour. Patrice lives in Los Angeles.

CATHERINE RUSSELL, singer and mandolin player, began working with Cyndi Lauper's group in May 1993, and in August played in Donald Fagan's group—he worked with Steely Dan. Russell is the daughter of Caroline Ray and the late bandleader Luis Russell.

*ALI RYERSON, flautist and group leader on "Blue Flute" and "I'll Be Back," Red Baron albums, lives in Connecticut.

SAFFIRE: THE UPPITY BLUES WOMAN, a trio with Gaye Adegbalola, guitar and harmonica, Andra Faye Macintosh, bass, mandolin, and violin, and Ann Rabson, piano and guitar, played in the fourteenth Annual "Women In Jazz" series, outdoor summer concerts, 1993, on the World Trade Center's plaza. The series always features the blues. In 1993, other groups were Gretchen Langheld's House Afire, the Charmaine Neville Band, Jane Ira Bloom, and Ifeachor Okeke's quintet. (Charmaine Neville, a singer and third-generation musician in the New Orleans Neville family, plays percussion instruments, including cowbell.) Saffire: The Uppity Blues Women's albums are "Broadcasting," "Hot Flash," "The Uppity Blues Women," Alligator.

LIESL SAGARTZ, lead triumpeter in Diva, left the University of Cincinnati's College Conservatory of Music to play trumpet for three months on a TV show in Madrid, Spain, then played for the Carnival Cruise Lines in the Caribbean and subbed in a big band at the Blue Wisp club in Cincinnati.

SHARA SAND, trombonist, in Kit McClure's band until 1992, left music to get her doctorate in clinical psychology. She played on "Some Like It Hot" and with opera companies, touring Italy and Spain, and dinner theater, summer stock, and new music groups. She has recorded with the Gay Men's Chorus and for children's albums.

Because she found it difficult to make a living, sometimes playing for $20 a night, riding long distances on the subway, she decided to regard music as an avocation.

NOREEN (GREY) SAULS, pianist and singer, who often works with her husband Earl Sauls, a bassist, played with trumpeter Howard McGhee from 1981 to 1987 in clubs and the Kool Jazz Festival. She plays in clubs in New York and New Jersey, teaches jazz piano and voice at William Paterson College in Wayne, New Jersey, and writes for the professional, highly technical journal, the *Piano Stylist,* which has become a section in *Keyboard Classics,* for which she also writes, along with *Sheet Music* magazine. Her book, *Professional Stylings for the Solo Pianist,* was published by Ekay, Katonah, New York, 1992.

A professional since the 1970s, she has played on the recordings: "Keeping a Secret," led by bassist Stephen Roane, with Frank Strosier on alto saxophone, Mothlight Records, 1983; tenor saxophonist James Dean's "Generation," Muse, with Pepper Adams and Frank Foster, 1985; and Dean's "Ceora," Cexton Records, with Marlene Ver Planck and Claudio Roditi, 1989. "Think Positive," co-led by Noreen and Earl Sauls, with Kim Pleasant, drummer, features Rory Stuart, guitar, Shanti Records, 1990. That rhythm section has played at the Guinness Jazz Festival, with Charles McPherson on alto sax and Spike Robinson on tenor sax, in Cork, Ireland.

CYNTHIA SAYER, banjoist, plays many styles of music, including classical and traditional jazz. She has worked with clarinetist-saxophonist Ken Peplowski, trombonist George Barrett, and guitarist Howard Alden, among many others. She once played "Rhapsody in Blue" with the New York Philharmonic in 1993. She has toured often in Germany, Switzerland, and France lately, and in England in past years, where she appeared on the BBC, and in Japan and Canada.

Among her recordings is "The Bunk Project," with Woody Allen on clarinet and Eddie Davis as musical director, on Music Masters, 1993. On drums, the instrument she originally wanted to play, she has recorded with leader Tony Trishka on banjo. She also plays piano on some professional gigs.

IRENE SAZER, violist as well as violinist and a singer and composer, played viola with the Turtle Island String Quartet. She has her own band, which plays modern folk-rock with jazz influences and works in the Bay area.

*MARIA SCHNEIDER, composer and arranger (see the "Individualists" section), assisted Gil Evans in scoring the film, *The Color of Money,* arranged for Sting's European tour with the Gil Evans Orchestra, and received the International Association of Jazz Educators' Gil Evans Fellowship Award.

**DIANE SCHUUR, singer, pianist, and organist, who became a star in the 1980s, lives in the state of Washington. Among her GRP albums are: "Collection," "Deedling," "Diane Schuur and the Count Basie Orchestra" (also available as a video), "In Tribute," "Love Songs," "Pure Schuur," "Schuur Thing," "Talkin' Bout You'," "Timeless."

*HAZEL SCOTT, a celebrity as a pianist in New York and Paris, was the second wife of U.S. Representative Adam Clayton Powell, minister of the Abyssinian Baptist Church. She played at the Waldorf-Astoria Hotel in the last years of her life. She died in 1981.

*SHIRLEY SCOTT, pianist, organist, and teacher, led a trio in the Village Vanguard in summer 1993, where she reaffirmed her status, impressing audiences with her ease and swing. Saxophonist George Coleman, who has worked with her previously, sat in. She teaches piano and jazz history at Cheyney University in Pennsylvania and had an NEA grant in the early 1990s to transcribe Dexter Gordon's solos and compositions.

Her newest recordings, including her compositions, are an organ album, "Oasis," on Muse, and "Blues Everywhere" on Candid, with her trio, bassist Arthur Harper and drummer Mickey Roker. She has led about fifty albums and played as a sideperson on another ten to twenty. Among her older recordings are "Blue Flames," Shirley Scott/Stanley Turrentine (her former husband), on Original Jazz Classics; "For Members Only/Great Scott," on MCA Special Products, 1964; "Queen of the Organ," on Impulse!, and "Workin'" on Prestige.

**ELLEN SEELING, trumpeter and co-leader of Deuce with Jean Fineberg, was last known to be living in San Francisco, California.

LEE SHAW, pianist, who was inducted into the Oklahoma Jazz Hall of Fame in June 1993, worked primarily in a trio with her husband, Stan, a drummer, and bassist Skip Crumby-Bey. In the early 1980s, Stan booked artists at the Castilian Lounge, in Albany, for which the trio was the rhythm section. Guests were Zoot Sims, Thad Jones, Al Cohn, Budd Johnson, Frank Wess, Al Grey, Howard McGhee, Billy Mitchell, Urbie Green, Arnie Lawrence, and others. The trio also played in Canada, Austria, Germany, Holland, and Hungary in the 1980s.

Lee has been a guest on McPartland's show and played in the "I Love a Piano" series at the New School in New York. She teaches jazz piano and jazz history at a small liberal arts college, College of Saint Rose. Since her husband became unable to play in 1991, Lee plays in duos with a bass or a horn or as a soloist. She can be heard on "Lee Shaw OK!," recorded at a concert at Bartlesville, Oklahoma Community Center, on Cadence, 1983, during her month-long tour of Oklahoma colleges, universities, and jazz clubs.

DARYL SHERMAN, New York-based singer and pianist, performs solo and leads group in hotels and clubs such as Tavern on the Green. She also travels to play in Los Angeles and Europe. Some of her critically praised jazz albums are "I've Got My Fingers Crossed," Audiophile, in the 1990s; "Getting Some Fun Out of Life" with Loren Schoenberg, saxophonist, singer Barbara Lea, Dick Sudhalter, trumpet, Mel Lewis, drums, John Goldsby, bass, Audiophile, in 1990. Pianist Dick Katz's new album includes one of her tunes, "Samburan." With a vast repertoire and a strong and varied piano style, she has won the admiration of important critics.

NINA SHELDON, pianist and singer, has taught as a professor at the Peabody Conservatory and played at Cobi Narita's Universal Jazz Coalition and women's festivals. She played in the Kool Jazz Festival in New York in 1978 and in the Saratoga branch of the festival, and led the house band at the Village Gate for four years in the 1970s. She was in *Who's Who in Jazz* in 1985.

She left New York to live in Woodstock and plays professionally at the Hanah Country Inn in Margaretville, New York, in the Catskills. "Secret Places," her album on Plug Records, 1987, was named a top album of the year by jazz writer Herb Wong. She also works as a medical writer and editor.

TRUDY SILVER, New York-based pianist and composer, tours in the United States, South America, and Europe, playing solo and in duos and trios. She received her latest Meet the Composer grant in 1993 and has had one album as leader released, "Heroes, Heroines," on Under Open Sky label, 1987.

At Hunter College, she teaches music education, with course material inspired by her work with the Salt and Pepper Mime Company. With students, she has performed her original music at the Apollo Theatre and St. Peter's Lutheran Church. She also trains music teachers for work in public schools under the Arts Genesis program funded by the NEA and others.

**NINA SIMONE, legendary soul singer and pianist, author of her autobiography, has about two dozen albums available, some named for her hit songs dating back to the 1960s. "The Best of Nina Simone" is on the RCA Records label. A recent release is "A Single Woman" on Elektra Entertainment. She lives in Europe.

NANA SIMOPOULOS, electric guitar and sitar player, based in New York, playing world music with improvisations and rhythmic inventiveness, has made albums, "Wings and Air," on Enja, 1987; "Still Waters," on Enja, 1990; and "Gaia's Dream," on B+W Music, 1992, in England. They received very good reviews in the *Penguin Guide to Jazz,* 1992. She tours in the Untied States and Europe. At the Montreux Jazz Festival, Switzerland, she was selected to be on a compilation CD of the best music there in 1989, on the B+W label. Carol Chaikin, Barbara Merjan and percussionist Beverly Botsford, a North Carolinian, play in Nana's group at times.

*MELISSA SLOCUM, bassist, who played in Diva and Unpredictable Nature in 1993, was a member of the house band at Arthur's Tavern throughout the 1980s and early 1990s in New York.

CECILIA SMITH, vibraphonist, playing at Lincoln Center Out-Of-Doors in August 1993, led her quartet in her own compositions and several by John Lennon, Paul McCartney, Pat Metheny, and Sonny Rollins. She teaches at the Berklee College of Music.

RHONDA SMITH, acoustic and electric bassist in Montreal, has played in Canadian pop and jazz festivals.

**GINGER SMOCK, violinist, plays and works in Las Vegas.

*CAROL STEELE, a percussionist, is based in New York.

**LENI STERN, guitarist, leads the albums, "Closer to the Light" and "Secrets" on Enja, "Next Day" on Passport, and "Ten Songs," 1992, and "Like One," 1994, on the Lipstick label. In recent years, she has been profiled in *Jazziz, Down Beat,* and *Musician* magazines. She lives in New York.

PEGGY STERN, pianist, in the New York area, traveled with Lee Konitz in the 1990s. When she played with him at the Atlantic Jazz Festival, Halifax, Nova Scotia, the reviewer wrote: "Stern playing outside of the changes . . . shimmers like an aurora borealis light show." She has worked with many well-known jazz musicians in clubs, concerts, and festivals—for example, with Diane Schuur and Stanley Turrentine in 1991. She has been a guest on "Piano Jazz" and leads her own septet featuring Dick Oatts. Among her recordings are "Lunasea," with Lee Konitz, Soul Note, 1992, and "The Jobim Collection," Philology, 1993. She has also played with Konitz on a trio album on the Philology label.

**VIVIAN STOLL, vibraharpist and percussionist, plays in the Harp Band with Nydia Mata in the New York area.

*STRAIGHT AHEAD, an all-women's quintet of instrumentalists and singers organized in Detroit in 1987, records for Atlantic Records. Members are Regina Carter, violinist, Cynthia Dewberry, flautist, Marian Hayden-Banfield, bassist, Eileen Orr, pianist, keyboardist, and Gayelynn McKinney, drummer. "Look Straight Ahead," 1992, was their first album. Their second, "Body and Soul," 1993, showcases the group playing mainstream acoustic, pop-fusion jazz, and pop-rap—often with a soulful r&b underpinning. All studied music in conservatories and colleges. Hayden-Banfield is the daughter of a bassist. McKinney's uncle is jazz bassist Ray McKinney.

The group was a finalist in 1987 in the annual Sony Innovators competition. In 1989, Straight Ahead played at the Montreux Jazz Festival. When "Body and Soul" was released, the group performed in Sweetwater's, a Manhattan club, and began a promotional tour.

*CAROL SUDHALTER, reeds player, group leader, lives in Queens, New York.

MONNETTE SUDLER, guitarist, made three albums for Steeplechase in the late 1970s, and has worked with saxophonists Arthur Blythe, Grover Washington, Frank Wess, drummer Philly Joe Jones, and pianists Kenny Barron and Cedar Walton. To raise her family, she remained in Philadelphia, where she plays in clubs, concerts, and festivals. She toured Berlin with the Change of the Century orchestra in the late 1980s, recorded as leader on "The Other Side of the Gemini," Hardly Records, early 1990s, and in summer 1993, led a quintet at Damrosch Park, Lincoln Center, in a series highlighting Philadelphia-based jazz players.

MAXINE SULLIVAN, singer, who became a star with her record, "Loch Lomond" in 1938, died in New York in the 1980s. She sang in public, to critical acclaim, until the last weeks of her life. When she played trombone in public, she was criticized for not being able to play it as well as she could sing. She turned to playing a small, pocket trumpeter— virtually in secret.

BARBARA SUTTON CURTIS, stride pianist and sister of stride pianist Ralph Sutton, has been playing piano professionally for many years. Sackville Records in Toronto, Canada, released her CD, "Solos and Duets," in 1993, including tracks of her playing with Ralph, and with bassist Reggie Johnson and drummer Jake Hanna. She lives in Ukiah, California.

FRANCESCA TANKSLEY, pianist, has played with Billy Harper's group since 1983, doing U.S. State Department tours to Southeast Asia, South America, Canada, and Europe. She played for three Harper CDs, two of which present her composition, "Dance in the Question"—on the CD "Destiny is Yours," Steeplechase, and on "Live On Tour in The Far East, Vol. One," Steeplechase, "Volume Two" is the newest CD. She appears in a documentary, *Women in Jazz—Styles,* hosted by Marian McPartland, produced by Burrill Crohn. She leads her own trio and has played in Cobi Narita's jazz festivals and on Erica Lindsay's debut album, "Dreamer," Candid Records, 1990.

MARTHA TAYLOR, trombonist, Diva's bass trombonist, travels between classical music, jazz, and rock and roll. While an undergraduate at the University of Michigan, she played in the Ann Arbor and Detroit Civic Symphony Orchestras. From a family of pianists—her father and brother are professional church organists—she couldn't play piano well. She chose to play trombone in the fourth grade, when the class bully challenged her by saying that a girl could never play trombone. She has taught at the University of Massachusetts, directed bands at Southern State Connecticut University, and teaches at Fairfield University and at a Fairfield elementary school. She also plays trombone in the Greater Bridgeport Symphony Orchestra.

NORMA TEAGARDEN, pianist in the "trad" jazz style, was working at the Washington Square Bar and Grill, San Francisco, on Wednesday nights, for eighteen years by 1993. Born April 28, 1911, she had been playing for over sixty years. "I have a whole wall full (of awards)," she said. The most recent was a performing arts award from the Eighth Annual San Francisco Jazz and All That Art on Fillmore Festival, July 1993. She has a merit award for outstanding public service from San Francisco's Mayor Diane Feinstein in 1980. The city also celebrated her with a Norma Teagarden Day. Other honors have been a certificate from California State University in Northridge and a Senior Achievement Award for outstanding work performance.

She toured London, Liverpool, and other English cities with an American band in 1986 and played in Holland in the 1980s. "A Hundred Years From Today" has been reissued as a CD on the Grudge label, 1990. It was taped at a Monterey Jazz Festival concert featuring Norma, her trumpet playing brother Charles, her brother Jack, the trombone star, and their mother, Helen, a pianist. Norma plays in annual festivals—Pismo Beach in October, Monterey in March, Sacramento in May, all in California, and San Antonio, Texas in August, all in 1993, and several more.

CECILIA TENCONI, flautist and tenor saxophonist, born in Argentina, based in New York since 1987, plays in the group Arrow, for pop Caribbean music, and Alma y Vida for Latin music, especially *candombe* music from Uruguay, and Pe de Boi and Amazonas, Brazilian bands, and with her own band, named Cecilia Tenconi and Los Gatos, in such clubs as S.O.B., the Village Gate, and Nell's. She has also worked with Latin jazz pianist and composer Eddie Martinez, Latin percussionist Patato Valdez, and drummer Portinho from Brazil. With Arrow and others, she has traveled to a dozen festivals in the United States and South America.

As a fifteen year old in Buenos Aires, she played flute as soloist with the National Radio Orchestra. She didn't pick up the sax until she came to New York. "There are no women saxophonists in Argentina," she says. In the United States, where she is generally accepted, she finds ways to deal with difficulties based on gender, because jobs are definitely available to her. She has played on Arrow albums on Island Records—"Soca Dance Party" and "Model T Bambam," and on her husband, pianist Dave Kikoski's album, "Persistent Dreams," Triloka Records, in the 1990s. She and her husband gave a concert at the San Martin Theater in Buenos Aires at the invitation of the American Embassy. Among the best jazz flautists, she has exceptional technique and a buoyant, swinging style; her music is vivacious and melodic. Her tenor saxophone is mellow and flowing.

*LESA TERRY, violinist, who was a prominent soloist in the Broadway show *Black and Blue,* played in the orchestra for *Camelot* in summer, 1993. With many prestigious credits in classical music, she is a member of the Uptown String Quartet.

*SUE TERRY, alto saxophonist, lives in New York.

**SUE TERWILLIGER, guitarist with Kit McClure and others, lives in the New York area.

**BARBARA THOMPSON, saxophonist, from England, has played in the United States. Some recordings are "Barbara Thompson's Paraphernal," Breathless, and "Songs from the Center of the Earth," Black Sun/Celestial Harmonies.

**TERRI THORNTON, pianist and singer, plays in many clubs and tours to Europe.

*SUMI TONOOKA, pianist, composer, group leader, and recording artist, lives in Woodstock, New York.

JOYCE TOTH, trumpeter with Kit McClure and Diva, subs in Broadway orchestras for shows such as *Les Miserable, Cats,* and *Kiss of the Spider Woman,* and works in salsa, classical jazz, ethnic groups, and in classical orchestras, because she enjoys variety. She is on a tape led by Tom Pierson for "Planet of Tears," and she recorded for Louie Ramirez's album, "King of Latin Vibes," on the Sugar Records label, 1991, and on McClure's album.

She has played for jingles, for a cartoon with a classical score for PBS, and she worked as assistant musical director, playing and arranging for a television show in Madrid, Spain. Though busy, she's aware of the discrimination against women. "There's always a little feeling," she says. One leader, to whom she was sent as a sub, cried out: "Oh, you're a girl!" She has also had gotten opportunities to work because she's a woman, she says.

*AKUA DIXON TURRE, classical cellist, composer, and improviser, who with her sister, Gayle Dixon, a violinist, plays in Quartette Indigo, is married to jazz trombonist Steve Turre. Among Akua's many engagements in jazz, classical, and new music, she plays in the Neo-Bass Ensemble. (See KAREN ATKINSON.) She has been on the soundtrack for Spike Lee's *School Daze* and Turre's album, "Fire and Ice," featuring the Quartette Indigo, 1988. She had a Rockefeller grant to compose "The Opera of Marie Laveau," presented at the Henry Street Settlement House Playhouse, in the late 1980s.

Quartette Indigo has recorded for Carmen McRae albums and others and for the album of Dizzy Gillespie's film, *Winter in Lisbon.* Akua arranges or composes most of the quartet's music. She has had Meet the Composer commissions for the Brooklyn Philharmonic and other orchestras and two NEA grants for composition and performance in the 1980s.

In July 1993, Quartette Indigo played for James Blood Ulmer's album for guitar and string quartet, for release on the DIW label. Akua sang on "Attica Blues Big Band," an Archie Shepp album, late 1970s, and on Steve Turre's album, "Right There."

SOOZIE TYRELL, violinist and singer, has played on Buster Poindextor's album "Buster Goes Beserk," on RCA, and has worked with Carol King, Bruce Springsteen, and Judy Collins.

ELLEN URYEVICK, harpist and percussionist, in the New York area, plays Latin jazz with the Harp Band, with Nydia "Liberty" Mata, and in other groups. Regarded as an innovator for Latin jazz harp playing, she has worked with Arnie Lawrence, jazz saxophonist.

SARAH VAUGHAN, legendary singer, died in 1990. She often sat down and played for herself in performances.

*BERNADINE WARREN, drummer, from East St. Louis, Illinois, sat in with Chuck Berry and also played with Ike and Tina Turner at the Club Manhattan, when all of them were starting careers. She plays in parks, on boat rides, in clubs and for dances in New York. She has worked with Gloria Coleman playing organ along with guitarist Grant Green. She and Gloria worked in saxophonist Red Prysock's trio. Bernadine has played with the Big Apple Jazzwomen for the women's festivals produced by Cobi Narita and for special events in 1993. She played in the Kool Jazz Festival in Willene Barton's group in the early 1980s.

Her gospel albums have been done with the White Rock Baptist Church choir with Shirley Caesar, the Five Blind Boys, the Institutional Choir of Philadelphia, all on the Hobb label, and the Gospel All Stars formerly with James Cleveland, when she was working for Speedy Warwick and John Bowden. She also did gospel concerts, one of them with Dorothy Norwood at the JFK Memorial, opening for the Rolling Stones and Stevie Wonder in Washington, D. C. She has toured in Canada, Greenland, and Europe.

MAMIKO WATANABE, pianist, was a ten-year-old prodigy studying at the Yamaha Music School Program in Japan, when she flew from Japan to make her debut at Carnegie Hall, in the fortieth anniversary celebration of Peanuts, "Jazzin' It Up with Snoopy," in October 1990.

MARY WATKINS, pianist, is in the San Francisco area.

ANGELA WELLMAN, trombonist, lives in the San Francisco area.

NEDRA WHEELER, acoustic and electric bass player, has worked with many successful musicians, including violinist Karen Briggs, pianist Kenny Kirkland, and drummer Jeff Watts, and Melena, a Cuban-born percussionist. Nedra played in a duo with Cedar Walton as a tribute to Nelson Mandela at the Sony Pictures studio. With her own quartet, she plays for colleges and special events and subs for Kenny's group at the Bel Age in West Los Angeles. She has broadcast from Las Vegas over NPR and played in a concert broadcast live over KPCC, Pasadena, from the Wadsworth Theatre at U.C.L.A.

Her CD, "Gifts," on the Splashing Sun Label, 1989, includes pianist Billy Childs, Ravi Coltrane, soprano and tenor saxes, and others in an octet. She composed six songs and arranged all the music. She also recorded with the Harper Brothers, on "Artistry," Polygram, 1990, appeared with them on CBS's "Sunday Morning" with Dr. Billy Taylor, and toured with the group in the United States, Argentina, Japan, and Canada. She recorded many times with Alice Coltrane, with Bob Dylan in 1984, and played for the soundtracks of *Malcolm X* with Branford Marsalis in 1992 and *Menace To Society* and *Chick Peas*. With Karen Briggs and Al "Tootie" Heath she traveled to Bulgaria in 1990, where they appeared on TV and made a video, *Life in 33/16, the Life of Milcho Leviev*, a pianist, arranger, and a U.S. citizen born in Bulgaria.

Another recording is in a compilation in tribute to Miles Davis, with trumpeter Marlon Jordan, drummer Jason Marsalis, saxophonist Mark Turner, and pianist Richard Atkins, Columbia, 1992. She has played on the album, "Murder in Metropolis," with Torch, a rapper, Wild West label, 1993. She has also toured with rock artist Pat Benatar; they appeared on the "Tonight" show with Johnny Carson. She has also played with Ella Fitzgerald, Kenny Burrell, Billy Higgins, Elvin Jones, Eddie Harris, Teddy Edwards, Donald Byrd, and Kenny Garrett. And she has worked on TV shows "Roseanne," "Major Dad," "Bob Newhart," and "Fame."

LILLY WHITE, who plays soprano, alto, and tenor saxes, and composes, came from Aurora, Illinois to New York in the early 1980s. She works primarily with Jimmy McGriff and also played with Jay McShann. As a sub, she played in Mario Bauza's big band, and recorded with Jorge Degas, a Brazilian bass player, on an album to be released. In 1993, she was working with her own quintet, Actual Proof, and writing for a new group. Actual Proof has played at Visiones in New York and Trumpets in Montclair, New Jersey. The new group made its debut at the Knitting Factory in August 1993. Her album, "Somewhere Between Truth and Fiction," was released on the Knitting Factory Works label, 1994.

PATTI WICKS (GREY), singer and pianist, who worked in New York for many years, moved from Long Island to Maine in 1990, where she plays solo and with duos and trios in the Bar Harbor-Blue Hill area. Cecil Payne, baritone saxophonist, and Frank Morgan, alto saxophonist, have played with her there.

MICHELE WILEY, singer with an exquisite voice, accompanied herself at the piano at Casa Bella in Manhattan's Little Italy, playing for a few years, with trumpeter Johnny Parker, beginning in 1992. In May 1994, the duo attracted a critic for *Hemispheres* magazine.

JESSICA WILLIAMS, pianist, keyboardist, experimentalist, recorded solo albums in 1993—"Live at Maybeck Hall, Vol. 21," for Concord, and "The Next Step," on the Hep label in Scotland. She has recorded many praised albums, including "And Then There's This," on Timeless, in

1991; an album of synthesizer music, "Heartland," Ear Art, 1990; "Epistrophy: The Charlie Rouse Memorial Concert," Landmark, 1989; "The Golden Light," Quanta, 1989; "Nothin' But The Truth," Black Hawk, 1986; and "Update," the Clean Cut label, 1983. "Orgonomic Music" was also on Clean Cut in 1981.

Recognized as a brilliant pianist and innovator, she is working on her third symphony for synthesizer. Her NEA grant in 1988 was for production and performance of her composition, "Tutu's Dream," for Bishop Tutu. She received four grants from the Sacramento Metropolitan Arts Commission for performance and composition between 1985 and 1990. She also received a Meet the Composer grant in 1989 to compose and arrange a Thelonious Monk tribute for a big band and string orchestra. In 1983, she placed first in the Talent Deserving Wider Recognition category in *Down Beat*. She tours to play in jazz festivals, concert halls, and clubs in Europe and the northwest United States. In 1993, she was living in Capitola, near Santa Cruz, California.

*MARY LOU WILLIAMS, who died in 1981, composed, arranged, and taught at Duke University and in private classes in New York, serving as a role model and inspiration for all musicians. Some albums are "Best of Mary Lou," on Pablo; "Live at the Cookery," on Chiaroscuro, 1975; "The Mary Lou Williams Quartet featuring Don Byas," GNP/Crescendo, and "Town Hall '45: The Zodiac Suite," Vintage Jazz Classics, 1945. She has been written about in the jazz histories.

SUE WILLIAMS, acoustic and electric bassist, and teacher, plays many styles of music, including a great deal of jazz, in New York. A member of the group, Sue Terry and the Holy Terrors, she has also recorded with rock groups—Richard Hill and the Voidoids, and with The Lovelies.

CASSANDRA WILSON emerged as an important jazz singer in the 1980s with such albums as "Blue Skies" and other primarily of original compositions that earn her critical acclaim. She played piano to accompany herself for the hymn "Amazing Grace" on her 1993 Columbia album, "Dance to the Drums Again." She studied piano for six years and started her career as a singer and guitarist. Her album "Blue Light 'til Dawn" was issued on Blue Note in 1993. She performs concerts at Town Hall, Lincoln Center, and other famous halls.

WINDS OF JAZZ, a Philadelphia-based women's jazz saxophone quartet, was founded as a quintet in 1990 by Dutch-born Lisa Westerterp, who plays alto sax and clarinet, with Kathy Kilpatrick, on bassoon, flute, and tenor sax, Lynn Riley, on soprano and alto saxes and flute, and Trish Valiante, on baritone sax and flute. Susan Doherty on alto and tenor saxes and flute was in the original group. It made its New York debut at Lincoln Center's Damrosch Park in August 1993. Although it rarely plays in clubs, because it works without a rhythm section, the quartet has played in the Mellon Jazz Festival, the Presidents Weekend Festival, at the Philadelphia club The Painted Bride, and for a new cable TV company, Black Movies and Entertainment, based in Washington, D.C.

Lisa had a Meet the Composer grant in 1990. She has been artist-in-residence at the Philadelphia Community Center.

*SHERRY WINSTON, flutist and group leader, leads the albums "Love Is. . . ," Warlock Records, 1991; "Love Madness," Head First, 1992, and "Do It For Love," K-Tel, 1989, originally on Pausa Records, 1986. She has played in clubs, toured to promote her recordings, and led groups for events for *Emerge* magazine, Coors Beer, Anheuser Busch, American Express, and others. In 1992, she performed with Ramsey Lewis at a benefit performance on BET's "Black Entertainment Tonight" show. In August 1993, she performed in a concert with Grover Washington. She was nominated for an NAACP Image Award in 1989, received the Eubie Blake Award in 1991, the Pathways for Youth award, 1991, and Howard University Alumni Awards, 1984, 1989.

*ELISE WOOD, flautist, often works with pianist John Hicks, with whom she records. "New Dawn," on Maple Shade, was scheduled for release in 1994, with Hicks, Walter Booker on bass, and guest trumpeter Jack Walrath. Elise also plays with a ten-flute orchestra and other groups in New York.

*TRACY WORMWORTH, electric bassist, has played in the studio for "The Cosby Show," and worked for Sting and the B52s.

JEANETTE WRATE, drummer and percussionist in Maiden Voyage and Jazz Birds, recorded with the band Big World for two CDs, one of which is "Angels" on the 9 Winds label.

KATIE WREEDE, violist, is based in Oakland and played with the Turtle Island String Quartet.

SHIZUKO YOKOYAMA, pianist, played with the Mercer Ellington orchestra for three years until 1991. She leads a trio, sometimes with her husband, drummer Fukushi Tainaka. She also plays with the George Gee swing band. She's on at least one recording with Ellington, "Music Is My Mistress."

*RACHEL Z, keyboardist with Steps Ahead, made her debut album as leader, "Trust the Universe," Columbia, 1993.

This list covers most of the best known players in major cities and samples the country.

Special thanks go to bassist Kim Clarke for helping to compose the following list of musicians who were inadvertently omitted above: ANNETTE A. AGUILAR, a founding member of Chevere in San Francisco, where she played with pianist Patricia Thumas, trumpeter Helena Jack, drummer Bonnie Johnson, and Mayhew, Franks, and Dreyer listed above, now plays percussion in jazz and Latin Brazilian jazz bands and timpani in orchestras; jazz and pop guitarist RONNIE CROOKS; electric bassist MYRA SINGLETON; electric guitarist DEBBIE KNAPPER in jazz, pop and folk groups and the all-women's group Ibis; CAROL COLMAN for fourteen years with Kid Creole and the Coconuts; bassist and singer MADELINE KOLE; KERIANN DIBARI, clarinetist, who also plays flute and tenor in the orchestra for "Beauty and the Beast" and Kit McClure's band; LIZZ (DOUBLE Z) CHISHOLM, electric bassist and singer, primarily an r&b musician, with her own album "In Z Mood" on Quest/Reprise; ELYSA SUNSHINE, singer and electric guitarist who also plays keyboards, viola and violin; AMINA MAJIED, jazz and classical trombone player; ANDREA GURLEY, trumpeter; PAMELA BASKIN-WATSON, singer, pianist, composer and arranger of choral music and tunes recorded by Betty Carter, Art Blakey, altoist Bobby Watson, and drummer Victor Lewis; LAFORREST COPE, pianist; LISETTE WILSON, keyboardist, with an album "Unmasked" on Atlantic; VALERIE GHENT, singer and keyboardist; vibes player VERA AUER; pianist BONITA SARGENT; DOTTI ANITA TAYLOR, flautist and pianist, who plays in the World Flute Choir, and as an accompanist for singers; and bassist JUNE SEGAL. Also, NANCY KENNEDY, pianist and composer, received an artists' fellowship from the New York Foundation for the arts in 1994.

/ / / Bibliography

American Women in Jazz, by Sally Placksin, Wideview Books, New York, 1982.

Black Women in American Bands and Orchestras, by Antoinette Handy, Scarecrow Press, Metuchen, N.J., and London, 1981.

Jazz Women at the Keyboard, by Mary Unterbrink, McFarland & Co Inc, Publishers, Jefferson, N.C., and London, 1983.

Stormy Weather, by Linda Dahl, Limelight Editions, New York, 1984.

Periodicals consulted were primarily the *Daily News, The New York Times, The New York Post,* and *Newsday,* in New York, and *Down Beat* magazine, *Jazz Times, Los Angeles Times, The New Yorker, CD Review,* and *Jazz Jz.*

Abercrombie, John, 133
Abrams, Muhal Richard, 160
Acuna, Alex, 145
Adams, Oleta, 149
Adderley, Cannonball, 163
Aguabella, Francisco, 147
Airto, 144
Akiyoshi, Toshiko, 8, 24, 76, 169, 210
Alden, Howard, 154
Alexander, Monte, 93
Alive!, 66
Allen, Geri, 22, 33–36, 37, 42, 46, 73, 133, 135
Almeida, Laurindo, 115
Anderson, Laurie, 60
Ariel, 25
Armatrading, Joan, 58
Armstrong, Lil Hardin, 8
Armstrong, Louis, 13–14, 56, 119, 187
Arnett, Gia, 70
Arriale, Lynne, 101, 197
Ash, Paul, 62, 64, 65
Astoria Big Band, 122, 123
Atherton, Paula, 104, 105
Atkinson, Karen, 84
Atkinson, Lyle, 84
Austin, Lovey, 22
Avakian, George, 59
Aznavour, Charles, 91

Bailey, Donald, 112, 157, 159
Bailey, Mildred, 195
Bailey, Sheryl, 70
Baker, Chet, 57, 175
Baker, Leslie, 85
Balliett, Whitney, 183
Bang, Billy, 160
Barbieri, Gato, 149
Barron, Kenny, 22, 38, 48, 116, 161
Barton, Willene, 25, 26, 29, 30, 31, 63
Bartz, Gary, 136

Basie, Count, 9, 21, 151, 152, 176, 208
Baum, Jamie, 69
Beiderbecke, Bix, 118, 120
Beirach, Richie, 162
Belafonte, Harry, 52, 186
Belgrave, Marcus, 22, 35, 36
Bellson, Louis, 198
Bennett, Tony, 192
Benoit, David, 135
Benton, Brook, 90–91
Bernhard, Sandra, 39
Bienenfeld, Lolly, 3–4, 68
Big Apple Jazzwomen, 63
Blackman, Cindy, 10–11, 45, 129, 136–42
Blake, Eubie, 193
Blake, John, 37, 40
Blake, Ran, 120
Blakey, Art, 29, 44, 140–41, 179, 180, 205
Blakey, Evelyn, 25
Blanchard, Terence, 18, 48, 164
Bley, Carla, 8
Bloom, Jane Ira, 68, 124–27
Bobè, Eddie, 157, 159
Bofill, Angela, 22, 145, 149
Bonet, Lisa, 91
Booker, Walter, 165, 166
Bostic, Kysia, 101
Boswell Sisters, 63
Bowie, Lester, 159
Bown, Patti, 8, 16, 19, 21–22
Boy George, 149
Brackeen, Charles, 179
Brackeen, Joanne, 8, 16–17, 29, 44, 53, 57, 63, 161, 163, 178–82, 204
Bradford, Kirt, 102
Brandy, Carolyn, 66, 129
Brecker, Randy, 202
Bricktop, 48
Brookmeyer, Bob, 167, 169
Brooks, Bernice, 81, 129, 130

Brown, Clifford, 102
Brown, Donald, 44
Brown, Garnett, 132
Brown, Lisa, 121
Brown, Ray, 112
Brown, Ruth, 69, 188
Brown, Tom, 145, 149
Brubeck, Dan, 101
Brubeck, Dave, 15
Bryant, Clora, 208
Bunnett, Jane, 17, 115
Burrell, David, 101
Burrell, Kenny, 41, 53, 101
Burton, Gary, 192
Bushkin, Joe, 153
Butler, George, 45
Butts, Jimmy, 118
Byrd, Charlie, 95
Byrne, David, 60

Callender, Red, 151, 154
Capers, Valerie, 24, 26
Carmichael, Judy, 150–56
Carrington, Sonny, 131, 132
Carrington, Terri Lyne, 10, 15, 43, 44,
    110, 129, 130, 131–35, 136, 138, 164
Carrol, Phil, 53
Carroll, Barbara, 193
Carrott, Bryan, 89
Carter, Benny, 57, 106, 198, 199
Carter, Regina, 85
Carter, Ron, 18, 47
Caruso, Carmine, 106, 107
Castleman, Charles, 40
Celebration, 25
Chaikin, Carol, 4, 97, 104, 105, 130
Chaloff, Margaret, 36
Chaloff, Serge, 36
Chapman, Stephanie, 79
Chevere, 102
Chic, 121
Clapton, Eric, 149
Clarke, Kim, 45, 47, 81, 83, 90, 202
Clarke, Stanley, 144
Clayton, Buck, 106
Clayton, Jay, 63
Cline, Nels, 112
Cobb, Jimmy, 141, 165
Cohn, Al, 57, 132
Cohn, Joe, 103
Cole, Nat King, 50, 177
Cole, Natalie, 10
Coleman, Cecilia, 209
Coleman, Ornette, 29, 180

Coleman, Steve, 133
Collazo, Julio, 147
Collins, Joyce, 210
Colon, Willie, 144
Coltrane, John, 14, 56
Condon, Eddie, 192
Connell, Robin, 123
Connick, Harry Jr., 48
Connor, Chris, 53
Copeland, Aaron, 159
Copeland, Keith, 131
Coppola, Johnny, 102
Coryell, Larry, 70, 93, 94, 140, 174
Cosby, Bill, 11, 69, 90–91, 101, 103
Cowings, Marion, 103
Cuenca, Sylvia, 12, 129, 136–37
Cunningham, Bradley, 110, 113, 160–63
Cunningham, Wendy, 17, 48
Cuscuna, Michael, 140
Czercowski, Sarah, 48

Dahl, Linda, 47
Davis, Eddie "Lockjaw," 8
Davis, Jean, 25, 26, 27, 29, 30, 31
Davis, Miles, 11, 43, 44, 47, 56, 58, 84,
    88, 102, 108, 141, 173, 196, 199
Davis, Richard, 32
Davis, Walter, 205
Debriano, Santi, 116, 159
Deffaa, Chip, 198
DeFunkt, 45
DeJohnette, Jack, 132, 178
DeMello, Beatriz, 14
DeRosa Dianne, 9
Deuce, 15, 50, 64
Diva, 3, 4, 5, 14, 68, 70, 73, 75–76,
    80–82, 83, 97, 100, 105
Dixon, Fostina, 9
Dixon, Gayle, 40, 70
Dixon, Lucille, 83
D'Lugoff, Art, 3
Dodgion, Dorothy, 19, 20, 21, 24
Dodgion, Jerry, 20, 21
Doky, Niels Lan, 133
Dolgin, Hana, 117
Donaldson, Lou, 11, 100, 115
Donegan, Dorothy, 8, 10, 15–16, 17, 21,
    183–89
Donnelly, Nancy, 129
Dreyer, Laura, 104–5
Drifters, The, 139
D'Rivera, Paquito, 49
Drummond, Billy, 17, 43, 45
Drummond, Ray, 159

Duchin, Peter, 63
Dudziak, Ursula, 89
Dunham, Katherine, 147
Durham, Bobby, 103
Durham, Eddie, 21
Duvivier, George, 132
Dyson, Kit, 18

E., Sheila, 11, 66, 129
Edison, Harry "Sweets," 112, 198
Eldridge, Roy, 15, 155
Elias, Eliane, 45, 160, 201
Ellington, Duke, 2, 43, 60, 63, 75, 108,
    110, 124, 157–58, 159, 190, 192, 195,
    197, 198
Ellis, Herb, 95
Enriques, Bobby, 205
Ertegun, Ahmet, 58
Ertegun, Nesuhi, 58
Escovedo, Pete, 66
Esen, Aydin, 93
Essen, Erik Von, 112
Evans, Anita, 169
Evans, Bill (pianist), 31, 52, 57, 92, 161,
    164, 178, 193
Evans, Bill (reeds player), 165
Evans, Gil, 130, 159, 168, 169
Evans, Sue, 10, 14, 18, 79, 83, 129, 130

Faddis, Jon, 47, 49, 130, 132
Farlow, Tal, 95
Farmer, Art, 53, 115
Farrell, Joe, 57
Fauber, Stephanie, 9, 18, 68, 70–72, 79
Feather, Leonard, 92, 111, 193
Fedchock, John, 169
Fettig, Mary, 208
Fields, Joe, 140
Fineberg, Jean, 15, 29, 50, 63, 67, 68,
    120
Fitzgerald, Ella, 10, 44, 124
Flack, Roberta, 10
Flanagan, Tommy, 63, 155, 161, 193
Flory, Chris, 154, 156
Fluijs, Ben, 112
Folson, Eileen, 40
Foote, Lona, 49
Fox, Mimi, 70
Franks, Rebecca Coupe, 11, 15, 68, 97,
    100–103, 105, 106, 207
Freelon, Nnenna, 49
Freeman, Sharon, 9, 13
Frink, Laurie, 73, 103, 105–9, 167

Frishberg, Dave, 57
Fulman, Ricki, 26

Gabriel, Peter, 149
Garner, Erroll, 130, 175
Gaye, Marvin, 66, 159
Gensel, John Garcia, Rev., 61
Getter, Jane, 84–85
Getz, Stan, 43, 133, 134, 179, 180
Gilbert, Peggy, 208
Gilberto, Astrud, 57
Gillespie, Dizzy, 9, 14, 26, 39–40, 41, 42,
    49, 62, 76, 88, 110, 132, 157, 159,
    195, 199, 208
Gioia, Ted, 209
Glaser, Joe, 187
Glass, Philip, 129
Goines, Lincoln, 84, 96
Goldstein, Linda, 50, 51, 54–60, 202,
    205
Gomez, Eddie, 163, 165, 178
Gonzales, Nelson, 144, 147, 149
Gonzalez, Babs, 185
Goodman, Benny, 106, 108, 196
Gordon, Dexter, 9, 20, 180
Gordon, Lorraine, 48
Gordon, Max, 48, 56
Grappelli, Stephane, 69, 115
Grauer, Joanne, 210
Green, Freddie, 151, 155
Grey, Al, 11, 14, 103, 111, 141, 198
Gumbs, Onaje Allen, 145

Haden, Charlie, 180
Hadley, Dardanelle, 8
Haggerty, Terry, 149
Hall, Arsenio, 133–34
Halvorson, Kathy, 70, 104
Hamilton, Chico, 115
Hammond, Doug, 205
Hampton, Lionel, 27, 204–5
Hampton, Paula, 25, 26, 27, 28, 30, 31
Hampton, Slide, 27
Hancock, Herbie, 44–45, 56, 168
Hanna, Roland, 32, 41, 114
Harewood, Al, 30
Hargrove, Roy, 48
Harlow, Larry, 121
Harlow, Rita, 121
Harper, Billy, 68
Harris, Barry, 43
Harris, Gene, 106
Harrison, Donald, 49, 164
Hart, Billy, 157

Hashim, Mike, 154, 156
Hathaway, Lalah, 135
Hawes, Hampton, 164
Hay, William, 193
Hayden-Banfield, Marion, 83
Haynes, Roy, 31, 116
Heath, Jimmy, 159
Helman, Ron, 45
Henderson, Eddie, 166
Henderson, Joe, 17, 43, 44, 56, 136, 137,
    140, 141, 179, 180
Henderson, Skitch, 3, 154
Hendricks, Jon, 58, 103, 150
Hendrix, Jimi, 160
Herman, Woody, 169
Hersch, Fred, 96, 126, 127, 162
Hewitt, Sandi, 26
Hicks, John, 15, 69, 114, 161
Higgins, Billy, 141, 165, 180
Hill, Buck, 173–75, 176, 177
Hines, Earl "Fatha," 150–51
Hinton, Milt, 101, 198
Hirschfield, Jeff, 96
Hittman, Jeff, 117
Hofmann, Holly, 208
Hoggard, Jay, 101
Holiday, Billie, 44, 119, 120, 177, 208
Holland, Dave, 133
Holzman, Adam, 85
Hope, Bertha, 63, 161, 165–67, 203
Hope, Elmo, 166
Horn, Shirley, 8, 10, 173–77, 205
Horne, Lena, 188
Hubbard, Freddie, 30, 56
Hutcherson, Bobby, 43
Hutton, Ina Rae, 4
Hyman, Dick, 130, 153, 193
Hyman, Phyllis, 89

International Sweethearts of Rhythm, 4,
    21, 74, 76, 83
Interplay, 105
Isis, 25

Jackson, Gene, 159
Jackson, Oliver, 111
Jacquet, Illinois, 57, 131
Jamal, Ahmad, 62, 175
Jansen, Nadine, 8
Jarreau, Al, 134, 135
Jazz Babies, 63
Jazz Birds, 111, 112
Jazz Sisters, 24, 74
Jensen, Ingrid, 3, 67, 97

Jeske, Lee, 174
Johnson, Anita, 81
Johnson, J. J., 44
Johnson, James P., 151
Johnson, Reggie, 162
Jones, Elvin, 140
Jones, Hank, 47, 93, 94, 155, 161
Jones, Harold, 151
Jones, Jonah, 3
Jones, Philly Joe, 141
Jones, Quincy, 19, 177
Jones, Rodney, 91
Jones, Thad, 4, 18, 31, 71–72, 79, 167,
    169
Jordan, Duke, 31
Jordan, Sheila, 63

Kalesty, Kim, 103
Kay, Connie, 138
Kay, Stanley, 3–5
Kaye, Carol, 209
Keane, Helen, 50, 51–55, 57, 60, 66, 72,
    103, 178–79
Keillor, Garrison, 156
Kemp, Emily, 66
Kessel, Barney, 95
Khan, Chakha, 149
Kidjo, Angelique, 148
Kinnon, Liz, 112
Kirk, Dorthaan, 49
Kirk, Rahsaan Roland, 49, 131
Kirkland, Kenny, 46, 88–90, 89, 90, 91,
    145
Kokubu, Hiroko, 63
Korsmeyer, Karen, 83
Kravitz, Lenny, 11, 140
Kressman, Eric, 201

LaBarbera, John, 4
LaFaro, Scott, 164
Laine, Cleo, 192
Lake, Oliver, 158
Langsjoen, Britta, 97
Larkins, Ellis, 193
LaSpina, Steve, 165
Lateef, Yusef, 41
Latin Fever, 25, 121, 145
Lauper, Cindy, 149
Lawson, Janet, 63
Ledgerwood, Lee Ann, 135, 160–65
Lee, Peggy, 192
Lee, Spike, 41
Leitch, Peter, 9, 50
Lester, Sonny, 4

Levine, Sylvia, 50
Levy, Morris, 187
Lewis, John, 153, 193
Lewis, Mel, 4, 18, 31, 71, 79, 83, 105, 106, 167, 169
Liepolt, Horst, 17
Lightsey, Kirk, 10, 79, 116, 161, 205
Lincoln, Abbey, 63, 125
Lindsay, Erica, 67, 68
Liston, Melba, 8–9, 10, 20, 22, 25, 63, 67–68, 206, 208
London, Barbara, 25
Lundvall, Bruce, 58
Lundy, Carmen, 145
Lutcher, Nellie, 208

Mabern, Harold, 62
Machito, 106
Maiden Voyage, 4, 14, 15, 104, 110, 112, 113, 208, 210
Mainieri, Mike, 45
Makovicz, Adam, 54
Mance, Junior, 3, 9
Mandel, Johnny, 177
Manne, Shelly, 57
Margolin, Steve, 174
Maria, Tania, 200, 202–203
Maricle, Sherrie, 4, 97, 130
Marsalis, Branford, 45, 89, 130, 139, 164, 173
Marsalis, Wynton, 88, 140, 173, 195
Martinotti, Bruno, 119–20
Mata, Nydia, 129
Maxwell, Jimmy, 107, 108
Mayerl, Billy, 192
Mayhew, Virginia, 3, 15, 68, 97, 100, 101, 102–103
Mazur, Marilyn, 11, 129
M-Base, 133
McBee, Cecil, 58
McCarron, Jill, 4
McClair, Carolyn, 49
McClane, John T., 186–87
McClure, Kit, 4, 14, 24–25, 45, 68, 73–74, 75–82, 105, 109, 115, 129, 167
McClure, Ron, 105, 136, 163
McCorkle, Susannah, 49–50, 96
McFerrin, Bobby, 50, 55, 57–60, 203
McGhee, Howard, 28
McLagan, Kent, 125, 127
McLawler, Sarah, 63
McLean, Jackie, 103, 141
McManus, Jill, 24, 25, 28–29, 31–32

McNeeley, Jim, 43
McPartland, Jimmy, 192, 195, 196, 197–98
McPartland, Marian, 10, 15, 16, 21, 47, 155, 156, 159, 190–200, 196, 199, 206
McRae, Carmen, 10, 110, 173, 177, 191
McShann, Jay, 153
McSweeney, Mary Ann, 83, 112
Mehegan, John, 28
Merjan, Barbara, 104, 130
Milano, Lynn, 25, 26, 27, 30, 31
Miller, Mulgrew, 43, 137, 195
Mingus, Charlie, 30, 70, 104
Mintzer, Bob, 106
Mitchell, Red, 111, 162
Moffett, Charnett, 45, 137
Mofsie, Louis, 32
Monk, Thelonious, 14, 36, 37, 44, 45, 48, 151
Monroe, Diane, 33–34, 40–41
Montgomery, Wes, 70, 84, 92, 93, 94, 95
Moody, James, 46, 114, 115, 132
Moore, Eddie, 159
Morgan, Lee, 44, 108
Moten, Benny, 152
Moye, Don, 159
Mraz, George, 162
Mulligan, Gerry, 29, 106, 108
Murphy, Rose, 187, 188, 189

Naranjo, Valerie, 64, 129
Narita, Cobi, 12, 37, 60–65, 122, 130, 132
Nasser, Jamil, 62
Niemack, Judy, 63
No Soap Radio, 85
Nottingham, Jimmy, 31

O'Gilvie, Victor, 100
O'Hara, Betty, 112, 208
Osborne, Jeffrey, 145, 146
Osborne, Mary, 84, 208
Osby, Greg, 133
OTB, 43
Owens, Jimmy, 62
Ozay, 205

Pace, Pat, 164
Palermo, Ed, 106
Palmer, Robert, 26, 80–81, 82
Palmieri, Eddie, 106, 147
Parker, Charlie "Bird," 41
Pastorius, Jaco, 146
Patterson, Ann, 15, 208

Persip, Charli, 9, 10, 13, 67, 69, 97, 103, 205
Peterson, Oscar, 44, 175, 185
Peterson, Ralph, 205
Petroff, Audrey Hall, 85
Pierson, Tom, 167
Placksin, Sally, 183, 187
Plattner, David, 59
Porter, Cole, 43, 48, 63, 122
Potter, Chris, 198, 199
Powell, Benny, 64
Pozo, Chano, 157
Priester, Julian, 159
Prince, 66, 148
Puente, Tito, 144
Pullen, Don, 141
Purim, Flora, 144

Quartette Indigo, 85

Randle, Vicki, 130
Ray, Carline, 63, 64, 69, 73
Redd, Vi, 208
Reid, Rufus, 38, 41
Reiner, Carl, 113
Reiner, Estelle, 113
Reinhardt, Django, 120
Reitz, Rosetta, 21, 49
Remler, Emily, 70, 84, 92–96, 153, 174
Rich, Buddy, 3
Riekenberg, Dave, 166
Riley, Ben, 38
Rios, Orlando "Puntilla," 157
Rivers, Sam, 141
Roach, Max, 39–40, 41, 42, 85, 88, 141
Roach, Maxine, 33–34, 40–41, 70
Robinson, Janice, 25, 26, 27
Robinson, Scott, 167
Roditi, Claudio, 49
Rodney, Red, 116, 198
Rollins, Sonny, 78
Roman, Jack, 193
Roney, Wallace, 36, 137, 139
Rosewoman, Michele, 156–60
Rosnes, Renee, 11, 17, 43–44, 46, 47, 161
Ross, Diana, 145
Rowles, Jimmy, 44, 109, 110, 111, 112, 113, 161
Rowles, Stacy, 109–13, 208
Royal, Marshall, 151
Rucker, Ellyn, 210
Rushen, Patrice, 11, 33, 38–39, 42, 133, 135, 209

Russell, George, 64, 70, 106
Ruth, Brown, 186
Ryerson, Ali, 69, 115–16

Sam and Dave, 80
Sample, Joe, 135
Sanborn, David, 133
Sanchez, David, 45
Sanders, Pharoah, 132
Sandoval, Arturo, 49
Santamaria, Mongo, 55, 144
Santana, Carlos, 11, 144
Santana, George, 33
Santos, Moacar, 57
Schneider, Maria, 108, 167–69
Schwarz, Gerard, 107
Scott, Alma, 195
Scott, Hazel, 8, 15, 21, 193, 195
Scott, Shirley, 8
Seeling, Ellen, 15, 29, 50, 63, 67
Shavers, Charlie, 31
Shaw, Woody, 132
Shearing, George, 161, 200
Sheldon, Nina, 25, 29
Shihab, Sahib, 102
Short, Bobby, 193, 197
Shorter, Wayne, 11, 29, 33, 44–45, 91, 133, 135, 203
Shure, Al B., 137
Sickler, Don, 166
Simich, Milan, 45
Simmons, Norman, 103
Simone, Nina, 10
Sims, Zoot, 57
Sinatra, Frank, 44
Singleton, Marge, 19–20
Singleton, Zutty, 20
Sloane, Carol, 53
Slocum, Melissa, 3, 9, 13, 47, 63, 73, 83, 203–5
Smith, Carrie, 186
Smith, Derek, 153
Smith, Marvin "Smitty," 93, 133, 139
Snow, Valaida, 85
Soy, Rosa, 121
Spaulding, James, 62
Spaulding, John, 62, 63
Speziale, Marie, 108
Spitalny, Phil, 4
Stamm, Marvin, 167
Staton, Dakota, 63
Steele, Carol, 10, 83, 129, 143–49, 205
Steig, Jeremy, 115, 163, 165

Stern, Leni, 70, 84
Stern, Mike, 70, 84
Stewart, Slam, 130
Sting, 69, 88, 90
Straight Ahead, 14, 76, 85
Strayhorn, Billy, 157
Sudhalter, Carol, 15, 63, 64, 69, 72, 115, 117–23, 167
Summers, Donna, 26

Tabackin, Lew, 210
Tankesley, Francesca, 68
Tatum, Art, 184
Taylor, Arthur, 140
Taylor, Billy, 63, 155, 193, 197
Taylor, Creed, 52
Teagarden, Jack, 19
Teagarden, Norma, 19–20, 104
Terry, Clark, 3, 9, 12, 16, 41, 96, 103, 110, 132, 136, 185
Terry, Lesa, 41
Terry, Sue, 3, 9, 13, 53, 67, 68–69, 97, 103–4, 130
Terwilliger, Sue, 84
Thiele, Bob, 69, 115–16
Thielemans, Toots, 173
Thomas, Gary, 135, 137
Thomas, Sybil, 145
Tipton, Billy, 19
Tjader, Cal, 55
Tonooka, Sumi, 33, 36–38, 42, 64, 203
Townsend, Robert, 11, 39
Tristano, Lennie, 193
Troup, Stuart, 101
Turre, Akua Dixon, 40, 70, 204
Turre, Steve, 49, 70, 204
Tyner, McCoy, 168

Ullman, Michael, 193
Ulmer, James Blood, 10
Universal Jazz Coalition, 60, 62, 64–65, 122
Unpredictable Nature, 4, 97, 204–5
Uptown String Quartet, 34, 39, 40, 41, 70, 85
Urbaniak, Michel, 89

Vaché, Warren, 154
Valentin, Dave, 129
Vaughan, Sarah, 10, 15, 44, 150, 192
Vega, Estaban "Chacha," 147
Vejmola, Larry, 117
Velvet Glove, 112
Viola, Joseph, 124

Waitresses, The, 88, 89–90
Waits, Freddie, 157
Waller, Fats, 43, 151, 152, 192
Walton, Cedar, 43, 44, 193
Warren, Bernadine, 130
Watanabe, Sadao, 145
Watrous, Bill, 111, 189
Watrous, Peter, 183, 189
Watts, Andre, 188
Wein, George, 49, 62–63, 111
Weiskopf, Walt, 167
Wellstood, Dick, 32, 152, 153
Werner, Kenny, 169
Wess, Frank, 114, 176
Wheeler, Nedra, 83
White, Barry, 79
White, Lenny, 85
Wiggins, J. J., 103
Wilder, Alex, 194
Wilder, Joe, 18
Williams, Buster, 43, 44, 93, 140
Williams, James, 43
Williams, Leroy, 166
Williams, Mary Lou, 8, 15, 21, 22, 28, 37, 151, 189, 200–01, 193
Williams, Sue, 83
Williams, Tony, 47, 139, 140, 141
Williams, Vanessa, 148
Willis, Bruce, 149
Willis, Larry, 104, 140
Wilson, Brian, 149
Wilson, Cassandra, 10, 133
Wilson, Gerald, 20, 208
Wilson, Jack, 122
Wilson, John S., 183, 185
Wilson, Nancy, 10, 163
Wilson, Teddy, 191, 193
Winburn, Anna Mae, 4
Winckelman, Matthias, 159
Winds of Change, 9–10
Winston, Sherry, 49, 115
Winwood, Steve, 144, 146, 149
Wood, Elise, 69, 114
Wood, Vishna, 114
Workman, Reggie, 157
Wormworth, Jimmy Jr., 89
Wormworth, Jimmy, Sr., 90
Wormworth, Tracy, 11, 46, 69, 83, 84, 87–91, 134
Wrate, Jeanette, 112, 129, 208

Young, Graham, 109

Z., Rachel, 9, 11, 18, 44